THE GREATEST LETTER EVER WRITTEN

To Don and Pat,
Dear Dear Friends
of Frances and me!
  —Frenchy
  5/5/2012

First Book As A Gift To Any One Delivered Un-Arrington to my Home at 10:15 AM on the 5th of May

THE GREATEST LETTER EVER WRITTEN
A STUDY OF THE BOOK OF ROMANS

FRENCH L. ARRINGTON

Unless otherwise indicated, Scripture quotations are taken from the *New King James Version*. Copyright © 1979, 1980, 1982, 1990, 1995, Thomas Nelson Inc., Publishers.

Scripture quotations marked KJV are taken from the King James Version of the Bible.

Scripture quotations marked NASB are taken from the *New American Standard Bible*®. Copyright © The Lockman Foundation 1960, 1962, 1963, 1968, 1971, 1972, 1973, 1975, 1977, 1995. Used by permission.

Scripture quotations marked NIV are taken from the *Holy Bible, New International Version*®. NIV® Copyright © 1973, 1978, 1984 by International Bible Society. Used by permission of Zondervan Publishing House. All rights reserved.

Scripture quotations marked NLT are taken from the *Holy Bible, New Living Translation*, copyright © 1996, 2004, 2007 by Tyndale House Foundation. Used by permission of Tyndale House Publishers, Inc., Carol Stream, Illinois 60188. All rights reserved.

Scripture quotations marked Ph. are taken from *The New Testament in Modern English** by J. B. Phillips. Copyright © 1958, 1959, 1960, 1972 by J. B. Phillips. Reprinted with permission of Macmillan Publishing Company. *Revised Edition.

Scripture quotations marked RSV are taken from the *Revised Standard Version* of the Bible. Copyright © 1946, 1952, 1971 by the Division of Christian Education of the National Council of the Churches of Christ in the USA. Used by permission.

Managing Editor: Lance Colkmire
Editorial Assistant: Tammy Hatfield
Copy Editor: Esther Metaxas
Technical Design: Tammy Henkel
Cover Design: Michael McDonald

Library of Congress Control Number: 2012935869
ISBN: 978-1-59684-652-4

Copyright © 2012 by Pathway Press
1080 Montgomery Avenue
Cleveland, Tennessee 37311

All rights reserved. No part of this publication may be reproduced or transmitted in any form or by any means, electronic or mechanical, including photocopying, recording, or otherwise, or by any information storage or retrieval system, without the permission in writing from the publisher. Please direct inquiries to Pathway Press, 1080 Montgomery Avenue, Cleveland, TN 37311.

Visit *www.pathwaypress.org* for more information.

Printed in the United States of America

*This book is dedicated to
two distinguished leaders in the church:*

Frances Lee Treadaway Arrington

A librarian, teacher, wife, mother, grandmother, and friend who touched the lives of so many people, greatly impacting the kingdom of God. During her fifty-eight years of service as a teacher, librarian, and director in colleges and universities and in church and public libraries, she provided support and inspiration to thousands of students, educators, families, businesspeople, writers, and Christian leaders as they have endeavored to learn, grow in faith, and develop their talents in service to God. It gives me great joy to celebrate my late wife and ministry partner and her contributions to God's work.

Dr. Daniel L. Black

A Bible scholar par excellence, whose weekly expositions of the Scriptures have taught many of God's people the Word of God for more than twenty-seven years. I am pleased to recognize his contributions to the kingdom of God and to count him as a dear friend and colleague in the ministry.

Table of Contents

Foreword 9
Preface 11
With Gratitude 13

INTRODUCTION

Why Study Romans? 15
- Romans and the Early Church 16
- Romans and Church Renewal 17
- The Greatness of Romans 21
- Romans and the Holy Spirit 24

ROMANS OVERVIEW

A Look at Paul's Letter to the Romans 27
- The Apostle Paul, Author of Romans 27
- About Paul's Writings 30
- Occasion and Date of Paul's Letter to the Church in Rome .. 31
- Reasons for Paul's Letter to the Church in Rome 33
- The Christian Church in Rome 38
- Emphases of Paul's Letter 42

PART ONE—Romans 1:1-17

Opening of Paul's Letter 51
- Paul's Greeting   Romans 1:1-7 52
- Paul's Thanksgiving   Romans 1:8-10 60
- Paul's Plans for Travel   Romans 1:11-15 62
- Theme of Paul's Letter   Romans 1:16-17 64

PART TWO—Romans 1:18—3:20

The World's Need of Salvation 71
- Paul's Warnings to the Gentiles   Romans 1:18-32 71
- Paul's Warnings to the Jews   Romans 2:1-11 81
- Conscience and the Gentiles   Romans 2:12-16 88
- Blessings and Weaknesses
  of the Jews   Romans 2:17—3:8 92
- All Have Sinned   Romans 3:9-20 106

PART THREE—Romans 3:21—5:21

God's Plan of Salvation 113
- Salvation Through Faith   Romans 3:21-31 113
- Abraham and David: Examples
  of Salvation Through Faith   Romans 4:1-12 123

- The Promise: Grace and Faith Romans 4:13-25 131
- Justification and Love Romans 5:1-11 138
- Adam and Christ Romans 5:12-21 149

PART FOUR—Romans 6:1—8:39
God's Plan for Sanctification 163
- Freedom From the Dominion of Sin Romans 6:1-23 164
- Freedom From the Law Romans 7:1-6 181
- A Defense of the Law Romans 7:7-25 186
- Life in the Spirit Romans 8:1-11 197
- Privileges for God's Children Romans 8:12-17 208
- The Glorious Hope Romans 8:18-30 215
- Assurance of Salvation Romans 8:31-39 230

PART FIVE—Romans 9:1—11:36
Salvation and Israel 243
- Paul's Love for Israel Romans 9:1-5 245
- God's Sovereign Purposes and Choices Romans 9:6-13 252
- God's Sovereign Will and Mercy Romans 9:14-29 260
- Israel's Reliance on the Law, Rather Than on Faith Romans 9:30-33 271
- All People Invited to Salvation Through Faith Romans 10:1-13 276
- Revelations About Faith in Israel's Teachings Romans 10:14-21 284
- God's Salvation Plan for the Faithful of Israel Romans 11:1-10 295
- God's Salvation Plan for Non-Jews Romans 11:11-24 303
- Completion of God's Salvation Plan for Israel and the World Romans 11:25-32 311
- Paul's Praise to God Romans 11:33-36 317

PART SIX—Romans 12:1—15:13
The Christian Life 325
- True Worship in Changed Lives Romans 12:1-2 326
- Service Within the Fellowship Romans 12:3-8 332
- Standards for Daily Living Romans 12:9-13 341
- Christians' Response to Non-Christians Romans 12:14-21 346

- Christians and Civil
  Government .... Romans 13:1-7 352
- Love Fulfills the Law .... Romans 13:8-10 359
- End-Time Urgency .... Romans 13:11-14 363
- Personal Freedom and
  Respect for Others .... Romans 14:1-12 367
- Acting in Love Toward
  One Another .... Romans 14:13-23 375
- Characteristics of Christian
  Fellowship .... Romans 15:1-13 382

PART SEVEN—Romans 15:14—16:27
Closing of Paul's Letter 391
- Paul's Travel Plans .... Romans 15:14-33 391
- Commendation of Phoebe .... Romans 16:1-2 401
- Personal Greetings .... Romans 16:3-16 404
- Final Caution .... Romans 16:17-20 409
- Greetings From Paul's
  Fellow Workers .... Romans 16:21-24 413
- Closing Words of Praise .... Romans 16:25-27 416

SUPPLEMENTAL RESOURCES

Appendices 423
A – The Apostle Paul, Author of Romans 423
B – Paul's Missionary Work and His Letters (map) 424
C – Paul's First Missionary Journey (map) 426
D – Paul's Second Missionary Journey (map) 427
E – Paul's Third Missionary Journey (map) 428
F – Justification/Sanctification 429
G – Practices That Nurture Our Faith and Holy Living 430

Glossary 435
Bibliography 469

Foreword

What printed work can compare to Paul's Epistle to the Romans? Of the thirteen epistles (by most counts) that came to us from Paul's pen, Romans is his most profound theological treatise, and could doubtlessly be argued as the most important to today's church. Why would I say that? Because Paul himself warned us that "the Spirit explicitly says that in later times some will fall away from the faith, paying attention to deceitful spirits and doctrines of demons" (1 Tim. 4:1 NASB). Romans provides a firm doctrinal foundation for a church that finds itself surrounded by false doctrines, heresies, and even demonic misinterpretations.

There is much in Christian history that testifies to the significant influence of the Book of Romans. Aurelius Augustine, whose early years were characterized by loose living and rebellion, received Christ as Savior in AD 386 after reading a passage from this epistle. Centuries later, John Wesley was so moved by this letter that he called it his "gateway to heaven."

Someone has said that the Book of Romans is the Declaration of Independence, Constitution, and Bill of Rights for the Christian believer. If all of the Bible except the Book of Romans was lost, scarcely any fundamental doctrine would be lacking. It is a weighty book that should be carefully and prayerfully studied by every believer and accurately exegeted by every minister of the gospel.

French L. Arrington, in writing this commentary, has once again excelled as a theologian and as an expositor. Arrington is not only qualified academically to pen this volume; he is qualified experientially as a teacher and as a gifted communicator. One cannot read Arrington without sensing that the author not only knows what he is writing about, but that he *feels* it and *lives* it. Those of us who are privileged to know the author personally and to count him as a friend know that the life behind the pen is one lived in humble submission to the Christ of the Scriptures. French L. Arrington and his late wife, Frances, have long been people filled "with all joy and peace in believing . . . [and who] abound in hope by the power of the Holy Spirit" (Rom. 15:13).

There are at least three things (in addition to the author's academic excellence) that make this commentary extraordinary:

First, this commentary takes complex subjects and makes them easy to understand and exciting to embrace. Arrington excels at making profound things simple and at making simple things profound!

Second, this commentary provides excellent balance in the biblical studies of *grace* and *faith*. Many books have been written on Romans that tend to tilt the scales either away from grace toward faith or away from faith toward grace. Arrington interprets Scripture with Scripture to avoid such biases that can lead to error at least, or heresy at worst. This balance is especially seen in his treatment of the subject of *sanctification*, and with his section on "Salvation and Israel."

Third, while commentaries on Romans abound, this volume is unique in that it comes from the heart and soul of a Pentecostal scholar. There was a time in history when that term (*Pentecostal scholar*) would have been considered an oxymoron. Though that prejudice has long been dispelled among those of informed intellect, should there be any still holding it, Arrington removes all doubt. This theologian embraces orthodoxy, while maintaining faithfulness to his personal and denominational pneumatology.

I have often said that Paul was obviously a preacher. He gives at least three benedictions in the Book of Romans; after two of them, he keeps on writing! As you read this volume, you may have many benedictions; after each, you will keep on reading!

"Now the God of peace be with you all. Amen" (Rom. 15:33).

James E. Cossey
Administrative bishop,
Church of God in Michigan
(former editor-in-chief of
Church of God Publications)

Preface

When I arrived at Columbia Theological Seminary in 1957, the professor who served as my faculty advisor had evaluated my college transcript. He had noted that in college I had a minor in classical languages, including four semesters of Classical Greek. On that basis, he recommended that I take as my first course in New Testament studies Paul's letter to the Romans. That course gave me a deep and constant appreciation for that epistle, for it opened up my understanding of the gospel and it took me directly to the risen and living Christ. Over the years, I have returned again and again to Romans for my own spiritual enrichment and have had the privilege to teach Romans at both the college and the seminary level since 1964.

In preparing this commentary my focus has been on the theological and practical implications of Romans for the church and the world. My aim has been to provide a commentary that is easy to read and to understand. The format has been designed to make this book useful in the church and other venues where the Word of God is taught and preached. As you will observe, the first portion, entitled "Why Study Romans?" is an introduction to this study and is followed by "A Look at Romans," an overview of Paul's letter to the Romans. Following the Overview, the text of Paul's letter is divided into seven parts. These major parts are then divided into smaller sections, each of which consists of the biblical text (NKJV), exposition of that text, keywords, a summary, and a life application. At the end of each major part of the book are reflection questions and a short Prayer. Additional information, maps, and resources are provided in the appendices, glossary, and bibliography.

The New King James Version is the primary version used for this study. This translation has been chosen because it is widely used and is more contemporary. When other versions, they are noted. I have spared no effort to get at the meaning of this most crucial letter, especially with the intent to provide help for those who are present in our worship services and classes and for those who preach and teach God's Word.

I have tried to keep the focus on the text of Romans and not on what scholars have said about it. I do refer to a few scholars where their observations are helpful, but I have been very selective. Any reference to them appears in parentheses in the text. The emphasis is on what Paul says and its significance for us today.

In the exposition of the text of Romans, an occasional Greek word appears. Those who know some Greek, I hope, will be glad to see them. Those who do not can pass over the Greek words without losing any of the thought in a single sentence. Above all, I have tried to capture in readable English the heart of Romans and bring the readers along with me.

I pray that this book will provide the necessary help for Christians to have a greater appreciation and experience of the life-transforming power of the gospel. Paul's letter to the Romans sets forth the gospel more clearly than any other writing in the New Testament. When the church and its people have slipped away from the gospel, the Holy Spirit has used the message of Romans as a means of renewal and recovery. This letter has given the right perspective and help over the centuries of time; it can do the same today.

French L. Arrington, Ph.D.

With Gratitude

Many people have contributed to this work, and I am delighted to acknowledge my debt to those who have been of direct assistance and those who have offered encouragement. Mention must first be made of my immediate family: Frances, my beloved wife; our daughter, Athena, and her husband, Gary Hicks; our son, Lee, and his wife, Traci, and their two sons, Travis and Trent. Their interest in the commentary from the inception to the completion and their love have been a constant source of strength and encouragement.

I want to express special appreciation for my wife, Frances, my companion in life and ministry for more than fifty-six years. With much patience, she saw me through many writing projects. In addition to reading the manuscript for this project and offering considerable help in organizing the material, she assisted me with library research and answered my many computer questions. Thank you, Little Hon, for faithfully persevering and being so giving in your service to the Lord Jesus Christ and our family.

Likewise, I am so grateful to Athena, who read the entire manuscript and offered valuable formatting and editing ideas for the text and supplemental tables. I am greatly indebted to her.

I am also a debtor to Dr. James F. Cossey, former editor in chief of Pathway Press and now the administrative bishop of the Church of God in Michigan. Recognizing the great value of the letter of Romans to the church, he invited me to write this commentary. Dr. Cossey's friendship and constant support throughout the writing project are greatly appreciated.

Managing Editor Lance W. Colkmire has supervised the editing of the manuscript and the preparation of the accompanying technological teaching aids. I am grateful to him for his and his staff's expertise, under the direction of the publisher, Terry Hart.

To Dr. William A. Simmons, professor of New Testament and Greek at Lee University, I give special thanks for reading the manuscript and for his valuable suggestions and steadfast friendship through the years.

I must not fail to thank Dr. Ted R. Gee and his dear wife, Judy, who have been so gracious and kind to Frances and me through the years, especially in difficult times. Both of them have a keen interest in biblical studies and in this commentary.

I want to express deep appreciation to Pastor Gary W. Sears for his support and to Olive Ministries for providing office space for the completion of this writing project.

I am grateful also to Pastor Keith D. Bates, Administrative Bishop Donald R. Logan, Dr. Randy L. Eaton, Dr. David H. Gosnell, marketplace evangelist F. Kim Stone, Dr. Thomas J. Doolittle, Dr. Paul L. Lee, and Pastor Ronald M. Sharp for their encouragement and friendship.

I owe much to Pathway Press, and to Joseph A. Mirkovich, the former general director of Publications, for his commitment to publishing this book.

French L. Arrington, Ph.D.

INTRODUCTION

Why Study Romans?

- Romans and the Early Church
- Romans and Church Renewal
- The Greatness of Romans
- Romans and the Holy Spirit

What would the church be like without Paul's great letter to the Romans? Is there anything unique about this letter that makes it important for us to study it today? The purpose of this book is to answer these questions. In the following chapters, we will come to see why the Book of Romans has been so important to the church and why it continues to be a real asset for our own personal spiritual understanding today. **There is a unique quality of this book that has greatly impacted Christians throughout history and continues to impact us. From studying Paul's letter to the Romans, we can learn the content of the Christian faith like nowhere else in the New Testament.** In his letter, Paul opens vistas to the gospel, shining a light on what we can experience by embracing and living in the Good News of Christ. He profoundly shares with us an understanding of the impact of Jesus Christ on our lives and the world.

Paul's words are loaded with divine truth and require careful study and thought. Indeed the letter to the Romans is a theological jewel, but Paul's discussions in the letter are sensible and practical. In the first portion of the letter, the apostle Paul lays a mighty foundation and builds a strong superstructure. After he has completed chapters 1 through 11, he draws powerful conclusions, beginning with chapter 12, which show how the whole letter has pastoral and practical application for the Christian life, the church, and the world.

ROMANS AND THE EARLY CHURCH

The letter to the Romans has had a significant place throughout the history of the church. Since early in the Christian era, the church has recognized the importance of this letter. **The position it occupies in the New Testament indicates that the early church saw it as the most significant letter that Paul wrote.** Paul's letter to the Romans stands first among all his letters, not just because it is the longest, but it is the most ordered, complete, and comprehensive statement from his pen. Paul had written at least five letters prior to writing Romans (1 and 2 Thessalonians, Galatians, and 1 and 2 Corinthians). Most likely the letter has that position due to content, not age. Because of its content, **Romans has had a remarkable influence on the early life of the church and its theology.**

This influence of Romans on the early church can be seen in the writings of one of the great thinkers of the early church, **Irenaeus, bishop of Lyons in Gaul.** Irenaeus, who lived in the latter part of the second century, had a true affinity for Paul's teachings. **Irenaeus' doctrine of salvation was centered in Christ's life and death, and he emphasized the importance of the Holy Spirit as the means of living the Christian life.** Irenaeus' answer to the question of why Christ came from heaven was "that He might destroy sin, overcome death, and give life to man" (*Against Heresies*, III, 18, 7). Like Paul, Irenaeus saw the coming of Christ in the flesh as absolutely essential to salvation. On the basis of Romans 8:3-4, Irenaeus stated, "The law, being spiritual, merely displayed sin for what it is; it did not destroy it, for sin did not hold sway over spirit but over man. For He who was to destroy sin and redeem man from guilt had to enter into the very condition of man" (*Ibid.*, V, 15). **Irenaeus' teaching on salvation and the Christian life reflects the strong influence of Romans on the thinking of one of the most creative thinkers in the second-century church, who in turn has greatly impacted the belief and life of the Christian church.**

ROMANS AND THE EARLY CHURCH

KEYWORDS

Christian / Believer
A follower of Jesus Christ and His teachings, one who is personally devoted to Him and has the features of His character. A true Christian has a genuine saving faith in Christ.

Church (*ekklesia*)
The family of God, created by the Holy Spirit. The Christian church stands in unity with the people of God in the Old Testament (Matt. 8:11; Rom.11:16-28). In the New Testament *ekklesia* is mainly used in two ways:
1. The body of Christ/one body in Christ—The whole redeemed fellowship in heaven and earth (Matt. 16:18; Eph. 1:22)
2. A gathering of worshipers—An assembly, a gathering of people who meet to worship the Lord (Acts 19:39, 41)

Romans/The Book of Romans/Letter to the Romans/Epistle to the Romans
Paul's pastoral letter to the Christian church in Rome around the year AD 58. It is generally agreed that Romans is the most important letter that Paul wrote from a theological point of view. Written from Corinth during Paul's third missionary journey, his explanation of salvation is profound, and he applies the truths of God's grace and salvation broadly. There is no dispute among biblical scholars that the letter's claim of Paul being its author is true. Similarities between Galatians and Romans help to establish Romans as coming from Paul's pen.

ROMANS AND CHURCH RENEWAL

A number of instances can be cited where **the power of Paul's letter to the Romans has brought about life-changing experiences for individuals and provided impetus in the church for revival and renewal movements.** The message of Romans, by touching the lives of individuals and revitalizing the spiritual life of the church, **has restored an understanding of what God did and continues to do in Jesus Christ.**

One such individual who was touched by Paul's letter to the Romans was the **great church father Augustine** (AD 354-430). **It was through reading Romans 13:13-14 that he came to faith in Jesus Christ.** Augustine tells his story in his *Confessions*. At the time of his conversion, he was deeply distraught because his attempts to live a good moral life had been a failure. But on one occasion he was in a garden and heard a voice saying, "Take and read." The voice sounded like that of a child, and Augustine rushed back to where a friend was sitting in the garden. There he had left a copy of Paul's letters. Immediately he picked up the volume and read the first words that his eyes fell upon: "Let us walk properly, as in the day, not in revelry and drunkenness, not in lewdness and lust, not in strife and envy. But put on the Lord Jesus Christ, and make no provision for the flesh, to fulfill its lusts." He had no need to read further. Through these verses, God transformed Augustine and flooded his heart with the assurance that he was a child of God (VIII, 463-67).

Another remarkable example of the power of Paul's letter to the Romans is its role in the sixteenth century **Protestant Reformation**, which was the movement that led to the repudiation of the pope's authority and to the stand that the Scripture is the sole authority for faith and practice. At first, the movement's effort was to reform the existing church according to New Testament teachings. The church leaders' reluctance to reform then led to the subsequent establishment of Protestant denominations. This tremendous renewal of the church began while **Martin Luther** was a professor of Bible at a seminary in Wittenberg, Germany. **Luther, along with his students, began to read Romans and to set aside the misinterpretations that had been imposed on it by the church.** As Luther and his students did this, they began to grasp the true meaning of the gospel. Only gradually did Luther come to understand the revolutionary significance of what he was reading. At first the Book of Romans spoke to him personally, liberating his soul from the agonies and frustrations of doubt and establishing his Christian life on the solid and enduring ground of the gospel. But soon Luther became convinced that the teaching and practices of the church of his day were clearly in contradiction to the gospel, which he had first discovered in Romans and later in the whole of the Scriptures (Smart, 1972, 16-17).

Two centuries later, there was a great need for a spiritual awakening. **An evangelical movement** began under the leadership of

John and Charles Wesley and other Christians. Aware of the noticeable spiritual decline, **a group of people who were deeply troubled by the condition of the church gathered together in London, England. They met in a house on Aldersgate Street to listen to the reading of Luther's commentary on Romans.** John Wesley was present that evening. As he listened, his heart was "strangely warmed." The words of Paul, interpreted by Luther, brought the heartfelt, transforming power of the gospel to bear on Wesley's life. From that time on, he was profoundly influenced by Paul's message to the Romans, particularly as he developed his theology and preached the gospel. Through the ministry of Wesley, the spiritual awakening that began in England reached America and had a tremendous impact on revitalizing the life of the Christian church. But more than that, it changed the way the entrance into the Christian life was viewed by a majority of American churches. **Many churches began to emphasize faith as being vital to a conversion experience, to transforming and regenerative change, and to entering the kingdom of God.** Romans, therefore, played a key part in the spiritual and theological renewal of the church in Europe and America.

The immense influence of Romans in America reached beyond the time of John Wesley and the great Wesleyan revival. The letter to the Romans continued to have a growing significance through a pastor by the name of **Karl Barth** (1886-1968). During the First World War, Barth was a young Swiss pastor who became deeply dissatisfied with the way liberal scholars in German universities were presenting the gospel. As a result, he began to study Romans and preach and teach it. A man of amazing ability and vitality, he wrote two commentaries on the letter to the Romans prior to leaving his ten-year pastorate for a professorship. The second was more explosive and influential than the first. **In his commentaries, Barth proposed the idea that the Christian faith was usually blended with the present-day national culture. The result of such blending was that values of faith and values of the world were often viewed by the church as being the same.** This blending of the gospel and the world's values reinforced the self-confidence of modern people, but it failed to remind them that they were under divine judgment and called to repentance. **He wanted humankind to understand what God thought about them and the way that God had come to them. God's Word had become flesh in Jesus Christ.** Christianity was not a human religion, but divine revelation—not the word of man, but the Word of God. For Barth, the message of Romans is this: *Let God be God*.

Barth is identified with Romans more than any other person in the history of the church. Over a span of sixty years, he wrote three commentaries and many studies on specific passages of the letter. The effect of his influence was felt beyond Switzerland and Germany and had a decisive impact on some areas of church life in America. His second commentary caused many to rethink their approach to the Scriptures and their understanding of the faith. **This expansion in thought and understanding had a profound effect on the Christian church.** Throughout his life, Barth remained a student of God's Word and continued to grow in his grasp of the faith. But never did he think that he had fully fathomed the depth of God's message in Romans. In the preface to *A Shorter Commentary on Romans*, his third commentary, he says, "After all, there is always something new to learn from the Epistle of Romans" (1959, 8).

A number of people have paid tribute to Barth for his Christ-centered, Trinitarian approach to the Scriptures. There is no doubt that many have been inspired by him to look in a fresh way at Paul and to come to a deeper understanding of what God has done in Christ and to be more committed to the truths of the gospel.

ROMANS AND CHURCH RENEWAL

KEYWORDS

Protestant Reformation
A Christian religious movement in the sixteenth century under the leadership of Martin Luther's teaching, which resulted in the reconstruction of Western Christianity according to the norms of Scripture and the separation of Protestant churches from the Roman Catholic Church. Opposition from the Roman Catholic leadership led Luther to emphasize the sole authority of the Scriptures and Paul's doctrine of justification through faith.

THE GREATNESS OF ROMANS

Earlier we observed that Romans occupies the honor of first place among Paul's letters. There is no doubt that the apostle spoke to his day. However, since more than nineteen centuries exist between his time and ours, we must ask why Paul's writings, and particularly his letter to the Romans, are the living Word of God for all times. Does Paul speak directly to us, person to person, and to all who will listen to him? By way of answer, let it be said that **the apostle Paul was more than simply a character in the New Testament; he was specially chosen by God and inspired to share the Word of God with all generations.** Though dead, he is still relevant to modern life and speaks to us. Through his letters, Paul enters rather easily into our modern world and serves well as a guide to our understanding of the saving work of Christ and to our receiving salvation. In his letter to the Romans, **Paul teaches that we have been made for fellowship with God**, but sin has separated us from Him. We cannot save ourselves from the deadly grip of sin, but God's grace in Christ bridges the chasm between God's holiness and our sin. **Now through faith in Christ, we can be put in a right relationship with God and be forgiven of our sins.**

No wonder the message of Romans has been used by the Holy Spirit as a major source to bring about spiritual revivals in the church and to have a continuing influence on God's people. **This letter takes us to the living heart of the gospel.** As the name of the letter indicates, Paul wrote it to a church in a city known as Rome. At the same time without knowing it, he wrote it to the whole world and for all the ages, supporting the efforts of cross-cultural ministry and providing a key to understanding the Bible. **So even though this great letter was addressed to the saints in Rome during the first century, its message is eternal, and its mandates are universal.**

Themes of Romans

The letter to the Romans covers several universal themes:
- **Our Need for Salvation.** Romans affirms that people of all times and nations are sinners and are in need of salvation.

- **God's Grace and Our Faith.** It also points to the fact that neither the law of Moses nor any work by humans has ever been, nor can ever be, the means of salvation.
- **Scope of Salvation.** Paul tells us in Romans that the scope of salvation is broader than individual souls and the church, for it includes the renewal of creation (Rom. 8:19-21). Sin and grace are universal and can be traced to their ultimate sources in Adam and Christ. The only hope for all of humankind—whether Jew or Gentile—is total trust in Christ for salvation.
- **Christian Service.** Regarding believers' discharging their duties, Paul asserts that love is the key characteristic in relating to the state, the church, neighbors, brothers and sisters in Christ, and themselves. Indeed, Paul lived in faith before God; and with great spiritual insight, he taught that total trust in Christ frees us to love God and neighbor.

A Message for All Times

The letter that Paul wrote to Rome plumbs the depths of the human heart and human existence. It deals with the decisions and destiny of all people and is marked by great energy and eloquence. Its arguments flow like a broad and deep river—quiet—but its current moves forever onward. **Romans is a relentless flow of divine truth, often with the writer's earnest and warm feelings and his keen sense of its relevance to human life** (Stifler, 1960, 20).

Too often, Paul is thought to be an abstract thinker, saying too much about the future and not enough about the present. **While Paul does emphasize the importance of the future life in heaven, he also understands that in the present, Christians should already be living the End-Time life, reflecting that they are citizens of heaven—a new people should live a new life.** To use a technical term, this is frequently called "*eschatological* (End-Time) existence"—the future life begins here for those who trust in Christ as their Savior. Indeed, we already experience the reality of "the gospel of God" that Paul talks about in Romans (1:1).

Why Study Romans?

What can we conclude from the study so far? The greatness of Paul's letter to the Romans has been hailed by many over the years. **Paul's letter to the Christians in Rome is his masterpiece.** In it he shows the connection of the gospel to all humankind and to all creation. Martin Luther described it as "the chief book in the New Testament and the purest gospel." John Knox, a modern American professor, says that it is "unquestionably the most important letter ever written." A Scottish New Testament professor by the name of A. M. Hunter declares it to be Paul's *magnum opus*. These are only a few examples, for many have ranked Romans as the greatest letter in the literature of the world. This estimation of greatness may appear to be a bit overstated; but **when we consider the remarkable influence that Romans has had on the church and the world for twenty centuries, it is right to describe Romans as the greatest letter ever written.** It is hard to overestimate the value of Romans. Just the way it transformed the lives of Martin Luther, John Wesley, and millions of others, the Holy Spirit still uses the truths of Romans to transform the lives of men and women. We can safely say that its day is not over. Paul's words in Romans will continue to have a vast influence until Jesus Christ comes again.

THE GREATNESS OF ROMANS

KEYWORDS

Christian Service (by all believers) (*diakonia*)
Actions and work through which followers of Christ express God's love, peace, and joy, benefiting others and the world God created

Faith
A response of a person to God, in which there is a trusted reliance on Him and faithfulness in life to Him

Gospel
Good News about Christ and eternal life

Grace (*charis*)
Unearned favor and blessings from God

Salvation
God's work in bringing people to eternal life

ROMANS AND THE HOLY SPIRIT

We know that the entire Bible is the inspired Word of God (2 Tim. 3:16) and requires the illumination of the Holy Spirit in order to understand the messages of the books of the Bible (1 Cor. 2:6-16). The Bible is the work of men to whom the Word of God was revealed in various ways. God guided and inspired them to write what sometimes they themselves did not understand. Though the books have human authors, they are divine in origin. The books were produced under divine inspiration, that is, "God-breathed" (2 Tim. 3:16 NIV).

The letter to the Romans is no exception. **The Holy Spirit inspired Paul and revealed to him the great truths of Romans.** Since the truths given by God must be understood by the help of God, **we need the help of the Holy Spirit to grasp the full significance of the gospel in Romans and to be able to apply it to our own lives and to teach others what Christ can do for them.** This study may whet your appetite for more, and you may ask for more. Just as Barth said, "There is always something new in Romans." So as we study, we should feel free to get the help we can from other sources. Even though the Holy Spirit may choose to enlighten us through those whom He has already enlightened, we also need to seek the Holy Spirit's aid through prayer. The Holy Spirit is crucial to our understanding "the deep things of God" (1 Cor. 2:10-16). Indeed, **the Holy Spirit and careful study will enhance our grasp of the grand perspective of Romans and its message from the living God for all times.**

Now we are going to take a look at some important facts about Romans which will help you to understand better what Paul wrote to the Roman Christians. As you embark on the journey through Romans, and sit at the feet of Paul, the greatest theologian and missionary of the church, my prayer is that the Holy Spirit will bless and enrich you and strengthen your commitment to our Lord.

Why Study Romans?

ROMANS AND THE HOLY SPIRIT

KEYWORDS

Bible
The collection of holy writings (Scriptures) that Christians use as their guide for life and which consists of sixty-six books—thirty-nine in the Old Testament and twenty-seven in the New Testament

Doctrine
A body or system of beliefs and teachings; also refers to the central theological themes of Scripture, particularly including the teachings given by Jesus and the apostles. "Sound doctrine" is vital to the Christian life (1 Tim.1:10; Titus 2:1). The early Christians devoted themselves to "the apostles' doctrine" (Acts 2:42).

Holy Spirit/The Spirit
The third person of the Godhead. The Spirit is equal to and works with the Father and the Son, calling people to Christ and His saving grace, bestowing spiritual gifts, and giving guidance, power, and peace for the Christian life.

INTRODUCTION—WHY STUDY ROMANS?

SUMMARY

Importance of Romans in the Christian Church
No other book in the Bible has influenced the church as much as Romans, which furnishes a valuable key to understanding both the Old Testament and the New Testament. The influence of the great doctrinal truths of this letter had become apparent in the second century. God used Romans to transform the heart and thinking of Augustine. It also provided the impetus and biblical basis for the Protestant Reformation, and later for the spiritual awakening under the leadership of the Wesley brothers. Through the years, Romans has been used by pastors and Bible teachers everywhere.

Factors That Make the Book of Romans Great
- The most complete statement of Christian doctrine in the Bible
- Exciting and relevant
- Confronts the mind of humans with the truth of God
- Encourages discipleship and godly living
- Speaks to anyone who will listen

The Holy Spirit's Role in Our Understanding
Only by the Holy Spirit can the heart of the biblical message be penetrated. Therefore, the Spirit's role in illuminating and interpreting Scripture is indispensable. The Spirit is the ultimate author of the Bible, and we need the aid of the Spirit, the great revealer, to understand the truths of Scripture.

LIFE APPLICATION

You are about to embark on one of the most significant studies in your lifetime. This letter is filled with truths that will nurture your soul and enable you to live a more godly life because of what God has done for you in Christ. On the pages of Romans, you will find spiritual and practical truth that will help you to understand the rest of the Bible. Approach this study with prayer and a keen sense of dependence on the Holy Spirit.

REFLECTION—INTRODUCTION

1. What can you tell us about the early influence of the letter of Romans in the church?

2. What significance did Paul's letter to the Romans have for Luther, Wesley, and Barth?

3. Can you identify a few of the major themes in Romans?

4. How would you explain the greatness of Romans?

Prayer

Our Father, we begin this study with the desire to grasp the doctrinal principles and truths of Romans. By the Holy Spirit, open our hearts and minds so that we do not only understand the truth but that we also allow the teaching of Scripture to direct our daily walk with You. May the truths of the Bible take root in our lives and may the Holy Spirit empower us to share the gospel. Amen.

ROMANS OVERVIEW

A Look at Paul's Letter to the Romans

- The Apostle Paul, Author of Romans
- About Paul's Writings
- Occasion and Date of Paul's Letter to the Church in Rome
- Reasons for Paul's Letter to the Church in Rome
- The Christian Church in Rome
- Emphases of Paul's Letter

Our main concern in this study, *The Greatest Letter Ever Written*, is to understand Paul's message to the Romans and its relevance for the church and the world today. The focus will be on the text of Romans and the thoughts of its author, who claimed to "have the mind of Christ" and to "have the Spirit of God" (1 Cor. 2:16; 7:40). In order to enhance our study, we will first look briefly at a few matters about the Book of Romans—its author (the apostle Paul), his ministry, his purpose for writing, and the background of the Roman Christians.

THE APOSTLE PAUL, AUTHOR OF ROMANS

Most biblical scholars are in agreement that the author of Romans was the apostle Paul, formerly known as Saul of Tarsus. Paul was born about AD 3 during the reign of Caesar Augustus and was executed in AD 67 under Nero. From his letters and the Book of Acts, we know several facts about Paul's life:

1. **He was born to devout Jewish parents in the Greek city of Tarsus in Asia Minor.** Paul's parents had retained the language and customs of the Jewish people, and in keeping with

Jewish custom, they had him circumcised on the eighth day of his life (Phil. 3:5; cf. 2 Cor. 11:22). During his early life, Paul lived in the Roman province of Cilicia, the capital of which was Tarsus. This province was located between the Black, Aegean, and Mediterranean Seas. The city of Tarsus was a center of commerce and intellectual life, famous for its great university. It was also well known for the manufacture of felt from goats' hair, which was used for the making of tents. Paul was a tentmaker by trade.

2. **He was a very conscientious, religious Jew, who was proud of his people and their place in history.** He believed that his people had and would continue to play a significant role in the history of humankind. Even after the life, death, and resurrection of Christ, he believed that Israel had a special place in the purpose of God (Rom. 9–11).

3. **At an early age, Paul's family probably brought him to Jerusalem in order for him to study to become a religious leader.** Eventually, he was trained as a rabbi in the school of the Jewish teacher Gamaliel (Acts 22:3; cf. 5:33-42).

4. **He surpassed many of his contemporaries in devotion and zeal for the faith of his fathers** (Gal. 1:13-14). Before his conversion to Christ, Paul became an ardent persecutor of the Christian movement. This zealous period of violence came to an abrupt end when the Lord confronted Paul on his way to the city of Damascus. On that occasion, Paul was traveling to Damascus with the intent of imprisoning Christians and bringing them back to Jerusalem. During the Lord's confrontation, Paul was not only converted, but also called to preach the gospel and to be an apostle to the Gentiles (Acts 9:1-19).

5. **As a result of Paul's life-changing experience, he became a courageous, pioneering missionary for Jesus Christ.** Assisted by others, he carried the gospel into the Roman/Greek world on three missionary journeys (Acts 13:1–14:28; 16:6–18:23; 18:24–19:20).

6. **Paul's missionary work involved reaching out to Jews, as well as Gentiles.** Paul's missionary strategy was to go first to the synagogues (Acts 18:1-4). This practice grew out of his conviction that salvation was for the Jews and that the gospel which

he preached should first be offered to the Jews (Rom. 9:1-4). To the end of his life, Paul persisted in his desire to see his people accept Christ as their Savior. We can conclude that Paul had this ongoing desire based on the fact that during his third missionary journey, he planned to travel to Jerusalem in order to deliver funds from the Gentile churches to the needy believers there, and then continue on to Rome and Spain (15:22-33).

7. **Paul suffered and died for his missionary efforts.** As Paul was writing to the Romans, he was not expecting to arrive in Rome in chains. However, later when Paul was in route to Rome and he stopped in Jerusalem to minister and deliver funds, the Jews accused him of religious heresy and political sedition. Roman authorities arrested and held him in custody for two years and then sent him to Rome as a prisoner (Acts 21:26–27:1). Tradition says that Paul was executed in AD 67, most likely at the hand of Nero.

THE APOSTLE PAUL, AUTHOR OF ROMANS

KEYWORDS

Apostle (*apostolos*)
A person whom a sender dispatches with authority to fulfill a mission

Gentiles
A biblical term used to describe people who were not Jews

Gospel (see p. 23)

Jews/Israelites/Hebrews
The *Jews* were Abraham's descendants who were also called *Hebrews* or *Israelites*. The term *Jews* refers to national origin, while the term *Israelites* indicates membership in the covenant community based on God's promises to Jacob.

Missionary
A person who is especially sent by God to preach the gospel and to do the work of the church

Salvation (see p. 23)

> **SUMMARY**
> For biographical information about Paul, see:
> - *The Apostle Paul, Author of Romans*—Appendix (A) on page 423
> - *Paul's Missionary Work and His Letters*—Appendix (B) on pages 424-425
>
> For maps of Paul's missionary journeys, see:
> - Appendices (B, C, D, E) on pages 424-428.

ABOUT PAUL'S WRITINGS

Paul's Writing Style

Paul's comments are not academic exercises or theological treatises, but messages from God to His children. Paul's letters to the churches are similar and also have characteristics that were common among other letters of his day. The letter to the Romans, however, is unique even among Paul's letters, due to the fact that the recipients of the letter were a church that Paul did not establish nor had ever visited. Because Paul was writing to a church where the majority of the Christians did not know him personally, he felt compelled to declare to them the gospel in a complete manner. Like his other letters, Romans shows that Paul took his readers seriously and was very careful in interpreting the gospel for them.

Among the factors that affected Paul's letter writing style was his desire to address concrete issues within each church. In the case of the Roman congregation, because the church was not established by him, he was not as knowledgeable about their particular concerns and problems. Because of this lack of knowledge, Paul in his letter to the Romans is more general in his approach. He does not identify any adversaries by name or deal directly with any opponents. Romans is a genuine letter containing valuable information and spiritual insights. It contains warm, personal correspondence that addresses broader issues, like the tensions between Jewish and Gentile Christians in the Roman church. Although scholars do not consider Romans to be a "treatise in systematic theology" (that is, a comprehensive statement of all his theological beliefs), the depth of its spiritual insight is great and was valuable for the Roman Christians, as well as for Christians today.

When studying Paul's correspondence, some parts may require careful thought in order to understand their meaning (see 2 Peter 3:15-16). Information about Paul's religious and cultural background and that of his readers will help us understand the gospel that had been revealed to him.

Paul, like most people of his day, dictated his letters to a scribe. After completing the dictation, he would add his own signature. In Romans 16:22, Tertius, the scribe, added his greeting before closing this letter. This use of a scribe may explain why at places in Paul's letters the meaning is difficult to understand—probably because the scribes who recorded his dictations were inexperienced in inscribing letters of such theological depth and complexity. It is not hard to imagine that Paul, inspired by the Spirit, dictated the text, while his scribe rushed to record every word. We have no way of knowing if the letters were taken down in longhand or some form of shorthand, but his letters are products of what the Holy Spirit inspired him to say to the church of his day and to believers across the centuries.

OCCASION AND DATE OF PAUL'S LETTER TO THE CHURCH IN ROME

As we read a letter, it is normal to want to know as much as possible about the author, the receiver, and the occasion that prompted the writing of the letter. **Paul wrote his letter to the Romans in AD 58 while he was on his third missionary journey, during his stay in the city of Corinth in Greece.** *For map of locations of churches that received letters from Paul, see Appendix (B) on pages* 424-425.

Review of Paul's Missionary Journeys

A brief review of Paul's three journeys will place the writing of Romans in the context of his ministry:

First Journey—Island of Cyprus and Southern Asia Minor. The first campaign, lasting about three years, took him through the island of Cyprus and then to Asia Minor, where he planted churches in the cities of Antioch (Pisidia), Iconium, Lystra, and Derbe (Acts 13:1–14:28). *For map, see Appendix (C) on page* 426.

Second Journey—Asia Minor and Europe. The second journey, also lasting about three years, took him across Asia Minor, revisiting the churches he had planted on the first journey. He then crossed into Europe and established churches in the cities of Philippi, Thessalonica, and Corinth (Acts 16:6–18:23). *For map, see Appendix (D) on page* 427.

Third Journey—Asia Minor, Europe, and Macedonia. The third journey covered much of the same route as did the second and involved a long stay in the city of Ephesus. Leaving Ephesus, Paul traveled westward through Macedonia. He came to Greece (Corinth), and while he was there he wrote Romans (see 15:24-33). At that time, he planned to deliver to the needy Christians in Jerusalem the funds received from the Gentile churches. (This collection is referred to by scholars as the "Pauline Collection".) Luke records the third journey in Acts 18:24–19:20. *For map, see Appendix (E) on page* 428.

A Time of Transition

The apostle Paul wrote his magnificent letter to the Romans at a time when his ministry was in transition and his life was at a turning point. During his third missionary journey, Paul remained in Corinth for three months, where he wrote his letter to the Romans. Since near the end of the letter Paul says to the Roman Christians, "But now I am going to Jerusalem to minister to the saints" (15:25), **he must have penned the letter just before he departed for Jerusalem.** These events would have placed him corresponding with the Romans in AD 58, about thirty years after Jesus' death and about twenty years after his conversion experience on the Damascus road.

At the end of his third missionary journey, as Paul was completing his ministry in the eastern Mediterranean world,

he now was thinking about ministry in the West, planning to visit Rome and to preach the gospel in Spain. The controversies that he had encountered in the Corinthian and Galatian churches were now behind him. His stay in Corinth for three months is the only time we have an indication of Paul's being on vacation and relatively free with some extended time to rest (Acts 20:1-3). We can imagine then that Paul must have written this marvelous letter to Roman believers on a quiet backstreet in Corinth.

REASONS FOR PAUL'S LETTER TO THE CHURCH IN ROME

In Paul's letter, he indicates that he had a growing desire to visit Rome, but no doubt he also had other reasons for writing to the Roman Christians. These additional reasons for writing have been debated by biblical scholars. Their debates frequently have focused on whether or not Paul was attempting to address particular problems among the Roman believers. An examination of these scholars' discussions reaches beyond the scope of this study. However, by examining the content of his letter, we can conclude Paul's main reasons for writing (1:9-15; 15:22-29). The words in his correspondence reflect that the purpose of his letter comes from both his situation and that of the Roman believers.

Paul's Introduction of Himself and His Message (1:1-17)

Though Paul had never been to Rome, he did have apostolic authority over the Roman church. He was the "apostle to the Gentiles," which gave him universally binding authority (11:13; Gal. 2:8). **As a result of this more distant relationship with the Christians in Rome, he took great care when he drafted his letter to them, immediately identifying who he was and explaining the general content of the letter.** In his introduction he gave a lengthy and logical explanation of his ministry and preaching, along with his general concerns, but he never lost sight of his Roman readers. At the opening of this letter, he expresses his eagerness to preach the gospel to the Roman Christians (1:15) before he deals at length with some disagreements that had arisen between those who were stronger in faith and those who were weaker in faith (14:1–15:13). Moreover, the tone of Paul's introduction indicates that he may have suspected that false rumors in Rome about himself and his ministry had circulated. Criticism regarding his preaching a law-free gospel had spread widely throughout Jewish communities. This criticism could have preceded him before going to Rome. In some measure, Romans may be an attempt to counteract any rumors that might have characterized him as being a dangerous and divisive person, whose teaching led to immoral living (6:1ff; 12–14). To say the least, it was good for Paul to explain his role in preaching the gospel. Romans clarified his teaching for those who knew him only by rumor and criticism, which would help to pave the way for his arrival, and then he would continue on to Spain with Roman support.

Pastoral Encouragement for the Church (1:11-12)

The apostle Paul wanted to encourage and strengthen the Roman believers. Although he had never set his foot in Rome, Paul and the Romans were not complete strangers to each other. In Romans, Paul declares that the faith of the Roman Christians "is spoken of throughout the whole world" (1:8) and that they "are full of goodness, filled with all knowledge, able also to admonish one another" (15:14). Most likely some of Paul's coworkers were among those who had started the Roman church and were included in the twenty-six recipients to whom he sends greetings in chapter 16. No doubt, Paul felt some pastoral responsibility toward them (1:11; 15:14-16). From Paul's comments, it appears that the believers in Rome had been hoping for a visit from the apostle. As he told them, he had intended to come to them earlier, but had always been prevented (1:13; 15:18-23), apparently because of his ministry in the East. Perhaps he sensed that they were becoming impatient, so he assured them that he was on his way to see them after the delivery of the funds for the needy Christians in Jerusalem. Warm, mutual feelings characterized the relationship between Paul and the Roman believers. **Because Paul had the heart of a pastor, in his letter he expressed a genuine heartfelt concern for them.**

Appeal for Financial Support (15:24)

Paul's missionary plans included reaching out to the Western world as far as Spain, and he wanted the Christians in Rome to assume some responsibility for that Spanish missionary work. With this goal in mind in his letter, **Paul asked the Roman church to support his missionary efforts to the farthest parts of the West, where the gospel had not been preached.** His words deserve close examination:

> Whenever I journey to Spain, I shall come to you. For I hope to see you on my journey, and to be helped on my way there by you (15:24).

One precise purpose for his writing this letter is indicated by his words "to be helped on my way there by you," which literally reads in the Greek, "by you to be sent there." The word "there" refers to Spain, and "to be sent" is almost a technical missionary term, meaning "to send forth," not just with prayer and good wishes but also with food and money (cf. Acts 15:3; 1 Cor. 16:6; 2 Cor. 1:16; 3 John 6). **Apparently in addition to prayers and good will, Paul was hinting for the Roman believers to give financial support to aid his Spanish mission and to help him make travel arrangements for the journey. Very likely, one reason for his drafting the letter and carefully explaining the gospel was to convince them that his mission to Spain was worthy of their support.**

Preparation for a New Home Base (15:23-24, 28)

During his ministry in the East, Paul's base had been Antioch in Syria. Normally, he returned to Antioch upon concluding a missionary journey; but **now anticipating preaching in the West, Paul would need another home base for the second phase of his ministry.** The ideal city for it would be Rome—it was the capital of the entire Roman Empire, and its great armies and its political system dominated the whole civilized world.

From the great city of Rome came many lines of communication, and people constantly traveled to and from the city. Evidently, Paul was convinced that Rome would be a strategic home base for his future ministry, and he hoped that the strong church in that city would share his vision for the mission into the West (Smart, 1972, 23-24).

Request for Prayer (15:30-31)

In view of his upcoming visit to Jerusalem to deliver the funds for the Christians who were in need, Paul was somewhat anxious about his arrival in the center of the Jewish world. As his request for prayer reflects, he was uncertain if he would encounter trouble when entering Judea. Doubting what kind of reception awaited him, he wrote, "Now I beg you, brethren, through the Lord Jesus Christ, and through the love of the Spirit, that you strive together with me in your prayers to God for me, that I may be delivered from those in Judea who do not believe, and that my service for Jerusalem may be acceptable to the saints" (15:30-31). **His first concern was about his enemies: "those in Judea who do not believe."** Such hostile unbelievers had tried to kill him on a previous visit (Acts 9:29). The apostle wanted to be assured of the Roman Christians' prayers before undertaking the dangerous mission to the Holy City. **The second deep concern was whether the Jewish believers in Jerusalem would receive the financial gift from the Gentile churches.** The Gentiles had given the money with gladness, and the gift was not simply something that the Gentiles owed to the mother church (Rom. 15:26-27). It is unclear why the Jewish believers might not have graciously received the gift. But it is well to remember that the gift was from Gentiles, and the traditional Jewish belief was that anything that a Gentile had touched was unclean. As Jewish Christians who continued to observe their traditional religious practices, they could have refused the gift.

Another possible reason that the Jewish believers might have rejected a monetary gift was that they might have thought it to be a bribe from the Gentiles—that the Gentiles gave it to Paul in order to convince him to preach a gospel that was free of Jewish law. Some Jewish believers were unhappy with Paul's message.

Such attitudes might have prompted Paul to request that the Romans pray that the gift would be received with gladness, in the same spirit in which it was given. Paul's intent was to minister to the needs of the Christians in poverty and to show that the Spirit's love was at work in the Gentile churches. Paul, therefore, asked the Roman believers to keep him in prayer that no harm would come to him and that the Jewish believers would be pleased to receive the monetary gift from the Gentile churches.

Explanation of the Gospel (1:15; 15:29)

Earlier the Lord had spoken to Paul and said, "Be of good cheer, Paul; for as you have testified for Me in Jerusalem, so you must also bear witness at Rome" (Acts 23:11). In the opening chapter we read, "So, as much as is in me, I am ready to preach the gospel to you who are in Rome also" (Rom. 1:15). Until Paul arrived in Rome, the letter to the church would substitute for his personal presence and would inform those who did not know Paul personally about the nature of what he preached. However, Paul's expectation was that whenever he reached Rome, he would preach "both to Greeks and to barbarians, both to wise and to unwise" so as to "have some fruit among you also" (1:13-14). **The apostle Paul desired to be active as an evangelist while in Rome and to share the gospel with anyone who would listen to him.** The Roman Christians knew what to expect of Paul while he was among them. **It turned out that he did not arrive in Rome as an evangelist, as he desired, but as a prisoner in chains (Acts 28:16).**

ABOUT PAUL'S WRITINGS

KEYWORDS

Holy Spirit/The Spirit (*pneuma*) (see p. 25)

Missionary (see p. 29)

Paul's Letters and Missionary Journeys
For maps, see Appendices (B, C, D, E) on pages 424-428.

> **Rome**
> The capital of the Roman Empire, which dominated Europe and the Mediterranean world from 44 BC to AD 1453, commanding respect of millions of people

> **SUMMARY**
>
> **Characteristics of Paul's Writings**
> - Inspired by the Holy Spirit
> - Included letters of encouragement to churches
> - Addressed general spiritual issues
> - Addressed areas of concern to particular churches
> - Complex and thought-provoking
>
> **Time Frame in Which Paul Wrote His Letter**
> - AD 58 (about 30 years after the death and resurrection of Jesus, about 20 years after Paul's conversion experience on the Damascus road)
> - During Paul's third missionary journey, while staying in Corinth
> - At a time of transition in his ministry—just before heading to Jerusalem and then west to Rome
>
> **Reasons for Paul's Letter to the Romans**
> - Introduce himself and his message
> - Encourage the Christian church in Rome
> - Ask for financial support
> - Prepare for a new home base
> - Request prayer
> - Explain the gospel (Good News about Christ)

> **LIFE APPLICATION**
>
> Paul's letter to the Romans is the key to our understanding the rest of the Bible. A solid grasp of Romans will be very useful to us in building our faith and becoming a devoted follower of Jesus Christ.

THE CHRISTIAN CHURCH IN ROME

Establishment of the Roman Church

The Christian church had been securely established in Rome by the time Paul wrote his letter. In fact, it had been in existence for "many years" before Paul wrote Romans (15:23) in AD 58. **The church had existed before AD 49, the year the Roman emperor Claudius expelled the Jews from the**

city of Rome because of riots that centered around *Chrestus* (Suetonius, "Claudius," 25, in *The Lives of the Twelve Caesars*). The disturbance arose because of the teaching of *Chrestus* (Christ), indicating that the Christians were preaching the gospel in Rome. Conceivably, among those who might have been expelled from the city of Rome were Aquila and Priscilla, who later became Paul's coworkers (Acts 18:1-4; 1 Cor. 16:19). Although the Jewish Christians were expelled, the Gentile Christians remained free to continue in Rome, unaffected by the decree of Claudius. After the emperor's death, the decree was lifted (AD 54), and the Jews were free to return to Rome.

The exact year the church in Rome was established and the identities of the founders are unknown. As we have already observed, Rome was the center of the Roman Empire and attracted visitors and settlers from all across the empire and beyond. People were attracted to Rome for various reasons—such as business, religion, and politics. Most likely, among those who came to Rome were a few people who were carriers of the new Christian faith. **The Book of Acts leads us to think that Christianity began to penetrate the imperial city soon after the outpouring of the Holy Spirit on the Day of Pentecost.** Present at that celebration were Jewish "visitors from Rome" (Acts 2:10), who, following the outpouring of the Holy Spirit on the disciples, heard Peter preach his great sermon. **Some of the Jewish visitors from Rome could have been among the three thousand converts, and upon returning to Rome they started the church there.**

Furthermore, **the constant movement of people in and out of the imperial city might have included Christians from churches planted by Paul**, since Rome was cosmopolitan in character and engaged in trade with the East as well as the West. Three cities—Antioch, Corinth, and Ephesus—where Paul spent much time, were actively engaged in trade with Rome. **It was almost inevitable that some Christians would have ventured to Rome and could have had a part in establishing the church.**

As is evident, there is uncertainty as to who established the church in Rome, but we can be fairly sure that it was not planted by one of the twelve apostles. Although some traditions within Christianity believe the church in Rome was founded by Peter, there is no indication in the Scriptures that Peter ever visited Rome. Also, Paul makes no mention of him in his letter to the Romans. **If Peter had planted the Roman church, surely Paul would not have slighted him and would have referred to him in the introduction of his letter to the Roman believers.**

Diversity of the Roman Church

There is one other matter about the church in Rome: What was the background of its members? **When Paul wrote to the Roman Christians, the church was predominantly Gentile, but there was also a strong Jewish influence in the church (chs. 2-3; 9-11).** There was a large Jewish community in the city of Rome and a strong body of Jewish believers in the broader Christian church, but the Roman church included both Jews and Gentiles. Paul implies that the majority of the Roman believers were Gentiles (1:5; Barrett, 1991, 21-22). **Of the 26 people mentioned in chapter 16, only about 15 percent of them were Jewish.** This figure also suggests that the vast majority were Gentiles. Though in the minority, the Jewish believers would have had a considerable influence.

THE CHRISTIAN CHURCH IN ROME

KEYWORDS

Disciple
Any person who follows Jesus Christ and His teachings and endeavors to continue to learn more about His ways and to grow in their relationship with Him. The term disciples also refers to the twelve followers of Jesus who traveled and worked with Him during His life on earth.

Gentiles (see p. 29)

Jews/Israelites/Hebrews (see p. 29)

Roman Church / Christian Church in Rome

The church to whom Paul writes the Book of Romans. The beginning of the church remains unknown. Paul speaks of having long desired to visit the church (Rom.15:23) and that its faith was well known. Probably the church was established by Jewish missionaries who went to Rome after being converted on the Day of Pentecost (Acts 2:10). The majority of the Roman Christians were Gentiles, many of whom were from the lower strata of society. At the time Paul wrote to the church, there were also some Jewish Christians among the church members. Paul had a number of friends and acquaintances in the church, although most of the believers in Rome had never met Paul.

SUMMARY

The contents of Romans reveal that Paul had a number of reasons for writing the letter to a church that he did not plant and had never visited. He wrote to the Roman Christians to introduce himself and his message and to gain their favor and cooperation.

Paul's other letters deal with special problems that had arisen in the congregation to which the letter was addressed, but Romans is more general and deals with general questions. The Roman church was a diverse congregation with a number of Jewish Christians, but the majority of the believers were Gentiles.

The letters of Paul included in the Bible are not only personal, aimed at particular situations and places, but they also are authoritative documents. At the opening of Romans, Paul identifies himself as an apostle—one whom Christ appointed to proclaim the Good News of salvation. Therefore, Paul's message in Romans bears the authority of God himself.

LIFE APPLICATION

The Christians in Rome were a diverse group of people, coming from various social, economic, religious, and educational backgrounds, just as today believers come from diverse backgrounds. As a result, just as the Roman believers did, we experience tensions and conflicts in our fellowship with one another. But God's love, poured out in our hearts by the Holy Spirit, can enable us to respect each other and resolve the problems of relationship.

EMPHASES OF PAUL'S LETTER

Paul's Primary Concerns

A number of concerns shaped the apostle's point of view. A reading of Romans discloses that Paul had several theological concerns, but he mostly emphasized the four that appear to have a dominant influence in Romans. A brief review of these overarching themes will aid our understanding of Paul's message and its relevance to us.

The Gospel (Good News About Christ)

The apostle opens Romans with an emphasis on the gospel or its cognate verb *evangelize* (1:1-2, 9, 15) and likewise closes the letter with this same emphasis (15:16, 19; 16:25; Moo, 1996, 29). As well as bracketing the body of the letter to the Romans, the word *gospel* is given first place in the summary statement of the letter: "For I am not ashamed of the gospel . . ." (1:16-17). In these verses, mention is made of salvation, Jews and Gentiles, and justification by faith. These themes and several others are dealt with in Romans. All of this means that **Paul's chief goal in this letter is to explain the gospel.** For him the gospel is nothing more than what God revealed about Himself in Christ, which is Good News for a lost and despairing world. **The *gospel*, therefore, encompasses the various topics in Romans, and the letter is a summary of the gospel as Paul preached it. The Good News is wide in scope and touches all areas of our relationships and life.**

The Righteousness of God

In the gospel, the righteousness of God is revealed. The term *righteousness* (*dikaiosune*) often means, in Paul's letters, "justification" or "a right relationship"; and the verb (*dikaioo*)—which comes from the same root—means "to justify" or "to declare righteous." These words come from the courtroom and are legal terms. They do not express abstract ideas, but the saving goodness of God in Christ, basic to our experience here and now. **By the action of justification, God—as a judge might do—declares us righteous in His sight and brings us into a right**

relationship with Himself. Paul's own conversion is a marvelous example of the justifying, saving righteousness of God. Through Jesus' encounter with him on the road to Damascus, he was brought into a personal relationship with the Savior and called to be an apostle (Acts 9:1-9). From his own experience, Paul understood that God's righteousness is what God does to set us right with Himself. **In short, *justification* is God's activity of setting things right and forgiving sins through the sacrifice of Jesus Christ on the cross.**

This phrase *righteousness* of God, which is a major theme in Romans, has its roots in the Old Testament. In Psalms and the Book of Isaiah, *righteousness* and *salvation* are more or less used as synonyms, meaning God's saving, justifying activity. From the same point of view, Paul says, "The righteousness of God is revealed from faith to faith" (Rom. 1:17). **Paul's use of the term *righteousness* indicates an activity of God, rather than an attribute of God**. This usage refers to the righteous God in action, justifying, and delivering all who have faith in Christ. By believing on Christ who died for our sins, God—in His grace—sets us in a right relationship with Himself. Indeed this gives a glimpse of God's amazing grace. In our courtrooms, a judge must condemn those who are guilty, declaring their punishment. When the guilty come into God's court and approach Him with faith in Christ, He declares them to be forgiven of their sin. Using the language of the courtroom, Paul says that God declares right, acquits, and forgives the ungodly (4:5). Then, does *justification* mean "to make righteous"? No, it means "to declare, to treat as righteous." It means not only the forgiveness of sin, but also the gift of a right relationship with God. **As the result of sins being forgiven, the Holy Spirit enters the hearts of believers; and with the believers' cooperation, the Spirit enables them to live the Christian life**.

The Law

For Paul, the law was a revelation of God's will and primarily consisted of the law of Moses (Torah). It was not an abstract legal system, but was based on the will of the personal, living God (Whitely, 1964, 158). The apostle described it as "holy" and says it was meant to "bring life" (Rom. 7:10, 12). **The law is God's gift and, therefore, good.** For this reason, there is nothing wrong with the law as such. However, according to Paul, no person can be justified in God's sight by keeping the law (3:20). The law, by defining sin—"you shall" and "you shall not"—makes humans aware of what sin is and may even incite some people to sin (3:20; 5:20; 7:5, 7). **The purpose of the law was never meant to be salvation through works, but was intended to prepare us to receive the promise of salvation in Christ (5:20; Gal. 3:17, 24).** After all, no person can be saved "by works of law" or by observing any written code (see 3:21-26).

At the heart of Paul's assessment of the law was legalism, not a criticism of the law itself. Legalism is the attempt to find salvation through the law by living according to its rules and regulations. Convinced that salvation can be earned, the legalist hopes to get to heaven by doing good works. The effort is motivated by a belief that through one's own strength, a person can obey a code of conduct in order to win God's favor and earn salvation. **The letter to the Romans is Paul's emphatic rejection of legalism.**

There is also another viewpoint regarding *the law* issue. There are a number of scholars who think that Paul's intent in his letter to the Romans was not to address legalistic Jews who believed that good works would get them to heaven, but rather to speak to Jews who believed that they would be automatically saved by grace, based on God's covenant with the nation of Israel. This view has been called "the new perspective on Paul." According to this view, good works are not the means to becoming justified/saved, but the means of remaining in the saving covenant relationship (Dunn, 1988). **For some Jews, keeping the law was an expression of their love to God for saving them by His grace.**

First-century Judaism was pluralistic; all Jews did not believe the same thing. Undoubtedly, there were those Jews who were not legalistic, and did not view obedience to the law as the means of securing salvation. However, this view that obedience to the law was the means for maintaining salvation was not generally held and practiced. **So, the most natural way to read Romans is that Paul was addressing legalistic Jews who believed that by keeping the law they would earn for themselves a place in heaven.** From beginning to end, Romans includes teaching about justification and its consequences in the life of the believer. A pressing question in Romans is; How can a person be saved and come to have a harmonious relationship with God? As Paul and many others since him have found, a harmonious relationship is only through faith in Jesus Christ. Paul rejects the legalist's approach to salvation. Paul's argument in Romans is, therefore, that salvation is received by faith and the proper response to God's saving grace in Christ is living the Christian life. This truth separates the reception of justification/salvation from the works of the law.

The Two Ages

In Jewish thought, a sharp division was made between *This Age* and the future referred to as *the Coming Age*. For Paul, though, the Future Age had already broken into the Present Age. This reality occurred through Christ's life, death, resurrection, and the outpouring of the Holy Spirit (Arrington, 1977b, 113ff.). **The ministry of Christ and the presence of the Holy Spirit introduced the Coming Age into this Old Age of sin and death, modifying the rigid distinction made between This Age and the Coming Age.**

As long as the First Coming of Christ lay in the future, people could only look forward to His Coming, and therefore the new age of life was called the Coming Age. **Now that the Coming Age has dawned, we live in the period of salvation history where the two ages overlap.** Neither has This Age of sin and death been completely destroyed, nor has the Coming Age been realized in its fullness. Both of these realities will be fully realized when Christ comes again. Since the two ages overlap, it is proper to describe the biblical view of last things as *already/not yet*. To state it another way, God's End-Time work has "already" begun, but "not yet" has it been completed and will not be until He brings the Present Age to its end.[1]

As a foundation of Romans, the two-ages idea emerges in chapter 1 and continues to appear throughout Paul's letter, especially in 5:12-21. **In chapter 5, Paul places Adam and Christ in contrast: Adam represents This Age** by reason of his transgression, bringing the reign of sin and death into the whole world. In contrast, **Christ introduced the beginning of the Age to Come**, triumphing over sin and death, and providing deliverance from sin and granting life for all humankind.

Nevertheless, those who are in Christ have a new quality of life. They have already experienced the quickening power of Christ's resurrection among those who are spiritually dead in trespasses and sin. **Indeed, God has brought among us a new era grounded in a new relationship with Him, which is made possible by His saving work through Christ**. Therefore, salvation is a present experience and also a future hope. When salvation is finally and fully realized, This Age of sin and death will give way to the Coming Age of eternal life. Sin and sorrow will pass away, and eternal joy and bliss will be the experience of God's people. The old will be finished and all things will become new.

---

[1] Christ himself essentially taught the same truth, but He expressed it in a different way. Christ spoke of the kingdom of God as being both present (Matt. 4:17, 23; Luke 4:43) and future (Matt. 24; Mark 13; Luke 21). The presence of the Kingdom was evident in Christ's providing the benefits of salvation, deliverance from demons, and healing those who were sick or disabled.

MAIN EMPHASIS AND UNITY OF THEMES

The main emphasis of Romans is *justification by faith*. Although Paul emphasizes the importance of justification in his letter, just as many churches do today, he also emphasizes additional important Christian truths. In fact, we need to listen to the teachings of Romans in their entirety, not just to the first chapters on justification. **After the first five chapters, the letter goes on to include many more important truths that are applicable to our spiritual lives**. Despite the multiple topics that Paul covers, Romans is a unified letter with an unbroken unity. All of Paul's discussions flow from his understanding of the saving work of Christ. Because his main foundation is Christ's saving grace, Paul declares truths by which all humankind can live from age to age. The Christian life begins with being justified in God's sight. From that point, the entire Christian life is the outworking of faith in Christ and the empowerment of the Spirit (Rom. 8:1ff.). Thus, Romans does not consist of a collection of unrelated ideas, but a rigorous, consistent line of thought with intense harmony. **Step-by-step, Paul explains the great truths of salvation in Christ**. As Paul develops his Spirit-inspired train of thought, we need to observe carefully as he builds his message.

EMPHASES OF PAUL'S LETTER

KEYWORDS

Already / Not Yet Doctrine
Through the First Coming of Christ and His ministry on earth, the beginning of the Future Age has moved into the Present Age. Until Christ returns, the Future Age penetrates the Present Age and the two ages overlap.

Forgiveness by God
God's act of pardon or remission of sin

Gospel (see p. 23)

Grace (*charis*) (see p. 23)

Justification (*dikaiosune*)
God's act of declaring a person to be righteous

Justified by Faith (*dikaioo*)
The condition of having been forgiven and pardoned by God due to one's trusting in Christ for salvation

The Law (*Torah*)
Sacred Scriptures recorded in the Hebrew Bible (Old Testament) that give Jewish religious rules for living and authoritative regulations, specifying the relationship between God and His people. The law (*Torah*) was delivered by an authorized spokesman, such as Moses, a prophet, or priest. The moral law, essentially summarized in the Ten Commandments, had a prominent place in biblical revelation.

Legalism
Having hope for salvation based on human effort, rather than relying on God's grace

Righteousness of God/Righteousness of Faith (for believers) (*dikaiosune*)
The state of being in right relationship and standing with God, which is a gift from God to all believers

Salvation (see p. 23)

Sin
Anything contrary to the will and character of God

This Age/The Coming Age (The Two Ages)
The biblical view of history in which there are two orders of existence: this age of sin and death and the coming age of grace and life. **This Age**, also referred to as *The Age of Adam*, is dominated by sin, evil, and demonic powers and is doomed to pass away. **The Coming Age** (*The Future Age*), which was initiated into *This Age* during Christ's First Coming, will be fully realized when Christ returns in glory. Now the two ages overlap, and there is an *already/not yet* distinction. This overlap will continue until Christ returns in power and glory. At that time, *This Age* of sin and death will be destroyed (1 Cor. 2:6-7), *The Coming Age* will be fully realized, and those who believe in Christ will share in the full benefits of salvation.

SUMMARY

The apostle Paul wrote Romans from Corinth in AD 58 as he was planning to take to Jerusalem an offering given by the Gentiles churches for the needy Christians in the Holy City. We do not know who planted the church in Rome, but the evidence points to Jewish Christians converted on the Day of Pentecost (Acts 2:10). At the time Paul wrote Romans, his ministry was coming to an end in the East, and he was planning to go to Rome and then on into Spain to preach the gospel in the West. So he wrote to the Roman Christians to prepare them for his visit.

In his letter, the apostle introduces himself and his message, which emphasized such themes as the gospel, righteousness of God, law, and the two ages. He places a heavy emphasis on justification by faith along with several other important Christian truths.

LIFE APPLICATION

Paul's godly zeal to share the gospel with others is a wonderful model for us. God gave Paul and us the greatest message in the world, the Good News about Jesus Christ and eternal life. God expects those of us who are Christians to share the Good News with family, friends, coworkers, those in the marketplace, and others with whom we come in contact every day. The gospel is a powerful message that can save us from the misery of sin and lead us to eternal life.

REFLECTION—ROMANS OVERVIEW

1. What are some of the things about the person of Paul and his ministry that strike you as being significant?

2. How would you define the gospel? Why is it so important today?

3. Briefly summarize the circumstances of Paul when he wrote his letter to the Roman Christians.

4. State your understanding of the origin of the church in the city of Rome.

5. Of the six reasons for Paul's writing Romans, which two or three appear to be the most significant as far as his future ministry was concerned? Explain.

6. If someone were to ask you to explain to them the doctrine of *justification by faith or the doctrine of the two ages*, how would you respond?

7. How would you describe the people in the church in Rome? What group made up the majority?

8. In light of the way Paul uses the phrase "righteousness of God" in Romans, what is its significance?

Prayer

Dear Lord, we have begun our study of this power-packed letter and pray that the Holy Spirit will help us to understand the great truths of Romans and to apply them daily to our lives. Amen.

PART ONE—ROMANS 1:1-17

Opening of Paul's Letter

- **Paul's Greeting**
  Romans 1:1-7
- **Paul's Thanksgiving**
  Romans 1:8-10
- **Paul's Plans for Travel**
  Romans 1:11-15
- **Theme of Paul's Letter**
  Romans 1:16-17

In his letter to the Romans, Paul's words are alive and bursting with divine truth. As Martin Luther said about the words of Paul, "They are living things, with hands and feet." **Paul's words are masterfully expressed but also sensible and practical.** We can understand and apply Paul's teachings to our lives today through thoughtful examination of his teachings and reliance on the Holy Spirit.

Many people have assumed that Paul's letters are difficult to understand and that the greatest of them, the letter to the Romans, is the most challenging of all. Any book that deals seriously with the issues of life and death, God and humankind, and sin and salvation cannot be understood by casually skimming through it as one might the daily news. **Such a book must be read carefully with a mind open to God's transforming power. Paul did not write his letter to theologians or biblical scholars, but to a local church made up of believers from various walks of life—to people like all of us in the Christian church today.**

Characteristics of Paul's Communication
- His words are spiritual truth.
- His words are practical for daily life.
- His words are thought-provoking.
- His words are understandable with guidance from the Holy Spirit.

It is still true today that anyone who reads and studies Romans carefully with a keen sense of dependence on the Holy Spirit can get to the heart of Paul's message.

PAUL'S GREETING
ROMANS 1:1-7

> ¹ Paul, a bondservant of Jesus Christ, called to be an apostle, separated to the gospel of God ² which He promised before through His prophets in the Holy Scriptures, ³ concerning His Son Jesus Christ our Lord, who was born of the seed of David according to the flesh, ⁴ and declared to be the Son of God with power according to the Spirit of holiness, by the resurrection from the dead. ⁵ Through Him we have received grace and apostleship for obedience to the faith among all nations for His name, ⁶ among whom you also are the called of Jesus Christ; ⁷ to all who are in Rome, beloved of God, called to be saints: Grace to you and peace from God our Father and the Lord Jesus Christ.

Most correspondence written during Paul's time opened with the name of the sender, the name of the recipient, and a short greeting. In his letters, Paul followed that practice, and as a practical missionary, he expanded the opening of his letters to express his faith, like many other New Testament writers did.

Paul, a Slave of Christ

Paul begins his greeting to the Roman church by identifying himself as a Christian—"a bondservant [*doulos*, slave] of Jesus Christ." The word *slave* does double duty, expressing humility and authority. By using the term *bondservant* (or slave) at the outset, Paul avoids approaching his readers with a haughty attitude and affirms his total commitment to Jesus Christ; but as a slave of Christ, he had authority and influence in the church. This word *slave* was used in Old Testament writings to describe some of the great men of faith (Josh. 1:2; Jer. 7:25; Amos 3:7). Jeremiah and the prophets were servants of Jehovah. Paul, although born many years later, belonged to that noble succession of servants of the Lord, who were known for their devotion to God.

During the apostle's day, to be a slave meant to be owned and directed by a master (*kurios*, lord). Thus, one of Paul's favorite titles for Jesus Christ was *Lord*. **Because Christ had purchased Paul with His own blood, Paul gave absolute loyalty to Him**

as his Lord and Master. An important distinction should be noted here, however. In the ancient world the life of a slave was usually harsh and difficult; but when Paul speaks of himself as a slave of Christ, all harsh overtones of the term *slave* fade away. He delighted in doing the will of his Lord. Paul was much like the Old Testament love-slave who took great pleasure in serving his master, so that even when the slave had an opportunity to go free, he chose to remain with his master. A hole was bored in the lobe of his ear, signifying that he was a slave by choice (Deut. 15:12-17). **As a love-slave, Paul knew that Christ had bought him with a price, and he took great delight in choosing to serve his Lord. In the same way, all Christians have been purchased by Christ's blood and become servants of Christ by free choice.**

Moreover, the phrase "bondservant of Jesus Christ" may have had a great significance for the Christians in Rome. During Paul's time, it was the practice of citizens of Rome to declare with whom their allegiance lay. Archaeological research has uncovered inscriptions from the Roman Empire in which individuals were described as a "slave of the emperor." In his letter to the Roman church, **Paul was pleased to write that he was "a slave of Jesus Christ" (1:1 NLT).** Indeed he was a slave of the King of kings and the Lord of lords! **In a paradoxical way, belonging to Christ Jesus is true freedom.** "Thank God for the privilege of being freed from slavery to sin and Satan, that we might be Christ's slave and His alone" (Earle, 1974, 13).

Paul, an Apostle

Paul also identifies himself as one who was **"called to be an apostle." This word *apostle* refers to someone given full authority for a particular purpose.** By identifying himself as a slave and as an apostle, Paul appropriately introduced himself to the church in Rome. Behind Paul's reference to his being called to be an apostle stands the dramatic experience that he had on the road to Damascus (Acts 9:1-9). In that encounter with the Lord, he was both called to salvation and to ministry. These were interlocking realities, both received at the time of his conversion. **Paul's ministry did not originate with himself but was the result of God's calling him.** Abraham had been called by God

(Gen. 12:1-3), and so was Isaiah (6:8-9). Thus Paul knew that he was doing the will of God because of having received a calling as many individuals of old. He had been called by Christ to share the Good News with the Gentiles.

Paul, Set Apart to Tell the Good News

Keenly aware of the miracle that God had performed in his life, Paul understood that he was "separated to the gospel of God." The verb *separated* means "set apart." In the Old Testament, the prophets were set aside by God for their work. God spoke to Jeremiah and told him that before his birth, he had been set apart—sanctified and appointed a prophet to the nations (Jer. 1:5). Paul declared that before his own birth, he too was set apart for the purpose of sharing the Good News (Gal. 1:15). The circumstances of his life prior to his conversion involved his being born and raised to become a member of the Pharisees, a distinguished group of Jewish people who were considered to be "the separated ones." **Following his conversion, Paul concludes that just as he was set apart as a Pharisee, now he truly is set apart as a Christian.** God had separated Paul for a specific purpose: the preaching of the gospel (vv. 16, 23). Paul knew that the Good News that gripped his heart and was the content of his message did not originate with humankind but with God.

Paul devoted himself to the task of preaching the gospel wherever he went. Although the gospel that Paul preached (Good News about the Messiah, Jesus Christ) was news during his day, it was not unexpected news, since the Jewish people were expecting a Messiah to come one day. **This Good News of Christ had been promised many years earlier by the prophets of the Old Testament (Rom. 1:2).** Truly the gospel is consistent with God's promises to Israel. It can, therefore, be said that the Old Testament is essentially a Christian book—a Christ-centered book—because it speaks of Christ, the Messiah, the Anointed One, who was to come. Paul's use of the Old Testament in his letters reminds us that Paul would have never dispensed with these holy writings—not because they were a great source for religious history, but because they point to Christ. **Through the birth, life, and resurrection of**

Jesus Christ, the prophetic promises about the First Coming of Christ are now fulfilled.

The Content of Paul's Good News

In his telling of the gospel, **Paul emphasized there were two major characteristics of Jesus Christ that make it possible for God to fulfill His promises through Jesus (v. 3):**

First, Jesus was God's Son. The expression "concerning His Son" implies the preexistence of Christ; that is, the relationship of Christ with the Father before Jesus came into this world (Phil. 2:5ff.). Christ's sonship is eternal. Human believers, on the other hand, become children of God at the moment they believe in Christ and are immediately adopted into the great family of God with all the rights and privileges of being His sons and daughters (Rom. 8:15-17).

Second, Jesus was a man—a Jewish descendant of David. Even though Christ was the eternal Son of God, He came into the world as a member of the human race. In His physical being, Jesus Christ came through the lineage of the royal line of David, Israel's greatest king. However, Jesus was greater than David—He was David's Lord (Ps. 110:1; Acts 2:34-35).

Jesus Christ was the Son of God from all eternity and became the Son of Man by a human birth. He shared our nature fully, except that He was free of sin (see Rom. 8:3; 2 Cor. 5:1). After Jesus Christ's death on the cross, God declared Him to be His Son by raising Him from the dead. **Through the events of Jesus' death and subsequent resurrection, God affirmed that Jesus had died for the sins of the whole world.** These holy events demonstrated God's love in a tangible way, so that humankind could know beyond a doubt that Jesus was the very Son of God. The term for *resurrection* (*anastasis*) was often used in Greek inscriptions for the creation of a monument. "The resurrection of Jesus Christ was God's monument to the deity of His Son, erected to confirm the faith of all generations to come" (Earle, 1974, 16).

Jesus, who was crucified, was raised by the Holy Spirit (cf. Rom. 8:11). The term *Spirit of holiness* is a Hebraic way of speaking of the Holy Spirit. By the Spirit or in the sphere of the Spirit,

Jesus Christ was raised "in power" (1:4 ESV). **During His earthly ministry, Jesus was the Son of God embodied in weakness**; His divine glory and power were hidden, except on the occasions when His teachings provoked amazement and He did miracles. **But from the Resurrection forward, He was the Son of God in power.** His teachings and resurrection affirmed who He was. If He had not risen as He had predicted (Matt. 17:9; cf. Luke 24:46), Jesus would have been considered to be a false prophet. The resurrection of Christ changed our world, and it will never be the same again. **Because of who Jesus was and what He did, Christians are who they are—saved from the power of sin and death.**

The Roman Christians, a Blessed People

Paul recognized that the Roman Christians were a blessed people, and in addressing them, he used three phrases that reminded them of that fact (1:6-7):

First, the Roman Christians were called of Jesus Christ. The phrase "called of Jesus Christ" (v. 6) could be rendered, "called to be possessions of Christ." The Roman believers were like Paul: they were slaves of Christ, no longer their own master, owing Christ their obedience, bought with a price (1 Cor. 7:23). Jesus was their Lord. Like the great apostle, the believers in Rome had been called to salvation. In responding to their summons, they had become the property of Christ.

Second, the Roman Christians were beloved of God. This was true because they had experienced God's redeeming love in Christ. God had delivered them from the dominion of darkness and transferred them into the kingdom of His beloved Son (Col. 1:13). Christ is God's beloved Son and thus the object of His Father's love. All who are in Christ are likewise objects of the Father's love. They are dear to the Father as His eternal Son is.

Third, the Roman Christians had received a divine call to be saints (hagioi, holy people). At the heart of the word *saints* is the idea of separation, alluding to the fact that Israel had been designated to be a holy people. The Roman readers of Paul's letter were in the world, but they were not to be of the world. They were set apart by a holy God. As His people, they were to be holy in character. *Saints* is Paul's favorite term for Christians and strongly implies that believers are to become more and more holy in character, more like God, whom they worship and serve.

Paul, Blessed by God's Grace

Indeed the believers in Rome had been blessed. Paul had a share in God's blessings, too. He had received grace and the gift of apostleship (v. 5). No doubt in Paul's case, he viewed grace and apostleship as being closely related. **All Christians receive the gift of grace (*charis*), which means "unearned favor," and like Paul, all Christians also receive an additional spiritual gift to use in Christian service (1 Cor. 12:7-11).** Grace and merit are contradictory. If a person merits or earns something, the ground for receiving it is not grace. The sheer generosity of the giver is the ground for receiving grace. **Grace is a gift the receiver can never earn or deserve by anything he or she does.**

Paul was aware that all that he had received from God was a matter of divine generosity. Grace excludes all boasting except about what God has done in Christ. **Paul also received a specialized grace—apostleship (*apostole*). His ministry as an apostle can very well be described as a spiritual gift (Eph. 4:7-11).** However, he was not called to be a Christian and then an apostle. He received his call to be a Christian and an apostle at the same time—while on the road to Damascus. As an apostle, Paul was a personal representative of Christ; and although he never numbered himself among the twelve apostles, he did insist on equal apostolic authority (Gal. 1:1). He also thought of his apostleship as being just as much a gift from God as the saving grace he had received.

Christ had called Paul to be His personal representative among the nations (Gentiles). His mission was to call Gentiles to "obedience to the faith" for Christ's sake (Rom. 1:5; 15:18). He traveled over land and sea calling men and women to Christ and bringing them into a trusting submission to Christ. As Paul traveled from place to place, he proclaimed the gospel in "word and deed," with supernatural signs and wonders done by the power of the Holy Spirit accompanying his ministry (15:18-19). Truly Paul was called to serve Christ by dedicating his full energies to the telling of the gospel.

Paul blesses his readers, before moving on to his next topic. As was common in Paul's letters, he pronounces "grace

. . . and peace" upon his readers (1:7). His choosing to combine both *grace* and *peace* in a single greeting was most likely due to the fact that the church in Rome was composed of both Jewish and Gentile believers. The word *grace* (*charis*, a variation of *chairein*) was a typical Gentile greeting, whereas *peace* (Hebrew, *shalom*; Greek, *eirene*) was the greeting used by the Jews. In the New Testament, *grace* is given a new significance to mean God's spontaneous, unearned favor and is a term that includes all of God's saving work and blessings in Christ. *Peace* is the outworking of grace, not simply in the sense of the absence of war, conflict, and strife but also in the sense of inner calm and total well-being of the individual. **The source of the blessings of peace and grace is "God our Father and the Lord Jesus Christ" (v. 7; cf. Num. 6:24-26).**

ROMANS 1:1-7

KEYWORDS

Apostle (*apostolos*) (see p. 29)

Bondservant/Slave (*doulos*)
A person who renders service freely or because of obligation. In the New Testament, the emphasis is on obedience to Christ. Paul uses the term *bondservant* or *slave* to describe his total dedication to Christ. Such dedication is called for in Romans 12:1 as our "reasonable service."

Flesh
1. Sinful living
2. Physical body or lineage
3. Natural human limitations

God/Godhead
The spiritual entity and social being comprised of three persons—Father, Son, and Holy Spirit—who is all-powerful, all-knowing, infinite, eternal, and unchangeable in being, wisdom, and glory

God the Father/the Creator
God is Father and the Creator (originator and maker) of all things in the universe. God is Father to humankind by creation (Acts 17:28-29); Father of Israel (Isa. 63:16) because He created the nation; Father of Christ in a special sense because His Son is a revelation of the Father (Matt. 11:27; John 14:6-7); and Father of believers because they are children of God (Rom. 8:15-16). The term *Father* indicates a relationship.

Opening of Paul's Letter

God the Son
A title indicating that Jesus shares the nature of God, united in being with the Father

Gospel (see p. 23)

Grace (*charis*) (see p. 23)

Holy
1. Applied to God—God's separation from sin in any form or degree
2. Applied to the law and God's Word—The sacred nature of God's law and Word
3. Applied to humans—God sets individuals or groups apart to serve Him, and as a result they have a holy standing.

Holy Spirit/The Spirit (see p. 25)

Jesus Christ
The Son of God, who suffered and died for the sins of humankind (Mark 1:1)

Roman church/Christian Church in Rome (see p. 41)

Saints (*hagioi*)
The people of God, holy or dedicated ones

Separated
A term often used to make a distinction between God's people and those who are not

SUMMARY

The opening of the Book of Romans reveals that it is a letter from the apostle Paul to the Christians in Rome. This opening followed the typical form; but as other writers of the New Testament, Paul lengthens the introduction. He mentions a number of themes:

- his apostolic authority
- the fulfillment of the Old Testament in the gospel
- the gospel of salvation centered in Jesus Christ
- Christ the incarnate and resurrected Son of God
- the obedience involved in faith
- his mission to the Gentiles

Paul then identifies his readers and pronounces a blessing on them.

LIFE APPLICATION

Although all Christians are to engage in ministry for the Lord, we, as individuals, are to pursue full-time ministry only if God has called us and set us aside for this type of concentrated Christian service.

> A preacher, pastor, or other full-time minister needs to have an absolute conviction that God has called and separated him or her for this special purpose.
>
> All Christians are called to serve—not necessarily as apostles or pastors, but by going and telling the Good News of Christ and sharing His love wherever God may lead them. If you are convinced that God has called you to do a work, do not wait until the church tells you to do it or until the church helps you to do it. Go and do it, blessing others with God's grace and peace.

PAUL'S THANKSGIVING
ROMANS 1:8-10

> 8 First, I thank my God through Jesus Christ for you all, that your faith is spoken of throughout the whole world. 9 For God is my witness, whom I serve with my spirit in the gospel of His Son, that without ceasing I make mention of you always in my prayers, 10 making request if, by some means, now at last I may find a way in the will of God to come to you.

Paul gives thanks to God for the Roman Christians. In all his letters, except Galatians, Paul offers a prayer of thanksgiving for the readers. Perhaps his lack of expression of thanksgiving in his letter to the Galatian Christians was a result of their tendency to embrace an understanding of a gospel that was radically different from the truths that Paul had taught them. But in regards to his Roman readers, Paul had no difficulty finding something for which to be thankful. Word concerning the Roman church's faith—news of the church's commitment to Christianity—had circulated through "the whole world," that is, the Roman Empire (v. 8). Therefore, **Paul's thankfulness was not simply gratitude for the Roman believers' private, personal faith, but also for the church's strong public expression of faith.** The Roman church had already made its presence felt and had served well by spreading the Good News of Christ. The progress of this Christian gospel in Rome was widely known in the world of that time. The Roman church was not a weak, ineffective church; it was a strong, Christ-affirming church, and for this Paul was thankful.

In verse 9, Paul's thanksgiving quickly merges into prayer. Although Paul had never been to Rome, he had prayed for the Roman church. Because he was not able to be present and show his love, he had appealed to God, whom he believed would hear his earnest prayers on behalf of the Roman church. Perhaps Paul kept a prayer list that included names of some of the Roman believers. Also, when he bowed before God, he most likely would have prayed, "Lord, I want to go to Rome." We do not know how long he had desired to visit the city. Months before he wrote this letter, Paul expressed his intention of going there (Acts 19:21). Nor do we know what delayed him, unless it was his ministry in Asia and Greece. Even though he had not been able to go to Rome, Paul recognized it was the will of God that governed his life and authorized his ministry.

ROMANS 1:8-10

KEYWORDS

Gospel (see p. 23)

Pray/Prayer
An element of worship, and the communication between God and His people

SUMMARY

As typical, Paul follows the greeting of his letters with a thanksgiving. He gives thanks for the Roman believers' faith, which "is spoken of throughout the whole world" (v. 8) and tells them about his prayers for them and his desire to visit them.

LIFE APPLICATION

Paul prayed constantly for the Roman Christians. Offering his prayers "through Jesus Christ" (v. 8), the apostle is a marvelous example for us to follow in our prayer life. As Christians, our prayers and thanksgiving are to be offered through Christ.

Our Savior is in heaven where He is making intercession for us (Rom. 8:34). Having not forgotten us, Christ is constantly concerned about us and prays on our behalf. Our awareness that now He is at the right hand of God as our intercessor should prompt us to pray for others and for ourselves.

PAUL'S PLANS FOR TRAVEL
ROMANS 1:11-15

> 📖 ¹¹ For I long to see you, that I may impart to you some spiritual gift, so that you may be established— ¹² that is, that I may be encouraged together with you by the mutual faith both of you and me. ¹³ Now I do not want you to be unaware, brethren, that I often planned to come to you (but was hindered until now), that I might have some fruit among you also, just as among the other Gentiles. ¹⁴ I am a debtor both to Greeks and to barbarians, both to wise and to unwise. ¹⁵ So, as much as is in me, I am ready to preach the gospel to you who are in Rome also.

Paul's first stated purpose for going to Rome was to impart "some spiritual gift" to the church in Rome (v. 11). The word *spiritual* implies that the gift was from the Holy Spirit. Paul's desire was that the Holy Spirit would work through him and bestow on the Roman Christians the necessary gift(s) to strengthen the church. No doubt, Paul recognized that the Holy Spirit is the One who distributes the gifts (1 Cor. 12:7-11). In Romans 1:11, Paul is using a shorthand way of saying it, assuming that the readers would know what he meant. In himself, Paul had no power to impart spiritual gifts, but he could lay hands on the people and pray that the Holy Spirit would bestow gifts for the edification of the church. There is no specific indication of which gifts Paul had in mind; but turning to Romans 12:6-8 and 1 Corinthians 12:7-11, 28-30, we can get a good idea. The gifts of which Paul speaks in Romans 1:11 were for the purpose that the believers might be "established," which means to be strengthened by God. Upon his arrival in Rome, Paul wanted the Holy Spirit to work through him so the Christians would become more rooted and grounded in the gospel. His expectation was that God would make a strong church stronger.

Both the Roman believers and Paul would benefit by his going to Rome (v. 12). The church and Paul would be mutually blessed. Some scholars have understood Paul's statement about their both being encouraged to be an example of Paul's tact and his wanting to avoid arousing the displeasure of the Roman believers. While this might have been one of his motives for making the statement, Paul knew he had something to offer them and said so. On the other hand, he also knew that their fellowship would strengthen and comfort him. Paul's words here are a good reminder to pastors to recognize that not only can they be a blessing to the congregation, but the congregation can also be a blessing to them.

Paul anticipated ministering to the Roman Christians so he could have some fruit (converts) among them, as he had among other Gentiles (v. 13). As an active missionary, Paul's aim was to prevent racial barriers and cultural differences from hindering his ministry. By the time the apostle wrote Romans, the word *Greeks* (v. 14) included Romans. The term had lost its national and racial meaning and had become a term indicating culture and language. The Greek language and culture had spread across the Roman Empire. During that time, the world was perceived as being divided into two major cultures—those who spoke Greek and those who did not. The term *barbarians* was used as a designation for the people who did not speak what was considered to be the beautiful, harmonious language of Greek, even though they might have been highly civilized. Moreover, the "wise" and "unwise" can be read as designations for the educated and the uneducated (v. 14). Therefore, at the beginning of Romans, Paul expresses his sense of obligation to the whole world—Greeks and barbarians, and the wise and unwise. He saw it as a personal responsibility: "I am a debtor. . . . I am ready" (vv. 14-15).

ROMANS 1:11-15

KEYWORDS

Brethren
A term used to refer to members of the same family (see Mark 1:16; 3:31), a race (Rom. 9:3), or a neighbor (Matt. 7:3), but the distinctive use in the New Testament is to express a spiritual relationship. All members of the Christian community are brothers (sisters). This relationship is not merely figurative, but is based on spiritual birth (2 Peter 1:10).

Gentiles
A biblical term used to describe people who were not Jews. Paul at times in his letter to the Romans, rather than referring to Jews and *Gentiles*, refers to Jews and *Greeks*.

Gift of the Spirit
Spiritual gift for Christian service (*charisma*; plural *charismata*)—a special gift given to individuals to empower them to do Christian service in the body of Christ and world (Rom. 1:11; 12:6; 1 Cor. 12:4, 9, 28, 30-31; 1 Tim. 4:14; 2 Tim. 1:6; 1 Peter 4:10).

SUMMARY

For how long Paul had been planning to go Rome we do not know, but months before he wrote this letter he had expressed his intention of doing so. His desire to visit them was so he could impart to them some spiritual gift and have fruit among them as he did among other Gentiles. We do not know what had prevented him from going, but likely it was his duties in Asia and Greece. At least three years passed after writing Romans before he finally arrived in the city as a prisoner (Acts 28:16). As an apostle of Christ, Paul felt an obligation to preach the gospel to as many people as possible regardless of their station in life.

LIFE APPLICATION

If believers in every city and community were to have Paul's profound sense of obligation to share the Good News about Christ, what an impact the gospel would have on our communities and the world!

THEME OF PAUL'S LETTER
ROMANS 1:16-17

> ¹⁶ For I am not ashamed of the gospel of Christ, for it is the power of God to salvation for everyone who believes, for the Jew first and also for the Greek. ¹⁷ For in it the righteousness of God is revealed from faith to faith; as it is written, "The just shall live by faith."

The Gospel, Paul's Message

The major theme of Paul's letter to the Roman Christians is "the gospel." Romans 1:16-17 summarizes the main message of this letter, indicating that **Paul wished to preach in every region possible, including Rome.** Paul states, "I am not ashamed of the gospel of Christ," indicating that he felt compelled to preach this Good News, and nothing could silence him. This Good News was that God had opened the way of salvation through saving acts in Jesus Christ.

Paul was proud to have the privilege of preaching and sharing this Good News about Christ, his Lord. Paul used the term *gospel* more than sixty times in his letters, including ten of those in Romans. The gospel is the accepted message of the Christian church, and its central truth is that God has provided a way of salvation through the gift of His Son. Anyone might have hesitated to be identified with a message that had as its subject a man crucified as a criminal (Barrett, 1991, 27f.), but Paul was glad to preach the gospel, even though it was "foolishness" to the Greeks and a "stumbling block" to the Jews (1 Cor. 1:23).

Why was Paul so proud of the gospel? His answer: "For it is the power of God to salvation for everyone who believes" (Rom. 1:16). Rome boasted of its military might, but Paul had something more powerful than the imperial armies—the gospel, which could make men and women safe for time and eternity. The Greek for *power* (*dunamis*) is the word from which English gets *dynamo* or *dynamite*. This term *power* indicates even more power than God's power revealed in nature, history, and miracles. Here *power* is "unto salvation" and refers to God's continuing ability and willingness to save whomever turns to Him in repentance and faith in Christ. **The saving power of the gospel is active and powerful in the present and the future.** As long as we continue to trust in Christ, the gospel assures us of eternal life at the end. Salvation is not something we will only enjoy in the End of Time, but it also delivers us here and now from the dominion of sin. It is no wonder that Paul was delighted to preach the gospel everywhere "for the Jew first and also for the Greek [Gentile]" (v. 16).

Righteousness and Salvation

Through the gospel, God's righteousness is revealed (v. 17). There are two basic kinds of righteousness: human righteousness and God's righteousness.

1. ***Human righteousness* describes personal character, indicating that someone is pious and good.** Such righteousness is achieved by one's own efforts apart from God. Though it may be worthwhile, a person secures human righteousness through his or her own strength and discipline. This righteousness is as good as the one who does the work and is bound by human limitations. The result is that mere human righteousness is inadequate to bring us into a right relationship with God.

2. ***God's righteousness* is revealed in the saving work of Jesus Christ.** We will observe the various ways Paul uses it in parts of this letter. When he speaks of God's righteousness, Paul does not have in mind God's nature and character, but His saving work in Christ. Certainly God is righteous in character, but the focus is on God doing right by putting men and women right with Himself. Through this process, people are given a new status before God and His law. *Righteousness* is, in fact, a term borrowed from the courts of law, where in biblical times its meaning had to do with the way the accused were treated—not with the guilt or innocence of the person. **The image is that in God's court, God (the Judge) forgives the accused (the sinner), who has faith in His Son. The righteous, forgiving God pardons the sinner, bringing that person into right standing with Himself, and that person is justified.** The result is a full pardon, and the sinner is set free. In short, **God forgives those who trust in Christ as though they have never been sinners.**

The Greek word for *righteousness* (*dikaiosune*) is translated "justification" in Romans 5:16. The Jews thought there would be no judgment until the Final Judgment. At that time a person on the basis of works would be either justified or condemned. In Paul's thinking, the future judgment in part has been brought forward into the present because Christians are now justified, declared right in God's court. Justifying grace means that the Coming Age penetrates into this Old Age of sin and death. **The only thing we can contribute to our salvation is faith in which we take God at His word and allow Him to save us.**

Salvation Through Faith

Ruling out good works as the means of salvation, Paul states that God's saving righteousness "is revealed from faith to faith"

(Rom. 1:17). In this Scripture passage in the Greek, the verb *reveal* is in the present progressive tense (*apokaluptetai*). This indicates that **God is engaged in ongoing saving work through the proclamation and acceptance of the gospel (the acceptance of the transforming truth about Jesus Christ).**

The appropriate response to the gospel is faith. Paul's phrase "from faith to faith" is a way of saying "on the basis of faith alone." **Only through faith can one receive Christ as Savior and live the Christian life.** From start to finish, salvation is a matter of faith. **Saving faith involves knowing that Christ died for our sins, believing it, and committing ourselves to Him as our Savior.** Christ is the Savior and the primary cause of salvation. Faith is the means, the instrument, by which we receive Christ and is, therefore, the secondary cause of salvation. To put it another way, faith is the empty hand of the beggar that receives God's priceless gift of eternal life. God provides salvation, and the Holy Spirit helps us to repent and believe. God, however, does not do this for us; we must repent and reach out our hand of faith.

Paul emphasizes his point by citing Habakkuk 2:4: "The just [righteous] shall live by his faith." In this passage, Habakkuk was prophesying that those who were faithful to God's instructions would survive the coming siege of Jerusalem. However, in Paul's time and way of thinking, the prophet's words had a dual meaning. Paul also understood Habakkuk's words to be a prophecy regarding faith as the means by which future generations would receive Jesus Christ (the Messiah). The following translation seems to fit Paul's view: "He through faith is righteous shall live" (RSV; Nygren, 1949, 85-92). **So faith is not just a way of living, or living in the presence of God at the end, but is also the means by which we enter into a right relationship with God.** For Paul, faith was a believing obedience. He did not only know what it was to be saved by faith, but he also knew what it was like to live by faith. Faith was the way he dealt with the practical issues of life. Paul's preaching of the gospel, his pastoral duties, addressing churches' spiritual problems, and his modest and humble lifestyle were all accomplished in the context of his walk of faith.

ROMANS 1:16-17

KEYWORDS

Faith (see p. 23)

Forgiveness (see p. 47)

Gentiles (see p. 29)

Gospel (see p. 23)

Jews/Israelites/Hebrews (see p. 29)

Judgment by God/God's Judgment
Being held accountable for one's wrongdoings (sins)

Justification (*dikaiosune*) (see p. 48)

Power (*dunamis*)
The ability to perform. In the New Testament, God manifested His power in Christ. Paul recognized the preaching of the cross as the power of God (1 Cor. 1:23-24) and that God's power succeeds in saving humans who have faith in Christ. The gospel as God's power is capable of achieving its purpose, the salvation of souls (v. 18).

Revealed/Revelation (verb–*apokaluptetai*)
This verb implies God's divine action to make effective salvation.

Righteousness (*dikaiosune*) (see p. 48)

Salvation (see p. 23)

Sin (see p. 48)

Sinner
A person who has violated God's will

SUMMARY

Paul is eager to preach the gospel in Rome because this Good News about Christ is the power of God that heals and brings eternal life. In the gospel, God is revealing His righteousness by which He puts people in a right relationship with Himself and leads them to salvation. The only thing that they have to contribute to this process is faith (Hab. 2:4). Faith is their action of trusting in God and His promises.

LIFE APPLICATION

Faith and a devotional life are essential for the Christian walk. Today we often see a decline in Christian commitment among those living in technologically advanced cultures. This spiritual stagnation frequently

> relates to our trying to meet our needs by filling our lives with work, activities, and technological endeavors. However, no matter what our culture may be, it is important for us to remember that faith thrives where time is devoted to prayer and Bible study and an ongoing commitment to follow the way of Christ.

REFLECTION—PART ONE
Romans 1:1-17

1. What did Paul mean by being "separated to the gospel of God" (v. 1)? Why is it important for a minister to have a profound sense that God has set him or her apart for a special purpose?

2. Paul speaks of Christ as being both divine and human. What does that mean, and why is it important?

3. In the life of the local congregation today, what do you think would happen if many of the people had a consuming desire, as Paul did, to share the gospel with others? What difference would such a desire make in your own life?

4. Throughout Romans, Paul refers to the Old Testament. What do you think of the Old Testament?

5. Paul was a man of prayer. He had prayed for the church in Rome, which he had never visited. What are some ways we should follow Paul's example?

6. Take a careful look at Romans 1:16-17, especially the keywords: *gospel*, *power*, *salvation*, *righteousness*, and *faith*. We will get better acquainted with them as we study Romans, but what is your understanding of them now?

Prayer

Dear Lord, grant us the kind of eagerness and earnest desire that Paul had—to share with others the message of God's saving work in Christ. Amen.

PART TWO—Romans 1:18—3:20

The World's Need of Salvation

- **Paul's Warnings to the Gentiles**
  Romans 1:18-32
- **Paul's Warnings to the Jews**
  Romans 2:1-11
- **Conscience and the Gentiles**
  Romans 2:12-16
- **Blessings and Weaknesses of the Jews**
  Romans 2:17—3:8
- **All Have Sinned**
  Romans 3:9-20

Every person is in need of God's transforming love, grace, and forgiveness—His salvation. God offers His gift of salvation and life though His Son, Jesus Christ. In Romans 1:16-17, Paul has introduced the theme of God's salvation as the main focus of his letter to the Roman church. In 1:18—3:20, Paul declares that all humans are in bondage to sin and no one is able to save himself, not even those who attempt to keep God's laws. To demonstrate people's need for God's grace, Paul first discusses the Gentiles, then the Jews, and concludes that all people have exposed themselves to God's judgment. **The only hope for the human race is the saving grace and mercy of God, which has been revealed in the gospel.**

PAUL'S WARNINGS TO THE GENTILES
ROMANS 1:18-32

In Romans 1:18, Paul begins the main discussion of his letter. Previously, in verses 16-17, he has taken the reader to the lofty heights of the saving power of the gospel. Now he explains to his readers that **while God's saving righteousness has** been at work in the world, there has been another process also taking place, namely the revealing of God's wrath in response to those who reject His truths and refuse to allow Him to direct their lives. One day both of these processes will be brought to completion—one ending in eternal salvation and the other in condemnation.

In his letters, Paul frequently uses the term *wrath* to describe God's response to being rejected. The word *wrath*, as Paul uses it, is not a burst of rage or an emotional disturbance in God, but it is His holy displeasure at sin and His punishment of it. **God in His wisdom and compassion despises anything that harms and separates Him from those whom He loves.** Sin is always a destructive force in lives and relationships, and it separates us from God.

We do well to remember that Paul wrote this letter to the Romans while he was in Corinth, a city notorious for corruption, licentious excesses, and vice. The morals of the culture were probably reflected in the spiritual condition of the new Gentile Christians within the Corinthian church, and Paul wanted to address those issues.

GOD'S RESPONSE TO UNGODLY LIVING
ROMANS 1:18-23

> [18] For the wrath of God is revealed from heaven against all ungodliness and unrighteousness of men, who suppress the truth in unrighteousness, [19] because what may be known of God is manifest in them, for God has shown it to them. [20] For since the creation of the world His invisible attributes are clearly seen, being understood by the things that are made, even His eternal power and Godhead, so that they are without excuse, [21] because, although they knew God, they did not glorify Him as God, nor were thankful, but became futile in their thoughts, and their foolish hearts were darkened. [22] Professing to be wise, they became fools, [23] and changed the glory of the incorruptible God into an image made like corruptible man—and birds and four-footed animals and creeping things.

God is displeased when people break His law and separate themselves from Him. The Old Testament prophets spoke about the wrath of God. When Israel was disobedient, God's wrath usually brought defeat and national disaster (Num. 25:3). In Romans 4:15, Paul talks about the law bringing about wrath. **It is our transgression of the moral law, our breaking of it, that makes us subject to God's displeasure and in need of saving grace.** Later in 5:9, Paul addresses our need for saving grace (salvation), telling us we are saved from condemnation through the sacrificial death of Christ. **God's holy displeasure at sin and His forgiveness in response to our repentance demonstrate that He has not withdrawn from this world. In fact, He is active in the lives of people and is concerned about us.** Therefore, Paul writes that God's wrath is being revealed from heaven against those who hold down and suppress the truth by their immoral living (1:18).

We can conclude that the "truth" to which Paul refers in verse 18 is the knowledge of God provided through creation, rather than the truth of the gospel, since the majority of the pagan world at that time would not yet have heard about Jesus Christ and His teachings. **Since the Creator had made manifest His eternal power and Godhead in creation and left His prints on what He created, the pagan world did not lack knowledge of God. That is, they could learn something about God from creation itself.** The pagan world's fault was that they suppressed the truth derived from creation and would not allow it to bear fruit in their lives. The heart of their problem was rebellion against God. When they knew God, "they did not glorify Him as God, nor were thankful, but became futile in their thoughts, and their foolish hearts were darkened" (v. 21). They denied evidence of a powerful and glorious Creator, and rather than pursuing knowledge of God, they embraced counterfeits in order to obtain happiness and pleasure. Their suppression of the truth ultimately led to a very dark and painful existence.

Creation clearly reveals that God is God. Creation does not provide the key to its own existence, but it does point to the One who is responsible for its existence. When we look at creation, our first impression is that of power. Have you ever gone out at night and looked up at the stars and the moon? As you contemplate the splendor and the vastness of creation and the fact that God stands behind it all, you will come away with a profound sense of God's greatness and His unlimited power.

God's invisible attributes are manifested in the visible world. In addition to pointing to God's power, creation also reveals the character of the Godhead, which theologians often refer to as *divine attributes.* God's attributes such as justice, goodness, and wisdom can be seen in creation. Sin has disrupted creation, and the natural world now exists under the burden of sin (8:19-22). Even so, creation still testifies to God's attributes and His perfection through its complexities, interconnections, and beauty. The order that prevails in creation—the sun shines and the rain falls on both the just and the unjust, and the seasons of the year occur in regular cycles—reveals the goodness and wisdom of God (Matt. 5:45; Acts 17:24-30).

Our knowledge of God through His creation is sufficient to hold us responsible for a lack of reverence or for worshiping anyone or anything in creation rather than our Creator. **The natural world reveals God's power, perfection, and His provision for His creation, but it does not have the power to save us. While knowledge of God's natural order is adequate to hold us accountable for seeking or not seeking God, that knowledge alone is not adequate to bring us into a relationship with God.** Only God's grace, expressed through Jesus Christ, can give eternal life. God, because of His love for the world, sent His Son to earth in the form of a human (that is, the form of one of His created beings) in order to demonstrate His love and to build the needed bridge between His created world and Himself (Gal. 4:4). **Today, God reveals His plan through His Word, the Holy Bible, and extends His grace and forgiveness through Jesus Christ. Through the Holy Spirit, He draws to Himself those who seek and pray to know their Creator.**

ROMANS 1:18-23

Creation
The world and everything in it, which God made by command, without using any previously existing material that He did not create

Divine Attributes
The perfections or characteristics of God

Forgiveness (see p. 47)

Glory of God
1. The sum total of God's perfections (attributes)
2. A special manifestation of God

Glory to God
An act of praise and worship by human beings for God

God/Godhead (see p. 58)

Ungodliness
A lack of reverence for God. Such a lifestyle shows disrespect for God and sacred things and manifests itself in a wide range of evil works.

Unrighteousness
An indication that one is not in a right relationship with God due to one's wickedness and unbelief, including a lack of both a right attitude and right conduct

Wrath of God
God's displeasure with rejection of Him; God's opposition to sin, the results of which are correction and punishment, from which God in His grace forgives and releases anyone who repents

SUMMARY & LIFE APPLICATION

See under "ROMANS 1:24-32," pages 80-81.

THE NATURE OF GOD'S WRATH
ROMANS 1:24-32

²⁴ Therefore **God also gave them up to uncleanness**, in the lusts of their hearts, to dishonor their bodies among themselves, ²⁵ who exchanged the truth of God for the lie, and worshiped and served the creature rather than the Creator, who is blessed forever. Amen.

²⁶ For this reason **God gave them up to vile passions.** For even their women exchanged the natural use for what is against nature. ²⁷ Likewise also the men, leaving the natural use of the woman, burned in their lust for one another, men with men committing what is shameful, and receiving in themselves the penalty of their error which was due.

> ²⁸ And even as they did not like to retain God in their knowledge, **God gave them over to a debased mind,** to do those things which are not fitting; ²⁹ being filled with all unrighteousness, sexual immorality, wickedness, covetousness, maliciousness; full of envy, murder, strife, deceit, evil-mindedness; they are whisperers, ³⁰ backbiters, haters of God, violent, proud, boasters, inventors of evil things, disobedient to parents, ³¹ undiscerning, untrustworthy, unloving, unforgiving, unmerciful; ³² who, knowing the righteous judgment of God, that those who practice such things are deserving of death, not only do the same but also approve of those who practice them.
> [*emphases added*]

Human beings naturally want to live by their own understanding and to make reason the sole guide of their lives. According to Paul, **even though God had revealed Himself in creation, many people did not take this revelation seriously and gave no honor to the One to whom the revelation pointed.** Instead, they worshiped the creature rather than the Creator. As a result, God allowed them to plunge deeper and deeper into sin. The biblical expression "God gave them up to . . ." is repeated three times (vv. 24, 26, 28).

In studying Romans, it is helpful to remember that Paul made his comments regarding sin within a cultural background of greed, neglect, and sexual abuse. People of his day even incorporated these practices into their religions. Most likely, the Roman church would have reached out to those caught in pagan religions, offering them freedom in Christ. As a result, many of the Gentile Christians in the Roman church would have been converts from pagan religions. These pagan religions from which they would have converted had a history of requiring followers to visit temples in order to participate in sacrifices and rituals. These rituals included sexual acts with temple prostitutes as a means for the people to worship, appease, and connect with their gods. The slaves who were prostituted at the temples most likely included both children and adults, some of whom were obtained through human trafficking. They were one of the primary sources of the temples' wealth (Henderson, 1988, 1249-63; Hallett, 1988, 1265-78; Krenkel, 1988, 1291-97).

By engaging in such abusive, selfish actions, the Gentile people would have dulled their consciences and would have carried heartache and disease back to their families and communities. **A culture that sanctioned practices outside God's laws would have resulted in the normalization of the sins that Paul lists in verses 29-32. Such prevalence of sin would have created a society full of distrust, fear, brokenness, disease, mental illness, and major dysfunction—ultimately a society of death.**

Because many converts in the church would have come to Christ believing that their harmful practices were normal, Paul's strong comments about wrongdoing and sin were necessary in order to convince these new Christians that their practices were unhealthy and would separate them from God. **In verses 24-32, Paul warns the Gentiles of what the results of ungodly living would be.** He begins with the three major ways that God responds to people who choose to engage in lifestyles contrary to His laws.

God's Response to Rejection of His Laws

1. ***"God . . . gave them up to uncleanness"*** (Rom. 1:24). Men and women were **consumed by their lust and gave their bodies to sensuality, engaging in degrading sensual behaviors.** The inevitable result of their refusal to honor God was that **they embraced a lie rather than the truth and worshiped things in creation rather than God.** God allowed the rebellious Gentiles to go in the direction they chose, pursuing a life of vice and sexual impurity.

* *Application*: Ignoring God is costly, for God will allow us to chase lies and selfish passions, which will ultimately lead to our traveling a harmful path in life devoid of the goodness of God.

2. ***"God gave them up to vile passions"*** (v. 26). These "vile passions" were **uncontrollable affections.** God had made humans to be much higher than the animals that He created. Even though human beings have been created in the image of God, we can descend to a level much lower than the rest of creation because we have the ability to choose. **Humans may choose to**

follow God or to walk away from Him, not honoring His laws and the order that He established in Creation (Gen. 1—3).

When we have no relationship with God, the results can be serious distortion of our relationships with one another. Paul refers to these distortions as being "against nature" (Rom. 1:26)—that is, being contrary to God's natural order. As an example, Paul refers to homosexual acts, the practice of men engaging in sexual relationships with other men, and women with other women. He draws attention to these particular actions not just because they are immoral (contrary to God's law), but because they are also a departure from God's design in creation. **Paul refers to any of our actions that don't agree with God's plan for His creation as being "against nature" (v. 26).** God in His wisdom created and designed woman to be with man. He fashioned both their bodies to complement each other for them to thrive within a loving, devoted relationship. **However, sin within individuals, families, and societies has caused great damage and has disrupted the created order of relationships. Sin can be defined in terms of personal relationships. It distorts relationships with God, with self, and with others.**

* Application: When people refuse to include God in the practical affairs of their lives, the results are not good. They displease God with their suppression of the truth, indifference, and lack of respect for Him, resulting in His giving them up to their ways, as He did in Paul's day.

3. *"God gave them over to a debased mind"* (v. 28). For those who rejected God, the end of the story was not just the worship of things in creation and abnormal sexual relationships. **As those who walked away from God plunged deeper and deeper in sin, they were unable to retain a true knowledge of God.** No longer did they have the capacity to distinguish between right and wrong or between God and idols. **As a result of their abandoning God, God respected their wishes and abandoned their minds.** They had lost the ability to understand the truth and to discern the will of God (cf. 12:1-2). So God is able to

overcome unbelief and obstinacy to accomplish His will. (See Paul's references to Esau, Israel, and Pharaoh in Romans 9–11.)

Application: Stubborn refusal to follow God's way and persistence in sin are dangerous matters, because God will eventually abandon habitually resistant people to their wicked ways. God's Spirit will not always strive with humankind (Gen. 6:3), and present judgment is a foretaste of the Final Judgment.

Results of Disobedience

In Romans 1:29-31, Paul gives us a list of vices which provide a commentary of what he means by *ungodliness* and *unrighteousness*. The clause "being filled with all unrighteousness" (v. 29) introduces this catalogue of evils and indicates that Paul wants this list read as a whole. The focus of this list of sins is on the whole range of human depravity rather than on each vice that comprises the list. **Each of these vices can be placed in one of the following categories: idolatry, sensuality, or social strife.** The particular sins listed are examples of what the results can be when people go their own way, and God in His displeasure gives them up to their selfish desires. **Men and women can sink spiritually to such a low level that they not only do evil things, but they "also approve of those who practice them" (v. 32). In such a spiritual state, people contribute both to their own death, and to the death of others.**

Application: God has revealed Himself in Christ and also in creation. **To ignore God has terrible consequences.** The vices of Paul's day are common in the secular, undisciplined culture in which we live. Much of North American culture is without Christ. **But God is still a just God, now as in the first century: God is still God and gives people over to their sinful desires and behavior and allows the effects to gnaw away at them like a cancer.**

ROMANS 1:24-32

KEYWORDS

Evil
The opposite of good and is the cause of loss and suffering. Several kinds of evil can be identified: religious evil, moral evil, social evil, and natural evil.

God, The Father/The Creator (see p. 58)

Judgment by God/God's Judgment (see p. 68)

Unclean
Contamination by physical, ritual, or moral impurity; the opposite of purity and sanctity in relation to God and His will

Unrighteousness (see p. 75)

Wrath of God (see p. 75)

SUMMARY

To show that the whole world is guilty before God and in need of salvation, Paul begins his discussion with the Gentile (pagan) world. These were not followers of Christ, but people who had a knowledge of the invisible God through what He had created; however, they deliberately turned their backs on this revelation, refusing to treat God as God and to give thanks to Him for His goodness. They worshiped parts of creation and other gods. The inevitable result was the wrath of God, in which He gave them what they wanted, giving them up to their sin and allowing them to plunge deeper into sin and darkness. Their hardened spiritual condition is described in the closing verses of this section and shows where persistence in the rejection of God leads.

LIFE APPLICATION

Paul's Warnings. As in Paul's time, many practices of our culture are also a departure from God's laws. Even though some actions that do not agree with God's laws may feel normal to us, and actually feel freeing or healing, eventually our pursuing a path that is not in agreement with God's teachings will lead to our being separated from Him. We will no longer be able to distinguish between what is good for us and others, and what is not. Because such practices lead to our becoming separated from God's goodness, they will eventually plunge us into a life of death, despair, and meaninglessness. Their false promises for feeling better or for being connected to something larger than ourselves will not hold up over time.

> **Hope in Christ.** The Christian church today, like the church of Paul's day, has Good News for people who are hurting and looking for answers. We all share a common condition—we have been hurt and broken by sin and are in need of Jesus Christ's love, forgiveness, and healing (3:23). Through the power of His Spirit, God uses the Christian community to lovingly befriend, instruct, and pray for those who are struggling with sin and are searching for answers. God calls us to be compassionate agents of Christ, leading people to Him for healing from past abuse and damaging inclinations. Because Christ heals both victims and wrongdoers who come to Him for help, there is hope for all.
>
> **Walking With God.** We would all be wise to pay attention to Paul's warnings. If we do not submit to God and walk with Him, after a time, God will respect our wishes for a life apart from Him and will allow us to go our own way. Such a life without God's goodness and healing can only lead to personal destruction and deep pain for those around us. On the other hand, when we walk with God, we will enjoy a whole life that offers joy and healing for ourselves, as well as for others to whom we minister.

PAUL'S WARNINGS TO THE JEWS
ROMANS 2:1-11

In chapter 2, Paul continues his discussion of the wrath of God. In the preceding chapter, he painted a grim picture of the spiritual state of many people in the Gentile world. Now Paul speaks to the Jews. **The shift from addressing the Gentiles to addressing the Jews marks a new phase of Paul's discussion. The Jews thought they occupied a privileged position in the sight of God, but Paul informs them that they too are subject to the judgment of God, just as are the Gentiles.** (*Please note*: As we are reading this passage and some others in Romans, in order to make the meaning more relevant for us today, we can substitute the term *Jew* with either *moralist* or *religious person*.)

Moralistic people often do not think of themselves as being in need of God's forgiveness, nor as being subject to His wrath without forgiveness. Paul, however, indicates that **all people are accountable to God for their actions, and that no one can justify himself or herself through good deeds.** Just as were the

Jewish leaders of biblical times, moralists and all other people are responsible to God for how they live. **All people must rely on God for their eternal salvation. Paul's purpose in verses 1-11 is to close off the imagined escape from God's examination.**

SELF-RIGHTEOUSNESS WITHIN THE JEWS
ROMANS 2:1-5

> ¹ Therefore you are inexcusable, O man, whoever you are who judge, for in whatever you judge another you condemn yourself; for you who judge practice the same things. ² But we know that the judgment of God is according to truth against those who practice such things. ³ And do you think this, O man, you who judge those practicing such things, and doing the same, that you will escape the judgment of God? ⁴ Or do you despise the riches of His goodness, forbearance, and longsuffering, not knowing that the goodness of God leads you to repentance? ⁵ But in accordance with your hardness and your impenitent heart you are treasuring up for yourself wrath in the day of wrath and revelation of the righteous judgment of God.

In verses 1-5, Paul indicates that the religious Jews had no right to set themselves up as judges of the Gentiles. **In the New Testament, the verb *judge* has two meanings. It can mean "to condemn" (see Matt. 7:1; Rom. 2:1) or "to distinguish"** (see John 7:24). In the first usage, *condemn*, Scripture forbids us from judging others. In the second usage, *distinguish*, as used by Jesus in John 7:24, indicates that we are responsible for evaluating or discerning certain matters in life. Humans in general often err in their judgment of others' spiritual conditions, but in Romans 2, Paul is dealing with the self-righteous attitude of some of the Jews. The particular Jews of which Paul speaks had a practice of condemning others for the very actions of which they themselves were guilty. **If individuals know that others' actions are wrong, their knowledge can be an indication of discernment.** However, **if they themselves do what they have determined to be wrong, they have essentially judged and**

condemned themselves. This was precisely what the Jews of whom Paul speaks had done. Knowing the law, they had condemned the Gentiles, but they themselves were guilty of breaking the same laws (v. 3).

In what sense were these Jews guilty of what the Gentiles did? It should not be taken that the Jewish people engaged in the same sexual practices that were a common part of the Gentile culture. Isolated cases may have been found among them, but the Jews as a whole were known for their high ethics and moral purity (Barrett, 1991, 43-44). Behind the sins of the Jewish leaders stood the sin of idolatry, at the heart of which is often the human ambition to assume the role of God. **By judging, these moralistic Jews were trying to play the role of God.** Judging was God's business, not theirs. **They were judging the Gentiles for their idolatrous acts, while at the same time they were engaging in the idolatrous act of setting themselves up as God and judge.** Only God had the right to determine the destiny of the Gentiles. The Jews did not occupy the privileged position of judge like they thought. They too were sinners and subject to God's judgment.

As a result of their self-righteousness, these Jews had contempt for God's mercy. Throughout their history, God had blessed the Jewish people and had been patient with them. Even so, at different times, the Jews had exhibited a general indifference toward God. In verse 4, however, in the statement "Do you despise the riches of His goodness," Paul is not referring to these past periods of indifference, but to the indifferences that these particular Jews were currently showing toward the message of the gospel—the message of God's mercy. Paul indicates that these moralistic Jews had taken for granted God's goodness, forbearance, and long-suffering. Just as God had dealt with the Jewish people throughout their history, attempting to *lead* them (*agei*, conative present, meaning ongoing "tending to lead") to repentance, God also had given these Jews many opportunities to repent. However, because of the hardness of their hearts, they, like the Gentiles, had failed to honor God and give thanks to Him (cf. 1:21).

By taking for granted God's kindness, those Jews who were prideful were storing up wrath that would break forth on them "in the day of wrath and revelation of the righteous judgment of God" (2:5). However, many Jews of Paul's day thought that they did not need to worry about God's wrath in the afterlife. At that time a common belief among the Jews was that the wicked received their reward in this life for the few good things they did, so that in the Final Judgment they would receive only punishment. The righteous, however, would receive punishment in the present life for any evil they might have done, so that life in the hereafter would be nothing but bliss (cf. Barrett, 1957, 45). **Even though God's goodness should have brought the self-righteous Jews to their knees in gratitude, there were those who did not repent.** Without repentance they were certain to face the full measure of God's wrath in the hereafter. The unrepentant and prideful religious were storing up wrath, and like a dam that has broken, God's judgment would one day break forth on them.

ROMANS 2:1-5

KEYWORDS

Jews/Israelites/Hebrews (see p. 29)

Final Judgment
The occasion when God will reward the righteous and condemn the ungodly

Judgment by God/God's Judgment (see p. 68)

Judgment by Humans
In the New Testament, the verb *judge* has two meanings:
1. One person's judgment of another—to condemn or harshly criticize
2. Judgment of spiritual matters—to distinguish or discern (John 7:24)

Repentance
Turning from sin and self-centeredness to God, asking for His forgiveness

Self-Righteousness
A critical and *holier-than-thou* attitude of being morally better than others. The self-righteous are sanctimoniously sure of their own righteousness.

The World's Need of Salvation

SUMMARY

Apart from the acceptance of the Good News of God's grace and mercy (the gospel), the moralistic Jews would be deprived of eternal life with God. They too were sinners as were the Gentiles and were subject to "the wrath of God," which will be manifested on the day of the Final Judgment. God had postponed His punishment of them in order to give them ample opportunity to repent and to receive the gospel. Since the moralistic Jews persisted in their unbelief and practices as did many of the Gentiles whom they condemned, they also exposed themselves to the same divine punishment.

LIFE APPLICATION

We who condemn others often fail to take our own guilt seriously and do not think that we ourselves need to repent and to receive God's forgiveness. God is not deceived by those of us who pretend to be on the side of righteousness. Like those Jews of Paul's day who were self-justifying and self-satisfied, as moralists we may also treat God's mercy and kindness as things we do not personally need. Such an attitude amounts to despising the riches of God's goodness and patience, an attitude which will provoke His wrath.

God may withhold His wrath for now, but there is coming a day when His righteous judgment will be manifested and all accounts will be settled. Now is the opportunity for us to repent of any self-righteousness. God is willing to forgive us. Let us take a moment to go to God in prayer to ask Him for His forgiveness for our judgment of others, and to give us compassion for them.

GOD'S IMPARTIAL JUDGMENT
ROMANS 2:6-11

📖 ⁶ Who "will render to each one according to his deeds": ⁷ eternal life to those who by patient continuance in doing good seek for glory, honor, and immortality; ⁸ but to those who are self-seeking and do not obey the truth, but obey unrighteousness—indignation and wrath, ⁹ tribulation and anguish, on every soul of man who does evil, of the Jew first and also of the Greek; ¹⁰ but glory, honor, and peace to everyone who works what is good, to the Jew first and also to the Greek. ¹¹ For there is no partiality with God.

All people, Jews *and* Gentiles, stand on equal footing before God. According to Paul, **God will judge everyone, and they must give an account of their actions (v. 6)**. Religious people are not immune to God's examination. Divine judgment looks at deeds, not privilege.

Some scholars have claimed that all that mattered to Paul was faith, that he did not consider a person's works to be spiritually important. This assumption is untrue. **The way that leads to eternal life is patience in doing well.** So what are good works? Paul's answer is "patient continuance in doing good" (v. 7). This means more than perseverance—it also means a willingness to look with hope to God beyond what we are doing to what God will do finally (8:25). This hope in God motivates us to seek "glory, honor, and immortality" (2:7). An essential component of the Christian life is doing good. **God promises eternal life to those who show evidence of genuine repentance and faith.**

Those who reject the truth of the gospel and follow evil bring upon themselves "indignation and wrath" (v. 8). God will treat all people the same in the Final Judgment. He will have no favorites, and no preferential treatment will be given to anyone (v. 11). Paul places great emphasis on grace and faith, but he clearly teaches that good works that are motivated by service to Christ are important in the Final Judgment (1 Cor. 3:10-15). The bottom line for the apostle is that genuine, good works are fruits of grace and faith (Gal. 5:22-23) and, furthermore, are initiated by the Cross and by the ministry of the Holy Spirit in the life of the believers (Rom. 8:1ff.). Consequently, through the Spirit ("fruit of the Spirit"), we have the privilege to "walk in the Spirit" (see vv. 1, 4) as a matter of worship throughout our life as Christians (12:1-2).

ROMANS 2:6-11

KEYWORDS

Faith (see p. 23)

Final Judgment (see p. 84)

Gentiles (see p. 29)

Glory
Glorification of humans—the resurrection state of the believer

God as Judge
God is the absolute judge of all the earth (Gen. 18:25; Rom. 3:6). His decisions are without prejudice or partiality.

Jews / Israelites / Hebrews (see p. 29)

Life / Eternal Life
A quality of being and living which is derived from God and is eternal

Tribulation
Trouble and suffering in this life

Wrath of God (see p. 75)

SUMMARY

The Jewish moralists of Paul's day, as well as moralists today, were imperfect people and were sinners. They had sinned just as their Gentile (pagan) neighbors had. The religious among them had condemned their Gentile neighbors; but since these pious Jews acted no better, they had exposed themselves to God's Final Judgment. God in mercy for them postponed His judgment, giving them an opportunity to change and to come to Him by repenting. However, the religious Jews ignored God's goodness and patience and shut themselves off from God, risking His displeasure and punishment in the Final Judgment.

Although neither the Jews, nor anyone else, can earn salvation by doing good, they are to do good deeds as an expression of their faith in God. In the Final Judgment, God will judge impartially each person's deeds, in order to reward Christians for their faithfulness and to make accountable those who have refused to accept Christ as their Lord and Savior.

LIFE APPLICATION

God will uphold His holy law and will judge us fairly. It is God's business to judge the world. God will give eternal life to those of us who, in our seeking for "glory, honor, and immortality," put our faith in Christ and persevere in reflecting His love through our actions.

We cannot be saved by works, but each of us lives either according to the flesh or according to the Spirit. Our choice is between seeking for worldly goals such as personal glory and self-reliance, or seeking for lofty spiritual goals such as the honor and glory of Jesus Christ. Those of us who do not have faith in God are being disobedient to God's truth. Instead of being obedient to the truth, we are pursuing our own interests, rather than God's plan for our lives. The results of such a choice will be that we will receive divine displeasure, wrath, tribulation, and anguish. Only faith in the living Christ can save us from these eventual realities. There is no special exemption for any of us.

Let us put our faith in Christ as the loving Savior and Lord of our life, who will forgive us and save us from our self-reliant inclinations—bringing us into an eternal life of meaning and purpose.

CONSCIENCE AND THE GENTILES
ROMANS 2:12-16

> 📖 ¹² For as many as have sinned without law will also perish without law, and as many as have sinned in the law will be judged by the law ¹³ (for not the hearers of the law are just in the sight of God, but the doers of the law will be justified; ¹⁴ for when Gentiles, who do not have the law, by nature do the things in the law, these, although not having the law, are a law to themselves, ¹⁵ who show the work of the law written in their hearts, their conscience also bearing witness, and between themselves their thoughts accusing or else excusing them) ¹⁶ in the day when God will judge the secrets of men by Jesus Christ, according to my gospel.

In this passage, Paul returns to his discussion of the Gentiles. In the previous verses, Paul has pointed out that **the Jews had the advantage of the law, which had been given to Moses on Mount Sinai, but the Gentiles did not have that law.** Then how could God be just and condemn the Gentiles? If God judged the Gentiles on the same grounds as the Jews, God would be a respecter of persons. The Jews had the Mosaic law; the Gentiles had only revelation in nature, but did not have the Mosaic law. The difference between Jews and Gentiles was more than race; it was also a matter of revelation. Here Paul states a principle by which God would judge those who have the Mosaic law and those who do not. He indicates that **the Jews would be judged by the law of Moses, and the Gentiles by the law written on their hearts (vv. 14-15).** Stated another way, if the Gentiles' deeds were right, there would be no detriment. This, of course, is a very huge *if*. Later in chapter 3, Paul observes that all have sinned and that both Jews and Gentiles are under sin.

Law Written on the Heart

God has written on the hearts of all people a basic law of right and wrong. Still, the Mosaic law is a more complete revelation of God's will than the law on the heart. **Romans 2:15**

indicates that the function of our conscience is to judge our own conduct by the law written on our heart, and it either accuses or excuses us. The conscience is best understood as that which distinguishes us from the animal kingdom and is an aspect of God's image in us. When the Gentiles did what the law stamped on their hearts required, they demonstrated God's law within, that is, they showed the effect of the inward law. Therefore, people who sinned without the Mosaic law would perish without it. Their final condemnation would not be the law of Moses, but the law implanted in the heart. **The law that the Gentiles had within them made them accountable for their actions.** Paul does not suggest that anyone has conformed completely to the law stamped on the heart. Verse 14 implies just the opposite. The word *when* (*hotan*, better translated "whenever") suggests that the obedience of the Gentiles to the law on the heart was occasional. Their obedience was the exception rather than the common practice.

Obedience to God's Law and Judgment

Nevertheless, Paul is confident that there is coming a day when everyone will appear before the judgment seat of God. **Those who are justified—that is, pardoned without punishment—will not be the "hearers of the law," but the "doers of the law" (v. 13).** Each Sabbath, the Jews heard the law in their synagogues, but just hearing and knowing the law were not enough—not enough to justify them in the sight of God. **Paul's emphasis is that the law requires that we respond to it with action, not merely listen to it.** For example, when traveling by car, on most of our roads there is a speed limit. Not only must we know the speed limit, but we are required to observe it. By doing what the speed code demands, we are considered "righteous" in regard to the governmental law. But as Paul makes clear, **we often fall short of perfect obedience to God's law.** One day when we enter God's court, **the only way we will receive a favorable verdict is through faith in God's Son, whose perfect obedience is credited to our account.** The Final Judgment will be according to what Paul calls "my gospel" (v. 16). Obviously there is some tension between the doctrine of judgment of works on the Final Day and the doctrine of salvation by faith. (The reading of *gospel* for *law* in verse 13 makes it more understandable for those who are followers of Christ.) Much of the tension disappears when we separate judgment of quality of Christian service from judgment in regards to the unsaved.

Divine judgment is part of the gospel. On the Day of Judgment, God will hold every person accountable and will make His final decisions according to the gospel which Paul preached. "The secrets of men" (v. 16) will come under careful examination. As we stand before God, He will know more about us than we know about ourselves. Nothing will be hidden from Him. Truly, He will know not just what our behavior has been and what our motives and thoughts have been, but even our faith in Him. **God's focus will be on our commitment to the gospel (that is, our relationship with Him through Christ) and the resulting purity of heart (see 1 John 3:19-21).**

Concerns About Verses 12-16

Before concluding this discussion about our conscience and our ability to keep God's laws, let us focus on two concerns that this passage raises:

1. **Function of conscience.** The first concern is the function of the conscience. **We should not assume that the conscience is an infallible guide.** In some passages of the New Testament, conscience is described as being unreliable: *weak, ill-informed* (1 Cor. 8:7, 10, 12), *seared* (1 Tim. 4:2), *defiled* (Titus 1:15), and *evil* (Heb. 10:22). However, in other passages it is described more positively, as being *good* (Acts 23:1; Heb. 13:18) and *pure* (1 Tim. 3:9; 2 Tim. 1:3).

For the Christian's conscience to be a reliable guide, it must be led by the Holy Spirit (cf. Rom. 9:1). As Christians, our conscience can err because of failure to live in complete conformity to the will of God. It is easy for us to become sidetracked by life challenges, societal pressures, or personal weaknesses. **A good conscience must be continually nurtured.** Paul indicates that the conscience functions in two ways—it accuses and excuses. The conscience cannot be an independent witness or authority. Only by obeying the voice of conscience which is in agreement with the Scriptures and guided by the Holy Spirit can we act consistent with the will of God.

2. **Those who have not heard about Jesus Christ.** The second concern is about those who have never heard the gospel. Can they be saved by living according to the voice of conscience? In light of Romans 2:12-16, the only answer that I can give is that **all people will be judged according to what they have done with what God has given them.** Scripture clearly teaches that there are degrees of punishment in judgment (Matt. 10:15; 11:22; Luke 10:12-15; 12:47-48). We know that **the Judge of all the earth is a loving, good, and just God, who will always do what is right (Gen. 18:25).** As Christians, the message we must preach and teach is that **the only way to be assured of salvation and eternal life with the Lord is faith in Jesus Christ.** This is the message of the New Testament and the message that Paul traveled over land and sea preaching. The church has the same responsibility. We will leave those who have never heard the gospel in the hands of an all-wise and merciful God. All humans have sinned and will be accountable for wrongdoing.

ROMANS 2:12-16

KEYWORDS

Conscience
Moral awareness, the faculty in humans that makes them aware of right and wrong and is a dimension of the image of God in humankind

Gentiles (see p. 29)

Judgment by God (see p. 68)

Justification (*dikaiosune*) (see p. 48)

The Law (*Torah*) (see p. 48)

Sin (see p. 48)

SUMMARY

Unlike the Jews, the Gentiles had only a law written on their hearts, that is, an innate sense of right and wrong. The Jews would be judged by the Mosaic law, but the Gentiles only by the requirements of the law exhibited in their conscience. Because of their instinctual knowledge of God, when the Gentiles violated the moral law, they could not logically blame their failure on their lack of moral knowledge or the morals of their culture. Paul seems to be confident that God judges people on the basis of what has been available to them and not on the basis of what has not been available, but he is clear in 1:18–3:23 that all have sinned and are accountable for their deeds. This accountability to God includes a person's actions, as well as his or her acceptance of God's grace in Christ (2:13, 16).

LIFE APPLICATION

When any of us comes to Christ, offering Him our brokenness and repenting of our wrongdoings, Christ gives us His grace, forgiveness, and eternal life. Without repentance and God's grace, anyone can sin and perish whether they have heard God's law or not. A Jewish person who has heard the law of Moses read in a synagogue every Sabbath will be held accountable by God for not following their knowledge of the law. Another person (a Gentile) may have never attended a synagogue or a Christian church nor ever heard the Word of God, but that person has God's moral law in his or her conscience. Therefore, the person who has never heard the Word of God also will be held accountable for the law written on their conscience.

Either type of person (the one with the written law or the one only with the law inscribed on their conscience) who fails to live according to God's moral and perfect plan is subject to God's judgment. On the Final Judgment Day, however, God will examine the hidden chambers of each of our hearts. His decisions will not be made according to the law, but according to the gospel, which makes Jesus Christ and His cross the main factors in the Final Judgment. We are all accountable to God's Word; but as believers in Christ, we can have the assurance that when we stand before God, the verdict will be in our favor.

BLESSINGS AND WEAKNESSES OF THE JEWS
ROMANS 2:17—3:8

In this passage, Paul explains that a Jewish person who practiced his religion in a self-righteous manner (application for today—a religious person who is hypocritically moralistic) was in the same predicament as the Gentiles.** In chapters 1 and 2, Paul has stated that all people are guilty before God and are under the bondage of sin. He has discussed the effects of this bondage on the Gentiles. Now he returns again to discuss the Jews and their bondage, listing their failures and their claims to a special standing before God.

THE JEWS' UNIQUE STATUS
ROMANS 2:17-24

> 17 Indeed you are called a Jew, and rest on the law, and make your boast in God, 18 and know His will, and approve the things that are excellent, being instructed out of the law, 19 and are confident that you yourself are a guide to the blind, a light to those who are in darkness, 20 an instructor of the foolish, a teacher of babes, having the form of knowledge and truth in the law. 21 You, therefore, who teach another, do you not teach yourself? You who preach that a man should not steal, do you steal? 22 You who say, "Do not commit adultery," do you commit adultery? You who abhor idols, do you rob temples? 23 You who make your boast in the law, do you dishonor God through breaking the law? 24 For "the name of God is blasphemed among the Gentiles because of you," as it is written.

The Jewish people have always had a unique relationship with God. Paul was very pleased to belong to this covenant people, the race to whom the Messiah was born. The Jewish religious leaders, as teachers of the truth and as having the law, thought of themselves as being distinct from all other nations. Paul does not dispute the unique position of the Jews and that there was some truth in their claims. In fact, Paul understood that they possessed "the oracles of God," the greatest privilege (3:2). **In Paul's day for some Jews, however, their special blessing had led to pride (2:17) and to claims inconsistent with the way they were living.** Paul, therefore, exposes their inconsistencies as hypocrisy (vv. 18-21). **In Paul's way of thinking, the Jews' privileges were not the issue, but their setting themselves up as judges of others was.** They failed to practice what they professed. Most likely, Paul's description of the Jewish religious leaders' way of thinking was consistent with the self-perception of most of the Jewish population of Paul's day.

In addition, **Paul observes that some of the Jews were guilty of the very things they told others not to do—theft, adultery, and idolatry (vv. 21-22).** Paul's wording in these verses might raise the question of whether or not the Jewish people in general and/or their religious leaders were guilty of the sins in a literal sense. No doubt, a few examples of these sins could have been found among the Jews in Paul's day, but the average Jew had not committed theft, adultery, and idolatry (according to the traditional way of understanding these terms). Though the nation of Israel and its people were known for high moral purity (cf. Matt. 5:21-48), **since all people have committed such sins in their hearts, the Jews could not claim absolute freedom from these evils.**

Sin in Jewish History

Below are examples of some unique ways that these sins had appeared in Jewish history:

- **Sin of Theft**

    Israel had robbed God of honor (Mal. 1:6ff.). At different points in history, **the Jewish people had failed to show God the high respect and esteem that were due to Him. On those occasions, they essentially had robbed God of His honor.** God is to be praised and honored for who He is.

- **Sin of Adultery**

    As the bride of God, Israel could not deny the charge of spiritual adultery. **Time and time again the people had pursued other gods and had been unfaithful to God, a spiritual form of adultery (Hos. 1—3; Jer. 3:6-25).**

- **Sin of Idolatry**

    Israel had been guilty of the sin of idolatry, a transgression of the first of the Ten Commandments (Ex. 20:3). The Jews' opinions regarding idols were well known. They viewed idols as an abomination and a horror, because they believed that devotion was to be only to the one true God. At points in past Jewish history, some among them had worshiped physical idols. Paul's reference to temple-robbing (Rom. 2:22) was a reminder of one of these earlier incidents. On an occasion when Israel was tempted to accommodate Canaanite culture, God instructed His people to destroy idols and forbad them from taking any gold or silver dedicated to idols (Deut. 7:25).

In Paul's day most of the Jews had never literally worshiped physical idols, but **through their pride, some Jews had set themselves up as judges (Rom. 2:1ff.). As a result, they assumed the role of God and denied Him their devotion by putting themselves in His place** (Barrett, 1991, 55-57). The Jews' exalting themselves as the final authority was nothing short of idolatry.

Effects of Our Sins on Others

We see that throughout their history, whenever the Jewish people dishonored God and broke His law, it had a detrimental spiritual effect on them, as well as others. In Romans 2:24, Paul refers to Isaiah 52:5, where the Babylonians had scorned Israel's God. To the Babylonian Gentiles, Israel's God seemed to be a very weak god, since the Israelite exiles living among them failed to live up to their own religious claims. **In response to their Jewish captives' behavior, the Babylonians reproached the name of God because they did not believe the God of the Jews was able to keep His chosen people from sinning.** These Gentiles judged God by what His people did. The same holds true today. **The world still judges God and the church by what His people do.** Whether true or false, the world's opinion often is that the Christian church is full of judgmental hypocrites.

ROMANS 2:17-24
KEYWORDS
Gentiles (see p. 29)

> **Jews/Israelites/Hebrews** (see p. 29)
>
> **The Law (Torah)** (see p. 48)
>
> **Sin** (see p. 48)

> **SUMMARY**
>
> Some Jews of Paul's day failed to practice what they professed. They were proud of possessing the law, but habitually broke it and caused others (the Gentiles) to doubt and dishonor God. While offering to guide others toward the light, the hypocrites among the Jews turned them away from God. They heartily approved the truths of the Old Testament, but did not consistently live by them.

> **LIFE APPLICATION**
>
> Having ready access to light and truth, we as Christians need to be cautious of developing pride and self-righteousness regarding those gifts. We need to be on guard against developing a condescending attitude toward those who might appear to be unconverted or unenlightened, and we should not regard them as foolish or as children of the Evil One. Instead, we should endeavor to see all people through the compassionate eyes of Christ.
>
> Those people who are well versed in the Scriptures have a great responsibility to be lights to those who are in darkness. In our concern for others' weaknesses, we must never avoid discerning and asking forgiveness for our own shortcomings.
>
> Verses 17-24 teach us two truths:
>
> 1. Superior knowledge does not necessarily make us good people.
> 2. It is risky business to profess something which we fail to live.

CIRCUMCISION AND THE LAW
ROMANS 2:25-29

> 25 For circumcision is indeed profitable if you keep the law; but if you are a breaker of the law, your circumcision has become uncircumcision. 26 Therefore, if an uncircumcised man keeps the righteous requirements of the law, will not his uncircumcision be counted as circumcision? 27 And will not the physically uncircumcised, if he fulfills the law, judge you who, even with your written code and circumcision, are a transgressor of the law? 28 For he is not a Jew who is one outwardly, nor is circumcision that which is outward in the flesh; 29 but he is a Jew who is one inwardly; and circumcision is that of the heart, in the Spirit, not in the letter; whose praise is not from men but from God.

Circumcision and Water Baptism

Paul moves on to discuss the inability of the law to save us from sin and death. A common belief among some Jews was that the rite of circumcision guaranteed entry into heaven, regardless of the character of the person. When thinking about these passages of Scripture, in order to make Paul's teaching more relevant for the Christian church today, we can substitute the term *water baptism* for "circumcision" and the word *Christian* for "Jew." Paul affirms the importance of water baptism for the life of faith (6:1-14). In the New Testament, for followers of Christ the ordinance of water baptism replaced the Old Testament ordinance of circumcision. Some Christians have believed that baptism (like the Jews' idea about circumcision) is a means of salvation. **Water baptism, while being a very important act of obedience, is not the agent of salvation—faith in Christ and a relationship with Him are.**

Obedience to the Law

The external rite of circumcision was a covenantal identity marker for the Jews, but it did not have the power to commend one to God apart from faith and obedience (2:25; 4:1-12). **For Paul, doing the things that the Mosaic law required did not mean conformity to the details of the law, but fulfilling the trust relationship to which the law pointed. What was important was faith rather than observing particular commandments.** Outward circumcision had little spiritual value unless it was accompanied by faith and good works. Since to violate the trust relationship to which the law pointed was to render circumcision as uncircumcision, the Jew who was unfaithful to His covenant commitments was no better than the unbelieving Gentiles. In fact, Gentiles who converted to Christ fulfilled what the law pointed to by the virtue of their faith (2:26-27). **The need for obedience and a relationship with God puts Jews and Gentiles (all people) on the same level before an impartial God, making salvation dependent only on faith in Christ.**

The Jewish person of Paul's day might have replied that Paul's argument does not make sense and that no one could possibly keep the law without circumcision. What becomes clear is that the keeping of the law involved faith and not simply the observance of commandments such as circumcision. **Faith must come first, and then true obedience becomes possible.** In light of Paul's argument, outward circumcision becomes irrelevant to one's spiritual standing with God. **What the law teaches us is to live in a humble, believing dependence on God.**

Paul's Definitions of *Jew* and *Circumcision*

Paul proceeds to clarify God's purposes and intentions for the Jewish people and the rite of *circumcision* by explaining what a true Jew and true circumcision are. Paul proposes that "they are not all Israel who are of Israel" (9:6).

True Jew

- **The true Jew was not the outward Jew.** As a public person, the Jew was marked by the works of the law, and as a result, some Jews made an open display of their religion. They thought membership in a nation assured them of the privileges of being a child of God.
- **In contrast, the true Jew is a faithful Jew.** This reference is not about the religiously private Jew, who never talked about religion or participated in public religious observances, but one who was declared to be in a right relationship with God. Another way to state it is that **through faith one becomes a true Jew, a true child of God, a child of Abraham through faith in Jesus Christ (Gal. 3:26).** According to Paul's explanation, followers of Christ, who through faith have a relationship with God, can also be considered genuine Jews. (We should not take this to mean that Paul teaches that the Christian church has replaced the nation of Israel. As we will note, according to Romans 9–11, the Jewish nation has a special place in God's plan, which will be realized in the End Time.)

True Circumcision

- **True circumcision is not circumcision in the flesh.** Outward circumcision was a mark of belonging to a nation. That mark was made with a sharp knife and was a physical rite. God had given the rite as a sign of His covenant with Israel, and God was free to set it aside. For the Christian, water baptism has replaced circumcision.

- **In contrast, circumcision of the heart is true circumcision.** Those who trust God have their hearts transformed (circumcised) in the new birth. This assures them that they are truly children of God (Deut. 10:16; 30:6).
- **True circumcision is not in the letter.** The letter of the law is manipulated by sin to bring death (Rom. 7:6; 2 Cor. 3:6f.). The gospel frees us from the condemnation of the law and leads to life.
- **In contrast, true circumcision is of the Spirit.** Only the Holy Spirit can administer true circumcision, which is the transformation of the heart. In His renewing work, the Spirit cuts out evil from the human heart. Since the Holy Spirit removes sin from Christians' hearts, as people who have faith in God, they are considered to have real circumcision (cf. Phil. 3:3). **The Spirit's work in their hearts is nothing short of a miracle.**
- **The true people of God are inward Jews and have received circumcision of their hearts.** Their "praise is not from men but from God" (Rom. 2:29). Ultimate approval will depend on their Creator, not on human appraisal. Paul has exposed the error of the Jews who were relying on appearances and seeking the approval of others. It is possible for us to be very religious and do many of the things that Christians normally do, yet remain outside of a relationship with God, lacking assurance of eternal life with Him. A devotion to religion and even to a high morality are not enough. Religious devotion and virtue may be the means by which men and women try to save themselves. **True Christians are defined not so much by outward marks, but by inward submission of their hearts and lives to Christ.**

ROMANS 2:25-29

KEYWORDS

Circumcision

The removal of the foreskin on the male organ. For the Jewish people, this holy ritual had the distinct meaning of being the sign of the covenant that God made with Abraham. Circumcision was a confirming seal/sign of the salvation Abraham received by faith. (Gen. 17:11). In Romans 3:30, Paul refers to "the circumcised by [*ek*, out of] faith and the uncircumcised through [*dia*, through] faith." These are two ways of expressing the same truth—that *true circumcision* is primarily a condition of the heart that is the result of faith in the one *true* God. Circumcised (Jews) and uncircumcised (Gentiles) both stand in a right relationship with God on the basis of faith. The entire human family's access to righteousness is through Christ.

Covenant (*diatheke*)

A compact or agreement between two parties that is mutually binding on each other

Faith (see p. 23)

Flesh (see p. 58)

Holy Spirit/The Spirit (see p. 25)

The Law (*Torah*) (see p. 48)

Transgression

A deliberate violation of a revealed command

Water Baptism

An ordinance of the church which is a sign of death to the old life and resurrection to a new life with Christ (Rom. 6:1-6). Water baptism also serves as a seal/sign of believers' right standing with God through faith in Christ.

SUMMARY

Some Jews, although they received the honorable, physical mark of circumcision, failed to have faith in God, which would have compensated for their not keeping the law. True circumcision is not a mark in the flesh, but rather the transformation of the heart by the Holy Spirit.

Furthermore, being a true Jew (a child of God) is a matter of faith rather than a matter of membership in a nation. The real Jew's heart has been "circumcised" by the Spirit. A child of God stands right in the sight of God and receives praise from Him.

LIFE APPLICATION

The external practices of Christianity should spur us to a closer relationship with God and living right, just as the external mark of circumcision should have motivated the Jews to trust in God.

Our participation in worship, celebration of the Lord's Supper, and receiving the ordinance of baptism should be clear signs of our humble dependence on Christ. However, these spiritual practices have little value without our having faith in God. We would be wise to remember that we can do many things that Christians normally do and still be in a sinful state. Observing the rules and practices of Christianity is no substitute for giving our hearts to Christ and living for Him.

THE MOST IMPORTANT ADVANTAGE OF THE JEWS
ROMANS 3:1-8

> **¹ What advantage then has the Jew, or what is the profit of circumcision?** ² Much in every way! Chiefly because to them were committed the oracles of God. ³ For what if some did not believe? Will their unbelief make the faithfulness of God without effect? ⁴ Certainly not! Indeed, let God be true but every man a liar. As it is written:
>
> > "That You may be justified in Your words,
> > And may overcome when You are judged."
>
> **But if our unrighteousness demonstrates the righteousness of God, what shall we say?** Is God unjust who inflicts wrath? (I speak as a man.) ⁶ Certainly not! For then how will God judge the world?
>
> ⁷ For if the truth of God has increased through my lie to His glory, why am I also still judged as a sinner? ⁸ And why not say, "Let us do evil that good may come"?—as we are slanderously reported and as some affirm that we say. Their condemnation is just.
>
> [emphases added]

In Romans 2:25-29, Paul may have seemed to have denied any special position to the Jews. Expecting Jewish readers to misunderstand his words, Paul assures them that he recognizes that God has given the Jewish people special advantages and blessings. The nation of Israel could not be reduced to the level of other nations. To deny them their blessings would have accused the Old Testament Scriptures of lying or God of failing to carry out His plan. In Romans 3:1-8, Paul addresses these concerns. **This passage should be read as a conversation between Paul and an imaginary Jewish opponent.** This questioning technique that Paul uses here is also used elsewhere in the letter to the Romans, especially in chapters 10 and 11. Likely on his missionary journeys, Paul had encountered such opponents, who asked these very questions. Paul's opponents may have thought Paul was teaching that evil actions did not matter because of his teaching that God could bring good out of evil actions.

Opponent's Questions for Paul

The opponent's first question: "What advantage then has the Jew, or what is the profit of circumcision?" (v. 1). Another way to state this question is, "Is there any good to being a Jew by natural descent or profit to being circumcised?" That is, does Paul's gospel do away with the benefits of being God's chosen people? **Paul's answer is that the Jews (or we could say, the Christian church) had been blessed "much in every way" (v. 2).** The Jewish people's main advantage was that they had been entrusted with "the oracles of God," referring to the Old Testament. God had written a basic moral law on the hearts of all people (2:12-16), but the chosen people had also received the inspired Scriptures. In the Scriptures, God had revealed Himself to them and had made known His plan. **The Jewish people had an unchangeable revelation, carefully recorded in Scripture.** They could read it and know God's will. In the inspired Word, they had the promise of the coming Redeemer; but later when the Messiah came, many did not recognize Him and rejected Him. As a result, those individuals had squandered many of their advantages. Here, mention is made of only one advantage (being entrusted with the oracles of God), but in 9:4-5 several more are listed.

**The opponent's second question: "But if our unrighteousness demonstrates the righteousness of God, what shall we say?" (3:5). Stated another way, "Does human unrighteousness bring out more clearly the righteousness of God?" One school of thought was that the purpose of spiritual darkness was so God's light could be seen more clearly. If that were true, then people in their disobedience would have done God a favor, and He would be unjust to judge the sinner. This argument does not change the reality that God's judgment of the world remains a universal fact (v. 6). Therefore, Paul objects to the opponent's reasoning, which makes sin and wickedness no longer mean anything. There would be no ground for judgment; every sinner could plead that his sin gave God an opportunity to manifest His saving grace and made God's goodness stand out more brightly.

Such reasoning is based on a false principle—"Let us do evil that good may come" (v. 8; cf. 6:1-14). Another way of putting it is, "People like to sin and God likes to forgive sin. So let us sin more and more in order to make God's goodness shine brightly and to please and honor Him." This argument is known by theologians as the *antinomian* (against rule, law, or regulation) *perversion* of the gospel. **Because Paul preached a law-free gospel (justification by faith apart from works), no doubt, some of his critics had charged that Paul had encouraged people to sin vigorously and had promoted ungodly lifestyles (3:7-8; 6:1).** Sternly disagreeing with this charge, Paul explains that for those who turn away from God in unfaithfulness, or those who take an antinomian position, the condemnation pronounced on them is just. **Paul's position was that since sin separates us from God, one cannot live in deliberate ongoing sin and have a real relationship with Christ.**

Paul's Response to His Opponent

In response to the questions posed to him, Paul offers four basic Christian truths:

1. **God will fulfill His promises in the Old Testament regardless of people's unbelief (3:3).** God had not broken faith with the Scriptures that He had entrusted to Israel. **Whatever Jews (or Christians) may or may not do, God will keep His**

promises. In no way does the unfaithfulness of humankind set aside the faithfulness of God (v. 4; for a full discussion of this, see Romans chapters 9—11). Throughout history, God has worked through a remnant which has remained faithful to Him.

2. **There is a coming judgment (vv. 4-6).** At the Final Judgment, everyone will receive rewards or punishment based on their faithfulness or unfaithfulness. In verse 4, Paul cites Psalm 51:4, which depicts a courtroom scene in which God and human beings plead against one another. **God and humans will both present their cases, and God will be vindicated as the Judge of all humankind.** Those people who are repentant and honor God will *justify* God; that is, they will declare and demonstrate that God is a just God, and that what He speaks is right and true. Here *justification* does not refer to humans being justified, but the vindication of God himself before all those who have failed to honor Him and all religious substitutes for genuine obedience to Him. On Judgment Day, God is certain to leave the court justified.

3. **Punishment is a certain response to evil (vv. 5-7).** God may bring good out of evil, but that does not relieve from guilt the person who does evil. If it did, then that would encourage us to do evil, hoping that good would come from it. Such a false assumption would destroy the distinction between right and wrong.

4. **God does give special advantages to some people, but along with those advantages come added responsibilities and service expectations (v. 2).** The Jews had been made custodians of the Word of God. Among us are those who, like the Jews, have significant advantages—such as having been dedicated at an early age to the Lord, having been raised in the church, having godly parents, or having been instructed in the moral law and the gospel at a young age. For those people, their advantages make it easier for them to come to faith in Jesus Christ and require them to use their advantages to serve God and others.

The World's Need of Salvation

ROMANS 3:1-8

KEYWORDS

Antinomian Perversion
A system of thought that erroneously teaches that Christians are entirely free of moral law as a rule for life, due to the fact that they are justified by faith alone

Chosen by God
Chosen (people of Israel)—The nation whom God chose to be His light to all nations, and through whom He sent His Son, the Messiah Jesus Christ, into the world to offer grace, healing, and salvation to all people

Evil (see p. 80)

Justify God
Declaring God to be right. To *justify* God is to acknowledge that He is just and His ways are right.

Oracles of God
Hebrew Scriptures. In Jewish writings, designates the Hebrew Scriptures and most naturally refers to the Old Testament.

Righteousness (*dikaiosune*) (see p. 48)

Unrighteousness (see p. 75)

SUMMARY

The Jewish people had the advantage of having "the oracles of God"—the Old Testament. As a consequence, they were taught more thoroughly and precisely about God than the Gentiles, who had only the law that was written on their hearts. This advantage had not made the Jews any more righteous than the Gentiles. The Jews, therefore, had no legitimate reason to think they were superior spiritually. God has remained faithful to His Word, while both Jews and Gentiles have been continually unfaithful. The charge that God's judgment is unjust is false, since He acts in justice and grace, treating all people equally. No one will escape judgment, and God will be true to all of His promises.

LIFE APPLICATION

Like the Jews, Christians have been entrusted with God's Word. We have the truth, the oracles of God. Through the Bible, God has made known what He expects of us. For us it is a great privilege to be able to read the Bible and to know the will of God, and the Bible also tells us about God's love and the way of faith.

> As we continue our study of Romans, the way to come to faith in Christ and to live the Christian life will become clearer. As Paul tells his people, religion apart from Christ—churchmanship, piety, and good deeds—will not save our souls. Only a relationship with God through Christ, as described in the Bible, can provide us that assurance.

ALL HAVE SINNED
ROMANS 3:9-20

> ⁹ What then? Are we better than they? Not at all. For we have previously charged both Jews and Greeks that they are all under sin.
>
> ¹⁰ As it is written:
>
> > "There is none righteous, no, not one;
> > ¹¹ There is none who understands;
> > There is none who seeks after God.
> > ¹² They have all turned aside;
> > They have together become unprofitable;
> > There is none who does good, no, not one."
> > ¹³ "Their throat is an open tomb;
> > With their tongues they have practiced deceit";
> >
> > "The poison of asps is under their lips";
> > ¹⁴ "Whose mouth is full of cursing and bitterness."
> > ¹⁵ "Their feet are swift to shed blood;
> > ¹⁶ Destruction and misery are in their ways;
> > ¹⁷ And the way of peace they have not known."
> > ¹⁸ "There is no fear of God before their eyes."
>
> ¹⁹ Now we know that whatever the law says, it says to those who are under the law, that every mouth may be stopped, and all the world may become guilty before God. ²⁰ Therefore by the deeds of the law no flesh will be justified in His sight, for by the law is the knowledge of sin.

In the previous verses, Paul has answered the question "What advantage then has the Jew?" by declaring, "Much in every way!" (3:1-2). **Now in verse 9, Paul returns to this line of thought by raising the question, "Are we better than they [Gentiles]?" His reply is "Not at all."** Here Paul seems to take back what he has just said. The point that he is making when he responds "Not at all" is that the advantages of the Jews will not make any difference when they stand before the judgment seat of God. **All human beings, Jews and Greeks (Gentiles) are "under sin" (v. 9). This is Paul's first mention of** *sin* **in Romans, and he describes sin as an oppressive power. To be "under sin" means to be in a Christless condition, controlled and dominated by the oppressive power of evil.** The means by which Paul was able to discern the Jews' and Gentiles' condition of spiritual bankruptcy (being "under sin") was by observing how their behavior measured up to the requirements of the law as recorded in Scripture. Scripture attests to the guilt of all humankind. Therefore, there is no salvation outside of the gospel—not even for the Jews, who, like Abraham, could have been saved by believing God's promises fulfilled in the gospel.

The Human Condition

To show that all persons, both Jews and Gentiles, are in the same condition, Paul, in Romans 3:10-18, cites passages from the Psalms and Isaiah. These passages describe the character, speech, and conduct of human beings.

- **Human Character**

> As it is written: "There is none righteous, no, not one; there is none who understands; there is none who seeks after God. They have all turned aside; they have together become unprofitable; there is none who does good, no, not one" (vv. 10-12; cf. Ps. 14:1ff.).

The fact is that all Jews as well as Gentiles have not only collectively but also individually turned aside from God. The terms *none*, *all*, and *together* indicate that there is not a single righteous person. **Sin has gone throughout the entire human race. No one can stand right with God apart from His justifying grace (Rom. 2:11-24).**

- **Human Speech**

> "Their throat is an open tomb; with their tongues they have practiced deceit"; "The poison of asps is under their lips"; "Whose mouth is full of cursing and bitterness" (vv. 13-14; cf. Ps. 5:9; 10:7).

As a result of sin, people's speech is filled with threats of violence and destruction and with deceptive, smooth talk

and flattery. In short, their lips are as deadly as the poison of a snake. Their speech is vulgar and violent.

- **Human Conduct**

  "Their feet are swift to shed blood;" "destruction and misery are in their ways; and the way of peace they have not known." "There is no fear of God before their eyes" (vv. 15-18; cf. Isa. 59:7f.).

People's wickedness is expressed not only through speech, but also through deeds and actions. Romans 3:18 sums up the cause of human sins: "There is no fear of God before their eyes." To have no fear of God means that **God was not a part of their thinking.** If God had been before their eyes, it would have meant that God was in their thoughts. **Their minds were devoid of the fear of God, which resulted in their engaging in self-destructive behaviors.** The fear of God, therefore, had nothing to do with directing their lives.

The entire human personality—inward and outward—has been radically affected by sin. Indeed all are "under sin." There is no exception; and to make sure that his readers understood, Paul indicates there is no religious exception. Even "those [Jews] who are under the law" cannot plea that they are not sinners. **The law, referring to the passages Paul has cited from the Psalms and Isaiah, indicates that the world is guilty before God (v. 19). Paul has in mind a courtroom situation which includes the whole world as defendants. God is both the offended One and the Judge.** The defendants are given the opportunity to speak. But these defendants are overwhelmed by the weight of evidence against them so that every mouth is silenced. **The testimony of the Scriptures (the law) against them leaves everyone speechless before God and without any defense as in 1:18–2:1.**

The Solution for the Human Condition

The solution to the human predicament, however, is not by performing perfectly the deeds demanded by the law (3:20). The law was not given to enable people to work their way to salvation. On the contrary, it was given to make human beings aware of right and wrong and their need for God's forgiveness, grace, and salvation (5:20). **A right understanding of the law prompts us to rely on Christ for salvation.** In Paul's day, the Jews tried to make the law into something it was never intended to be. **The law has no power to save "good" or "bad" people or to make anyone righteous, but it does make clear what is sinful by defining right and wrong (7:7-12).**

Sin is a powerful, oppressive force in human beings. People not only need forgiveness, but also deliverance from the dominion of sin. **As broken and sinful as humans may be, Paul does not think that they are in a hopeless condition. He knows that humans are sinners, but also knows that Christ is a great Savior.**

As we move further in Romans 3, Paul will reveal God's solution for the human condition. We will see that even though God in His wisdom has shown us our brokenness, He has also revealed to us through His Son a way to receive His healing and salvation.

ROMANS 3:9-20

KEYWORDS

Under Sin
To be in a Christless condition, controlled and dominated by the oppressive power of evil

SUMMARY

All humans, Jews *and* Gentiles, are "under sin." The Old Testament teaches that the entire human personality has been affected by sin and that all people are equally guilty before God. The law has no power to make bad people good. It cannot justify them and bring them into communion with God. The purpose of the law is to reveal "the knowledge of sin"—to turn our hearts toward repentance.

LIFE APPLICATION

The Bible (law) paints a grim picture of humans apart from the saving grace of Christ. In our own strength, none of us can deliver ourselves from the oppressive power of sin. The law does not have the power to save us either. It can only tell us what God's will is and that we have failed to do it. If we respond to the law as we should, we will repent and look to Jesus, for He is our salvation.

REFLECTION—PART TWO
Romans 1:18—3:20

1. Divine wrath is the inevitable consequence of sin. How would you define God's wrath? Explain the way it is revealed.

2. What are the two characteristics (attributes) of God that are evident in nature (creation)? Explain each of them (1:20).

3. Paul describes a grim picture of society in his day. How would you characterize the sins listed in 1:28-32? Why are these sins in themselves God's judgment, His wrath?

   Being filled with all unrighteousness • sexual immorality •.wickedness • covetousness • maliciousness (v. 29)

   Full of envy • murder • strife • deceit • evil-mindedness (v. 29)

   They are whisperers • backbiters • haters of God • violent • proud • boasters • inventors of evil things • disobedient to parents • undiscerning • untrustworthy • unloving • unforgiving • unmerciful (vv. 29-31)

4. According to Genesis 2:18-25, God declared that a man and woman would live together in relationship as one flesh. Since men engaged in sexual relationships with other men, and women with other women (Rom. 1:26-27), why did Paul consider these acts to be unnatural and in violation of God's will?

5. Will the self-righteous as well as the unrighteous experience God's judgment? Relate your answer to Jewish critics of Paul's day and to those today who condemn others for doing the same things of which they are guilty.

6. What is your understanding of "the law written on the heart" (2:15 NIV)? Relate your answer to the principle: All people will be judged by what God has made available to them.

7. Explain the sense in which the Jews were guilty of the sins of theft, adultery, and idolatry.
8. What is the relationship between circumcision and water baptism?
9. How would you explain Paul's teaching that all people apart from Christ are "under sin" in terms of character, speech, and conduct?
10. What are a few of the ideas in Romans 1:18–3:20 that have impacted you? How have these ideas influenced how you think or live?

Prayer

Dear Lord, help us to prevail in prayer for those who are "under sin" and to extend compassion to them. Many are ensnared, blinded, and oppressed by the power of sin and are unwilling or unable to pray for themselves. Help us to unite in prayer for their deliverance and for the worldwide advance of the gospel.

And, too, we pray for our own spiritual condition:

Forgive us *of the carnal pride of exalting ourselves and human reasoning.*

Deliver us *from any temptation toward sensuality and to violate the sanctity of marriage.*

Keep us *from the sins that may arise in social and family relationships.*

Guard us *against a spirit of self-righteousness and looking down on others.*

Above all, our Lord,

Help us to listen *to our consciences on which the law is written and **to treasure** the Bible as our guide to eternal life.*

May our lives be pleasing to You, our heavenly Father. Amen.

PART THREE—Romans 3:21—5:21

God's Plan of Salvation

- **Salvation Through Faith**
  Romans 3:21-31
- **Abraham and David: Examples of Salvation Through Faith**
  Romans 4:1-12
- **The Promise: Grace and Faith**
  Romans 4:13-25
- **Justification and Love**
  Romans 5:1-11
- **Adam and Christ**
  Romans 5:12-21

God has revealed salvation in a new way—by grace through faith alone. In the Old Testament, God gave His laws to the people in order to teach them the difference between sin and righteousness, but these laws had no power to save and to bring one into a right relationship with God. In order to establish a relationship with His people, God has provided another way. In Romans 1:18–3:20, Paul has proclaimed that all people are sinners and that the law can do nothing but give them knowledge of their sin. He now prepares his readers for the development of his gospel message—that salvation is only possible through faith in Christ. **Desiring that his readers appreciate better the benefits of the gospel, Paul takes up the theme of the saving righteousness of God (1:16-17) and emphasizes that the only way anyone can benefit from it is by faith.**

SALVATION THROUGH FAITH
ROMANS 3:21-31

Everyone is in need of salvation. Like a skillful physician, Paul has diagnosed the human condition. Previously, he has examined the human race and has concluded it has a chronic spiritual disease (Rom. 3:9-20). The symptoms of this disease are ungodly attitudes, motivations, and actions, which indicate that all people are sinners and guilty before God. **The only cure for our souls is what God has done for us in Christ.** Apart from Christ we are under the wrath of God, and we can do nothing in our own power to save ourselves. In chapter 3, Paul offers us the only remedy for our condition.

> **Salvation**
> God's work in bringing people to eternal life. *Salvation* is the total work of God to bring humankind from a state of sin to a state of eternal life through Jesus Christ. People are saved when they believe in Christ. From that time, their salvation progresses; and finally in the future when Christ returns, the fullness of their salvation is realized.

THE SOLUTION TO THE SIN PROBLEM
ROMANS 3:21-26

> 21 But now the righteousness of God apart from the law is revealed, being witnessed by the Law and the Prophets, 22 even the righteousness of God, through faith in Jesus Christ, to all and on all who believe. For there is no difference; 23 for all have sinned and fall short of the glory of God, 24 being justified freely by His grace through the redemption that is in Christ Jesus, 25 whom God set forth as a propitiation by His blood, through faith, to demonstrate His righteousness, because in His forbearance God had passed over the sins that were previously committed, 26 to demonstrate at the present time His righteousness, that He might be just and the justifier of the one who has faith in Jesus.

The Righteousness of God Revealed

Verses 21-26 are most important for understanding Paul's gospel message. In the preceding chapters, he has described the desperate plight of the human race, but here Paul's opening statement is good news: "But the righteousness of God apart from the law is revealed" (v. 21). As we have already observed, "the righteousness of God" is God's saving activity, which is revealed

God's Plan of Salvation

in His mercy, love, and grace in Christ. **Both the law (Gen. 15:6) and the prophets (Hab. 2:4) bear witness of God's saving work in Christ.**

- *Revealed* (*apokaluptetai*). In Romans 1:17, the word *revealed* is in the present tense, meaning "is being revealed." This use of the present tense emphasizes that saving righteousness continues to be revealed when the gospel is preached.
- *Revealed* (*pephanerotai*). In 3:21, the Greek uses the perfect tense for the term "is revealed," indicating an accomplished fact in the past with abiding results in the present.

Both of the verb forms for the word *revealed* indicate that God's saving work in the gospel events—life, death, and resurrection of Christ—is still effective. In other words, the saving power of Christ has the power to save now just as much as it did when He died and arose. The blessings of salvation are received by faith, not by obedience to a moral code, which inevitably leads to wrath and condemnation. Faith directs us to depend on God for salvation and is the means by which we enter into a right relationship with Him.

Again Paul stresses that everyone is under the oppressive power of sin and is in need of a faith-relationship with God. **"All have sinned and fall short of the glory of God" (v. 23).** This verse means that **all unbelieving men and women lack what Adam had, namely the glory in which he was created** (Barrett, 1991, 74). Adam lost the divine radiance in which God clothed him because of his disobedience, and all humankind since then has done likewise. **Christians, however, already have had a measure of divine glory restored to them** (Rom. 8:18; 2 Cor. 3:18; 2 Thess. 2:14), **but full restoration will not come until they are completely transformed and their bodies are conformed to the glorious body of their Lord** (Phil. 3:21; 1 John 3:2).

God's Saving Process

In Romans 3:24-25, Paul endeavors to use language that adequately describes the saving process. He uses three terms

to emphasize the great cost of salvation to focus his discussion about salvation on the cross.

- ***Justified (dikaioo); noun, justification (dikaiosune)*—a legal term from the courts**

    The term *justification* pictures God as a judge in the courtroom. When a guilty person is arraigned by God, what will happen to him? Surely he will be condemned and punished. God knows that the sinner is not good enough to merit salvation. Nevertheless, **God treats the sinner who has repented as though he is not a sinner and declares him innocent.** God is the Judge, but He is not a vengeful judge determined to punish the guilty. On the contrary, when a person enters God's court with faith in Christ, the Judge will treat him or her not as a criminal but as a son or daughter. That is what justification through faith means. We can never justify ourselves; God can do it and does it. Forgiveness is possible only because of the cross.

- ***Redemption (apolutrosis)*—a term from the world of slavery**

    The term *redemption* conveys the idea of freeing someone through the payment of a price or a ransom (Morris, 1993, 179). In the ancient world, slavery was common. The practice was that when a slave wanted his freedom, he worked long hours and earned money for his extra work. The money he earned was deposited in a temple of a god. After years of saving money for his freedom, the slave then asked his master to go with him to the temple. The priest of the temple came out and offered the slave's master the money in exchange for the slave. The slave then became the property of the temple god, so to speak, and no longer belonged to any man (Deissmann, 1957, 172-74). Here is a picture of what Christ did. **Jesus Christ paid the price so that every person could be free of the dominion of sin.** Paul says to the Corinthian believers, "You were bought at [with] a price" (1 Cor. 6:20). The ransom was paid at the cross (Mark 10:45), and the Holy Spirit continues to apply the liberating power of the cross to those who come to faith in Christ.

- ***Propitiation (*hilasterion*)—a term from the temple sacrificial system***

    Some liberal scholars prefer to translate the Greek word as *expiation* rather than *propitiation* because of theological assumptions and because *expiation*, which means "to blot out sin and guilt," is more neutral and less offensive since it does not suggest that God is angry at sinners. ***Propitiation*** indicates that God's anger at ungodly people needs to be appeased. **Likely, *propitiation* includes both the blotting out of the guilt of sin and the appeasing of God's wrath. God sent His Son to make atonement, which involves the blotting out of sin and the turning away of God's wrath, which has been aroused by sin.** In the first three chapters of Romans, Paul has dealt with wrath and now indicates how God diverts wrath and judgment away from the believer. **God has pardoned the believer through Jesus Christ**, who has taken that person's place, receiving the weight of divine judgment on Himself on the cross. As a result, God's wrath was diverted from the guilty to the Innocent One.

    It is possible that when Paul wrote the explanation of God's merciful judgment, he had in mind the Day of Atonement (v. 25; Lev. 23:27-28; 25:9). Paul used the term *hilasterion*, which was the Greek equivalent for the Hebrew term used in the Old Testament for *mercy seat*, the lid on the ark of the covenant (Ex. 25:17-22). Yearly, the high priest went into the Holy of Holies and sprinkled blood on the lid of the ark, atoning for the people's sins. Paul is contrasting the old and the new place where God forgives sins and turns away wrath from believers (Davies, 1948, 237-41). The contrast between the ark and the cross is striking, as depicted in the letter to the Hebrews:

Places of Forgiveness	
The Ark	**The Cross**
Hidden away in the Holy of Holies (9:3-4)	Out in the open, up on a hill (13:12)

Only one man had access to it (9:7).	All have access to it (4:16).
Offering was repeated each year (10:1-4, 11)	Offering was once and for all, never needs to be repeated (7:27; 10:8-10).
Benefits through an animal's blood (10:3-4)	Benefits through Christ's blood (5:7-10; 9:12-14; 13:12, 20)
Benefits depended on ritual (8:3-5; 9:8-10).	Benefits depend on faith (4:14; 10:19-39; 11:1ff.).
Old mercy seat (9:4-5)	New mercy seat (6:19-20)
Confined to the walls of the Temple and the nation of Israel (9:1-5)	Reaches beyond the boundaries of Israel to the world (7:25-26; 8:1; 13:12-13)

Indeed a significant change has taken place in the way God deals with sin. We have access to the cross, and everyone is invited to kneel at its foot. **Christ offered one sacrifice, which accomplished what all the sacrifices of the past had failed to do.** In recognizing that sin had not been effectively addressed, Paul says God "had passed over the sins" of the past (Rom. 3:25). In His forbearance and patience, God did not require adequate punishment for sins committed before Christ came. From time to time God did judge sin, but generally He overlooked sins without condoning them. But through the cross, God took decisive action to deal with human sin. The way that He dealt with human failures showed His kind justice, in that He chose to bear the penalty of our sin through the person of His Son. In doing that, God did right in that He was both just and merciful.

God is both a demanding Judge and a forgiving Father. How is He a merciful God? His justice demands punishment for wrongdoing. God's Son took the penalty of sin so that the Father's mercy would forgive the sinner. In the cross, God's justice and mercy are united for a common end—the salvation of humankind. **Simply stated, we see in the cross both God's hatred of sin and His** saving righteousness. God is a moral being, and through the cross He is "just and the justifier of the one who has faith in Jesus" (v. 26). The cross, therefore, solves the problems of God's being just and holy on the one hand and loving and merciful on the other.

ROMANS 3:21-26

KEYWORDS

Believe
An attitude of the heart to accept something as being true and to rely on particular persons or things. In the New Testament, to *believe* is to have an active, personal trust in Jesus Christ and to depend on Him for salvation (Rom. 4:5; 10:10).

Faith (see p. 23)

Forgiveness (see p. 47)

Glory of God (see p. 75)

God as Judge (see p. 86)

Justification (*dikaiosune*) (see p. 48)

Justified by Faith (*dikaioo*) (see p. 48)

Propitiation
The act of atoning or of satisfying the wrath of God against sin. The need for propitiation arose because the sin of humankind offended the holiness of God. In the New Testament, the cross is the place of propitiation, since there the death of Christ fully satisfied the holy demands of God. In the Old Testament, the place of propitiation is the mercy seat where high priests sprinkled blood in atoning for the people's sins.

Redemption
Deliverance from some form of bondage secured by the payment of a ransom. Throughout the New Testament, redemption is a divine activity; its primary spiritual significance lies in the price that God paid to deliver humankind from the death that sin brings, through the death of His Son Jesus Christ on the cross.

Revealed (see p. 68)

Righteousness (*dikaiosune*) (see p. 48)

Sin (see p. 48)

> **SUMMARY & LIFE APPLICATION**
> See under "ROMANS 3:27-31" pages 122-123.

EXCLUSION OF BOASTING
ROMANS 3:27-31

> 27 Where is boasting then? It is excluded. By what law? Of works? No, but by the law of faith. 28 Therefore we conclude that a man is justified by faith apart from the deeds of the law. 29 Or is He the God of the Jews only? Is He not also the God of the Gentiles? Yes, of the Gentiles also, 30 since there is one God who will justify the circumcised by faith and the uncircumcised through faith. 31 Do we then make void the law through faith? Certainly not! On the contrary, we establish the law.

This section of Scripture emphasizes some truths that can be inferred from what Paul has previously said. Here Paul continues the pattern of dialogue with an imaginary Jewish adversary. Exactly what the Jewish representative might have said is not readily apparent, but what Paul says in his response is very clear.

Paul's Response to an Opponent

First, there is no room for boasting since the way to God is by faith alone (vv. 27-28). The Jews tried to keep every aspect of the Mosaic law. In so doing they developed an attitude of pride and boasted about their works. In response to this attitude of self-confidence, Paul describes *the law of faith*, terminology that only appears in the Bible in Paul's letters (v. 27). **This rule of faith means that in the kingdom of God there are no self-made people—no people who have saved themselves.** Paul's position is that every person is a sinner and no one can make himself right before God through works. The only way is faith, and faith excludes boasting (4:1-4).

Second, the way to God is the same for all people (3:29-30). If some people received salvation through observing the law and others through faith, would that not suggest there are two Gods? The idea of two Gods was repulsive to the Jews. They insisted on monotheism, and the heart of their creed was that God is one (Deut. 6:4). Since there is only one God, **all people stand before God alike and all must come to Him the same way—by faith.** Thus, Paul insists that the God of the Jews is also the God of the Gentiles. Contrary to what some Jews thought, God was not their own exclusive God. They, like all others, could only be right with God through trusting in Christ—again excluding boasting.

Third, the exclusion of the works of the law raises a serious question (Rom. 3:31). Does the insistence on faith do away with the law? Here, as is often the case, Paul seems to use the term *law* in a broad sense, including Jewish thought and practice as expressed in the Old Testament. Did faith destroy the very foundation on which Jewish life and religion rested? "Certainly not! On the contrary, we establish the law," says Paul (v. 31). The full significance of Israel's religion is affirmed in the gospel. God's promises in the Old Testament point to the gospel—the Good News of salvation through faith in Christ Jesus. **In the gospel, the Old Testament and the religion of Israel find their real meaning and fulfillment.** The Old Testament testifies to the need of justification by faith, and the moral law in particular convicts us of the need of faith. **Faith in Jesus does not replace the Old Testament Scriptures and the law; it fulfills them.** No disrespect is shown for the law, but Paul has established a truth—salvation through faith.

Justification Through the Cross

Human sin is rebellion against God. The cross is the only means by which sin can be effectively addressed. At the cross we see God bridge the awesome gulf that separated Him and the human race. In his careful use of language, Paul has sought to safeguard the great Christian truths of salvation. His conclusion is **"that a man is justified by faith apart from the deeds of the law" (v. 28). This statement means that every person with faith in Christ is released from guilt and fear and can**

walk through life with assurance of being a child of God. Paul tells us that as we stand before the cross, guilty and destitute, God lavishes His love and forgiveness upon us. We need only to come as we are. God's love is free and is for sinners. We do not need to be good, religious, rich, educated, famous, or wise. **The only requirement is that we trust the Savior and take Him at His word.**

ROMANS 3:27-31

KEYWORDS

The Cross
The Roman Empire's instrument for the most cruel and shameful punishment, and the climax to Christ's suffering for the salvation of humankind

Gentiles (see p. 29)

Jews/Israelites/Hebrews (see p. 29)

Justified by Faith (*dikaioo*) (see p. 48)

The Law (*Torah*) (see p. 48)

SUMMARY

Salvation is available, independent of the law and is received on the sole condition of faith in Christ. Just as the law and the prophets taught, salvation cannot be otherwise, for all are sinners in need of being delivered from the oppressive power of sin.

Salvation is a free gift and the result of the sheer goodness of God, since we are "being justified freely by His grace" (3:24). The total process of salvation centers on the cross whether it is expressed in terms of justification, redemption, or propitiation. Truly, God's way of saving people is not through their doing the works of the law but by faith alone. The biblical doctrine does not replace the law (Old Testament), but it fulfills its true purpose.

LIFE APPLICATION

Salvation through faith in Christ eliminates all basis for spiritual pride. When we become Christians, we simply receive salvation as an unearned gift from Him.

The only possible solution to the problems of sin and brokenness in our lives is salvation provided through faith in Jesus Christ. Our own actions of righteousness or good works are ineffective in securing

> forgiveness for us. We are only forgiven and set free when we put our faith in the Lord Jesus Christ, who died on the cross for us. Jesus brings healing to the brokenness that sin has caused, and His forgiving grace reaches us in our deepest spiritual needs.

ABRAHAM AND DAVID: EXAMPLES OF SALVATION THROUGH FAITH
ROMANS 4:1-12

In Romans 3:21-31, Paul emphasized justification through faith. Now in chapter 4, because he is eager for his readers to understand the importance of this doctrine, **Paul points to Abraham and David as prime examples, showing that salvation through faith is scriptural.** As Paul has said, the gospel affirms the Old Testament, but not the religion of salvation by works (3:31). Earlier, Paul observed that the Old Testament law and prophets had testified to God's saving righteousness, which is proclaimed through the gospel (v. 21). Now turning to Abraham, **Paul carries us back about four thousand years, and shows us that the way that God justifies a person has always been the same.** Before coming to faith, Abraham lived in Ur of the Chaldeans, a region controlled by idolatry and perishing in paganism.

ABRAHAM SAVED THROUGH FAITH
ROMANS 4:1-5

> [1] What then shall we say that Abraham our father has found according to the flesh? [2] For if Abraham was justified by works, he has something to boast about, but not before God. [3] For what does the Scripture say? *"Abraham believed God, and it was accounted to him for righteousness."* [4] Now to him who works, the wages are not counted as grace but as debt. [5] But to him who does not work but believes on Him who justifies the ungodly, his faith is accounted for righteousness.

Paul's comments in this passage are most likely a response to an adversary, who has argued that Abraham was saved because of good works (vv. 1-2). Like an experienced lawyer, Paul asserts that the patriarch did not earn his salvation, but received grace—God's saving favor. Abraham had reasons to be proud of his exemplary life, but from God's point of view he had no grounds for having pride.

Abraham as an Example

Why did Paul use Abraham as an example to support his side of the debate about salvation? The answer seems to be twofold:

First, Abraham was known for his moral excellence. The Jews thought of him as the father of their nation and a friend of God. In their minds, Abraham towered above all others and was esteemed for his exemplary lifestyle. It was a common belief that the patriarch kept all the law before it was even given. To support this view, a reference was made to Genesis 26:5, where God assured Isaac that He would bless him because "Abraham obeyed My voice and kept My charge, My commandments, My statutes, and My laws." Abraham had not received the law of Moses; he lived before the time of Moses. He had no Bible, but he was a model for living. Since Abraham, a good man, was not saved by works, his example provided Paul the scriptural support for teaching that no person can be saved by good works. If salvation by works would have been possible, Abraham would have been saved that way.

Second, Abraham was actually justified through faith. In Romans 4:3, to support his argument, Paul cites Genesis 15:6. This verse is the foundation for Paul's understanding of salvation: "Abraham believed God, and it was accounted to him for righteousness."

Definition of Accounted (*Logizomai*)

The word *accounted* (*logizomai*), a bookkeeping term, can also be translated *reckoned, imputed,* or *credited*:

- **At times, the word *accounted* was used in reference to ancient kings who kept a roll of their subjects.** There were two lists in the book. One consisted of those who had been faithful and the other of those who had been disobedient and rebellious. Paul may have had in mind that his readers' names were on the list of the disobedient in God's book. However, due to what Christ had done for them and their faith response to Christ, God had taken their names off the list of the disobedient and added them to the list of the obedient. **God, the King of kings, through Christ, has reckoned, imputed, and credited His followers as being loyal subjects.**

- **The word *accounted* was also used when a person kept a record of what his debtors owed him.** As unbelievers, we all withheld obedience that should have been given to our Creator, therefore placing ourselves in debt to God. Simply stated, our sins created a balance against each of our names in God's book. Since none of us could repay this debt, God's Son paid it off for us. **Because of our trust in Christ, God has blotted out our debt. Now we are no longer debtors.**

Gift of God's Grace

Long ago, **God removed Abraham's debt.** The phrase "accounted it to him" in Genesis 15:6 does not refer to rewards for Abraham's good works or to his personal merit, but to his believing what God had promised him. Paul draws a sharp distinction between wages and gifts (Rom. 4:4). God gives what cannot be earned as wages. Salvation can only be secured by trust in God "who justifies the ungodly" (v. 5). **No human judge should declare a guilty person innocent, but God does what we may see as unthinkable because of His redeeming work through Christ. In His court, God declares the ungodly to be innocent and forgives their sins.** No other person can free someone from sins. Through His acts of forgiveness, God expresses His divine grace. Apart from Christ, all people are sinners, needing to be reckoned or imputed righteous in God's sight. **When people put their faith in God, He extends His grace to them and pardons and declares them to be righteous, imparting to them His Holy Spirit.** The indwelling Holy Spirit renews and transforms their lives, enabling them to live the Christian life.

> **ROMANS 4:1-5**
>
> **KEYWORDS**
>
> **Account/Impute (verb *logizomai*)**
> Greek bookkeeping term—translated *account, reckon, impute* or *credit*. This term basically means "to set down to one's account"; that is, God credits to the account of the believer the righteousness of Christ.
>
> **Believe** (see p. 119)
>
> **Flesh** (see p. 58)
>
> **Gift**
> The basic meaning is "gratuity, a free gift." In the New Testament, the term *gift* signifies God's supreme gift of His Son to humankind (John 3:16; 2 Cor. 9:15). Furthermore, the Holy Spirit is the promised gift of the Father, sent by His Son to believers (Acts 2:33).
>
> **Grace** (see p. 23)
>
> **Justification (*dikaiosune*)** (see p. 48)
>
> **Righteousness (*dikaiosune*)** (see p. 48)
>
> **Ungodliness** (see p. 75)
>
> **SUMMARY & LIFE APPLICATION**
>
> See under "ROMANS 4:9-12" page 131.

DAVID TESTIFIED TO THE SAME TRUTH
ROMANS 4:6-8

> 6 Just as David also describes the blessedness of the man to whom God imputes righteousness apart from works:
>
> 7 "Blessed are those whose lawless deeds are forgiven,
> And whose sins are covered;
>
> 8 Blessed is the man to whom the Lord shall not impute sin."

Paul follows his comments about Abraham's righteousness with the story of David, Israel's greatest king. Previously, Paul has used Abraham as an example of religious piety, and now he uses David as an example of repentance. **Both men were dependent on God's saving grace.**

Recipients of God's Grace

In verses 7 and 8, Paul quotes the words of David from Psalm 32:1-2. The important word *impute* or *account* that he used earlier in verse 3 also appears in verses 6 and 8. In verse 8, the emphasis is on God's refusing to impute or to reckon a person's sins against him. Again this is a matter of God's undeserved grace and faith in Him. **David pronounces a person who has received God's grace as "blessed," which means that God accepts that person and forgives his sin. Even though an individual has broken the law of God, because he has turned to God with faith, his sins are not counted against him.** In fact, they are remitted, forgiven, and he is blessed.

Even though Abraham, the father of the Jewish people, was known to be a man of good character and works and would have greatly influenced King David, David does not talk about God's accepting good people because of their goodness. Instead, he indicates that God forgives their badness. **The fact is that God saves both the morally upright and the morally bad if they turn to Him.** Apart from Christ all people are sinners, needing to be reckoned or imputed righteous in God's sight.

The bookkeeping term *impute* should not be pressed too much to make it appear that salvation is nothing more than book work on the part of God. Equal emphasis needs to be placed on the impartation of the Holy Spirit. **The indwelling Holy Spirit renews and transforms the lives of believers, enabling them to live the Christian life (8:1).**

ROMANS 4:6-8

KEYWORDS

Account/Impute (verb *logizomai*) (see p. 126)

Forgiveness (see p. 47)

Grace (*charis*) (see p. 23)

Imputation of Righteousness
An act of God by which the believer is declared righteous before the holy God

Imputation of Sin
God's holding humans accountable for their sins

Righteousness (*dikaiosune*) (see p. 48)

SUMMARY & LIFE APPLICATION
See under "ROMANS 4:9-12" page 131.

ABRAHAM SAVED BEFORE CIRCUMCISION
ROMANS 4:9-12

> [9] Does this blessedness then come upon the circumcised only, or upon the uncircumcised also? For we say that faith was accounted to Abraham for righteousness. [10] How then was it accounted? While he was circumcised, or uncircumcised? Not while circumcised, but while uncircumcised. [11] And he received the sign of circumcision, a seal of the righteousness of the faith which he had while still uncircumcised, that he might be the father of all those who believe, though they are uncircumcised, that righteousness might be imputed to them also, [12] and the father of circumcision to those who not only are of the circumcision, but who also walk in the steps of the faith which our father Abraham had while still uncircumcised.

In Romans 2, Paul has already discussed circumcision and has indicated that **true circumcision is a matter of the heart.** The issue here in chapter 4 is how God's forgiveness is related to circumcision. A similar issue for Christians is what water baptism has to do with salvation. The Jews thought that circumcision was of utmost importance. To them a man could not be a true Jew without that physical mark, even though he was a Jew by descent. Paul, however, uses Abraham as an example of one whose sins were forgiven before receiving circumcision. Abraham's acceptance by God is told in Genesis 12:1-3 and 15:6, but he was not circumcised until later, which is recorded in 17:10-11. The patriarch did not receive the circumcision mark until about fourteen years after God called him and he had entered a right relationship with God. **Abraham's circumcision was a seal of his righteous standing before God, a standing which Abraham had already acquired through faith.**

The terms *sign* and *seal* (Rom. 4:11) mean about the same thing. Here seal means that circumcision confirms by a visible sign that Abraham was already justified by faith. Normally a sign is not constructed for a business or a city that does not actually exist, meaning, therefore, that Abraham received the sign of circumcision *after* being saved.

Circumcision and Water Baptism

As the reality of Abraham's salvation preceded the outward sign, so does the faith of a believer precede water baptism. **Abraham's circumcision was symbolic of what God had already done in his heart. In like manner, water baptism is symbolic of what believers have experienced in Jesus Christ.** The reality precedes the sign. Abraham was circumcised because God commanded it. Believers are baptized in water because the Lord commanded it. **Outward circumcision did not guarantee the fact of salvation, nor does water baptism. Only faith in God (Christ)—a believing obedience—did and still does guarantee right standing with God.** Substituting the *outward* for the *inward* has disastrous spiritual consequences.

Paul's Conclusions Regarding Abraham

Paul came to two conclusions:

First, Abraham is the father of those who believe (Rom. 4:11). What made Abraham great was his being the father of people of faith, not his being the father of a nation of circumcised people. When God called him, Abraham became a believer—a believing Gentile. Understandably, first and foremost, he was the father of those who obey and take God at His word. Truly Abraham was the spiritual ancestor of all of the people of God. He was the father of believing Gentiles and also the Jews, who had not only been circumcised but believed too.

Second, physical descent from Abraham does not guarantee one's standing with God. Just because a Jewish person could trace his lineage back to the patriarch did not mean that he was a true son or daughter of Abraham. One becomes a real descendant of Abraham by faith, not birth (Gal. 3:7). Circumcision and birth are not enough. No religious observances are sufficient without following Abraham's example of faith—the true mark of a God-human relationship.

Thoughts for Christians Today

Many Jewish people thought that the mark of circumcision and being descendants of Abraham assured them of God's blessings. Likewise, Christians can become complacent and satisfied. The temptation is strong for us to become smug and self-righteous, seeing our religion as a harbor of safety and as the basis for congratulating ourselves for being so well-pleasing to God. A remedy for such an attitude is to keep in sight the fact that God's purpose for calling us is to serve the world and to make a difference in our time. That was Israel's calling too, but the fact that at various points in Jewish history many lost sight of their calling should be a cautionary reminder for us Christians to continually remember God's grace in our lives.

ROMANS 4:9-12

KEYWORDS

Account/Impute (verb *logizomai*) (see p. 126)

Believe (see p. 119)

Circumcision (see p. 100)

Righteousness (*dikaiosune*) (see p. 48)

Seal/Sign
In the ancient world a seal or stamp served to give authenticity or authority to letters, documents, or commands. At times the imprints of seals were placed on merchandise or other items as proof of ownership. *Circumcision* was a confirming seal/sign of the salvation Abraham received by faith. The visible sign or mark of circumcision was given to Abraham as a seal/proof of his right relationship with God. Likewise, *water baptism* serves as a seal/sign of believers' right standing with God through faith in Christ.

> **Water Baptism** (see p. 100)

> **SUMMARY**
>
> Abraham was a good man, who was in right relationship with God (saved) through his faith, not by keeping the law. In fact, the patriarch lived before the law was given to Moses. Abraham believed God's promises, and God justified him or accounted him righteous in His sight. Unlike Abraham, David was not consistently a man of good character. Using his power as king, he flagrantly broke God's laws. Later, King David discovered (as Abraham had known) justification by faith.
>
> Abraham was justified before he was circumcised. Therefore, he is the father of both the uncircumcised Gentiles who believe in God and the circumcised Jews who follow the patriarch in his faith. Furthermore, God saves the circumcised (in Christianity, those who are water-baptized) and the uncircumcised the same way. Through faith, God saves both the morally upright and the morally bad.

> **LIFE APPLICATION**
>
> Many Jews believed that Abraham was saved because of his perfect obedience and good works. Paul told them that they were in error. Abraham received salvation by trusting God. Moreover, he received the blessings of salvation before circumcision. That is, no religious rite or human work saved him, nor will save us.
>
> Faith was the way of salvation in the Old Testament and remains the same for us today. The outcome of our faith in Christ introduces the Holy Spirit into our lives and leads us to godly living.

THE PROMISE: GRACE AND FAITH
ROMANS 4:13-25

God promised a glorious future to Abraham and his descendants, but the fulfillment of that promise did not depend on their keeping the law. God's promise to His people was made out of the sheer goodness of His heart. For at the time that God promised to Abraham an heir and many descendants, He had not yet given the Mosaic law (Gen. 17:5; 18:18; 22:17-18). It was God's goodness and Abraham's faith in God that enabled Abraham and his descendants to share in the promise. The blessings of the promise reached far beyond Abraham's time and even beyond Paul's time. It is an End-Time promise. **When God's promise is ultimately fulfilled, the patriarch's descendants will inherit the whole world (Rom. 4:13), a way of saying that they will inherit this earth and all the benefits of salvation will be theirs.** Their blessings will be determined by "the righteousness of faith." We know that blessings are determined through faith rather than law, because the law was given centuries after Abraham. **God's grace and human faith have always been the ground for salvation.** Of course, Abraham's walk with God illustrates that faith is a believing obedience (1:5).

FAITH AND LAW
ROMANS 4:13-17

> [13] For the promise that he would be the heir of the world was not to Abraham or to his seed through the law, but through the righteousness of faith. [14] For if those who are of the law are heirs, faith is made void and the promise made of no effect, [15] because the law brings about wrath; for where there is no law there is no transgression.
>
> [16] Therefore it is of faith that it might be according to grace, so that the promise might be sure to all the seed, not only to those who are of the law, but also to those who are of the faith of Abraham, who is the father of us all [17] (as it is written, *"I have made you a father of many nations"*) in the presence of Him whom he believed—God, who gives life to the dead and calls those things which do not exist as though they did.

Paul makes a forceful point: **"If those who are of the law are heirs, faith is made void and the promise is made of no effect" (v. 14).** The issue is, **What determines who the heirs to the promise are?** A promise is not a contractual agreement. If you were to enter into a contract, agreeing to do some work for someone, you and your employer would be bound by the terms of the contract. You know that you will be paid provided you keep your side of the contract. **Becoming an heir to God's promise rests on faith, not on a contract that requires the**

keeping of the law for salvation. If it were true that one could become an heir to the promise by observing a code of rules, then *faith* and *promise* would have lost their meaning. The promise of salvation involves both faith and grace. **Salvation is a gift received by faith; it cannot be earned.**

Functions of the Law

Clearly the law is unable to determine who the heirs of salvation are. The law has its place and has two vital functions (v. 15):

First, the law defines transgression. The consequence then of the law is transgression, since no one can keep God's laws perfectly. If there were no law against stealing, it would be impossible to transgress it. Enacting a law makes it possible to break it. **The law of God, therefore, identifies human disobedience as transgression.**

Second, transgression of the law brings about God's holy displeasure (His wrath). Disobedience to God's law brings about His judgment. Due to humans' inability to keep the law perfectly, we are subject to condemnation and wrath. Rather than qualifying us, the law disqualifies us for the inheritance of salvation. **Simply stated, God's law is designed to make us aware of our spiritual and moral bankruptcy.** The law tells us what is right and what is wrong, but it lacks any power to enable us to do good and avoid evil (8:3). **God's law has no power to save us.**

God's Promise of Salvation

No one has the capability of earning salvation. **God's promise of salvation is for everyone, "not only to those who are of the law, but also to those who are of the faith of Abraham, who is the father of us all" (4:16).** The patriarch is the father of both Jewish and Gentile Christians. Abraham had a relationship with God, not because of who he was, but because of his trust in God. As a believer, Abraham confirmed the gospel—that salvation is by faith, and he serves as an example of how God saves human beings. **Down through history, believers have trusted in God as Abraham did, and God has graciously accepted their faith and brought them into close relationship with Himself.** Between the time of Abraham and Christ, God has not changed His way of saving (bringing us into a right relationship with Himself). **In Christ, God continues to do today what Abraham trusted Him to do in his day.**

God the Creator and Life-Giver

The God that Abraham believed is the God who makes alive the dead and calls into existence those things that do not exist (v. 17). **God not only justifies the ungodly, but also gives life to the dead and brings into being things that did not previously exist. God is both the Creator and Life-Giver.** From a broad viewpoint, this truth indicates that justification is a life-act as well as an act that frees us from guilt for having done wrong. God is always the God of the living and of those who will be raised to eternal life (Schweizer, 1970, 248). The reality of the resurrection assures us that God is greater than death. **At the beginning of the world, God created life; and at the end of the world, He will bestow everlasting life on all those who trust in Christ.** The reality of this life-giving promise anchors our faith in the Creator and Life-Giver.

ROMANS 4:13-17

KEYWORDS

Faith (see p. 23)

God, The Father/The Creator (see p. 58)

Grace (*charis*) (see p. 23)

Judgment by God / God's Judgment (see p. 68)

The Law (*Torah*) (see p. 48)

Promise
In Scripture, that which God declares that He will bring to pass

Righteousness (*dikaiosune*) (see p. 48)

Transgression (see p. 100)

Wrath of God (see p. 75)

SUMMARY & LIFE APPLICATION
See under "ROMANS 4:18-25" page 138.

THE MAGNITUDE OF ABRAHAM'S FAITH
ROMANS 4:18-25

> 📖 ¹⁸ Who, contrary to hope, in hope believed, so that he became the father of many nations, according to what was spoken, *"So shall your descendants be."* ¹⁹ And not being weak in faith, he did not consider his own body, already dead (since he was about a hundred years old), and the deadness of Sarah's womb. ²⁰ He did not waver at the promise of God through unbelief, but was strengthened in faith, giving glory to God, ²¹ and being fully convinced that what He had promised He was also able to perform. ²² And therefore *"it was accounted to him for righteousness."* ²³ Now it was not written for his sake alone that it was imputed to him, ²⁴ but also for us. It shall be imputed to us who believe in Him who raised up Jesus our Lord from the dead, ²⁵ who was delivered up because of our offenses, and was raised because of our justification.

In order to explain the nature of faith, again Paul takes us back to the story of Abraham. **God had promised Abraham that he would be the father of multitudes (4:17).** He and Sarah, his wife, were beyond the age of childbearing—Abraham being a hundred years old and Sarah ninety (Gen. 17:17). For them to have children was unthinkable.

Abraham's Hope

Even at Abraham's advanced age, **"contrary to hope, in hope" he believed that God would carry out His promise (Rom. 4:18).**[1] The phrase "contrary to hope, in hope" (*par'*

---

[1] Paul has emphasized Abraham's faith despite the continuing barrenness and age of his wife. Abraham believed that God would give him a son in his old age, but in his impatience and desire to make it happen according to his own time frame, instead of waiting for God to produce a son through Sarah, Abraham had a child with an Egyptian handmaid, Hagar (Gen. 16:1-6). We know that during this time period, Abraham's faith was weak, because Hagar's son was a product of human effort (cf. Rom. 9:6-9). It is never right to try to accomplish God's purpose in ways that do not include sincere prayer, patient hope, and the leading of the Holy Spirit.

elpida ep' elpidi) **literally means "beyond hope, in hope."** The two mentions of the word *hope* are different.

The first use of the word *hope* ("contrary to hope") indicates human hope. When human hope is exhausted, it is then that God-given hope comes into play.

The second mention of the word *hope* ("in hope believed") indicates a God-given hope that looks to God. When Abraham looked at his situation, it was bleak. Even though Abraham had no human hope that he and Sarah would ever have children at such an advanced age, in hope he turned to God, who had given him the promise of many descendants.

The patriarch recognized God as the All-Powerful One "who gives life to the dead and calls those things which do not exist as though they did" (v. 17). **Abraham took God at His word, indeed a marvelous example of faith.** The description of Abraham in verse 21 gives us a good definition of faith: Abraham "being fully convinced that what [God] had promised He was also able to perform." **When we turn to God, there is always hope, just as there was for Abraham.**

According to Genesis 15:5 and Romans 4:18, there is more to the story. God told Abraham to look at the stars and then said, "So shall your descendants be" (v. 18). Facing his situation, he showed no weakness in his faith (v. 19). Abraham was a striking contrast to those who are described as "weak in faith" in Romans 14 and 15. However, his faith was not a blind faith. "He did *not* consider his own body, already dead" (4:19). On the basis of the best and oldest original manuscripts, we should omit the word *not*. This omission of the word *not* actually is an indication that Abraham's faith was even more striking if he *did* consider his body already dead. **Abraham, though considering his body dead as far as reproduction, believed that God could give him a son.** He was unwavering in his hope in the promise God had given him. **Strengthened by his confidence in God's power, Abraham gave glory to God.** His faith in God was just the opposite of the actions of the Gentiles in 1:21. They, like all humankind, had sinned and needed to turn to God in faith, as Abraham did.

Abraham recognized God as God—that He was the Creator and Life-Giver. Unwavering in his faith, he believed God's promise, even though his belief went against human experience and human hope. Considering Abraham's splendid example of faith, **we are inspired to look beyond the hopelessness of human circumstances and to rejoice in God's power which is able to overcome the difficulties of life and give us victory.**

Our Hope

Finally, Paul concludes his discussion of Abraham's hope by saying that all that has been written about Abraham applies to us in regard to our salvation (Rom. 4:23-24). The God who gave His word to Abraham, and in whom we have believed, is the same God "who raised up Jesus Christ our Lord from the dead" (v. 24). Abraham lived before Jesus' resurrection, and we live after it. **Abraham's salvation lies in store for all those who believe in the God who raised Jesus from the dead.** This truth is even clearer and more powerful since we live on this side of the Resurrection.

To end this section, Paul quotes what was probably a part of an early Christian confession (a declaration of religious belief): "who was delivered up because of our offenses, and was raised because of our justification" (v. 25). The verbs *was delivered up* and *was raised* are what we call *divine passives*, implying that God was the active agent. This confession unites the death and the resurrection of our Lord and sees the two events, though separated by two days, as an inseparable action of God in providing salvation for us. **Through a single action (Jesus' death and resurrection), God has provided justification, which results in the forgiveness of our trespasses.** The bottom line is that belief in the death and resurrection of Jesus secures justification and forgiveness of our sins. **When we believe in the Savior, the Creator and Life-Giver makes us new creatures, or "a new creation" (Gal. 6:15), and indeed we are "in Christ Jesus."**

ROMANS 4:18-25
KEYWORDS
Account/Impute (verb *logizomai*) (see p. 126)
Faith (see p. 23)

Glory to God (see p. 75)

Hope
Confidence that God will do what He has promised

Justification (*dikaiosune*) (see p. 48)

Promise (see p. 134)

Righteousness (*dikaiosune*) (see p. 48)

SUMMARY

The promise that God gave Abraham will finally be fulfilled when his spiritual descendants inherit the whole earth (another way of describing the full benefits of salvation). The fulfillment of the promise to Abraham and his descendants does not depend on observing the law, but on faith. The impossibility of keeping the law results in humans' having to face divine judgment (*wrath*, v. 15). The promise, therefore, must depend on faith so that it may reach all believers, the spiritual descendants of Abraham.

The patriarch acknowledged the creative power of God, and his hope remained unwavering—"contrary to hope, in hope" (v. 18)— even though his personal circumstances seemed to invalidate God's promise. Without hesitation, Abraham believed God's promise to give him a son (Isaac). As Abraham was justified by faith, the same lies in store for all who believe in the creative power of God through which Jesus was raised from the dead to put us in a right relationship with God (v. 25).

LIFE APPLICATION

Abraham's trust in God confirms for us that we also can place our hope and trust in God. We, too, can have assurance that God will keep His promise. Like Abraham, when we put our faith and hope in our Creator and His promise, fulfilled through Jesus Christ, we can fully enjoy God's blessings. We can rejoice in the fact that Christ died for our sins and arose from the dead in order to forgive our transgressions and give us life. For us, who live after the resurrection of Jesus, this truth is even clearer and more powerful. Indeed we should rejoice in the life-giving power of our Savior.

JUSTIFICATION AND LOVE
ROMANS 5:1-11

Being justified by faith affects our daily lives. Paul has already devoted a great deal of time and thought to the doctrine of justification, but he recognizes that it is very important that we know what our stand with God is. Can we really believe that our sins have been forgiven? What about our failure to keep God's laws perfectly? What about our struggles and suffering? Can pastors assume that their congregations understand what *justification by faith* means and just build on that knowledge? It is very doubtful that they can just build upon current understanding without further foundational instruction. Biblical teaching about justification is needed, since it is just as relevant to the modern church as it was in Paul's day. *Justification* is a theological word that has been around a long time, but it matters greatly. **The ability of the church for an effective life of holiness and mission rests on the assurance that we have been justified on the basis of grace and through faith.** Justification is not the only factor in the Christian life, **but everything in the Christian's life depends on justification, even heaven.**

BENEFITS OF JUSTIFICATION
ROMANS 5:1-5

> ¹ Therefore, having been justified by faith, we have peace with God through our Lord Jesus Christ, ² through whom also we have access by faith into this **grace** in which we stand, and rejoice in **hope** of the glory of God. ³ And not only that, but we also glory in tribulations, knowing that tribulation produces perseverance; ⁴ and perseverance, character; and character, hope. ⁵ Now hope does not disappoint, because the **love** of God has been poured out in our hearts by the Holy Spirit who was given to us.
>
> [*emphasis added*]

Chapter 5 begins with the word *therefore*. This word *therefore* transitions the reader from the previous discussion about faith and its resulting justification to an introduction to marvelous benefits that belong to those who have been justified. **The blessings of peace, grace, and hope are all benefits of justification that assure believers that they have a right standing with God.**

Peace

The first, immediate benefit of justification is *peace*: "We have *peace* with God" (v. 1). Paul's focus here is not on *receiving* peace from God, but *being* at peace with God. Apart from justifying grace, a person's relationship with God is that of hostility. **Reconciliation has been made by God through Christ, and believers have the assurance that they are at peace with God and can enjoy this peace.** This kind of peace is an objective reality, not a subjective, inner feeling. **In other words, peace is a harmonious relationship with God.** The by-product of this relationship is a deep feeling of inner well-being and peace with others (Eph. 2:14).

Grace

The second benefit of justification is *grace*: "We have access by faith into this *grace*" **(Rom. 5:2).** Although Paul has already emphasized grace (3:24; 4:1-4, 16), the repeated emphasis on grace in chapter 5 is striking. **Paul's emphasis on grace is an indication to us that the "amazing grace" of which we often sing actually defines our existence as the people of God.**

Access to Grace

Through faith in Christ, we have *access* or (*an introduction* into) grace. During biblical times, the word for *access* (*prosagoge*) was used in two ways:

- **The term *access* was used for introducing a person to royalty.** Paul may have in mind that Christ introduces the Almighty God. **Christ opens the door so that we can come into the very presence of God.** Through Him we can come boldly to the throne of grace so that we can receive mercy and grace in the time of need (Heb. 4:16). Even now, Christ gives us access to the Father. At this moment, He is at the right hand of the Father in heaven interceding for us (Rom. 8:34).
- **The term *access* was also used to refer to entry into a harbor.** Some scholars think that is the way Paul used it (Moo, 1996, 300-01). The idea is that **we have been**

storm-tossed by sin and troubles, but through Christ a way into the harbor of God's grace has been opened. Nothing could have saved us from making shipwreck of our lives had Christ not guided us into God's harbor of divine grace. The destination is God's saving grace— "access by faith into this grace in which we stand" (5:2). Grace is God's saving work in Christ. As believers, "we stand" (perfect tense of *histemi*, durative in force), indicating a continuing condition or sphere in which we daily live. **As we stand daily in God's grace, our lives are being transformed.** Therefore, this condition of grace is not something that is going to happen, but is a here-and-now reality. This reality includes more than justification; it means that we benefit daily from all the blessings conveyed to us by God in Christ.

Hope

The third benefit of justification is *hope*: "We . . . rejoice in *hope* of the glory of God" (v. 2; cf. 8:18-24). Biblical hope is free of doubt about our ultimate future. It is the absolute confidence that what is hoped for will come. This expectation is the profound assurance of seeing and experiencing the glory of God (1 Thess. 4:13-18). At the Second Coming of Christ, our bodies will be transformed and our salvation perfected. Paul rejoices in the hope of sharing in the glory of God. **Glory is the final End-Time consequence of our justification.**

Hope During Suffering

In addressing the benefit of hope, Paul goes on to deal with suffering and adversities that may appear to deny God's justifying grace and love (Rom. 5:3-4). Anticipating the completion of his salvation on the Last Day, Paul has a hope that results in joy. But taking it another step, he says that the same joy is available even amid trials and tribulations. **Suffering is a time of testing, but in the sphere of grace there is value in suffering (8:28).** Paul knew from his own experience the benefits of troubles. Through the thorn in his flesh, he experienced the sufficiency of God's grace (2 Cor. 12:7-10). He had been beaten, stoned, and left for dead (Acts 14:19-20). Such afflictions do not contradict justifying grace, for God uses them for our benefit. They humble us and cause us to depend on Him. We actually mature in tribulations, though they hurt and are painful. We can understand why people rejoice when troubles and afflictions pass; but Paul says that we glory amid tribulations. All people have troubles and adversities, but these are tribulations in Christ and for His sake.

To prove that afflictions produce valuable spiritual fruit for believers, Paul makes three observations (Rom. 5:3-4):

1. **Tribulation and suffering produce perseverance, or patience.** Because of our hope in God, the hardest trials can produce patience. **Suffering for our faith, we look beyond the present circumstances to the future when what God has already begun will be completed.** The confident expectation that we shall finally experience fully the magnificent transforming glory of God proves to be a real source of strength and patience. **We look to God, not to ourselves, which produces perseverance in us.**

2. **Perseverance produces character (see 1 Peter 1:7).** The word *character* (*dokime*) refers to the process of testing. It was used for the testing of gold through fire. As it passed through the fire, all the base metals were removed. **When Christians meet trials and troubles, relying on God who gives them patience and endurance, they become purer and stronger in character.**

3. **Character produces hope.** This is the end of the process. Out of the experiences which produce character comes hope. The experiences of life may easily drive nonbelievers to despair, but difficult experiences will help believers depend more on their hope in God. The basis of our hope is not in that our character has proved to be strong but, by endurance and patience, we have learned to rely on God. **Afflictions and trials find their meaning in God because they teach us to look away from ourselves and look to God in hope.**

The Love of God in Our Hearts

Love—The Basis of Our Relationship With Christ

God's love is basic to our entire relationship with Christ: "the *love* of God has been poured out in our hearts" (Rom.

5:5). Hope emerges out of endurance and character. What if this hope is nothing more than wishful thinking? What if there is no solid basis for it? Paul's response is that **"hope does not disappoint" because it rests on the love that God has already given us**—"the love of God has been poured out in our hearts by the Holy Spirit." **The verb *has been poured* (*ekcheo*) is in** the perfect tense, signifying a past event with abiding results and emphasizing the abundance of God's love brought to our hearts through the Holy Spirit. The same verb is used to describe the first believers when they were filled with the Spirit on the Day of Pentecost (Acts 2:17; cf. 10:45). Paul's description may refer to what Pentecostals call *baptism in the Spirit*. The impact of this experience continues to reverberate in the day-to-day lives of Spirit-filled believers (Johnson, 1999, 725). The experience gives them profound assurance of God's love and the hope of their future glory.

Love—Producing Hope During Suffering

Far from disappointing us, **God's love that fills our hearts fortifies our hope and fills our hearts with the assurance of salvation.** Suffering and hope have a close relationship. Trouble and trials are not contrary to God's justifying love and our hope of glory. God does not protect all His people from misfortune, but He does give us grace that will see us through those times. **When our physical blessings—health, prosperity, and security—are taken away, we emerge strengthened in endurance, character, hope, and God's love. This process in which we are conformed to the likeness of Christ is called** *sanctification*, which Paul deals with extensively in Romans 6–8 and in 12:1–15:13. Indeed the continuous work of God's justifying grace results in granting value to suffering.

Grace is only fully experienced when we come to a place of desperation. Pentecostals have rightly emphasized the power of God to deliver from troubles and distress. What they have not always stressed is the sufficiency of God's power to strengthen our endurance. As Johnson notes, "This continuous work of grace is just as miraculous, if not more so, than a singular act of deliverance that lifts a person out of difficulty. **He [God] always** delivers the believer, but sometimes He delivers us through the affliction rather than out of it" (1999, 724). The enduring of trials produces a quality of perseverance, which is not a resignation to fate but is an acceptance of Christ's suffering and accompanying learning and growth that are essential to the Christian life (2:7; 5:3-4; 8:25; 15:4-5).

ROMANS 5:1-5

KEYWORDS

Baptism in the Spirit
The powerful Pentecostal anointing by the Spirit that one may experience subsequent (after) conversion. To be Spirit-anointed is to be endowed with power for witnessing and evangelizing (Luke 4:18; Acts 1:8).

Glory (see p. 86)

Grace (*charis*) (see p. 23)

Holy Spirit/The Spirit (see p. 25)

Hope (see p. 137)

Jesus Christ (see p. 59)

Justified by Faith (*dikaioo*) (see p. 48)

Love (*agape*)
The expression of God's goodwill and mercy for everyone, initiated by and lived by deliberate choice, rather than by mere emotions or affection. God is the source of *agape love*, and without Him, this Christian love is impossible.

Peace (Hebrew, *shalom*; Greek, *eirene*)
A condition of being whole or of being complete and sound

Pentecost/Day of Pentecost
One of the three major feasts in early Israel. It was also known as the Feast of Harvest, Weeks, and Pentecost. This feast was celebrated in early summer, fifty days or seven weeks after the first day of unleavened bread. On the first Pentecost after the resurrection of Jesus, the Holy Spirit was poured out on the church. This event was the beginning of the fulfillment of Joel's prophecy (Joel 2:28-29).

Perseverance
The supreme value of fortitude and endurance despite the disadvantages caused by circumstances

Tribulation (see p. 87)

> **SUMMARY & LIFE APPLICATION**
> See under "ROMANS 5:6-11" page 148.

THE ULTIMATE EXPRESSION OF RECONCILING LOVE
ROMANS 5:6-11

> 📖 ⁶ For when we were still without strength, in due time Christ died for the ungodly. ⁷ For scarcely for a righteous man will one die; yet perhaps for a good man someone would even dare to die. ⁸ But God demonstrates His own love toward us, in that while we were still sinners, Christ died for us. ⁹ Much more then, having now been justified by His blood, we shall be saved from wrath through Him. ¹⁰ For if when we were enemies we were reconciled to God through the death of His Son, much more, having been reconciled, we shall be saved by His life. ¹¹ And not only that, but we also rejoice in God through our Lord Jesus Christ, through whom we have now received the reconciliation.
>
> [emphases added]

Christ's Death

Paul has spoken about the love of God, which we have experienced in our hearts through the Holy Spirit. Another way that God the Father demonstrated His love is through an event in history, the death of Christ (v. 8). We have read and been told that Christ died for the ungodly, but when we consider the magnitude of human sin, can we actually *believe* in God's justifying love? As Paul discusses our condition without Christ, he considers the seriousness of our sin: "When we were still without strength" (v. 6); "while we were still sinners" (v. 8); "when we were enemies" (v. 10). As unbelievers, we were both helpless and hostile; but more striking, we were "enemies," living contrary to God. It is for those who are broken, spiritually bankrupt and needy, for whom Christ died. Paul indicates that **Jesus Christ's death on the cross was personal: "Christ died for us"** at the time of

our greatest need. We were powerless, weak, and hostile; that is, ungodly (v. 6). **As an ultimate act of love, Christ died for the enemies of God—for those who least deserved it.**

Human Love and Christ's Love

Going on, Paul contrasts *human* **and** *divine love* **(v. 7).** *Human love* is usually conditional, while Christ's love is unconditional. Paul observes that someone would not want to die for a "righteous" person (that is, a person who strictly keeps the law, but who is coldly righteous). Perhaps one would be willing to die for a good, benevolent, and noble person, but no one would want to die for an ungodly, wicked, sinful person. But Christ did! Unconditional divine love stands in sharp contrast to human love. We were neither righteous nor good, but sinners. **Christ gave Himself for us sinners. Christ died in the place of the ungodly so we could be saved from wrath (divine judgment) through Him (v. 9).** In the face of this gift, how can any of us doubt God's love? The cross is an overwhelming demonstration of His love.

Justification and Reconciliation

Using different language in verses 10 and 11, Paul states again essentially the same truth. **The important words** *reconcile* **(*katallasso*) and** *reconciliation* **(*katallage*) appear for the first time in Romans. These terms are similar to** *justification*. They are great grace-words, but do not come from the law court as does the term *justification*. **The term** *justification* **indicates that God pronounces us righteous in His sight. The terms** *reconcile* **and** *reconciliation* **are used to describe the restoring of a friendship between two people whose friendship had been dissolved.** Likewise sin severed humankind's fellowship with God. It alienated God from human beings, and human beings from God. **God sent His Son to restore harmony between Himself and humankind. "God was in Christ reconciling the world to Himself" (2 Cor. 5:19).** Reconciliation on God's side is complete; but when we still remain enemies, we are not actually reconciled to God until we accept by faith His pardon of our sins. **To be *reconciled to God* means that our status has changed—from that of an enemy to that of a friend, just like Abraham (Isa. 41:8; James 2:23).**

Obviously **there is a close link between *justification* and *reconciliation*** in Romans 5. Observe the parallel between the two grace-words:

Justified (v. 9)	Reconciled (v. 10)
By His blood	By the death of His Son
We shall be saved.	We shall be saved.

God's act of justifying us is at the same time His act of reconciling us, which removes our hostility and restores our friendship with God.

Rejoicing

Our reconciliation rests on the shedding of the blood of God's Son on the cross. **From the beginning to the end, our new life in Christ depends on the cross. As justified/reconciled believers, we need daily renewal—a daily journey to the cross.** The Holy Spirit who dwells in us wants to take us there daily and show us the mystery of redeeming grace and love (John 14:17; 16:13). There at the cross we see proof of the reality of God's grace and its overwhelming mercies. **At the cross we receive grace that does not leave us powerless. It is grace that enables us to courageously live life—grace that enables us to walk and live in the Spirit, causing us to rejoice in our Lord Jesus Christ,** who took the penalty of sin in our stead so we could be reconciled to the Father (Rom. 5:11). There at the cross the church receives its message to the world: "Be reconciled to God" (2 Cor. 5:20).

ROMANS 5:6-11

KEYWORDS

Godly/Ungodly
Godly people have great respect for God and for sacred things, but the *ungodly* is Paul's picture of all who are without Christ.

Justification (*dikaiosune*) (see p. 48)

Reconciliation (*katallage*)
A restoration of personal relationship between God and human beings (Rom. 5:1-11; 2 Cor. 5:18-21) or between human beings

Salvation (see p. 23)

Sinner (see p. 68)

Wrath of God (see p. 75)

SUMMARY

We who are the beneficiaries of God's saving righteousness are at peace with God and have access daily to divine grace. We have an unshakable hope of one day sharing in full salvation in spite of the troubles and adversities encountered in this life. In addition to all of our blessings, we have evidence of God's love through our possession of the Holy Spirit.

God has also demonstrated His love through a historical event: the death of Christ. God intervened in the person of His Son in order to deal with the estrangement between Himself and humans, which was created by the sin of humankind. God through His Son has eliminated alienation between Himself and humankind, and we (Christians) are reconciled (the language of friendship) to God and have received the Holy Spirit, who is our pledge of final salvation.

LIFE APPLICATION

As believers, we are reconciled and at peace with God. We are beneficiaries of God's justifying, reconciling love in Christ. Despite any disciplinary testing or adversities that we might encounter in this life, God has a way of transforming these into blessings. His grace during these times includes the benefits of peace, grace, and hope.

Because of God's blessings, no matter what afflicts us here on the earth, we can go through life with joy, rejoicing in God. God's goodness is inconceivable goodness, humanly speaking. Those of us who are reconciled and remain faithful to him can have confidence in God's absolute pledge to us for our final salvation—a life with Him, free from suffering.

ADAM AND CHRIST
ROMANS 5:12-21

Paul now shifts his attention from the individual to the human race in general. This section is one of the most complex passages in the Bible. It has had a great influence on theology, and scholars have interpreted it in various ways. Behind this account stands the biblical record of Adam's fall (Gen. 3). **The question that Paul grapples with is this: How did the sin of the first man, Adam, affect the whole human race? Sin is more than an individual matter; it is a problem for all of humankind. Salvation meets not only an individual need but a need of the entire human race.** We may see this issue as purely academic, but **Paul wishes to consider justification in light of ultimate possibilities—the salvation of the entire human race. The cross is sufficient to save all humankind.**

Corporate Solidarity

For us to understand the corporate dimensions of justification, we need to keep in mind the Jewish idea of corporate solidarity. **The people of Israel did not think of themselves primarily as individuals, but rather members of a tribe and nation.** Biblical scholars call it *racial solidarity* or *corporate personality*. In the Old Testament, an example of solidarity is Achan (Josh. 7). In the Western world, people are often uncomfortable with the idea of solidarity because emphasis is placed on the individual. Group identity and responsibility are not the typical ways of thinking. **The typical Hebrew, however, understood that the human race was caught up with Adam in his sin.** During that time the entire human race was still considered to be one with Adam. From this viewpoint of solidarity, Paul saw Adam as a corporate personality representing the entire human race and his sin as an act of the whole human race. As a result, the human race is sinful, as well as each individual.

Sin in Our Lives

The concept of the sinfulness of the entire human race raises a question: How is it that one man's sin has affected us all? There are four basic views:

View #1: Adam's sin has had absolutely no effect on us.

We have all come into the world sinless, pure, and innocent, just as the first man did. And we have all sinned as Adam did, that is, on our own accord, not due to the influence of Adam. The only connection between our sin and Adam's is that his sin is typical of ours. Each of us has become our own Adam and has rebelled against God as he did. According to this view, Adam's sin and guilt were not passed on to future generations. However, this view is questionable since for Paul there is a close connection between Adam's transgression and the spiritual condition of the human race (see Rom. 5:12-19; 1 Cor. 15:21-22).

View #2: Adam was a representative of the human race.

Being the first man, God appointed Adam as our representative. Therefore, we are held accountable for his transgression, since he acted as the representative head of the whole human race. This type of representation would be similar to the president of a country leading that nation into war. Since the president is the people's representative, the citizens of that nation would be held responsible for what their president did. The point of this view of sin is that the whole human race is guilty of what its representative head did in the Garden of Eden. Since Adam was the human race's representative, all of humanity is essentially identified with him and has been held accountable for his rebellion against God.

View #3: The whole human race participated in the sin of Adam.

This view assumes not representative solidarity, as the one above, but real solidarity. The reason for this perspective is that at the time Adam sinned, the human race was in a sense there physically with Adam in his body, waiting to be birthed. Therefore, Adam and his offspring—the human race—are one. Because of this intimate connection, the entire race sinned in Adam. This view understands Adam as a *corporate personality*;

his transgression was not merely an act of one individual, but an act of the entire human race. The belief is that as a result, each of us participated in Adam's sin and rebelled against God when he did. In large measure, this interpretation depends on the rendering of a Greek phrase (*eph ho*) in Romans 5:12 as *in whom*, making the clause read, "in whom [Adam] all sinned." But both the *New King James Version* and the *New International Version* translate the same phrase as *because*, and so the passage reads, "because all sinned." If we choose the older Greek translation, "in whom all sinned," it still fails to make clear whether we actually participated in Adam's rebellion, or whether we sinned by our own individual acts. The idea of real solidarity may also be suggested in 1 Corinthians 15:22, where all are said to be united with Adam in death, but now by faith belong to the New Adam, who is Jesus.

View #4: We all have been affected by the sin of Adam.

According to this fourth view, everyone enters the world with a tendency toward sinning. The effect of Adam's sin is that it has weakened us morally and has made it easy for us to sin when temptation presents itself. This weakness in itself does not condemn us; the disposition to sin inevitably results in our sinning and condemnation, if we do not accept God's gift of grace. All people become sinners through the choices that they make, which break God's laws.

Our Responsibility

In regard to these various views, there is room for difference of opinion. Whatever view (except for the first one) we may embrace, Romans 5:12-21 reflects a close connection between Adam's sin and our spiritual condition apart from Christ. However, we do well to remember that Romans 1:18–3:23 emphasizes that people are under God's judgment because of their own sinning. In fact, **the letter to the Romans overall and the Bible as a whole teach that God judges people for their own conscious acts of sin. That is why Scripture calls on us to repent of sins we have committed in this life.**

THE TWO AGES
ROMANS 5:12-14, 18-19

> ¹² Therefore, just as through one man sin entered the world, and death through sin, and thus death spread to all men, because all sinned— ¹³ (For until the law sin was in the world, but sin is not imputed when there is no law. ¹⁴ Nevertheless death reigned from Adam to Moses, even over those who had not sinned according to the likeness of the transgression of Adam, who is a type of Him who was to come.
>
> ¹⁸ Therefore, as through one man's offense judgment came to all men, resulting in condemnation, even so through one Man's righteous act the free gift came to all men, resulting in justification of life. ¹⁹ For as by one man's disobedience many were made sinners, so also by one Man's obedience many will be made righteous.

The central thought of Romans 5:12–21 is that **Adam's deed had a profound effect on the entire human race, but Christ brought grace and life in contrast to Adam's sin and death. The age of sin and death began with Adam, and the age of grace and life with Jesus Christ.** What Adam did in the Garden of Eden released sin and death into the world. **Sin is more than transgression of God's law; it is a power exercising control over human lives.** Sin is either evil behavior or it is a power that promotes such behavior. Death is more than physical death; it is a destructive power, including the Old Testament idea of separation from God. **Over and against the results of Adam's sin, Christ has brought grace and life.**

The Age of Adam

Throughout this passage, the fruit of what Adam did and the fruit of what Christ did are held up against each other. **Through Adam, sin entered as an encroaching army into the world, and death came as a result of his sin (v. 12).** He died and his descendants have been dying ever since. If he had not sinned, he would have been immortal. Adam's sin not only affected himself, but also the whole human race. Adam's sin set off a chain reaction and spread death throughout the world. Indeed, "death reigned" (*basileuo*, v. 14) like an evil dictator.

As a result of Adam's sin, **everyone comes into the world with a disposition to yield to temptation and to sin.** However, if there were those who did not sin, would they still die? In grappling with this question and the plight of humankind, **Paul distinguishes sin from transgression (v. 14). During the period between Adam and Moses, there was no law. God did not give the law until Moses' time.** Because God had not yet given the law, the sins committed by people who lived prior to Moses were similar yet different from those committed by Adam. **The people did not have specific commandments directly from God like Adam did in the Garden of Eden.** Adam had a commandment and disobeyed it. No more specific commands were given until the Mosaic law. From Adam to Moses, there was much evil done with the consequences of spiritual disaster. **In that period, since there was no law to transgress, the people were not held accountable in an explicitly legal sense or in an eternal sense for their sins.** But as Paul says, "Sin is not imputed [placed to their account] when there is no law" (v. 13). That is, they were not answerable to specific laws, because there was no law. Yet by nature, they sinned because they were sinners.

Paul then adds, "Nevertheless death reigned from Adam to Moses, even over those who had not sinned according to the likeness of the transgression of Adam" (v. 14). **Adam's failure started a chain reaction and the consequence was that even the people who did not live under Mosaic law died.** Possibly their death was also due to the violation of the moral law written on their hearts (2:12-16). We learn from the account of the Flood in Genesis 6 and 7 that although the people of Noah's day did not have the Mosaic law they were still held accountable during their lives on earth in that they had to face death, which sin causes. One thing becomes clear: **those who lived between Adam and Moses did not have the law to transgress, but even so, they still experienced the dominion of sin and death.**

Sin continues to be an ever-present and devastating reality in this world as a death-dealing power.

The Age of Christ

In Romans 5:18-19, Paul contrasts Adam and Christ. Because of Adam's disobedience, "all men" come under condemnation; but **Christ's obedience on the cross brings to "all men" the free gift of grace and justification which leads to life.** Some scholars have interpreted "all men" to mean universalism (all people will be saved), based on verse 18. But Paul in this context makes it clear that only those who receive the gift of righteousness (justification) will be saved (v. 17), making "all men" in verse 18 refer to *all believers*. The believers are the ones who "will reign in life through the One, Jesus Christ" (v. 17). No doubt, the reader has observed that Paul uses the words *all* and *many* in this passage without any significant difference. Both *many* and *all* are inclusive terms, but God's saving grace involves a person's choice. Paul's lengthy discussion of God's wrath against sinful humanity and God's provision of salvation through faith in Christ would make no sense if on the Final Day all people regardless of their personal desire and choices will be saved (1:16–5:11).

Looking at Jesus from one perspective, He was a man like Adam (v. 18). **Jesus as man obeyed God.** From another perspective, **Jesus was more than a man; He was God, and His saving work on the cross was God's gift to us.** The misdeed of Adam got us all in trouble, but Christ's good deed brings salvation and life. Indeed, what Adam and Christ did had far-reaching consequences. Adam initiated the reign of sin and death, and **Christ initiated the reign of righteousness and life.** Standing with Adam leads to death, but **standing with Christ leads to life.** The age that Adam introduced placed the human race under the dominion of death, but **the age that Christ introduced places all who trust in Him under the dominion of life. Jesus Christ offered a new beginning to the human race.** Paul summarizes this truth in his statement in verse 19: "For as by one man's disobedience many were made sinners, so also by one Man's obedience many will be made righteous."

Adam	Jesus Christ
Man who disobeyed God	Man who obeyed God
Man whose disobedient acts caused harm to all of humanity	God who did saving work on the cross for all of humanity
Unleashed an age in which sin and death reigned	Initiated the reign of righteousness and life
Standing with Adam leads to death	Standing with Christ leads to life

ROMANS 5:12-14, 18-19

KEYWORDS

Account/Impute (verb *logizomai*) (see p. 126)

Condemnation
An unfavorable decision or sentence by a human or divine agent. People who love darkness rather than light come under God's holy displeasure or judgment. For those who are in Christ there remains no holy displeasure or divine judgment. For them Christ has borne God's holy displeasure toward their sins.

Corporate Solidarity
The principle of the human race being in unity with Adam in his sin (Rom. 5:12-21; 1 Cor. 15:22, 45). Being united with Adam in his disobedience to God, the entire race suffered the dire consequences of Adam's sin. What Adam did was more than an act of an individual; it was a corporate act of the human race.

Judgment by God/God's Judgment (see p. 68)

Justification (*dikaiosune*) (see p. 48)

The Law (*Torah*) (see p. 48)

This Age/The Coming Age (The Two Ages) (see p. 48)

Righteousness **produces** *life.*
Righteousness is being in right standing with God and is a gift of God that brings a believer into a right relationship with Him. In so doing, God gives to the believer a spiritual and moral quality of *life* that extends beyond physical death into eternity (2 Cor. 5:4; 2 Tim. 1:10).

Sin **produces** *death.*
A broad definition of *sin* is that it is anything contrary to the will and character of God. Adam's transgression of God's will brought *death* as a penalty. Since sin is universal, the presence of death is a necessary consequence (Rom. 5:12-14).

Transgression (see p. 100)

> **FULL SUMMARY & LIFE APPLICATION**
> See under "ROMANS 5:15-17, 20-21" pages 159-160.

THE SUPERIOR EFFECTS OF CHRIST'S SAVING WORK
ROMANS 5:15-17, 20-21

> 15 But the free gift is not like the offense. For if by the one man's offense many died, much more the grace of God and the gift by the grace of the one Man, Jesus Christ, abounded to many. 16 And the gift is not like that which came through the one who sinned. For the judgment which came from one offense resulted in condemnation, but the free gift which came from many offenses resulted in justification. 17 For if by the one man's offense death reigned through the one, much more those who receive abundance of grace and of the gift of righteousness will reign in life through the One, Jesus Christ.)
>
> 20 Moreover the law entered that the offense might abound. But where sin abounded, grace abounded much more, 21 so that as sin reigned in death, even so grace might reign through righteousness to eternal life through Jesus Christ our Lord.

The Old Age of sin and death is associated with Adam, but the Coming Age, already present in measure, is associated with Christ. The results of what Christ did were far superior to the fruits of Adam's disobedience. Adam brought *offence* (*paraptoma*, better translated *trespass*), which means that he stepped across the line and took what he had no right to take. In contrast, Christ brought a "free gift" through His cross, and it is in every way a greater thing (v. 15). In verses 15, 17, and 20 we find the word *grace* (*charis*). In connection with *grace* we note the words "much more" (vv. 15, 17), and then Paul tells us that "where sin abounded, grace abounded much more" (v. 20). The emphasis here falls on the lavishness of Christ's grace and blessings. Jesus Christ's act of grace through the cross did not just balance Adam's disobedience, but overbalanced the results of Adam's sin. The believer is not simply brought to a state of innocence, but receives the infinite righteousness of Christ.

Grace and Salvation

Adam initiated a torrent of sin that spread throughout the world; but where sin increased, grace increased even more (*hupereperisseusen*), so that all who belong to Christ may enjoy salvation (v. 18). Saving grace will not just restore humanity to its original whole and sinless state that existed in the garden prior to Adam's sin. **Our state in heaven will far exceed the glory of the Garden of Eden.**

Power of Grace

Both sin and grace are worldwide in scope; however, divine grace is more than sufficient to overcome the power of sin. **God's grace is dynamic and exercises liberating power from the oppressive power of sin.** In verse 20, Paul returns to the law of Moses and states that "the law entered that the offense might abound," meaning that **the law was given by God so that the full power of sin would be evident.** The commandments from God clearly defined sin and thus stimulated sin's attractiveness.

Human nature is such that often when people are told not to do something, they fix their minds on the forbidden action even more. Also, the increase in the number of laws creates the context for an increase in transgression. **Paul tells us that even though people had responded in rebellion to laws that were meant to protect them and their sin had then increased, God's grace continued to grow even more.** Sin has power to exercise control over human lives—"sin reigned in death"; but grace has more power and delivers human lives from the oppressive power of sin. Grace is more than adequate to deal with the sin problem; it "reign[s] through righteousness to eternal life through Jesus Christ our Lord" (v. 21).

Our Response to Grace

When surveying the superlative excellence of divine grace through the cross, our hearts are moved to praise God and

offer thanks to Him. Grace not only brings us life now (v. 18), but also eternal life (v. 21). In brief, as believers, we are "already" saved; but "not yet" has our salvation been completed. God's plan of salvation is a matter of grace from beginning throughout all eternity, in accordance with the definite plan and foreknowledge of God (Acts 2:23).

Observations

Before we turn to Romans 6, a couple of observations are in order:

1. **Paul's comparison between Adam and Christ shows that Adam was a historical person.** Paul's treatment of Adam as a human person in history, not as a fictional or symbolic person, indicates the importance of our understanding that Adam was a man who actually existed (1 Cor. 15:22, 45-49).

2. **Through Christ, God empowers us to take control of our lives so that sinful drives and desires no longer control us**. God's empowerment is what Paul calls *grace*, which is dynamic and sufficient to enable us to live the Christian life as the empowerment of the Holy Spirit in grace (Rom. 5:21). Grace must be received through faith in Christ. At our first birth we have no control over our association with Adam, but we do have control over our second birth—a birth out of heaven that puts us "in Christ" and provides us with life beyond our wildest imagination. **Sin and death took hold of Adam, and his wrongdoing ultimately dragged us into a world of sin and death. In contrast to Adam, Christ did right and delivered us out of that realm of Adam's sin with all its pain and trouble, into the kingdom of God. Christ also bestowed on us the most extravagant gift of eternal life.**

ROMANS 5:15-17, 20-21

KEYWORDS

Condemnation (see p. 155)

Corporate Solidarity (see p. 155)

God's Plan of Salvation

Gift (see p. 126)

Grace (*charis*) (see p. 23)

Jesus Christ (see p. 59)

Judgment by God/God's Judgment (see p. 68)

Justification (*dikaiosune*) (see p. 158)

Life/Eternal Life
A quality of being and living which is derived from God and is eternal. Such life is imparted to those who follow Christ in faith (Rom. 6:4; 1 John 5:12) and extends into eternity beyond physical death.

Righteousness (*dikaiosune*) (see p. 48)

Salvation (see p. 23)

SUMMARY

The life of the non-Christian is a life of continual bondage to sin. Only God's great message of salvation conveyed by Jesus can bring deliverance. Paul discusses the origin of sin in the human race. He contrasts the disobedience of Adam (through whom sin and death came upon all humankind) with the obedience of Christ, who is the source of salvation and life. Adam's sin had disastrous consequences for all of humankind, introducing sin and death into the human race. Through Adam's transgression, an oppressive power entered into the world and has disposed all humans to sin and rebel against God.

Between Adam and Moses' time, the law of Moses had not been given. Even though the people did not have the law, there was much evildoing and death prevailed. Adam's sin had started a chain reaction, and sinning has been going on until now.

In contrast to the effects of Adam's sin, Christ's saving work is far superior. Divine grace that provides salvation resulted from the cross of Jesus Christ. Adam brought condemnation upon all, but Christ by His obedience has secured eternal life ("justification of life," v. 18) for all who believe in Him. The reign of life through Christ overcomes the reign of death through Adam. Christ and His cross is God's gracious solution to the sin problem and have always been the solution. The Old Testament believers looked forward to Christ death on the cross, while we look back to His death.

Adam's Offense	Jesus Christ's Gift of Grace
Sin increased.	Grace increased more.
Sin is worldwide.	Grace is worldwide.
Sin is powerful.	Grace is more powerful and able to overcome sin.
Sin can have control over our lives.	Grace empowers us to take control over sin.
Sin brings about death.	Grace brings about life.

LIFE APPLICATION

Can we really believe that God loves all people? Can we believe that God will save people like you and me? Some may conclude that perhaps the gospel applies to some people—those who are naturally good or religious, or to great people like the apostles Peter and Paul, Luther and Wesley, or Mother Teresa. Does the gospel apply to common people such as you and me? Yes it does; the gospel applies to the whole human race. There is room at the cross for everyone. All can be justified through faith in the cross of Christ.

REFLECTION—PART THREE
Romans 3:21—5:21

1. Paul uses language from the courtroom (*justification*), the institution of slavery (*redemption*), and the temple sacrificial system (*propitiation*) to describe the process of salvation. How would you explain each of these terms so that a person who is not a follower of Christ could understand their significance?

2. What is your understanding of Paul's statement that God is "just and the justifier of the one who has faith in Jesus" (Rom. 3:26)?

3. Why do you think Paul used both Abraham and David to illustrate the doctrine of justification by faith?

4. What is the significance of Abraham's being justified by faith before he received the mark of circumcision?

God's Plan of Salvation

5. Is there any connection between circumcision and water baptism?

6. Do you think individuals can live in such a way that God is obligated to forgive them of their sins? Relate your answer to the principles of faith and law.

7. Discuss briefly the magnitude of Abraham's faith.

8. In Romans 5, Paul mentions three benefits of justification by faith: *peace, grace,* and *hope.* How would you relate each of them to your own experience?

9. How did Adam's sin affect us all? A review of the four views presented in the commentary may help you to answer this question.

10. Briefly state your understanding of the doctrine of the two ages (5:12-14, 18-19). How do they relate to Adam and Christ?

11. Compare and contrast Adam and Christ.

12. Describe the power of God's grace in your life.

Prayer

Our Father, we rejoice in the glorious triumph of Christ on the cross and cherish the eternal significance of His death and resurrection for ourselves and for the whole world. When we contemplate the benefits of the death of Your Son and the mystery of Your redeeming love, our hearts are filled with gratitude and praise. At Calvary, Christ paid it all for our salvation. Amen.

PART FOUR—Romans 6:1—8:39

God's Plan for Sanctification

- **Freedom From the Dominion of Sin**
  Romans 6:1-23
- **Freedom From the Law**
  Romans 7:1-6
- **A Defense of the Law**
  Romans 7:7-25
- **Life in the Spirit**
  Romans 8:1-11
- **Privileges for God's Children**
  Romans 8:12-17
- **The Glorious Hope**
  Romans 8:18-30
- **Assurance of Salvation**
  Romans 8:31-39

Through salvation, God brings us into a right relationship with Himself; through sanctification, God sets us apart for holy living and service, giving us the privilege of participating in the life of God. In Romans 5:1-11, Paul has discussed the benefits of justification. Now in chapters 6-8, he describes at some length salvation's effect on Christians (those who have been justified). A right relationship with God requires a decisive break with sin (ch. 6). This break from sin frees the believer from the condemnation of the law (ch. 7) and death (ch. 8) so that the believer can live in the power of the Holy Spirit and in hope. Chapters 6-8 also deal with what is known as *the doctrine of sanctification*—that is, Christian freedom from the dominion of sin, law, and death. As children of God, we are no longer slaves to the powers of sin, law, and death.

Freedom in Christ	
Romans 6	We are free from sin—yet we must resist its temptations.
Romans 7	We are free from law—yet we must live lawfully.
Romans 8	We are free from death—yet we long for the redemption of our bodies (cf. Nygren, 1949, 296).

FREEDOM FROM THE DOMINION OF SIN
ROMANS 6:1-23

Being justified by faith, we enjoy a right relationship with God. This right standing with God calls us to the great moral responsibility of living the Christian life. As a result, we are to begin growing and maturing in the Lord, laying aside those old patterns of behavior that displease Him. Scripture describes this process as *sanctification* (1 Cor. 1:30; 1 Thess. 4:3-4; 2 Thess. 2:13; 1 Peter 1:2). *Justification,* **more than just bringing us into a right relationship with God, produces the fruit of** *sanctification* (holy, sanctified living). In chapters 6-8, Paul discusses the fruit of justification, which is sanctification or holiness (cf. 6:19, 22; 15:16). **There is an inseparable connection between justification and sanctification.** Justification is a right relationship with God and is to be accompanied by right living. Sanctification has its beginning in a right relationship with God and is to be characteristic of the Christian life from then on.

With chapter 6, Paul begins the third major division of his letter to the Romans. In the first division, he spoke about the universal scope of *sin* (1:18—3:20); in the second, about *justification* as the way God deals with the plight of humankind (3:21—5:21); and now in the third division he discusses *sanctification,* or *holiness* (chs. 6-8). **Holy living is the logical and necessary outcome of being forgiven of our sins. Paul develops the doctrine of sanctification by explaining the believer's** *freedom* **from sin (ch. 6), the law (ch. 7), and death (ch. 8).** It is in chapter 8, in his discussion about death, that Paul deals directly with the topics of the *Holy Spirit* and *sanctification.*

In *justification*, God breaks the power of sin to condemn us. In *sanctification*, He breaks the power of sin to control us, providing a way for us to become holy in character. Paul devotes the first ten verses of chapter 6 to the topic of *positional sanctification*. In the middle of chapter 6, he begins his discussion of what we might describe as *practical, daily sanctification*. Paul's viewpoint is that from the *positional* flows the *practical*. **When God saves us, He instantly and *positionally* sets us apart as holy people to live for and to serve Him.** *Practical sanctification,* **however, is continuous and ongoing throughout the Christian life.** The combination of positional and practical sanctification brings about in our lives divine transformation into the likeness of Jesus Christ. Chapter 6 reflects very well both aspects of sanctification, one being the separation from sin and the other being dedication to a new life in Jesus Christ.

Positional Sanctification (Rom. 6:1-10)	Practical Sanctification (Rom. 6:11-23)
God's spiritual designation and ethical standard for Christians	Development of holy character
Completed	Dynamic
Entire	Ongoing/Progressive

Strange and contradictory as it may appear, Christians are to become what God says they are already. As for our position, we are already "sanctified" (1 Cor. 1:2, 30), but in practice we are "becoming sanctified" (Palma 1973, 172). As is characteristic of Paul's thought, underlying the doctrine of sanctification is the biblical structure *already/not yet. Already* God has declared believers holy, but *not yet* have they reached perfection. So sanctification is an in-advance realization of the Kingdom in the context or venue of individual Christian lives.

*For a comparison of **Justification** and **Sanctification**, see Appendix (F) page 429.

POSITIONAL SANCTIFICATION
ROMANS 6:1-10

> ¹ What shall we say then? Shall we continue in sin that grace may abound? ² Certainly not! How shall we who died to sin live any longer in it? ³ Or do you not know that as many of us as were baptized into Christ Jesus were baptized into His death? ⁴ Therefore we were buried with Him through baptism into death, that just as Christ was raised from the dead by the glory of the Father, even so we also should walk in newness of life.
>
> ⁵ For if we have been united together in the likeness of His death, certainly we also shall be in the likeness of His resurrection, ⁶ knowing this, that our old man was crucified with Him, that the body of sin might be done away with, that we should no longer be slaves of sin. ⁷ For he who has died has been freed from sin. ⁸ Now if we died with Christ, we believe that we shall also live with Him, ⁹ knowing that Christ, having been raised from the dead, dies no more. Death no longer has dominion over Him. ¹⁰ For the death that He died, He died to sin once for all; but the life that He lives, He lives to God.

Grace and Sin in the Life of the Believer

In chapter 6, Paul returns to his conversation with the imaginary Jewish opponent, following up on Romans 3:7-8. Previously in 3:7-8, Paul has responded to a question from his opponent about whether or not sinning would give God the opportunity to forgive: "Why not say, 'Let us do evil that good may come'?" (v. 8). His opponent's rationale for asking the question was that sin must be good if it produces something as wonderful as grace. Perhaps as Paul wrote the statement, "Where sin abounded, grace abounded much more" (5:20), he was reminded that this matter was not settled, prompting him then to raise the question, **"Shall we continue in sin that grace may abound?" His answer is "Certainly not!"—sin has no place in the life of faith (6:1-2). Grace will abound even more if it is contemplated in terms of not only producing a right relationship with God, but also a new life.**

Effects of Justification on Sin

Paul gives three reasons why justifying grace does not encourage sinning:

1. **Christians have died to sin (6:2).** God has set believers apart from sin. In fact, they are united by faith to Christ, who died to free them from sin. **Their relationship with God calls for a reordering of their lives which frees them from old sinful patterns of living.** To be dead does not mean that believers have ceased to exist. A dead body has hands and feet, but in that state, it is insensitive to its environment. Likewise, death to sin is the condition of believers, who should be blind to sin's enticements and deaf to its voices. Just as a dead body is set off from the affairs of this world, so have believers been set off from sin. Believers owe sin absolutely nothing (Bruce, 1963, 136-37). **Death with Christ wipes the slate clean, and believers have already begun a new life with Christ.** They are people who have died to sin, so why should they live any longer in sin?

2. **Water baptism has moral significance (6:3-5).** In New Testament times, water baptism was the normal experience of those who confessed Christ as their Savior. It was a public affirmation of their faith. Paul refers to baptism as symbolic of the believer's death and resurrection. At that time, baptism was accomplished through immersion, which was and continues to be a fitting illustration of the believer's identification and union with Christ. **The act of baptism illustrates not only our union with Christ in His death, but also our union with Him in His resurrection.** When a believer descends into the water, it is like being buried in a grave; and when that person emerges, it is like rising from the grave. **At conversion, the believer is spiritually buried with Christ in death and raised with Him in newness of life. Baptism in water demonstrates what has happened in conversion—moving from one way of life to another.**

If we are "united together in the likeness of His death, certainly we also shall be in the likeness of His resurrection" (v. 5). Here, Paul handles carefully the idea of resurrection by using the future tense. **Resurrection is a present reality for the believers and a future hope.** As believers, we are already raised with Christ and "should walk in newness of life" (v. 4); but we "shall be in the likeness of His resurrection" (v. 5). Because of our participation in the death and resurrection of Christ, we have been raised to a new life—a life of discipleship. However, it is not until Christ returns that we will receive glorified bodies similar to Christ's resurrection body (Phil. 3:21). **The relationship we enjoy now with Christ calls for us to break with sin as sharply as a person who dies breaks with physical life, then to be resurrected to a new life in Christ—to be lived both in this world and the next.**

3. **The old self has been crucified with Christ (6:6-10).** Paul repeats the same idea in a different way, using phrases like *the old man* and *the body of death*. One interpretation is that the phrase *the old man* refers to the unconverted, unredeemed person who has evil thoughts, words, and actions; but here Paul is not speaking to that type of person, but to Christians in Rome. In Colossians 3:8-9, he urges Christians to put off the *old man*. **As believers, our old self has been crucified or nailed to the cross.** This does not mean that the self does not exist any longer. The power of the old self has been broken, but the old self is still capable of prompting ungodly desires, warped attitudes, and sinful behavior. **The lifestyle of the old self is undesirable,** which is suggested by the word *old*. This word *old* reminds us that over time the wear and tear of sin on our lives is neither attractive nor desirable. **The new person in Christ needs daily sanctifying grace and the help of the Holy Spirit to deal adequately with the old self, which remains capable of inciting attitudes, desires, and behavior displeasing to God.**

Christ's redeeming work is to transform *the old man* **by doing "away with" ("rendering inoperative,"** *katargeo***)** *the body of sin* **within him (Rom. 6:6).** Christ does this transforming work so that the body of sin cannot operate in our lives as it did before our conversion. In the context of the resurrection, *the body of sin* refers to the spiritual condition of humans who are under the control of sin. We must not think of Paul as holding a low view of the body. For him the body is a noble instrument made for noble things. **Paul urges Christians not to present their "members as instruments of unrighteousness to sin" (v. 13), but to present their bodies as living sacrifices to God (12:1), and reminds them that their body is the temple of the Holy Spirit (1 Cor. 6:19) and the temple of God (2 Cor. 6:16).** The body itself is not evil, but it can be dominated by the oppressive power of sin. The human body has emotions and desires that can result in evil, if controlled by sin. Doing away with the *body of sin* is putting out of action the sin-dominated aspects of a person's body and personality. **The power of sin is broken so that in our daily lives we are "no longer . . . slaves [to] sin" (Rom. 6:6).**

Through our union with Christ, we have been "freed from sin" (v. 7). In verses 4-8, Paul frequently uses the Greek term *sun* (*with*) to connect believers with Christ, and continues using that term in 8:17, 22. We can describe this union as a faith bond of believers with Christ. **Whenever the identity of believers is fused into the identity of Christ, believers must live out that identity in their personal life by walking in newness of life (6:4).**

Life in Christ

Unity with Christ in His death is not an end in itself. Christians firmly believe that they "shall also live with Him" (v. 8). Paul's use of the future tense in this passage does not weaken its application to the Christian life in the present (Morris, 1998, 254). **Christians have already entered into a new life and live with Christ day by day. The fulfillment of their hope of resurrection has already begun here during their life on earth.** In verse 8, the words "we believe" emphasize Paul's personal commitment and the commitment of other Christians to this truth. The Christians of Paul's day were living in the power of Christ's resurrection. The death and resurrection of Christ have secured for all believers that which is necessary for holy living. "For the death that He died, He died to sin once for all" (v. 10), says Paul. "Death no longer has dominion over Him" (v. 9). **Christ did something that need not be done again (Heb. 7:27; 10:12); Christ's resurrection was a decisive victory over death, securing life for each of us.**

ROMANS 6:1-10

KEYWORDS

Baptism into Christ Jesus
A phrase that refers to inward spiritual conversion. Water baptism, a symbol of *baptism in Christ Jesus*, has no power to save, but it pictures what happens at the time Christ is received in faith.

Believe (see p. 119)

Body of Sin/Body of Death
The human body (the whole personality) ruled by the power of sin

The Cross (see p. 122)

Death
Disunion of soul and body, or a state of separation from God

Disciple (see p. 40)

Freedom From Sin
Putting out of operation the dominion of sin in the life of the believer

Freedom in Christ
A supernatural blessing which delivers believers from destructive influence, such as sin, Satan, power of darkness, and condemnation by the law. This freedom is the grace that Christ preached (Luke 4:16ff.) and offered.

Grace (*charis*) (see p. 23)

Holy (see p. 59)

Holy Living
Living according to the teachings and example of Jesus Christ

Old Man
The sinful self

God's Plan for Sanctification

Resurrection

The coming forth from the dead in a resurrected body. The literal resurrection of Christ and the spiritual resurrection of believers have already occurred and should continue to occur as believers live the Christian life, but the literal resurrection of believers will not occur until the return of Christ.

Sanctification

The process of being made holy. Sanctification arises from a direct relationship with God, and its fruits are ethical and personal purity. In light of Scripture, in a positional sense, sanctification is complete; but in practice, it is still ongoing and a goal that can only be reached by the guidance of the Holy Spirit.

- **Positional Sanctification**—The status of anyone who, by faith, has been joined to Christ, breaking the dominion of sin
- **Practical Sanctification**—Result of a believer's being joined to Christ and striving, through the help of the Holy Spirit, for moral excellence in character and actions, following the teachings and example of Jesus Christ.

* For a comparison of Justification and Sanctification, see Appendix (F) page 429.

Sin (see p. 48)

Water Baptism (see p. 100)

SUMMARY & LIFE APPLICATION

See under "ROMANS 6:11-23" pages 180-181.

PRACTICAL SANCTIFICATION
ROMANS 6:11-23

[11] Likewise you also, reckon yourselves to be dead indeed to sin, but alive to God in Christ Jesus our Lord.

[12] Therefore do not let sin reign in your mortal body, that you should obey it in its lusts. [13] And do not present your members as instruments of unrighteousness to sin, but present yourselves to God as

> instruments of unrighteousness to sin, but present yourselves to God as being alive from the dead, and your members as instruments of righteousness to God. [14] For sin shall not have dominion over you, for you are not under law but under grace.
>
> [15] What then? Shall we sin because we are not under law but under grace? Certainly not! [16] Do you not know that to whom you present yourselves slaves to obey, you are that one's slaves whom you obey, whether of sin leading to death, or of obedience leading to righteousness? [17] But God be thanked that though you were slaves of sin, yet you obeyed from the heart that form of doctrine to which you were delivered. [18] And having been set free from sin, you became slaves of righteousness. [19] I speak in human terms because of the weakness of your flesh. For just as you presented your members as slaves of uncleanness, and of lawlessness leading to more lawlessness, so now present your members as slaves of righteousness for holiness.
>
> [20] For when you were slaves of sin, you were free in regard to righteousness. [21] What fruit did you have then in the things of which you are now ashamed? For the end of those things is death. [22] But now having been set free from sin, and having become slaves of God, you have your fruit to holiness, and the end, everlasting life. [23] For the wages of sin is death, but the gift of God is eternal life in Christ Jesus our Lord.

Two Components of Sanctification

Paul acknowledges that God, through the Holy Spirit, sanctifies His people (15:16). The work of God in the process of sanctification does not relieve the Christian of the responsibility of putting into practice what God has already done. **Sanctification has two components: the sanctifying action of God and the response of His people.** It is striking that both components are placed side by side in Leviticus 20: "I am the Lord who sanctifies you" (v. 8); "Consecrate yourselves, therefore, and be holy, for I am the Lord your God" (v. 7). Like the Old Testament, Paul sees sanctification as rooted in God's work, and as Christians we are to walk and live accordingly. The daily changes that occur as a result of sanctification depend on what God has done and continues to do through the Holy Spirit and, furthermore, our willingness to dedicate ourselves to doing God's will.

Being Alive to God (Rom. 6:11-14)

After Paul has characterized us as being a holy people "set free from sin" (6:18, 22), he encourages us to become what God has declared us to be—holy (vv. 11-14). **From a grammatical standpoint, Paul shifts from the indicative mood to the imperative—from telling us what God has done for us to telling us what we must do for ourselves. Paul urges believers to *reckon* (*logizomai*) themselves dead to sin and to be alive to God.** The word *reckon* is in the present tense, and so **Paul is calling us to examine ourselves and to die daily to sinful tendencies and temptations, living in obedience to God.** The result of this daily practice is that we learn to live for God as Christ does (v. 10).

Living for God is accomplished "in Christ Jesus our Lord" (v. 11). The phrase "in Christ" runs throughout Paul's writings and means that we have entered into fellowship with Christ, the Second Adam, as our spiritual head. In union with Christ, we are to live as though we have already entered the resurrection life (Bruce, 1963, 139). **Living in the resurrection life calls for us to make Christ the center of our daily living and to give ourselves to God each day.**

Aspects of Holy Living (Practical Sanctification)

Verses 12-14 draw some practical conclusions regarding a life focused on Christ. The word *therefore* indicates that holiness of life must be the result for those who trust in Christ. The two admonitions that follow indicate that holy living (sanctification) has negative and positive aspects.

- **Negative Aspect of Sanctification—Not Living as a Slave to Sin**

    In verse 12, we are told to stop allowing sin's desires and urges to have control of our mortal bodies. **Following conversion, Christians are tempted by sinful desires and can still sin through what they do and what they might neglect to do. They are to oppose sinful desires by seeking God and by being strengthened through the power of the Spirit (8:1-5) and the encouragement of the**

Christian community. Followers of Christ are to prohibit sin from ruling their mortal bodies. (Here in verse 12, most likely the phrase "mortal body" refers to the whole person: mind, body, and soul.) Sin seeks to establish its rule over the whole person, not just the physical body. We must fight against sin or we will find ourselves giving in to the desires of our egos and becoming slaves to sin again. **In order to fight successfully against sin and not to be its slave, it is necessary to implement the positive side of sanctification—nurturing our relationship with God and submitting to His instruction and to the empowering presence of the Spirit.** To return to the practice or the rule of sin places us in the grave danger of forfeiting our salvation, "for if you live according to the flesh you will die" (8:13).

- **Positive Aspect of Sanctification—Accepting God's Grace and Being Obedient**

We are to present ourselves as instruments to be used by God. **Christ calls for us to be obedient to God, rather than being manipulated and controlled by sin.** Therefore, we who are "alive from the dead" are to be "instruments of righteousness to God" (6:13). **Now being spiritually alive in Christ, believers are to use their energy and natural and spiritual gifts to promote righteousness.** This requires grace, and God gives everyone sufficient grace needed "to do what is right for the glory of God" (v. 13 NLT). The way Paul states it is "for you are not under law but under grace" (v. 14). The law has no power to deliver us from the oppressive power of sin, but grace is actually sufficient to set us free from the control of sin. **Under grace, sin no longer has dominion over us.** And so again, to know Christ personally is not only a spiritual experience, it is a way of living.

Some Christians, who presume upon God's grace, may consider themselves exempt from responsible living and free to continue acting in a sinful manner. A grave danger among some believers is the attitude, Why worry about sin since grace can so easily cover every stain of sin? (see vv. 15-23). **Believers are set free from keeping rules in order**

to receive salvation, but this freedom does not mean they have no obligation to God. Nevertheless, many may still ask, "If God is so forgiving, He will forgive anything; therefore, why not go on sinning?" **Obedience has a central place in the system of grace and faith.** At the beginning of this letter, Paul speaks about the "obedience to the faith" (1:5). Obedience is required, and it is an obedience that flows out of faith.

Slaves to Sin or Righteousness (6:15-23)

In addressing the issue of holy living, Paul uses an example from the institution of slavery, which his original readers would have easily understood. Slavery was widespread in the ancient world. Most likely, some of the Christians in Rome had been slaves. During that time, slave masters had total control of their slaves, even power of life or death. At no time were slaves free to do what they wanted to do. Every moment of their lives belonged to their master. The only normal thing that could free them from obligation to their master was death. This picture illustrates the Christian experience. **As unbelievers, we had been slaves of sin—our thoughts and deeds were sinful—but as believers we died to the old life of sin, and now we are to live as slaves of God.** For Paul, all human beings are slaves, ruled either by obedience to sin or obedience to God. **Whatever master we have determines our lives.** As Jesus said, "No servant can serve two masters" (Luke 16:13). You cannot serve God and sin; they are incompatible masters.

In Romans 6:17, Paul indicates to his readers that he understands that they have properly settled the issue of slavery to sin: "You were slaves of sin, yet you obeyed from the heart that form of doctrine to which you were delivered." The Roman Christians had become obedient to the gospel, which had been preached to them. **Paul tells them that as a result of believing the message of salvation, they were set free from sin and became slaves of righteousness (v. 18).**

In verse 19, Paul recognizes that the slavery illustration is imperfect and falls short of describing the Christian life. Uncomfortable with comparing the Christian life to slavery, he apologizes for using it. He explains that he made use of the analogy "because of the weakness of your flesh" (v. 19). He wants the Roman church to understand that he chose the illustration in order to make it easy for them to understand the importance of giving themselves wholly to God. In using the word *flesh* here, Paul is referring to natural, human limitations. Later in his letter to the Romans, Paul will use the same term to describe a spiritual condition, which is more a matter of choice. In the case of spiritual condition, the term *flesh* indicates a worldly orientation toward overindulging oneself, such as pursuing money, lust, power, or pleasure rather than God (7:5; 8:4-7).

- **Slaves to Sin**

    Paul was well aware that since putting on the character of Christ was a progressive matter, Christians continue to remain in danger of sinning. He reminds his readers that they had been "slaves of uncleanness and . . . lawlessness," indicating that their condition of slavery to the oppressive power of sin was a result of their own choices and behaviors (6:19). **Before coming to Christ, Paul's readers had become bond slaves to sin by making wrong choices, embracing lifestyles of impurity and disobedience to the law.** Choosing this manner of living leads to more of the same; sin affects the conscience and leads to more sin. When a person sins initially, he may be rather hesitant; but as that person continues in sin, it becomes easier for him to make wrong moral decisions. The cascading effects of sin results from using human will in a destructive manner, that is, people using their freedom to avoid restraint and submission (Käsemann, 1980, 182-84).

- **Slaves to Righteousness**

    Before hearing the gospel, Paul's readers had zealously used their freedom to pursue ungodly lives. Now he exhorts them to have the same zeal for living the Christian life. **Outside of Christ, people's lives have been characterized by increasing wickedness and impurity. Through their faith in Christ, the old life of sin has been broken. Now they are to serve righteousness, which increasingly leads to holiness** (*hagiasmos*, sanctification). To serve God's righteousness means to live in terms of a right relationship with Him. The fruit of a right relationship with God is sanctification, and the ultimate result of a right relationship with God is eternal life (v. 22).

Choosing Life or Death

Verses 21-23 state the crucial importance of sanctification. These verses remind all humankind, believers and unbelievers alike, of holy living, describing it in terms of life and death. Paul asks a rhetorical question of the believers in Rome: "What fruit did you have then in the things of which you are now ashamed?" His answer: "For the end of those things is death" (v. 21). **The fruit of sin falls totally in the unprofitable realm of death.** A vital aspect of living a holy life is being ashamed of our past evil thoughts and deeds. Such shame prompts us to avoid the damaging and sinful parts of our old lifestyle and leads to holiness of life. **Holiness leads to everlasting life (v. 22). Unbelievers have certain freedom, but true freedom flows out of being slaves of God. This allegiance to God results in our being made holy (sanctified), and this sanctification leads to everlasting life.** Paul's illustration from slavery is really applicable to the Christian life. We do well to remember that no one can be absolutely free. We are only free to choose whether we are slaves of God or slaves of sin.

In verse 23, Paul sums up his discussion about slavery and sin: "The wages of sin is death, but the gift of God is eternal life in Christ Jesus our Lord." This contrast between death and life indicates that God breaks the factors that keep us imprisoned in a life of death. The outcome of sin is death—for the believer as well as for the unbeliever—no exception is made. Only Christ can bring life to that which we have allowed to die. Paul's statement about the wages of sin serves as a strong warning to those who have believed, but who do not think that living in sin has deadly consequences. **The call of God to salvation requires separation from sin.** This separation begins with justification (new birth) and continues in sanctification throughout the life of the believer. The final outcome for a life dedicated to growing in God's holiness is eternal life, but the reward for a life focused on sinful pursuits is death. God does not pay wages. The eternal life that God gives us is absolutely free, but His gift demands faith that results in holy living. The implication is clear—to live in sin without repentance results in death for the believer as well as for the unbeliever.

God's Gift and Our Responsibility

Now we sum up the implications of what Paul has said in chapter 6. **Paul has emphasized both what God has done in salvation and our responsibility for the way we live. Maintaining a balance between the two is important.** Too much emphasis on the work of God may suggest that the way we live is unimportant. On the other hand, an overemphasis on our responsibility to God could lead to a religion of merely good works and ultimately to legalism. **At the heart of legalism is the assumption that we can save ourselves. The idea of sanctification is to keep in focus what God has done and is doing for us and our responsibility to live in a way that pleases Him.**

Ministering to Others

When ministering to those who do not know Christ, we should always begin by stating what God has done instead of telling them how to live. It is important for us to remember that people's lives are changed through God's grace and His actions, not through their (or our) following a set of rules or engaging in good behavior. **Once a person has received Christ, he or she is ready to begin to make lifestyle changes through God's grace and the guidance of the Holy Spirit.** By daily consecrating themselves to the Lord, over time people grow and mature in Him, being conformed more and more to the likeness of Christ.

Maturing in Our Faith

In our walk with God, it is important to remember that God accepts us while we are in sin. However, He does not continue to be accepting if we continue in sinful pursuits and

do not accept Him and welcome His healing and instruction in our daily lives. Through disrespect and habitual sinful actions, we bring about an estrangement in our relationship with God. Faith cannot sustain itself without personal devotion and commitment to Christ. God who has begun a good work wants to advance it (Phil. 1:6; 2:12-13). Quite frankly, Paul urges progress in our faith. "We do not grow away from the beginning of our faith, but more and more into it" (Thielicke, 1982, 40). A principal teaching of Romans is that in addition to responding to God's initial invitation to relationship with Christ, we need to continue growing in relationship with Him. **We begin our relationship with Christ through faith, and we stay in the relationship by continuing to trust in Him and to lead holy lives.**

In Romans 1:17, the phrase "from faith to faith" indicates that faith is all encompassing. **It is through faith in Christ that we initially receive salvation, and it is also through faith that we live godly lives.** Again, Paul reminds us of this truth when he says, "You stand by faith" (11:20). Faith always includes a personal commitment—a believing obedience. To illustrate it simply—if a person gets into a lifeboat during a rescue, that person is going to attempt to remain where it is safe and will not jump out into dangerous waters. With God's help, we must strive to stay in the lifeboat that Christ has provided for us. Progress in sanctification is not automatic for the Christian. The Bible is full of calls to action that result in spiritual growth. Faith cannot thrive without prayer and devotion to God. **Faith will thrive when we nurture our relationship with God through daily spiritual practices, focusing our lives on Jesus Christ, and relying on the Holy Spirit for help and guidance.**

ROMANS 6:11-23
KEYWORDS **Bondservant/Slave (*doulos*)** (see p. 58) **Death** (see p. 170) **Doctrine** (see p. 25)

Flesh (see p. 58)

Grace (*charis*) (see p. 23)

Holy Living (see p. 170)

Legalism (see p. 48)

Life/Eternal Life (see p. 159)

Righteousness (*dikaiosune*) (see p. 48)

Sanctification (see p. 171)

Sin (see p. 48)

SUMMARY

Through Christ, God has provided forgiveness for our wrongdoings and deliverance from bondage to sin. Salvation calls for us to make a sharp break with sin. There is a close connection between *justification* and *sanctification* because a right relationship with God is to be accompanied by right living.

Scripture teaches that sanctification has two components: *positional* and *practical*. The *positional* emphasizes that God breaks the power of sin to control the believer. Out of the positional flows the *practical*, which stresses the efforts of the believer, with the help of the Holy Spirit, to live a holy life on a daily basis.

Paul highlights the work of God in sanctification and emphasizes that sin does not have the power to control the believer. He teaches that the Christian is dead to sin and the old self is crucified with Christ. He also explains that *baptism*, our being immersed and lifted out of the water, illustrates our decisive break and death to sin and being raised to a new life.

To strengthen his point that Christians should keep free of sin, Paul speaks of two slaveries: slavery to sin and slavery to God (righteousness). As a slave gives obedience to only one master, so Christians are to give themselves exclusively to Christ and obey Him. Serving sin leads to death, whereas serving Christ leads to eternal life.

LIFE APPLICATION

When we come to Christ, we are to leave our prior sinful lives behind. At the point of committing our lives to Him, we receive the blessing of positional sanctification; that is, we are forgiven and placed in a right relationship with God, who makes us holy.

From that point on, we are to apply and nurture that holy standing and live out our sanctification in a practical manner. This means we

> are to rely on the Holy Spirit for help in doing these things. He will lead and guide us and give us the power to resist temptations.
>
> The Holy Spirit helps us to grow spiritually. As we mature, every aspect of our being will become more like Christ, who is our example for holy living. We move farther away from our old life as a slave into our new life as a willing servant of Christ—moving from death into a wonderful life in which we will enjoy a relationship with Christ forever.
>
> * For a list of **"Practices That Nurture Our Faith and Holy Living"** (practical sanctification), see Appendix (G) pages 430-433.

FREEDOM FROM THE LAW
ROMANS 7:1-6

> [1] Or do you not know, brethren (for I speak to those who know the law), that the law has dominion over a man as long as he lives? [2] For the woman who has a husband is bound by the law to her husband as long as he lives. But if the husband dies, she is released from the law of her husband. [3] So then if, while her husband lives, she marries another man, she will be called an adulteress; but if her husband dies, she is free from that law, so that she is no adulteress, though she has married another man. [4] Therefore, my brethren, you also have become dead to the law through the body of Christ, that you may be married to another—to Him who was raised from the dead, that we should bear fruit to God. [5] For when we were in the flesh, the sinful passions which were aroused by the law were at work in our members to bear fruit to death. [6] But now we have been delivered from the law, having died to what we were held by, so that we should serve in the newness of the Spirit and not in the oldness of the letter.

We understand the importance of being free from sin, but why should Christians be free from the law? The law is God's gift; it forbids sin and demands obedience, providing protection for God's people. **Obedience to the gospel, or obedience of faith, is different from obedience to law in the sense of legalism. The gospel calls for a new obedience, which is independent of legalistic efforts of trying to earn salvation.** Christians are to have nothing to do with legalism; they depend on Christ for salvation, not on themselves and their good works.

Paul does not belittle the law of God. In fact, he restates and emphasizes the law, especially the moral teaching of it (13:8-14). **He simply places the law in its proper perspective, making it secondary rather than primary.** His conclusion is that **the law is "holy and just and good" (7:12).** As Paul looks back on his life (as a devout Pharisee) before conversion to Christianity, **he finds the law to be inadequate to secure a right standing with God.** Few had the zeal for the law that Paul had, which is evident in his statement about his own relationship with the law: "concerning the righteousness which is in the law, blameless" (Phil. 3:6). However, in Paul's new life, he experienced a joy and peace that he had never known. This peace did not come from keeping a code of laws, but through faith in Jesus Christ (v. 9). **After Paul's acceptance of Christ, he enjoyed freedom from the dominion of sin and law, dying to the old life of sinning and of trying to earn salvation.** Through the cross, God has broken the tyranny of sin and the law (legalism) for the believer. As for the law, it has no authority over the dead and is unable to offer the Christian any power to live the Christian life. In living the Christian life, some people are attracted to a version of Christianity that tries to blend the Christian faith and dependence on law. However, the Christian has died to the law and is no longer under the authority of it, but now is under the authority of Christ. Paul develops this point about the authority of the law in Romans 7:1-6.

Death to the Condemnation of the Law

Romans 7 deals with the relationship between the law and sanctification. Paul uses an illustration from marriage, an institution governed by law. We must not try to press every detail of this illustration. Its purpose is to emphasize that death cancels all legal obligations. In his example, Paul discusses a wife, who is obligated to her husband as long as he lives. If the husband were to die, his wife would be free to remarry, and in doing so, she would not be committing adultery. **Through death, a wife's responsibilities to the relationship with her husband would end, and she would be free to start a new life. The point of this illustration is that**

unbelievers are bound to the law, and like a married woman, death must occur before their relationship with the law can be dissolved.

Upon becoming a believer, a person dies with Christ and that person's relationship with the law is broken. As a Christian, he or she is free from the condemnation of the law and from legalistic servitude to it. Now the believer is bound to Christ and is free to "bear fruit to God" (v. 4), which is the same as "fruit to holiness" (6:22), or *sanctification.* Just as Christ died, the believer, through faith, dies to his or her previous life in order to receive a new one. To the Christians in Rome, Paul says, "You also have become dead to the law through the body of Christ" (7:4). **On the cross, Christ's body died to the law; that is, He took the penalty due us for breaking God's law. Having died with Christ to the law, the believer is free to give himself or herself to Christ rather than to the law**—"to Him who was raised from the dead" (v. 4). The union between Christ and the believer will never be broken by Christ, for as resurrected Lord, He lives forever. **Christ's death and resurrection are reproduced in the believer. While Jesus Christ's death was followed by resurrection, the believer's death and resurrection with Him are to be followed by a new life. This life is characterized by "fruit to God"—a life abundant in spiritual fruit expressed through godly character and living.** In this life, believers only enjoy part of the benefits of Christ's resurrection; but when He returns, they will receive the full benefits of resurrection. This process reminds us once again of the biblical structure *already / not yet*.

Negative Consequences of the Law

Still keeping the law in view, Paul indicates that **the law may actually move our passions to sin (v. 5).** From time to time, the apostle indicates that the law is closely related to sin—"I would not have known sin except through the law" (v. 7). **God's law defines what is forbidden. By defining sin, the law can be a factor in people's focusing their minds on the forbidden, motivating them to break the very rules that are meant to protect them.** Some people even take pleasure in breaking the laws of

God. **Another way that the law might motivate even conscientious and devoted people to sin is that they might come to despair because of their inability to keep the law perfectly, and give up trying.** The point is that the prohibitions of the law can serve as an incentive to sin and make attractive what is forbidden. Hence, sinful passions are aroused and stimulated by the demands of the law. The resulting sin and wrong actions, instead of producing fruit that nurtures and sustains life, produce poisonous fruit that brings about death. This subject of the negative power of the law reoccurs in verses 7-25.

Christians have been set free from the old life of subservience to the law (v. 6). Before being delivered, God's people were held captive and could not escape the law. **The law informed them of God's will,** and as a result they had knowledge but nothing more. Their trouble was that **the law offered them no power to do God's will. They were "in the flesh" (*sarx*; v. 5).**

At different places in the biblical text, Paul uses the term *flesh* with various meanings. Here in verse 5, the word *flesh* has a broader application than just referring to the physical body. Paul uses it to describe a person under the dominion of sin, law, and death (Barrett, 1991, 137). In short, **to be "in the flesh" describes the condition of a person controlled by ungodly desires for personal acclaim, advantages, or power over others.** Such a person has a worldly (not a spiritual) outlook on life.

Freedom in the Holy Spirit Through Christ

In contrast to this lifestyle, which is controlled by evil desires or fear of being imperfect, believers have a life of freedom since they no longer are under the dominion of sin and the law. Though free persons, Christians are still to be obedient to God. **Bearing spiritual fruit in response to God's forgiveness and love lies at the heart of Christian freedom.** The way Paul expresses this truth is that "we should serve in the newness of the Spirit and not in the oldness of the letter" (7:6). The new life comes through the Holy Spirit, not through following the old legal code. **Having the Holy Spirit in our hearts, we are to serve the Lord and to devote ourselves to godly living.**

In verse 6, Paul introduces the concept of new life through the Holy Spirit. However, the wonderful details of the Spirit's sanctifying work—so essential to the Christian life—are not described until chapter 8. "Having died to what we were held by," we begin to grow and mature in our relationship with the Lord (7:6). **In Christ through the guidance and power of the Holy Spirit, we begin to bear the fruit of new life, the fruit of the Spirit (Gal. 5:22-23).**

ROMANS 7:1-6

KEYWORDS

Brethren (see p. 63)

Flesh (see p. 58)

Holy Living (see p. 170)

Holy Spirit/The Spirit (*pneuma*) (see p. 25)

The Law (Torah) (see p. 48)

Legalism (see p. 48)

Obedience to the Gospel/Obedience of Faith
A positive response and true respect for God's redemptive activity in Christ on behalf of humankind

---

SUMMARY

Freed from sin, the Christian is liberated from the demands of the law. Paul offers an example to help his readers better understand this spiritual freedom. He points out that at the time of death, all obligations to human law are canceled, such as a woman's obligations to her husband as long as he is alive. At his death, she is released from the marriage bond.

Similarly, the death of believers' old lives through faith in Christ releases them from the bond of legalistic servitude to the law and its condemnation. That bond is replaced by their bond to the risen Christ and the grace that He gives. United with Christ, they are to "bear fruit to God," which results in sanctified living by the help of the Holy Spirit dwelling in their hearts (7:4).

> **LIFE APPLICATION**
>
> Before his conversion, Paul had tried to use the law as a ladder to heaven, but when he became united to Christ by faith, his obligation to the law was completely severed. Christ frees us as believers from the law (legalism); that is, He frees us from the observance of a code of moral rules and regulations in order to earn salvation.
>
> When we live in Christian freedom, our lives have nothing to do with the pursuit of disobedience and sin, but have everything to do with our pursuit of "obedience to the faith" (Rom. 1:5). This kind of obedience is new and is independent of legalism. It is a gospel obedience, which means that we are finished with trying to earn our way to heaven through good works. We are free to give ourselves to Christ in obedience and service, with the assurance that God will guide and help us.

A DEFENSE OF THE LAW
ROMANS 7:7-25

In Romans 7:1-6, Paul has explained that believers are released from the bondage of the law when they are joined to Christ by faith. The law is the gift of God and is good, but the law is also an instrument of sin and death. **In verses 7-25, Paul continues his assessment of the law, following up on topics that he has discussed previously in his letter to the Romans: how God's good law can bring about His wrath (4:15) by arousing our sinful passions (7:5), motivating us to sin (5:20). Paul emphasizes once again that the fault lies not with the law, but with sin.**

Paul's Use of the Pronoun "I"

In this section of chapter 7, the personal pronoun appears about fifty times. Scholars have debated whether Paul is describing himself or using the pronoun to depict humankind in general. According to this latter view, the pronoun *I* includes Paul, but includes other humans, as well (cf. 3:7; 1 Cor. 13:1-3). If this is the meaning, in chapter 7 we have a description of an experience that Paul had and others had also. If we assume that Paul is strictly describing only himself, there still remains the debate as to whether or not he is referring to himself before his Damascus-road conversion or to himself after that experience. Verses 7-25 certainly sound autobiographical, reflecting Paul's own personal experience. Some argue that Paul's statements about his struggles refer to his life before conversion. On the other hand, those who argue for a post-conversion experience contend that his words are a true description of the struggle involved in the life of all believers. **There is room for differences of opinion, but my opinion is that Paul is describing himself *after* he met Christ and implied that the law continued to be an ongoing issue in his Christian life. The assumption is that no person is perfect, and that a Christian can continue to struggle with temptation, and be victorious.**

Paul did not see his experience as unique to himself. "Paul's autobiography is the biography of everyone" (Manson, 1967, 945). Paul states part of his autobiographical comments in the past tense (vv. 7-13) and part of them in the present tense (vv. 14-25). This shift in tenses may be due to Paul's identifying himself and humankind with Adam (vv. 7-13) and then showing the continuing effect of that relationship on the human race. **The struggle against sin is a present, reoccurring reality. No one is able by human strength to measure up to the demands of the law and gain victory. We must rely on the grace of God through Jesus Christ and the guidance and power given us by the Holy Spirit in order to live victoriously.**

THE STRENGTHS AND WEAKNESSES OF THE LAW
ROMANS 7:7-13

> ⁷ What shall we say then? Is the law sin? Certainly not! On the contrary, I would not have known sin except through the law. For I would not have known covetousness unless the law had said, "You shall not covet." ⁸ But sin, taking opportunity by the commandment,

> produced in me all manner of evil desire. For apart from the law sin was dead. ⁹ I was alive once without the law, but when the commandment came, sin revived and I died. ¹⁰ And the commandment, which was to bring life, I found to bring death. ¹¹ For sin, taking occasion by the commandment, deceived me, and by it killed me. ¹² Therefore the law is holy, and the commandment holy and just and good.
>
> ¹³ Has then what is good become death to me? Certainly not! But sin, that it might appear sin, was producing death in me through what is good, so that sin through the commandment might become exceedingly sinful.

Verses 1-6 of this chapter appear to have equated law and sin. Earlier Paul has said that the believer has died to sin. In verses 4 and 6, he has indicated that the believer has died to the law. **This connection between the law and sin raises a question: Is the Mosaic law sinful? Paul's immediate answer is "Certainly not!" (v. 7), but a more complete answer appears in verse 12, where he makes clear that the law is "holy and just and good."** Meanwhile, Paul points to the strengths and weaknesses of the Mosaic law. The Mosaic law is valuable, for it is the law that made him aware of what sin is and his need for God. **The law has a place in God's plan of salvation; it brings knowledge of sin, and yet it can also incite and intensify the desire to sin.**

Paul's Violation of the Law

Paul remembers the time that he was confident that he was keeping the commandments, because he considered himself *not* guilty of committing sins such as stealing, idolatry, or adultery. None of these commandments were his problem. **His stumbling block was the tenth commandment: "You shall not covet" (v. 7).** Paul thought that he was sinless; but when the true significance of the tenth commandment dawned on him, it exposed his sinfulness. Exodus 20:17 specifies a number of objects that should not be coveted: neighbor's house, wife, servants, and other property. Whatever the object may be, coveting is sinful, whether it is for power, position, fame, money, et cetera. At the heart of coveting is the exaltation of the ego. That was Adam's sin; he wanted to be like God. **Regardless of the object, coveting is the very essence of sin.**

The tenth commandment informed Paul of his spiritual condition, but **the root problem was not the commandment; it was sin.** As Paul explains, "Sin, taking opportunity by the commandment, produced in me all manner of evil desire. For apart from the law sin was dead" (v. 8). **Sin took the commandment and used it to motivate Paul to violate it, just as Satan took the commandment God gave Adam and used it to motivate Adam to rebel.** Sin had been dormant or dead, not that it did not exist but had been inactive until prompted by the commandment. Nevertheless, when the tenth commandment came, sin used it to motivate Paul to do the forbidden. The result: "Sin revived and I died" (v. 9).

The Purpose of the Law and Sin's Use of It

Sin sprang to life, and Paul lost his former sense of spiritual security, realizing that he was in the grips of sin. **The commandment that Paul thought would bring him life was used by sin to lead him to death (v. 10).** This descent into sin was no fault of the commandment. **God's purpose for the law is to define right and wrong, not to deliver us from sin. The law is weak since it gives us no help to overcome sin** and has no strength to deal with the deadly, God-opposing power of sin. **It can only judge us.**

As a judge, the law was intended to show us our need for God and to lead us to life (v. 10). The law is God's gift and is holy, just, and good (v. 12), because God is holy, just, and good. The law, therefore, is not evil, nor is it the same as sin. In verse 11, Paul says that **sin used the law as an instrument to deceive and kill him.** The term *deceived* implies that Paul received just the opposite of what he expected. Satan led Adam to think that he would be like God, but the deception of Satan led Adam to death. Likewise Paul expected life, but the deception of sin put him on the road to death. Simply stated, **sin can take the good and holy law of God and use it to bring about evil.**

As noble and worthwhile as our religious heritage (law) is, sin can take it and make it more important to us than God is. The temptation is to rely on what God has given us instead of on God. Anytime we give greater devotion to our religious tradition or heritage than to God, our religion has become an instrument of sin. The point is that sin can take the most valuable and loveliest things and use them to bring forth evil and death. Paul has placed the responsibility for evil where it belongs and has shown that God's law is holy and good, though it can be used by the deadly power of sin. The basic problem in living a holy, sanctified life is not the law but sin, which, in order to accomplish its ends, can work through God's gifts, the law, and other noble things such as generosity, loyalty, and patriotism. For example, sin as an active agent may incite a person to use a financial gift prompted by generosity to purchase drugs to feed an addiction, or in the case of Paul before his conversion, the power of sin prompted him to persecute Christians.

Sin is an oppressive power that causes evil behavior and wrongdoing. Sin can motivate people to use religion to try to surpass others and to use it as a means to gain personal superiority (see Gal. 1:14).

ROMANS 7:7-13

KEYWORDS

Covet
Excessive desire for something that rightfully belongs to another person. Such desire often lies in the realm of money, position, power, or honor.

Evil (see p. 80)

Holy (see p. 59)

The Law (*Torah*) (see p. 48)

Sin (see p. 48)

SUMMARY & LIFE APPLICATION

See under "ROMANS 7:14-25" pages 196-197.

INNER STRUGGLE
ROMANS 7:14-25

> 📖 ¹⁴ For we know that the law is spiritual, but I am carnal, sold under sin. ¹⁵ For what I am doing, I do not understand. For what I will to do, that I do not practice; but what I hate, that I do. ¹⁶ If, then, I do what I will not to do, I agree with the law that it is good. ¹⁷ But now, it is no longer I who do it, but sin that dwells in me.
>
> ¹⁸ For I know that in me (that is, in my flesh) nothing good dwells; for to will is present with me, but how to perform what is good I do not find. ¹⁹ For the good that I will to do, I do not do; but the evil I will not to do, that I practice. ²⁰ Now if I do what I will not to do, it is no longer I who do it, but sin that dwells in me.
>
> ²¹ I find then a law, that evil is present with me, the one who wills to do good. ²² For I delight in the law of God according to the inward man. ²³ But I see another law in my members, warring against the law of my mind, and bringing me into captivity to the law of sin which is in my members. ²⁴ O wretched man that I am! Who will deliver me from this body of death? ²⁵ I thank God—through Jesus Christ our Lord! So then, with the mind I myself serve the law of God, but with the flesh the law of sin.

Sin Working Through the Law

Now in verses 14-25, Paul reflects on the inner conflict that our reliance on the law rather than on God can generate. As someone has said, "A person can be a walking civil war." Paul addresses something very profound—the struggle between law and sin. Verse 13 has clearly stated the problem is not the law, but sin. **God's law is good, but it is sin that uses the good (the law) to lead people into bondage and despair. Even so, the law does provoke an inner struggle, which Paul proceeds to describe.** The struggle that he portrays certainly has application to many Christians as they pursue the path of holiness. F. F. Bruce seems to have stated it best:

> This unequal struggle against "the law of sin which is in my members" (as Paul calls it) has been the real experience of too many Christians for us to state confidently that Paul cannot be speaking autobiographically here—and in the present

tense too. Paul can entreat his friends "by the meekness and gentleness of Christ" (2 Cor. 10:1); but did this meekness and gentleness come to him naturally? There is good reason to believe that a man of his imperious zeal found it no easy matter to "crucify the flesh"—to win the victory over a hasty tongue, a premature judgment, resentment at any encroachment on the sphere of his apostolic service. The man who made it his daily business to discipline himself so as not to be disqualified in the contest of holiness, the man who pressed on to the goal of God's upward calling in Christ Jesus, knew that that "immortal guerdon" was to be run for "not without dust and heat." He was too constantly given to portraying the way of holiness as a race to be run, a battle to be fought, for us to imagine that victory came to him "sudden, in minute" (1963, 152-53).

As Paul sees it, there is no question about the goodness of the law—"the law is spiritual" (v. 14). **This gift of spiritual law from God reveals God's righteous demands and the sinfulness of humans, creating within people an internal conflict that cries out for resolution.**

Sin Working Through Human Weakness

Because of the weakness of human nature (the flesh), the law can never sanctify the Christian. In contrast to the spiritual law, Paul describes himself as "carnal" (*sarkinos*, unspiritual) and "sold under sin," which he did not intend for us to take as unique to himself (v. 14). **Humans live in bodies, which have appetites and desires, which though not evil in themselves, are easily perverted by sin.** Many people have failed to resist temptation and have fallen into the captivity of ungodly living.

Sin is a tyrant, but this fact does not free humans from responsibility. The way is open for Christians to live holy, sanctified lives. Yet there is something in Christians that Paul calls "the flesh" (*he sarx*, the carnal element, v. 18) that seeks to be independent of God. **Sin working through the flesh is always ready to take over and bring devastating results.**

Biblical Personalities Who Struggled With Sin
- **King David.** David yielded to lust and brought bitter tragedy to his family (2 Sam. 11:1ff.).

- **King Ahab.** The words "sold under sin" perhaps indicate that Paul never forgot what the Old Testament writer said about Ahab—he "sold [himself] to do evil in the sight of the Lord" (1 Kings 21:20). The power to which Ahab sold himself was stronger than he was. It was a power that was determined to control, sidetrack, and destroy him in any way possible.
- **The Apostle Paul.** From his own personal experience, Paul knew that sin could dominate every aspect of life (Rom. 7:14-25). Early in his life he had been gripped by pride and religion that cut him off from God and made him an enemy of Christ. After he became a Christian, his struggle against sin continued. In verses 14-25, the present tense is used to indicate this recurring pattern of struggle with sin. Here, Paul gives us a summary of his experience, and we do well to take to heart the description of his struggle.

    Paul found that sin can reign over all aspects of life. Even though his intentions were good and pure, he made a striking discovery that indwelling sin, operating through the flesh (human emotions, desires, and passions dominated by the power of sin), could create intense inner conflict. **His shocking encounter with sin's power made him aware that his devotion to God's law was used by sin to achieve its goals. Sin turned the law into a kind of slavery.** The law in itself is good and holy (v. 16), but **Paul kept the rules for the wrong reasons—not out of love for God but out of hope of receiving a reward for himself. Serious religious devotion can be taken captive by pride and self-righteousness. Sin knows no boundaries; sin can take the best of human endeavors and corrupt them.**

Temptation in the Life of Christians

In the course of Paul's inner conflict, his inner self (mind or reason) recognized the ideals of God's law (v. 22), but he found himself in "captivity to the law of sin" (v. 23). This *law of sin* (ongoing principle, reliable phenomenon, like the law of gravity) was of the same origin as the sin that won its battle with Adam and makes war against all Christians today, seeking to bring them under its captivity. **Like many souls who have accepted Christ as Savior, soon after conversion the Roman Christians discovered that the carnal mind was not dead, and they began to experience great spiritual trials and temptations.** With a profound sense of despair, they could have joined Paul and said, "O wretched man that I am! Who will deliver me from this body of death?" (v. 24). **God has broken the power of sin through the cross of His Son; however, believers are not perfect. Their sanctification has begun, but sanctification is a dynamic and ongoing process.** And so, the question is, "Who will deliver me [us] from this body of death?" Like Paul, we want to be delivered from sin and its consequences. **Sin is a deadly power that pulls us in different directions and creates in us conflict.** "The body of death" may be another name for "the body of sin" (6:6). It is because of sin that the human body is under the dominion of death. Sin uses the body as an instrument of death (5:12ff.). Paul knows the answer to his question: "I thank God—through Jesus Christ our Lord!" (7:25). **Christ and Christ alone is the answer to the sin problem. Complete deliverance will come only from God through Christ and His cross.**

What is striking about the end of chapter 7 is that Paul simply restates the human dilemma: "So then, with the mind I myself serve the law of God, but with the flesh the law of sin" (v. 25). Such a closing statement prepares Paul to offer a solution in the next chapter. The above verse identifies the Father through His Son as the deliverer. Chapter 8, then, with its glorious details shifts to the Holy Spirit. The empowering of the Spirit as described by Paul in chapter 8 reminds us that each person of the Holy Trinity is involved in our salvation and sanctification.

Human Weaknesses

Now let us sum up what Paul teaches us in 7:14-25. In chapter 6, Paul has described the position in which Christians find themselves in this world. **The Coming Age has dawned in the life, death, and resurrection of Christ, but the Old Age of sin and death remains. The two ages now overlap, and Christians experience tension because of living in two worlds. Though saved, Christians still struggle against the Old Age of temptation and sin, while they eagerly look forward to the redemption of their bodies (8:23).** Romans 7:7-25 is a vivid description of the struggle. From these verses, we can derive three Christian insights.

First, the basic problem for Christians continues to be sin. Sin, in distorting our motives, can use good and noble endeavors in order to accomplish its evil ends. Paul, for example, found that the power of sin made the law, God's gift, an instrument of death in his life. Sin, because of its evil use of the law, had the power to create conflict within Paul. Thus, he stated, "For the good that I will to do, I do not do; but the evil I will not to do, that I practice" (v. 19).

The law does not profess to have a remedy for a soul that is divided against itself. However, had it not been for the law, Paul would not have known what sin was (v. 7). Even so, sin was able to work through Paul's knowledge of the law, making his condition of internal conflict between good and evil worse. **The law is powerless to deal with the power of sin, even in the life of believers. Our temptation is to rely on laws, moral accomplishments, or religion; but our reliance on anything except God fails to solve the sin problem.** Romans 8 tells us much about that.

Second, knowledge in itself is inadequate to make a person good. The law distinguishes right from wrong and defines what God's will is. Knowledge fails to enable us to do good. **Knowing God's will prompts us to desire to do what He commands, but the law is powerless to help us. The fault is not in the law, but the problem is that God's own law is used by sin.** In the hands of sin, the law makes us prisoners of war—the good that we want to do, evil comes out of it. Knowledge is insufficient; we need something more. Romans 8 tells us that we are not left to ourselves.

Third, the human will is weak. What is decisive is not our intentions, but our actions. **A Christian may resolve to do good, but intending to do good and doing it are two different things.** Often our good, religious intentions fail to prevail. Our intentions may be sincere, but our performance may come far short of what we desire. **Touched by sin, we often fail to measure up to the ideal.** Our failures then result in inner conflict between reason and wrong desires.

In Romans 8, Paul tells us that "life in the Spirit" will make a difference in our being able to live the life that God has called us to—a life of sanctification.

ROMANS 7:14-25

KEYWORDS

Body of Sin/Body of Death (see p. 170)

Carnal (*sarkinos*, unspiritual)
A worldly orientation which manifests itself in opposition to God

Evil (see p. 80)

Flesh (see p. 58)

Holy (see p. 59)

The Law (*Torah*) (see p. 48)

Temptation
The enticement to sin—that is, to do what is contrary to the perfect will of God

SUMMARY

The holiness of the law and the extreme hideousness of sin come into focus in our struggle to live the Christian life. Christians are caught between two worlds: the world of sin and death, and the world of the Spirit and life. As a result of both worlds' trying to gain control, Christians experience a struggle in doing the will of God. The law offers them no power to live the Christian life. It defines sin, and in the process of defining it, the law may also provoke sin.

The law is not sin; it is holy, righteous, and good. But sin perverts the law, deceiving people to think that by the fulfillment of its requirements they will be in right standing with God. Sin takes advantage of God's holy law and leads individuals to keep rules for the wrong reasons—not because they love God but to win for themselves rewards. Sin can corrupt the noblest of human endeavors and use them for evil. No one can deliver himself from the oppressive power of sin. Jesus, and Jesus alone, is the answer.

LIFE APPLICATION

The law is good. But if we let sin work through the law, it will motivate us to strive to do God's will for the wrong reasons. Sin's use of the law makes the law incite all kinds of evil desires, such as coveting our neighbor's blessings, even our neighbor's spouse or home. It may also create the desire to gain control of God by obligating Him for blessings through good works and religion.

This perversion of the law is a work of sin, but the law is spiritual and demands obedience offered by our heart if we truly love God. Motives are very important. What we do may be good and promote the kingdom of God, but may be done out of the wrong motives and from the wrong relationship with God. The desire for such things as food, praise, sex, and possessions are normal, but overindulgence is sinful. The best of our human endeavors and desires can be corrupted by sin, but our constant reliance on God's grace ensures that we will please Him.

LIFE IN THE SPIRIT
ROMANS 8:1-11

¹ There is therefore now no condemnation to those who are in Christ Jesus, who do not walk according to the flesh, but according to the Spirit. ² For the law of the Spirit of life in Christ Jesus has made me free from the law of sin and death. ³ For what the law could not do in that it was weak through the flesh, God did by sending His own Son in the likeness of sinful flesh, on account of sin: He condemned sin in the flesh, ⁴ that the righteous requirement of the law might be fulfilled in us who do not walk according to the flesh but according to the Spirit. ⁵ For those who live according to the flesh set their minds on the things of the flesh, but those who live according to the Spirit, the things of the Spirit. ⁶ For to be carnally minded is death, but to be spiritually minded is life and peace. ⁷ Because the carnal mind is enmity against God; for it is not subject to the law of God, nor indeed can be. ⁸ So then, those who are in the flesh cannot please God.

> ⁹ But you are not in the flesh but in the Spirit, if indeed the Spirit of God dwells in you. Now if anyone does not have the Spirit of Christ, he is not His. ¹⁰ And if Christ is in you, the body is dead because of sin, but the Spirit is life because of righteousness.
>
> ¹¹ But if the Spirit of Him who raised Jesus from the dead dwells in you, He who raised Christ from the dead will also give life to your mortal bodies through His Spirit who dwells in you.

The magnificence of chapter 8 can hardly be overemphasized. With a strong emphasis on the victory of the Christian, **Paul continues to focus on sanctification,** as he did in chapters 6 and 7. **Chapter 6 stressed freedom from sin; chapter 7, freedom from law; and now chapter 8 stresses freedom from death.** Up to this point, Paul has mentioned the Holy Spirit only three times: "the Spirit of holiness" (1:4), the Spirit's pouring God's love into our hearts (5:5), and serving God "in the newness of the Spirit" (7:6). What Paul has said about holy living up to now leaves the doctrine of sanctification incomplete. **In chapter 8, Paul brings this doctrine to completion by focusing on the sanctifying work of the Holy Spirit in the life of the believer. It is interesting how Paul groups important concepts in chapter 8: (1) flesh/Spirit; (2) law of sin and death/law of the Spirit and life; (3) condemnation/fulfillment of righteous requirement; (4) carnally minded/spiritually minded; and (5) death/life and peace.**

Paul, in a grand way, tells about the boundless possibilities and realities of life in the Spirit. In chapter 8, there are about twenty references to the Spirit, distinguishing this chapter from the rest of Romans. More is said about the Holy Spirit in this chapter than in any other chapter in all of Paul's letters. Chapter 8 has been called "the Pentecost of Romans." **The liberating message is that God never intended for us to live the Christian life by our own efforts and in our own strength. God's provision for Christian living is in the person of the Holy Spirit, who is the Spirit of life, liberty, and hope. Through His ministry in our hearts, the Holy Spirit applies to us the saving benefits that**

Christ secured for us through His life, death, and resurrection. What Christ has won for us positionally, the Holy Spirit works in us practically and helps us to do God's will.

Victory in Christ

Romans 8:1-11 is closely related to 7:1-6. Chapter 7 ends in agony and a cry of desperation, but chapter 8 strikes the note of victory, beginning with the words "no condemnation" and ending with the words "we are more than conquerors through Him who loved us" (v. 37). For those who are alive in Christ, there is no condemnation. Verses 1 and 2 restate the doctrine of justification, using "in Christ" instead of "faith." **Christians are free because God sees them in Christ. The power of the law to condemn them has been decisively broken. Sin has been dealt with at Calvary, and through the indwelling presence of the Holy Spirit, the Christian can live victoriously.** Some manuscripts add "who do not walk according to the flesh, but according to the Spirit" to bring verse 1 in line with verse 4.

Two Laws

In mentioning the victory that Christians have, Paul refers to two laws: "the law of the Spirit of life" and "the law of sin and death" (v. 2). Most likely the word *law* in these phrases refers to a religious way of life and is broader than the rules and regulations of the Mosaic law.

- **"Law of Sin and Death."** Paul's intent in using the phrase "law of sin and death" is not to describe the law as being sin, nor to indicate that the law causes death. **The phrase "law of sin and death" indicates the manner in which sin uses the law to deceive people into thinking that salvation can be earned.** Attempting to follow rules instead of pursuing a relationship with God, ultimately leads to death, separation from God.

- **"Law of the Spirit of Life."** In contrast with "the law [religion] of sin and death," stands "the law of the Spirit of life" (v. 2). The Spirit's power and presence are life-giving in contrast to sin, which uses the law to bring death. **The**

Spirit frees us from the oppressive power of sin and from the grip of death. He actually provides the power and strength for us to do what we should, thus breaking the terrible cycle of sin (7:7ff). The Spirit does not work apart from Christ. As we are united to Christ by faith, the Spirit's presence is realized in our hearts. **Obedience to God can only be achieved by the life-giving power of the Spirit.**

In 8:2 Paul expresses his view of the Christian life: **(1) Through life in Jesus Christ, the Christian is set free from legalism**—the human attempt to please God and to try to earn salvation. **(2) Through our being united with Christ in faith and with the Holy Spirit in control, we are also set free from our old nature** (Bruce, 1963, 160).

God's Grace and the Law

Living the Christian life requires us to be free from the law and open to God's grace. How can we live such a life? Can we simply make up our minds to change our ways and become holy? Paul knew that was impossible and explains why: "For what the law could not do in that it was weak through the flesh, God did by sending His own Son" (v. 3). The law was all right—in fact, holy, just, and good (7:12). Paul has been careful to show that the law is good. The law "was weak through the flesh" because the law was dealing with fallen human beings who did not have the strength to resist temptation and to obey it. Many people have tried to make use of the law as a way of salvation, which it is not and can never be. **The law can guide us to Christ (Gal. 3:24) and guide our walk with God, if we rely on the Holy Spirit to teach us the intent of the law and help us apply it. Without God's grace and the Spirit's guidance, sin and the flesh will use the law to draw us away from God.**

Role of Christ in the Defeat of Sin

Sin and the flesh do not have the final word. **God sent His Son to do what the law could not do.** Human beings in all their efforts, even in their religions, had failed to climb up to God, so

God came down to them. **The whole purpose of God's sending His Son to the earth was to enter the domain of "the flesh" and to share our humanity.** Christ was not sinful. He was sinless. Although He "knew no sin," He became sin for us (2 Cor. 5:21).

Paul chose his words with care—"in the likeness of sinful flesh" (Rom. 8:3). He avoided two doctrinal errors: (1) the docetic teaching which denies that Christ had a physical body, and (2) the erroneous view that Christ had "sinful flesh." **Jesus Christ fully identified Himself with humankind, except that He was without sin.** When faced with temptation, Christ made the opposite choice that Adam did. Christ's coming as a man was only in the likeness of sinful flesh, not in the choices that He made. He came into the rough and tumble of human life and overcame every temptation to sin, unlike Adam. **God's Son came as a man; and during His sojourn on the earth, He broke the power of sin and remained untainted by it.** His precise purpose for coming was "on account of sin"; that is, to deal with the entire problem of sin by offering Himself as a sacrifice for it (Rom. 8:3).

Through His sinless life and His death on the cross, Jesus Christ as the God-man condemned sin in the sense of overthrowing or dethroning its power. His cross, as well as His life on the earth, left no doubt about God's attitude toward sin. **Christ's mission was not to condemn, but to save sinners.** He came "in the flesh" (human nature), and in this world where sin reigns, He condemned sin. **Like Christ, the Mosaic law condemned sin, but it could not overthrow the power of sin. The good news is that in the Final Judgment, God will ultimately and finally destroy sin.** In fact, judgment of sin has already begun with Christ's life and death, which initiated the overthrow of sin and will be God's grounds for abolishing all evil at the end of the present world order.

Our Freedom From Sin

For those in Christ, the power of sin is already broken (6:6-14), and they are free from condemnation (8:1). Evidently in these verses, Paul is thinking about more than simply the forgiveness for sins of the past, but also of a real liberation from the present power of sin. In other words, **we are delivered from the penalty of sin, as well as from sin's power.** Thus, sanctification is involved in believers' being free of condemnation. **God has made provision for the Christian to fulfill the requirements of the law through the help of the Holy Spirit (v. 4).** Only the Spirit can enable us to live according to the righteousness which the law requires. Our freedom in Christ does not remove the law, but it does make possible our doing what the law calls for in its commandments. Those of us who do God's will "do not walk according to the flesh, but according to the Spirit" (vv. 1, 4). Yielding to the Spirit allows God to give light and guidance so that we "may prove what is that good and acceptable and perfect will of God" (12:2).

Life in the Flesh vs. Life in the Spirit

Now Paul turns to describing two ways of living: *life according to the flesh* **(sinful human nature) and** *life according to the Spirit* **(vv. 5-8).** These lifestyles stand in sharp contrast, but Paul has already noted these two ways of living in terms of life and death or freedom and slavery. **The *flesh-life* produces slavery and death, and the *Spirit-life* produces freedom and life.** A comparison of Romans 8 and Galatians 5:13-25 discloses that these two passages have much in common. The terms *Spirit* and *flesh* are prominent in both. Of course, *Spirit* refers to the third person of the Godhead, but *flesh* is a term that is often misunderstood as referring merely to the physical body. Occasionally, Paul uses *flesh* to indicate the physical meaning, but he also uses it for other meanings. It may be helpful to review the three basic ways Paul uses the word *flesh* (*sarx*).

The Term "Flesh"

First, Paul uses *flesh* to refer to the physical body. He speaks of the flesh being circumcised (Rom. 2:28). God gave circumcision as an external sign and seal of the covenant (Gen. 17:11). Circumcision in relation to *the flesh* refers to a physical mark that Israelite men received. In contexts such as these, *flesh* simply means the physical body.

Second, Paul uses *flesh* to express lineage. He says that Abraham was the forefather of the Jewish people "according to the flesh" (Rom. 4:1) and that Jesus was the son of David "according to the flesh" (1:3). The Jews were descendants of Abraham, and Jesus from His physical side was a descendant of Israel's greatest king, David. In 9:3, Paul refers to non-Christian Jews as his "kinsmen according to the flesh" (KJV).

Third, Paul also uses *flesh* to refer to the tendency in human nature toward sin. Paul uses the term in this way in Romans 8:4-5, 8-9, 13. In these verses, *flesh* refers to the dark side of human nature and indicates a willing instrument of sin. Used in this manner, **we might describe *flesh* as being a vehicle of sinful desires,** or we might think of *flesh* as being similar to a beachhead from which an army might launch its military operations. In the human personality, the flesh provides the beachhead from which sin works to achieve its ends. **In theological writings, *flesh* is often referred to as *sinful human nature*.**

The sins of the flesh (sins of human nature) are various expressions of evil and include more than sexual sins. Paul gives a list of the sins of the flesh in Galatians 5:19- 21. Sexual sins are included, but also mentioned are such sins as hatred, strife, envy, murder, idolatry, witchcraft, and divisions. Many of the sins of the flesh destroy community.

Two Different Mind-sets

The two ways of life—life in the flesh and life in the Spirit—involve opposite mind-sets, different orientations in life. A mind-set does more than direct our thoughts. It is a commitment of our will and emotions to achieve a desired goal. **Life is open to the Christian to live either according to the flesh or according to the Spirit.** The flesh-life seeks fulfillment in itself and focuses on this world, which results in living apart from God. The Spirit-life focuses on the things of God (Rom. 8:5) and points us to life and purpose in God. **The contrast is not between life as a being of flesh and life as a spiritual being, but life lived according to the flesh and life lived according to the Spirit.** Christ lived in the flesh (in a human body); however, He did not live according to the flesh (according to human sinful nature), because He was conceived by the Holy Spirit, which made Him holy.

A life lived according to the flesh is dominated by sinful interests and concerns. Individuals who live such a life have deliberately set their minds on the lower things in life. The flesh-life may be controlled by harmful passions or ambitions. **It is out of touch with the Spirit—adrift from God, inconsistent, on and off with God, taking moral holidays.** For the Christian, the carnal mind is definitely a regression to being at "enmity against God" (v. 7). Such a lifestyle can lead only to death, separation from God (v. 6). **In these verses, Paul gives a strong warning to Christians. To live according to the flesh is spiritual suicide; it brings death now as well as at the end: "For the wages of sin is death" (6:23).** The flesh-life entombs us in death at the present moment as well as at the end. Those who are controlled by the flesh are already dead, even though they are going through the motions of living. They think that they have found life. God has another point of view. He pronounces them dead in trespasses and sin. They are dead even while they live (1 Tim. 5:6).

Just the opposite, **life according to the Spirit creates a new mind-set that trusts in God and submits to His will. It is important what a person thinks, for "to be spiritually minded is life and peace" (Rom. 8:6).** Here *peace* refers to the inner tranquillity of heart and mind, resulting from having peace with God (5:1). *Peace* is the opposite of *misery*, which results from being hostile to God. On the other hand, *life* is the contrast to *death*. **The person who has Christ and is led by the Spirit is on the journey of eternal life.** This is the miracle of grace—believers are no longer death-bound but are life-bound as they live according to the Spirit. To live otherwise, they fail to please God (8:8).

Paul has compared the two ways of life. The placing of his ideas opposite each other may bring them more in focus:

The Two Ways of Life	
Mind-Set According to the Spirit	Mind-Set According to the Flesh
On the desires of the Spirit	On the desires of the flesh

Is life	Leads to death
Is fellowship with God	Is hostility toward God
Is spiritual	Is unspiritual
Controlled by the Spirit	Controlled by sin

Sin works through human desires, emotions, and passions. **As Christians, we will have to deal with the presence of sin the rest of our days on the earth, but our approach to sin is from the place of freedom rather than bondage. "Where the Spirit of the Lord is, there is liberty" (2 Cor. 3:17).** The Spirit has freed us to please God and to live for His glory (Rom. 8:8).

The Holy Spirit and New Life

The apostle goes on to give a definition of a Christian. The decisive factor is that **a believer is "not in the flesh"—not controlled by the world of the flesh—but is indwelt by the Spirit of God (v. 9).** As soon as we come to Christ, the Holy Spirit takes up His residence in our hearts. The word *dwell* comes from the Greek for *house* (*oikos*). **At the moment of conversion, the Spirit takes up His abode with us and makes our hearts His dwelling place.** He moves in as an occupant, as we might move into a new home. Our hearts become His home. The indwelling presence of the Holy Spirit is foundational to the Christian life. Indeed, without the Spirit, we cannot be Christians. From the outset of the Christian life, the Spirit is our "Guest of honor." **Our relationship with Christ depends on the Spirit, and without the Spirit we do not belong to Christ.**

Observations About Our New Life

The presence of the Holy Spirit in believers testifies to the new life they enjoy. Yet Paul does not want to leave the impression that believers will necessarily avoid physical death. The apostle makes two observations which are related to this idea of new life (v. 10):

First, "If Christ is in you, the body is dead because of sin." Paul is referring to death of the physical, mortal body. We know this because immediately in the next verse, he refers to a resurrection of the body (v. 11), indicating that he has in mind experiencing a physical death. **Christians have not been fully redeemed, because creation has not yet been glorified; they still die a physical death, even though they have Christ dwelling in them.** The body dies because the law of death is ever present in the physical body. **Physical death invaded the human race through the transgression of Adam (5:12).** As a result, we begin to die the day we are born.

Second, "the Spirit is life because of righteousness." The living and quickening Spirit is the pledge of eternal life. **Life comes to believers through Christ's righteousness**—His whole life of perfect obedience (5:18). **The obedience of Christ is the means through which the Spirit annuls death and imparts eternal life.**

The Holy Spirit makes the future certain for believers (8:11). Our hope of resurrection rests on Christ's resurrection. In us dwells the same Spirit who raised Jesus from the dead (1:4). The divine Agent in Christ's resurrection will also be the same Agent who will raise us to eternal life. **The resurrection of Christ, a fact of history, was dependent on the Holy Spirit; our resurrection, a fact of the end of history, will depend on the Holy Spirit.** Therefore, Paul infers from a present reality (the indwelling presence of the Holy Spirit in believers) an End-Time reality (the resurrection of all believers). Some of the Corinthian Christians did not believe in a bodily resurrection. In other words, the body is laid aside and only the immortal soul survives (1 Cor. 15). But in writing later from Corinth, Paul affirms in this letter to the Romans that even the mortal body will be raised. Furthermore, **Paul specifies that life will be given to our "mortal bodies" (8:11). These very bodies that are now subject to death will be brought to life in the resurrection. Eternal life includes the whole person, not just the human spirit.**

Paul's Terminology When Referring to the Spirit

Before continuing, let me note one matter that may be confusing. Paul uses a number of expressions such as *the Spirit*, *Spirit of God*, *Spirit of Christ* (v. 9), *Spirit of life* (v. 10), and *Spirit of Him* (v. 11). These expressions have almost the same meaning. The use of these terms does not suggest there are no differences among the three persons of the Godhead, but it does indicate that each is fully God and they have an intimate relationship with one another.

ROMANS 8:1-11

KEYWORDS

Carnal (*sarkinos*, unspiritual) (see p. 196)

Condemnation (see p. 155)

Death (see p. 170)

Docetism
Teaching that denied that Christ had a physical body and erroneously proposed that Christ was sinful

Final Judgment (see p. 84)

Flesh (see p. 58)

Freedom from Sin (see p. 170)

Holy Spirit/The Spirit (*pneuma*) (see p. 25)

Jesus Christ (see p. 59)

Life/Eternal Life (see p. 159)

Sin (see p. 48)

SUMMARY

Christians enjoy a new life in Christ through the indwelling presence of the Holy Spirit. By faith they are united to Christ and are delivered from being condemned to death by the law (8:1; cf. 5:1). There is no condemnation for believers because God has sent His Son to bear the condemnation by becoming a sin offering.

The Holy Spirit imparts to believers spiritual life, and they are to live in the power of the Spirit, depending on His resources for victory over the flesh (sinful human nature) that draws them away from God. Through the Spirit, the moral requirements of the law can be fulfilled in the new life believers live. This new life requires us to avoid setting our minds on the things of the unbelieving world and setting our minds on the things of the Spirit. The former ends in death (separation from God) and the latter ends in life and peace.

Two paths are open: "life according to the flesh" and "life according to the Spirit" (8:1,4). Those who are controlled by the flesh live to please themselves, and those who are controlled by the Spirit live to please God. In fact, only those who have the Holy Spirit living within them are Christians, and the same Spirit who was instrumental in Jesus' resurrection will also raise believers from the dead.

LIFE APPLICATION

As believers we are "in Christ," clothed in His righteousness, and we have received the life-giving Spirit. Through the blessed Holy Spirit, we have been led to surrender our hearts to the Savior. From that moment of our surrender, the Spirit has indwelt us and has provided us power to resist temptation and live the Christian life.

Living a Christlike life can only be accomplished by walking according to the guidance of the Holy Spirit. If we fail to be led by the Holy Spirit, we will displease God. A life lived without relying on the Holy Spirit may not necessarily be devoted to unseemly pleasures and sins, but may simply be a life that pursues happiness and self-fulfillment apart from Christ. The spiritual consequences of a life without the healing of Christ are fatal. In contrast, being led by the Spirit ensures that our heart is focused on Christ and our mind is set daily on the things of God such as Bible study, prayer, and worship.

Are you walking according to the Spirit or according to the flesh? You cannot do both at the same time. If you do not have the Spirit, you are not a Christian. If you do have the Spirit, then Christ is alive within you. In walking in and relying on the Spirit daily, you will live a life that is focused on the things of God—a life that has eternal value.

PRIVILEGES FOR GOD'S CHILDREN
ROMANS 8:12-17

[12] Therefore, brethren, we are debtors—not to the flesh, to live according to the flesh. [13] For if you live according to the flesh you will die; but if by the Spirit you put to death the deeds of the body, you will live. [14] For as many as are led by the Spirit of God, these are sons of God. [15] For you did not receive the spirit of bondage again to fear, but you received the Spirit of adoption by whom we cry out, "Abba, Father." [16] The Spirit Himself bears witness with our spirit that we are children of God, [17] and if children, then heirs—heirs of God and joint heirs with Christ, if indeed we suffer with Him, that we may also be glorified together.

God's Plan for Sanctification

The primary obligation of Christians is to pursue the spiritual way of life (Manson, 1962, 964). **Their obligation is to yield in obedience and service to the Holy Spirit.** Christians are no longer debtors to the flesh (v. 12). In Christ, their debt recorded in God's book and created by their disobedience has been forgiven because through Christ, they have died to sin (6:1-14). **The fleshly, unspiritual life no longer has any claim on them. Now they are debt-free in God's book.**

With this freedom in mind, Paul warns the Christians against returning to their former lives, for if they do so, they will die (8:13). Death does not occur from committing a single sin, but **spiritual death will be the result if Christians habitually sin, living as though they are unsaved.** By persisting in unbelief and sin, they will return to a state of spiritual death, of being separated from God.

Being Led by the Spirit

On the contrary, if believers live according to the Spirit's leading, they will devote themselves to doing the will of God. In other words, they will "put to death the deeds of the body" (v. 13), renouncing their former sinful ways of living. **As a result of being indwelt and led by the Spirit, believers can live holy, sanctified lives.** Paul expresses it this way: "For as many as are led by the Spirit of God, these are sons of God" (v. 14). In Pentecostal and Charismatic groups, this is a popular teaching. The verb *are led* (*agontai*, present tense), can be translated "being led constantly and habitually," and the noun *sons* (without the article *the*) emphasizes character. **To bring out the full significance of this verse, translated directly from the Greek, verse 14 reads, "For as many as are being led constantly and habitually by the Spirit of God, these have the character of the sons [and daughters] of God."** Being led by the Spirit daily and hourly puts out of operation sinful desires and behaviors. **The Spirit's guidance, a parallel to walking "in the Spirit" (Gal. 5:16), assures that we can reflect through our character that we truly are God's sons and daughters.**

So again, Paul reminds us of a Pentecostal theme (being led by the Spirit) and a sanctification theme (living daily a righteous life). **The purpose of the Spirit's guiding us can be summed up in one word: *holiness*. God has called us to holiness and the Spirit directs us to holiness, which means being in communion with God and living as Christians should, and is a fulfillment of the Old Testament mandate, "Be holy, for I am holy" (1 Peter 1:16; cf. Lev. 11:44-45; 19:2; 20:7).**

Safe and Secure as God's Adopted Children

Spirit-led believers have not received a "spirit of bondage again to fear"; that is, the Holy Spirit does not intend for believers to be slaves who live in fear of judgment as if they were under the law (v. 15). Even though earlier Paul has said that believers become slaves of God, he does not want them to think they have to be in constant fear of God as many slaves were of their masters. The Spirit is not a spirit of bondage and, in fact, brings a profound sense of freedom. So quite to the contrary, **the Spirit is "the Spirit of adoption" who assures believers they are members of God's family with all the rights and privileges that children of God have (v. 15).** Previously Paul has used a number of grace words to describe salvation in Christ: *justification*, *reconciliation*, and *redemption*. These terms are closely related in meaning, but each emphasizes a different aspect of our relationship with God. Now Paul adds another grace word—*adoption* (*huiothesia*). The context of this word is family relationship, and the literal translation is "placing as a son." In Roman culture, *adoption* was a legal term, indicating a person's familial status or standing. Any son who was adopted had full family rights. Likewise in God's family, both adopted daughters and sons have full family rights.

Christ is the only begotten Son by nature, but believers are sons and daughters of God by adoption. **As members of God's adopted family, believers have a new status, a new standing.** Regeneration (the new birth) describes our spiritual transformation when we are brought into God's family. **The Holy Spirit joins us to the family of God.**

Adoption in Roman Culture

In the first century, the Jews did not practice adoption (Barrett, 1991, 163). No doubt, Paul has in mind the Roman procedure of adoption. The Christians in Rome would have been well acquainted with the Roman way of adopting children. **A brief review of adoption practices among the Romans may help us to understand Paul's concept of our adoption into the family of God (Deissmann, 1957, 167-178).**

- **The father's power was absolute.** The son was always a possession of the father as long as his father lived. This made adoption difficult because it involved passing the absolute control of a son from one person to another.
- **The adoption ceremony was carried out in symbolism.** Twice the father symbolically sold his son and bought him back, but the third time he sold the son he did not buy him back. The natural father's power was broken and the son came under the authority of another.
- **The adoption ceremony was carried out in the presence of seven witnesses.** If a man who adopted a son died and there was a dispute over whether the son was a legal heir, one of the witnesses could affirm that the adoption was authentic.
- **In Roman law, the adopted son's past was wiped out.** He was regarded as a new person who entered a new life. Legally, he had no obligation to his past debtors. According to the law, his debts were forgiven and his debtors had no claims against him.

Benefits of Adoption Into God's Family

What are the blessings of being members of God's family? What are the rights and privileges of addressing God as Father and seeing other believers as our brothers and sisters? What are the benefits of being members of "the household of faith" (Gal. 6:10)—"the household of God" (Eph. 2:19)? The blessings are amazing, reminding us of the multifaceted grace of God (1 Peter 4:10). The benefits of being God's children are incalculable.

- **Believers are under the authority of a new father (Rom. 8:15-17).** The old authorities—the dominion of sin and the powers of darkness—have been broken (6:14). Now as sons and daughters of God, believers live under a new authority. God has adopted them through Christ (6:1-14) and has initiated them into a new relationship with Himself. As true children of God, believers stand under the authority and the care of their heavenly Father, with Jesus as their brother.
- **Believers are children in a new family (8:16; cf. John 3:3-7).** They have full family rights, including the right of access to the Father (Rom. 8:15) and sharing with Christ in the divine inheritance (v. 17). Indeed, they are objects of divine love (5:5-8) and are brothers and sisters in Christ. Believers' membership in the divine family is made possible through the love of God the Father and His work through God the Son. First John 3:1 makes clear their new status: "Take a hard and fast look at the amazing love the Father has given to us, that we are called the children of God; and that is precisely what we are" (my translation). Our status in our new family should be an incentive to holy living to reflect the values and goals of God's family.
- **Believers have begun new lives (vv. 13-14).** Their old lives of sin and death have no rights over them. They have died to the old life of sin and evil, and they have the help of the Holy Spirit to overcome their inclinations and temptations to return to their old lives. By His matchless grace, God has wiped out their debts of sin, and their old lives no longer have any rightful claims over them. They have a new life in God's family.
- **The Holy Spirit gives believers assurance that they are God's children (v. 16).** To say it another way, the Holy Spirit touches the spirit of believers and testifies to them that they are sons and daughters of God, working in them as an inner voice in their minds. Believers do not have to wait until they get to heaven to know who they are. The Spirit not only joins believers to God's family, but He

God's Plan for Sanctification

also continually reminds them of their relationship with the Holy One.
- **The Spirit enables believers to address God as "Abba, Father"** (v. 15; cf. Mark 14:36; Gal. 4:6). In the early church, the cry *Abba* came from the lips of Christians in public worship or in private prayer. When individuals become believers, the Holy Spirit begins to teach them to cry "Father" (in Aramaic "*Abba*")—a term used by small children for their earthly father. *Abba* was a word of great intimacy, used in the family circle. The Jews did not normally use *Abba* in addressing God. They thought it would be irreverent to use such a familiar expression to speak to the Almighty King. Jesus, however, used the intimate *Abba* in approaching God in His time of distress (March 14:36). Likewise, in times of need, believers by the Spirit can cry "*Abba*, Father." This is their privilege as sons and daughters of God, and the Holy Spirit encourages them to cry out for help.
- **Believers are "heirs of God and joint heirs with Christ" (Rom. 8:17).** Their ultimate blessing lies in the future. They have already experienced a measure of their inheritance, but there is more to come. Even though they are now children of God, the full realization of their adoption into God's family will not be complete until one day in the future. When that day arrives, the completion of believers' adoption will include "redemption of [their] body" (v. 23). This new body will more adequately manifest their true character as "glory" because they are God's children. The resurrection of believers' bodies will bring to completion the ministry of the Spirit in adoption.

However, there is a condition believers must meet if they are to receive their full inheritance and share with Christ in His glory; they must share in His suffering (v. 17). Contrary to some popular teaching today, knowing Christ and having strong faith do not lift one above suffering. As a Christian, Paul suffered for the sake of Christ. Suffering was not abnormal in his life (2 Cor. 1:4-5; Phil. 3:10). Christians under the cross of Jesus can find meaning and comfort in suffering in this life, especially since such suffering assures them of their divine inheritance and sharing with Christ in His glory (Rom. 8:28ff.).

Responsibilities of Adoption

As adopted children, we have the responsibility of reflecting who our Father is. With the blessings of God come the responsibilities of living the Christian life, particularly since one day we will make our home with Him forever. To claim the presence of the Holy Spirit and to live contrary to our new nature is to deceive ourselves. The Spirit of adoption is the same Person whom Paul described earlier as "the Spirit of holiness" (1:4). As our guide and power to live the Christian life, the Spirit brings to our attention our spiritual roots and reminds us who we are. **The knowledge of who we are in Christ should have a great bearing on what we think and do.**

ROMANS 8:12-17

KEYWORDS

Adoption
Literally means "placed as a son or daughter." Adoption is an act of grace by God, which bestows on believers the status and blessings of membership in His family. This gracious blessing of adoption is received by all who trust in Jesus as their Savior and prepares them to live a new life in the family of God.

Brethren (see p. 63)

Children of God/Sons of God
The status and resulting privileges of sons and daughters received by people who have been adopted into the family of God.

Communion
A common sharing or participation in something. *Communion with God/Communion of the Saints*—In the present life, communion finds its highest realization in the fellowship of believers with the triune God. This blessed communion with God and with one another will reach its fulfillment through eternal fellowship in unity together with the triune God.

Flesh (see p. 58)

Glory (see p. 86)

Holy Spirit/The Spirit (*pneuma*) (see p. 25)

> **SUMMARY**
>
> Christians are to rely on the Spirit's guidance and strength to withstand harmful carnal tendencies of human nature. As followers of Christ and people of the Spirit, believers have no obligation to the flesh, but if they choose to live according to sinful tendencies, the ultimate result will be separation from God. The key to living a holy, sanctified life is being led by the Holy Spirit daily.
>
> Spirit-led believers have received the Spirit of adoption—the Holy Spirit—who grants them the incalculable rights and privileges as members of God's family. Under the constant guidance of the Spirit, believers can be assured of their status as God's sons and daughters, and can experience blessings from their Father.

> **LIFE APPLICATION**
>
> As Christians, we are to yield to the guidance of the Holy Spirit. No longer are we to live only for ourselves. As changed people, we are under a new obligation. Living as slaves to our human weaknesses (flesh) will only lead to spiritual death. Instead, we are to take up the cross of Christ. In so doing, we die to our old ways, which have been harmful to us and others and have separated us from God. In our new life, we yield to the guidance of the Holy Spirit.
>
> Attentiveness and submission to the Spirit are what make walking in the Spirit possible. As believers in Christ, we have a new manager, the Holy Spirit, who chooses the path we are to walk and who gives us the joyous assurance that we are now the children of God.

THE GLORIOUS HOPE
ROMANS 8:18-30

The effects of Adam's sin was cosmic in proportion. **God's redemption work through Christ will not only deliver us as Adam's descendants from the sin that was introduced on earth by Adam, but will also reach and deliver the whole creation from its deadly results.** The ultimate glory that believers will receive one day will be so stupendous that our present suffering and troubles, perplexing and unsolved problems, and unanswered questions and frustrations will appear to be so insignificant. **We look forward to the day when our bodies will be transformed and to the day of the coming of the new heaven and earth.** All our dreams will be surpassed. **As we wait, the Scriptures and the Holy Spirit give us hope by offering us a glimpse of what is about to come.**

THE SPIRIT OF HOPE
ROMANS 8:18-25

> [18] For I consider that the sufferings of this present time are not worthy to be compared with the glory which shall be revealed in us. [19] For the earnest expectation of the creation eagerly waits for the revealing of the sons of God. [20] For the creation was subjected to futility, not willingly, but because of Him who subjected it in hope; [21] because the creation itself also will be delivered from the bondage of corruption into the glorious liberty of the children of God. [22] For we know that the whole creation groans and labors with birth pangs together until now. [23] Not only that, but we also who have the firstfruits of the Spirit, even we ourselves groan within ourselves, eagerly waiting for the adoption, the redemption of our body. [24] For we were saved in this hope, but hope that is seen is not hope; for why does one still hope for what he sees? [25] But if we hope for what we do not see, we eagerly wait for it with perseverance.

Hope for Release From Sin and Suffering

One day, the turmoil of sin and death that Paul discussed in Romans 5:12 will be over, for the God of hope will free the world of all death and suffering. The Holy Spirit is the Spirit of hope, for He assures the faithful of the glorious future that awaits them. His indwelling presence gives us not only assurance of one day being completely released from the power of sin, but also being completely released from sin's presence.

The Christian life on this earth is a life of struggle and suffering. Paul himself was a frequent sufferer for the sake of the gospel. He tells us that our present suffering—our sorrow, adversities, unsolved problems, and turmoil—are nothing in comparison to the glory and victory to come (8:18). In 2 Corinthians, Paul also expresses the same conviction: "For our light and momentary troubles are achieving for us an eternal glory that far outweighs them all" (4:17 NIV). Suffering touches our lives as it did the Lord and His apostles. To share in Christ's glory requires us to share in His suffering. **The magnitude of the coming glory will more than compensate us for our suffering and troubles.**

Hope for All Creation

In addition to believers' looking forward to the future glory and to the new heaven and earth (Rev. 21:1—22:5), **the whole creation, both animate and inanimate, "eagerly waits for the revealing of the sons of God" (Rom. 8:19).** The picture is that of one eagerly looking for something with head turned toward heaven. J. B. Phillips graphically expresses this thought in his translation: "The whole creation is on tiptoe to see the wonderful sight of the sons of God coming into their own" (8:19).

Creation's Bondage

In verses 20-21, Paul indicates that the earth was "subjected to futility" and was in "bondage of corruption." Though Paul does not mention Adam, he has in mind here the sin of the first man. **Through the introduction of sin into the world, the God-created natural order was disturbed, starting a cascade of consequences. The entire natural order suffered because of Adam's disobedience, giving way to a world of futility, suffering, and hardship.** Paul personalizes creation and says that it longs to be free from decay and corruption (v. 21). Creation, however, was subjected to the consequences of Adam's sin "in hope" (v. 20). **Creation eagerly looks forward to the "revealing of the sons of God," and it awaits this healing event "in hope" (vv. 19-20).**

It may not be clear now who the true believers are, but the glorious return of Christ to the earth will remove all doubt as to their identity. **The future of creation is intimately tied to the future of believers.** The redemption of the natural order from futility and sin's vanity will accompany the consummation of believers' salvation. Thus, creation itself will share with believers' ultimate salvation and, until that time, shares in the hope of that day. **All nature shared in the fall of Adam, and Paul says that all nature will share in redemption and restoration.**

What is the reason for the hopeful waiting? The object of creation's hope is "the revealing of the sons of God" at which time creation will be set free from the bondage of change and decay. **"We [Christians] know" (v. 22) and can see the discord and decay in the natural world, and that it has been groaning in agony until now.** This groaning, which is similar to a woman's groans during the process of giving birth (Mark 13), is a sign of creation's bondage and hope. So as Paul suggests, creation utters concerted groans under the burden and consequence of sin.

God has not left creation without hope—hope that it will be returned to the service of God's glory (Arrington, 1977a, 1-20). Until that time we live in a fallen world. We come into the world with a disposition to sin, and as a result, there is a downward pull in our heart toward evil. Both good and bad come to us in this world. This is why at this time even believers suffer and die. There is a downward pull from without as well as from within. When we finally enter into full and complete salvation, God will set us free from any tendency to sin and from the oppressive evils of the world in which we live.

Christians' Role in Creation's Hope

The final redemption of believers and creation is in the hands of God. The only hope, therefore, is the Maker and Redeemer of both humankind and the natural order of the world. **In the meantime, the natural world is yearning, along with believers, for the transformation of the whole world. God's people must not turn inward and become increasingly engrossed in their own lives. Christians must recognize that the natural world is destined by God for redemption, and their responsibility is to care for His creation and to guard against carelessness and greed that pollute and destroy natural resources and create survival problems for future generations.** As we look around us, we can see and hear the groans of creation for the Coming Age and for deliverance of oppressive powers of decay and death. **Through the power of the Holy Spirit, we are to be healing agents of God in the world until the day of its full redemption,**

embracing and fulfilling Adam's mandate to "tend and keep" the garden (Gen. 2:15).

Hope From the Firstfruits of Our Redemption

What God has planned for believers and creation will far exceed our dreams. Like the natural world, we long for the Future Age. **In the present, we have already received "the firstfruits of the Spirit" (Rom. 8:23). The term *firstfruits* (*aparche*) may also be translated "first installment" or "down payment" and refers to the first part of a harvest that has been gathered. In verse 23, the word *firstfruits* indicates the indwelling presence of the Holy Spirit in our hearts.** The Spirit has *not yet* completed His work in us, but His initial work in salvation whets our appetite for more. **Now we enjoy the *firstfruits* or *foretaste* of the blessedness of eternal life.** Yet, we yearn for the full harvest, that is, for the completion of our adoption into God's family and the resurrection of our bodies. At the moment of our faith in Christ, we were adopted into the family of God. **Nonetheless, we still wait for the full benefits of God's children, particularly the redemption of our bodies.**

Another way to express this truth is, **"We were saved in this hope" (v. 24).** The statement "we were saved" appreciates what we have already experienced, and we as believers can speak about having been saved. **There is more to what we have already received, and so Paul adds, "in this hope" (*te elpidi*), which looks forward to the full realization of what Christ has done for us. We have been saved, but not completely—*already/not yet*—saved *in hope.*** To put our salvation in proper focus: **We are already "saved" (Eph. 2:8), but still in a sense we are "being saved" (1 Cor. 1:18), yet we are not fully saved until Christ returns (Matt. 10:22f.).**

The presence of the Holy Spirit does not exempt us from suffering, but it does sustain our hope and expectation for final salvation. **Hope will affect the way we live and will turn faith into perseverance (Rom. 8:25). The cultivation of holy perseverance enables us to remain loyal to Christ and to endure in the midst of suffering and tribulation for His sake.** What the Spirit has already done gives us the firstfruits of glory and hope of the full harvest yet to come. Through this type of hope from the Spirit, **we put no confidence in ourselves, but look beyond ourselves to God's fulfillment of His plan of salvation.**

ROMANS 8:18-25

KEYWORDS

Already/Not Yet Doctrine (see p. 47)

Creation (see p. 74)

Firstfruit
A term that describes the products of human labor, especially those that come from the soil at the beginning of the harvest, such as grain, flour, and fruit. The term is used figuratively in the New Testament. The first converts to Christ were described as *firstfruits* (Rom. 16:5; 1 Cor. 16:15), and the works of the Spirit are also described as *firstfruits* (Rom. 8:23).

Hope (see p. 137)

Perseverance (see p. 144)

SUMMARY & LIFE APPLICATION

See under "ROMANS 8:28-30" pages 229-230.

THE SPIRIT OF PRAYER
ROMANS 8:26-27

> 26 Likewise the Spirit also helps in our weaknesses. For we do not know what we should pray for as we ought, but the Spirit Himself makes intercession for us with groanings which cannot be uttered. 27 Now He who searches the hearts knows what the mind of the Spirit is, because He makes intercession for the saints according to the will of God.

In addition to being the firstfruits of our salvation, there is another way that the Holy Spirit gives hope and endurance. **While we wait for the return of Jesus Christ, the Holy Spirit gives us hope by interceding on our behalf. We need His intercessory ministry because of our weakness—"We do not know what we should pray for as we ought" (v. 26).** In verse 26, the word *weaknesses* refers particularly to our need of help with prayer. Our need for help grows out of our limitation of not knowing for what to pray. **The suffering of creation parallels the suffering of believers. Creation groans, we groan, and the Spirit groans.** Human needs can be so great at times; we may be stretched to the breaking point and not know for what to pray.

The Spirit's Groanings on Our Behalf

On those occasions when we do not know what to pray, the Holy Spirit moves in our prayer lives and "makes intercession for us with groanings which cannot be uttered" (v. 26). **In the New Testament, the noun *groaning* (*stenagmos*) occurs only here in Romans 8:26 and in Acts 7:34. It simply means "sigh" or "groan."** In Acts 7:34, *groaning* refers to the misery of the Israelites under the oppression of the Egyptians (cf. Ex. 2:24). **In Romans 8:26, the phrase "cannot be uttered" translates *alaletos*, which means "unutterable," suggesting that the groanings cannot be expressed in normal words.** In both passages, the term *groanings* is used to describe deep feelings expressed to God, indicating the intensity and sincerity of individuals. **When believers are weary, suffering, and unable to express their desires and burdens in words, the Holy Spirit comes to their aid, praying for them.** Such prayer was, and is, the work of the Holy Spirit who understands believers' desires and troubles.

Speaking in tongues may have been included in the groans too deep for words. Paul does not specify the content of the groans. A number of distinguished New Testament scholars, who are not Pentecostals or Charismatics by persuasion, think that Paul could have had in mind speaking in tongues (Käsemann, 1980, 240f.; Barrett, 1991, 168; Bruce, 1963, 175). Particularly, Käsemann has made a persuasive case that the term *groanings*, as it is used in verse 26, refers to believers speaking in tongues in early Christian worship. This view of the prayer ministry of the Spirit agrees with Paul's statement in 1 Corinthians 14:14, where he says, "If I pray in a tongue, my spirit prays, but my understanding is unfruitful." This verse has a striking similarity to "groanings which cannot be uttered" in human language (Rom. 8:26). Yet we are uncertain whether the word *groanings* refers exclusively or partly to tongues. **The evidence certainly points in the direction of tongues, but responsible interpretation requires us to use restraint and not identify the *groanings* exclusively as tongues.** Nevertheless, in praying in tongues, Paul says that his "mind is unfruitful" (NIV), which seems to be an excellent parallel to Romans 8:26.

Our Need for Empowerment

The Spirit's groanings on behalf of us is an example of the helping ministry of the Holy Spirit, indicating that **we need the Holy Spirit to empower our prayers.** When burdens and aspirations well up in our hearts and cannot be expressed in normal words, the Holy Spirit intercedes on our behalf with groans too deep for human words. **The Spirit makes up what is lacking in our prayers and gives intensity and sincerity to them.**

The Spirit's Praying According to God's Will

As believers we can have the assurance that the Spirit prays "according to the will of God" (v. 27). He always prays the right and needed way because He knows the future, He knows what is best for us, and He knows what God's will is. A vivid way to express the Spirit's intercessory ministry is that He has seen further down the path that each of us is traveling and knows where it will take us. As a result, **the Spirit knows all about our circumstances and God's will for us.** His prayers and guidance are always on the mark.

Moreover, we may not understand what the Spirit is praying, but God the Father certainly does. **"He [God] who searches the hearts knows what the mind of the Spirit is" (v. 27).** The expression "He who searches the hearts" indicates that God understands our innermost desires and needs. The reason is that He knows "the mind of the Spirit." **The Spirit dwells in the depth of our being, praying for us and making known to the Father our burdens and aspirations. His intercessory ministry sustains our hope in the midst of suffering and troubles so that we do not despair and fall into unbelief.**

Jesus Christ and the Holy Spirit as Intercessors

As believers, we also have a second intercessor, Jesus Christ (8:34; Heb. 7:25). Paul identifies both the Holy Spirit and Christ as our intercessors. Paul's comments indicate that there is a difference of location between the two. **The Holy Spirit dwells in the depths of our souls and prays for us, but Christ intercedes for us at the right hand of God in heaven. The Spirit's ministry of prayer occurs within our hearts, whereas Christ's intercessory ministry takes place in heaven.** Christ and the Spirit are not rival intercessors. **Both assure us of acceptance and fellowship with God.** What great assurance to know we have in our hearts an intercessor who always prays "according to the will of God" and an intercessor who sits triumphantly at the right hand of God praying on our behalf!

ROMANS 8:26-27

KEYWORDS

Groan
Holy Spirit—The Spirit *groans* on our behalf, clearly indicating the Spirit's prayerful intercession on behalf of believers. Believers do not pray alone, for the Spirit comes alongside and helps them. (Rom. 8:26—27).

Holy Spirit / The Spirit (see p. 25)

Intercession by the Holy Spirit
The Spirit lends assistance for believers in their weakness in prayer. Believers are capable of praying, but may not know how to pray for exact needs. Vital is the Spirit's prayerful intercession for them.

Pray / Prayer (see p. 61)

Saints (*hagioi*) (see p. 59)

> **Speaking in Tongues**
> Speaking in a language unknown by the speaker. In the Book of Acts, this manifestation is prompted by the Holy Spirit when a believer is filled with or baptized in the Spirit (2:4; 10:44-46; 19:1-7).

> **SUMMARY & LIFE APPLICATION**
> See under "ROMANS 8:28-30" page 229-230.

THE SAVING ACTIVITY OF GOD
ROMANS 8:28-30

> 📖 ²⁸ And we know that all things work together for good to those who love God, to those who are the called according to His purpose. ²⁹ For whom He foreknew, He also predestined to be conformed to the image of His Son, that He might be the firstborn among many brethren. ³⁰ Moreover whom He predestined, these He also called; whom He called, these He also justified; and whom He justified, these He also glorified.
>
> [*emphases added*]

God's Plan for Good

For believers, their ultimate peace and assurance is knowing that their salvation is in the hands of God. The apostle Paul explains God's purpose and plan and provides us with a sweeping picture of salvation. **From beginning to end, salvation is the work of God. God's divine purpose in salvation is to conform us completely to the likeness of Jesus Christ and to produce a large family** that shares in the benefits of Christ's resurrection, experiencing glory with Christ (v. 17).

According to this divine plan, we can have the assurance that "all things are working together for good to those who love God" (see v. 28). This promise is expressed from God's point of view. Our view is more limited, because we are unable to see the complete picture. The struggles and hardships of life can appear to be very negative and contrary to the fulfillment of God's plan.

However, when life is seen from the broadest perspective—God's perspective—it is evident that everything that happens to Christians in this life will work together for their good. **This working together for good does not happen because of our love for God, but because of God's purpose for our lives.** The working together of all things for good has a more firm basis than believers' love. Only here and in two other passages does Paul speak of believers' love for God (1 Cor. 2:9; 8:3). Normally, Paul reserves the word *love* to refer to God's love, not believers' love. Their love may vary from hot to cold, or strong to weak. There is a more firm basis indicated by the phrase "who are the called according His purpose" (Rom. 8:28). The true basis is not found in believers, but in God's purpose. By supplying *God* as the subject of the first phrase, "[God causes] all things [to] work together for good to those who love God," we understand that God will always bring about good, no matter what the circumstances are. **All things we experience are not good; sin and its results certainly are not good. But we can have the assurance that God is causing all the adverse circumstances and difficult experiences to work together (*sunergei*, present tense) habitually and constantly for good.** In fact, God coordinates all things in our lives. The cross of our Lord is a marvelous example. God was present and at work then, and He is today. **All that God does is directed toward the ultimate goal of good, which is to conform us to "the image of His Son" (v. 29).** With this kind of assurance and God's grace, we are able to maintain our sanity in the face of tragedy and suffering.

God's Plan of Salvation

In verses 29-30, we have a broad view of salvation. Here justification, sanctification, and glorification all come together. These verses have been a theological battleground. Do Paul's words here lead us to think that specific individuals' salvation has been predetermined by God? Or do they simply teach that God has provided a way of salvation for all people? **From the beginning, God's purpose has been to save men and women. Out of His great love, God took the initiative and put His**

predetermined plan of salvation in place, causing all things to work for good to those who love Him.

Giving a broad view of God's plan, Paul identifies a fivefold sequence: *foreknowledge→predestination→calling→justification→glorification.*

- **Foreknowledge and Predestination**

    The terms *foreknowledge* and *predestination* indicate that salvation reaches back into eternity in the past. Paul gives no definition or explanation of the two terms. ***Foreknowledge** and **predestination** probably mean the same thing and indicate that God predetermined in eternity to provide salvation for all humankind, so God preordained a process.*

- **Calling and Justification**

    In addition to the divine provision, the process of salvation continues with *calling* and *justification.* **The word *calling* emphasizes the importance of preaching the gospel and the inward drawing of the Holy Spirit to salvation** (cf. Gal. 1:6; Col. 3:15; 1 Thess. 1:6-10). ***Justification*** **results from responding to the call by faith in Christ.**

- **Glorification**

    The process of salvation reaches its climax in final *glorification*, but the continuation of salvation throughout the life of believers requires a human response. Final glorification means we will receive the final form of the gift of glory (a new body on the order of Christ's glorified body) at the Second Coming of Christ. Believers are now in process with radiant righteousness, being conformed to the image of Christ (2 Cor. 3:18); but when Christ returns, believers will be glorified in a more definitive form.

Our Part in the Salvation Process

Salvation depends on God's call through the gospel and our response. **The provision for salvation is completely a work of God, but we have a part to play in it by responding, then living it (Phil. 2:12-13). The Christian life is a Divine-human partnership.** Paul teaches that it is always through the response of faith that a person is saved or, to use Paul's language, *justified*. **There is no initial salvation without faith, and without continuing in faith, there is no future glorification.** Whatever else "from faith to faith" means, it certainly means that the condition for a right relationship with God from start to finish is faith (Rom. 1:17). **A basic teaching of the New Testament is that we get into salvation by faith and we stay in it by faith.** Just as Paul says, "you stand by faith" (11:20). Faith is the proper response to God's saving grace. Nowhere does Paul deny that a believer who persists in the practice of sin and returns to a life of unbelief cannot abandon the family of God and be cut off from salvation. There is no absolute assurance of final glorification apart from the obedience of faith (cf. 1 Cor. 10:12), for "if you live according to the flesh you will die" (Rom. 8:13).

God's Plan to Conform Us to Christ

According to Paul, God's predetermined plan of salvation is compatible with one's freedom to accept or to reject Christ. **The ultimate purpose of God's plan, according to Paul, is to conform believers to the image of His Son (v. 29).** This plan emphasizes believers' sanctification and their growing in likeness to Christ as they pattern their lives after the life that Christ lived while on this earth. In God's family, Christ is "the firstborn," the Elder Brother who is the model for the divine family (v. 29). All the other members are to be conformed to Him. So it follows that all God's children are to be like Christ, the preeminent One in the family of God. At the present time, we are being conformed to His death (Phil. 3:10). This conforming is a matter of character formation and sanctification, a growing conformity to Him in obedience (Rom. 12:1-2), and calls for us to be empowered and led by the Spirit. **Our conformity to Christ will be completed in the future at our resurrection.** On that occasion, we will receive bodies like Christ's glorious body (Phil. 3:21). Thus, Paul stresses that **God's plan calls for us to be Christlike by continuing in hope of final salvation and by living holy lives. One day when our salvation is complete, we will be in the perfect likeness of Christ.**

God's Plan for Glorification

Glorification will be the final outcome of our having suffered with Christ (Rom. 8:17) and having lived according to the Spirit rather than according to the flesh (vv. 12-13). There is no absolute guarantee of glorification without enduring in our faith to the end. Among the Christians in Rome were those who were tempted to lose hope because of present suffering, but Paul's words in Romans 8:18-25 underscore the importance of God's people being Christlike by maintaining hope for final salvation and by holy living. **When the final result is glorification, it will not be credited to human merit, only to God's grace. Glorification is not a question of salvation through works, but it is a consequence of our devotion to our relationship with God, expressed through sanctified living—our living out our salvation. Such a life requires the help of the Holy Spirit.** God has a grand design in everything, even in the setbacks and adversities of life. Some greater good will come from everything that happens. Glorification will be the final outworking of God's plan for believers who give their lives to God and accept and use the gifts that He gives them.

ROMANS 8:28-30

KEYWORDS

Called by God
Called to salvation (*kaleo*)—God's invitation to participate in the blessings of salvation

Foreknowledge
The foresight of an all-knowing God. Scripture presents God as knowing all things past, present, and future. It also describes humans as having freedom and moral responsibility. No attempt is made in the Bible to explain this mystery.

Glorification of Humans
The resurrection state of the believer. To some extent the believer shares now in glory (2 Cor. 3:18; 4:6). In the future state, the believer will have a new body on the order of Christ's glorified body (Phil. 3:21).

Justification (*dikaiosune*) (see p. 48)

Predestination
Divine foreordination of the future. Scripture leaves this doctrine undeveloped and does not teach that God determines the actions of an individual in advance. Both *foreknowledge* and *predestination* refer to the fact that God has an eternal plan which He has carried out by making provision for the salvation of all who receive Christ.

SUMMARY

When Christ returns to the earth, believers will share with Him in His glory, and their present hardships and sufferings will not compare with the heavenly bliss and happiness that they will experience then. The magnitude of this glorious future is indicated by the deliverance of the whole creation from the curse of sin, which was the result of Adam's disobedience. As all creation shared in Adam's fall (Gen. 3:17-18), so all the natural order will share in redemption and restoration on the Last Day.

Like creation itself, believers yearn for that day, and the indwelling presence of the Spirit gives them hope. On that day, the salvation of believers that has already begun will be completed by the resurrection of their bodies.

In the meantime, we do not always know for what to pray. The Holy Spirit comes to our aid and intercedes on our behalf "with groanings which cannot be uttered" (Rom. 8:26). Such prayer may very well include speaking in tongues. God always answers the requests of the Spirit in the affirmative because He always prays in accord with the will of God.

Being in control, God weaves together all things so that they work together for the good of His children. God has always done good. Starting before creation, He made provision for the salvation of all humankind. God's purpose has been for all who receive salvation to be conformed to the likeness of His Son, emphasizing the importance of spiritual maturation and holy living (sanctification). God's grand design will ultimately work itself out in our glorification.

LIFE APPLICATION

From eternity, God set out to produce a large family, each member of which would have the likeness and traits of His Son. To bring about His plan, God provided through His Son, Jesus Christ, for the salvation of all who believe in Him. This divine plan includes God's foreknowledge, justification, and ultimate glorification of anyone who comes to faith in His Son and lives a life devoted to serving Him.

For members of His family, God causes all things to work together toward good. Even the setbacks, troubles, and disappointments that we experience, the Almighty works them out finally for our benefit.

> We may not understand how this can be true, but we can have the assurance that the final outcome will be good. Ultimately, we will be glorified, given a new body and a new life with the Lord in eternity. God will bring everything to a good and proper conclusion.

ASSURANCE OF SALVATION
ROMANS 8:31-39

> 📖 ³¹ What then shall we say to these things? If God is for us, who can be against us? ³² He who did not spare His own Son, but delivered Him up for us all, how shall He not with Him also freely give us all things? ³³ Who shall bring a charge against God's elect? It is God who justifies. ³⁴ Who is he who condemns? It is Christ who died, and furthermore is also risen, who is even at the right hand of God, who also makes intercession for us. ³⁵ Who shall separate us from the love of Christ? Shall tribulation, or distress, or persecution, or famine, or nakedness, or peril, or sword? ³⁶ As it is written:
>
> > "For Your sake we are killed all day long;
> > We are accounted as sheep for the slaughter."
>
> ³⁷ Yet in all these things we are more than conquerors through Him who loved us. ³⁸ For I am persuaded that neither death nor life, nor angels nor principalities nor powers, nor things present nor things to come, ³⁹ nor height nor depth, nor any other created thing, shall be able to separate us from the love of God which is in Christ Jesus our Lord.

In the preceding verses, Paul has traced the order of salvation (*ordo salutis*)—the process by which God carries out His plan for saving men and women. Now in the passage before us (8:31-39), **Paul explains why what he has previously said in this letter should give believers comfort and confidence. These verses mark the end of a major section of the letter to the Romans and are the climax of Paul's description of God's saving activity.** In them, he sums up the superiority of Christ. Paul's thoughts reach magnificent heights as he celebrates God's power to sustain believers in the face of trials and troubles and to withstand powers that work against God's purpose. The triumphant celebration of God's power offers an answer to suffering and despair.

Assurance Because of the Cross

As is rather characteristic in Romans, **Paul raises a question: "What then shall we say . . . ? If God is for us, who can be against us?"** (v. 31; cf. 4:1; 6:1; 7:7; 9:14, 30). We could reply, "My neighbor, my employer, the tax-collector, or Satan." Any of these could be "against us." We may have enemies and face much opposition. **The real issue here is, Who can be against us** *effectively* **in regard to our salvation? The answer is, "No one."** So Paul's question is not, "Are we on God's side?" but, "Is God on our side?" He is, but that does not mean He is on our side in every human issue. As far as our salvation is concerned, He is on our side. **Not even Satan can successfully be "against us" (8:31). Our certainty that God is on our side and that Satan cannot defeat God is found in the cross (v. 32; Col. 2:15).**

As a reminder that our salvation and victory rest on the cross, Paul says that God "did not spare His own Son, but delivered Him up for us all" (Rom. 8:32). These are the same words God spoke to Abraham when the patriarch offered his son Isaac. God said to Abraham, "You . . . have not withheld your . . . only son" (Gen. 22:16; cf. LXX, the Greek translation of the Old Testament). Since all Jews would have been taught about Abraham's having offered his son to God, Paul uses Abraham's sacrificial action as an example of what God did through the cross.

God spared nothing, not even His Son, in undertaking to save men and women. The cross assures us of God's love and His willingness to "freely give us all things" (Rom. 8:32). How broad is the scope of "all things"? Does the phrase "all things" allude to only our salvation, or does it encompass our sovereignty over the entire creation? Jesus promised that the meek will inherit the earth (Matt. 5:5). **Previously, Paul has said that believers will inherit the world (Rom. 4:13); and in emphasizing essentially the same truth, he adds that we will be "joint heirs with Christ" (8:17). Yet our reign with Christ is not confined only to the future, but is realized even now in measure.** In 1 Corinthians 3:21-23,

Paul indicates that the world, life, death, and "things present or things to come" already belong to us. We come into our rule only through suffering with Christ (Rom. 8:17-19), and we exercise our responsibilities of leadership in love, not by military power or exploitation. As believers, our sovereignty, which gives us no claim to superiority, is occurring in the present, but will not be fully realized until Christ returns. When He returns, we will rule over the world under the lordship of Christ. **All that we enjoy in this life and in the life to come are and will be a result of God's grace.**

We have a paradox: God will give us all good things, yet we may suffer persecution and famine (v. 35). Nevertheless, after giving His Son, God does not shield us from all suffering. Any suffering that we must endure is small in comparison to God's giving His Son to carry the sins of the whole world. **The cross gives us profound assurance of God's love and blessings in whatever we face and have to endure.**

Indeed, the cross leaves no doubt that God is "for us" (v. 31). **The cross gives believers confidence that when they finally stand before God, He will be favorable toward them (v. 34).** In considering the Final Judgment, the theme of condemnation reappears (v. 1). Believers have been acquitted by the God of heaven. Who then has the right to condemn them? Satan has no right to bring any charge against God's people. They have already been declared "not guilty" by heaven's tribunal. **God's decision of justification is final, and Satan will not be able to overturn God's verdict regarding our sins.** When we stand before God in the Final Judgment, no one can condemn us.

On that day, we can have unshakable confidence because of what God has done in Christ. We can be confident that Christ is and will be our advocate, continuing to plead our cause. **Thinking of God as being "for us" (v. 31) prompts Paul to say four things about Christ (v. 34): (1) He died; (2) He was raised from the dead; (3) He is at the right hand of God; (4) He makes intercession for us.** Biblical scholars tell us that a creed of the early church, similar to today's *The Apostles' Creed*, included these statements about Jesus Christ:

[He] was crucified, dead, and buried.
The third day He rose from the dead.
He ascended into heaven,
and sitteth at the right hand of God, the Father Almighty.

Paul's first three statements concerning Christ are similar to this creed of the early church. It is striking, however, that his last statement is not "from thence He shall come to judge the quick and the dead," but "who also makes intercession for us" (v. 34). Likely, Paul intentionally made the substitution and is saying that one may think of Christ as being at the right hand of God as Judge, but it is not true that He is there to judge. Christ is there not to condemn us, but to plead our case before the Father and to ensure our acceptance (Barclay, 1955, 122-23).

Our Savior died, arose from the dead, and ascended into heaven triumphantly. Now He sits in the position of great authority and *intercedes* (Greek: present tense—indicating ongoing work) for us. **Since Christ is our High Priest (Heb. 5:5-11; 7:20-28) and Advocate in heaven, we do not need to represent and defend ourselves. What great assurance we have! God the Father has justified us and forgiven us of our sins, and both the Holy Spirit (Rom. 8:26-27) and Christ pray for us. The triune God—Father, Son, and Holy Spirit—are on our side.**

Christ's Superiority Over Troubles

The rest of this passage develops Paul's message of assurance with the help of two lists: the sevenfold summary of Paul's hardships (v. 35) and the tenfold list of powers that threaten God's purpose (vv. 38-39). In between the lists, Paul uses an example from the Old Testament as confirmation (Ps. 44:22). The love of Christ (Rom. 8:35) should not be seen as different from the love of God (v. 39; 5:5, 8). Using the most sweeping language, **Paul says that all experiences, all time, all adversaries, and all worlds cannot separate us from divine love, whether it is described as "the love of Christ" or as "the love of God" (vv. 35, 39).** The way to look at the relationship between God and Christ is in light of the last words of verse 39—"the love of God which is in Christ Jesus our Lord."

In verse 35, Paul gives us a list of troubles that cannot separate us from divine love. These troubles come out of Paul's own experience and were typical experiences of early Christians:

Troubles That Will Not Separate Us From God	
Tribulation (*thlipsis*)	Pressure, which results from disastrous circumstances and tragedies
Distress (*stenochoria*)	The narrowing of space, indicating that the heart is compressed or depressed by painful and stressful experiences
Persecution (*diogmos*)	Implies being pursued and persecuted by one's enemies
Famine (*limos*)	Most likely refers to hunger, which was common for early Christians, for missionaries traveling from place to place
Nakedness (*gumnotes*)	Deprivation due to persecution and Christians' having to flee for their lives
Peril (*kindunos*)	Suggests suffering inflicted by others and living in grave danger
Sword (*machaira*)	A symbol of capital punishment. When pursued and caught, the sword implies the final outcome.

Once again Paul has come back to the thought of suffering. He himself had experienced all these troubles and hazards except the last one, the sword. A reading of the Book of Acts and his letters discloses that from time to time his life was in grave danger. Later Paul expresses his confidence that the sword would not separate him from Christ's love (Phil. 1:20-23). All that he has endured for the sake of the gospel has been incapable of disrupting his relationship with Christ. Paul reminds his readers that God's faithful people are always exposed to suffering because of their beliefs. For biblical support, in Rom. 8:36 he cites Psalm 44:22: "For Your sake we are killed all day long; we are accounted as sheep for the slaughter." **It is because of their trust in Christ that God's people have faced adversaries and troubles. Suffering has been the sure mark that they belong to God.** The love of Christ has separated them from the world.

As they have lived under the cross, they have been stigmatized and persecuted by the enemies of the cross. Their enemies have pursued them "all day long," from morning to night, and they have been "sheep for the slaughter."

Troubles and suffering, however, are not merely experiences that Christians must endure, but they are occasions for victory. As Paul looks back on his trials and troubles for the sake of Christ, He says, "Yet in all these things we are more than conquerors through Him who loved us" (Rom. 8:37). Believers are "more than conquerors"; that is, they have victory that is more than just victory. It is overwhelming victory. Such great confidence in being victorious is expressed by one who had more than his share of tribulations and adversaries (vv. 17-18; 2 Cor. 1:8-11; 11:22-33). **In the midst of adversity and sorrow, and demonic threats from all sides, Christians in hope of resurrection can have "the joy of conquerors"** (Käsemann, 1980, 251). In light of the resurrection, why should Christians sink into despair?

Christ's Superiority Over Other Powers

Having completed the summary of his own personal hardships, Paul goes on to identify ten powers over which Christ has superiority. Verses 38-39 form a single sentence in which the apostle answers in a magnificent way the question in verse 35, "Who shall separate us from the love of Christ?" **The apostle enumerates the powers that may threaten believers' relationship with Christ, but cannot prevail:**

Powers That Will Not Separate Us From God	
Death nor life	Neither events in this life nor physical death can separate us from God.
Supernatural powers	Neither good or bad angels, nor evil principalities and powers can separate us from Christ.
Things present nor Things to come	Nothing in our present life or in eternity can separate us from God.
Height nor depth	Nothing in the cosmos—that is, the expanses of space can separate us from God.

- **Neither death nor life can separate us from God.** The list of Paul's personal hardships ends with death (sword), and the second list begins with death. For those who choose to live apart from God, death means separation from God. Physical death is the final attack of sin, but for those in Christ, physical death cannot destroy their relationship with Him. To live with Christ is to die with Him. Thus death does not separate us from Christ, but brings us into the very presence of Christ (Phil. 1:23).
- **Supernatural powers cannot separate us from God.** In life on this earth and in the afterlife, neither good nor bad angels, nor evil principalities and powers have the power to abolish our relationship with God. Demonic powers do wage war against God's people (Eph. 6:10ff.) and have some power in this life, but these powers were mortally wounded by the cross and cannot prevail spiritually against the followers of Christ (Col. 2:15). They will ultimately be defeated (1 Cor. 15:20-28).
- **Neither things present nor things to come can separate us from God.** This time frame includes all time and eternity. The Jews divided time into two ages: This Age and the Age to Come. Nothing in the Present Age can separate us from God. When the Coming Age dawns in its fullness, there will be nothing in eternity that can sever our relationship with the Savior.
- **Neither height nor depth can separate us from God.** *Height* and *depth* are astrological terms and reflect that the ancients believed that humans were controlled by the position of stars under which they were born. The word *height* was used to describe the time when the star was at its highest, and it was thought to have great influence over a person. When at its *depth*, the star was at its lowest point. It was believed that at the *depth*, the star had no influence, but that it would regain that influence as it rose again. What Paul likely means in Romans 8:39 is that nothing in the expanses of space, height or depth, can sever us from God's love.

- **No other created thing can separate us from God.** To be sure that he left nothing out, Paul adds "any other created thing" (v. 39).

God is more powerful than death-and-life experiences, than supernatural beings, than things in time and eternity, than things imagined and real in space, and anything else in all creation.

Assurance of Our Salvation

What Paul has said about believers' security in Christ does not make believers' faith and personal perseverance in the Christian life unnecessary. He tells believers that the future is taken care of by God, giving them assurance that troubles and disasters cannot sever them from God's love. The security enjoyed by believers is not the kind whereby they can be content and cease striving for the crown of eternal life. Nothing that Paul says eliminates unbelief and sin as real dangers to believers' salvation. **All who hear the gospel have the freedom to make a decision for Christ, but that is not enough—we must persevere in that decision** (Bloesch, 1968, 87). Clearly for Paul, the gift of salvation is not limited to a few people predestinated to eternal life. All the resources of heaven are available to everyone through the gospel.

Is it possible for believers to fail to utilize the gifts and resources of the Holy Spirit that God makes available to them? Perhaps we should let the apostle answer this question. Writing to Christians, Paul warns them with these words: "If you live according to the flesh you will die; but if by the Spirit you put to death the deeds of the body, you will live" (8:13). **To return to the life ruled by sin (the flesh) means that the believer fails to use the resources provided by God. Such a lifestyle leads the believer to death. Death does not result from committing a single sin from which one repents, or from struggling with sin and then growing in an area of weakness, but results from engaging in ongoing sinful habits or lifestyle without any repentance.** The many rich spiritual benefits God provides to believers lift Paul to great heights of praise and celebration, especially when he thinks about the assurance of our salvation.

Nowhere, however, does Paul deny that the chain of events described in verses 29-30 (predestination→calling→justification→glorification) cannot be broken by unbelief and disobedience. **Believers can ensure their security in Christ by submitting to God and seeking His help to eliminate sin from their lives and to live holy lives that glorify Him.**

Before concluding our study of the grand words of Romans 8, let us review briefly what Paul has said about the Holy Spirit. A large part of the chapter is devoted to the ministry of the Holy Spirit and can be summed up as follows:

Characteristics of People Who Walk in the Spirit	
v. 4	The requirements of the moral law are fulfilled through people who walk in the Spirit.
vv. 4-5	They live according to the Spirit.
vv. 5-6	They have their minds set on the things of the Spirit.
v. 14	They are led by the Spirit.

What the Spirit Does for Believers	
v. 2	Sets them free from the law of sin and death
v. 9	Dwells in them
v. 11	Will make alive their mortal bodies in the resurrection
v. 14	Leads them
v. 16	Bears witness to their spirits that they are God's children
v. 26	Helps them
v. 26	Prays for them
v. 29	Conforms them to the likeness of God's Son

ROMANS 8:31-39

KEYWORDS

Elect of God
The term *elect of God* refers to believers. The biblical term *elect (election)* is a corporate category, and does not indicate the selection of specific individuals for salvation.

God's Plan for Sanctification

God as Judge (see p. 86)

Intercession by Jesus Christ

At the right hand of God, the risen Christ intercedes on behalf of believers (Heb. 7:25). Christ and the Holy Spirit, as well as believers, are in the position to converse with the heavenly Father, who hears and is attentive to them and the needs they express. We need Christ's intercession because His prayers assure us that He is not in heaven to condemn us, but to help us.

Principalities and Powers
Demonic forces and agencies

SUMMARY

Romans 8:31-39 is a magnificent conclusion to Paul's argument in the preceding chapters. God has demonstrated His love in that "Christ died for the ungodly" (5:6-8). The God of the entire universe is "for us" (8:31).

All foes and powers, even the most formidable ones on earth and in hell, cannot prevail against God. Since that is true, misfortunes and hardships cannot sever believers from their relationship with God. For Paul and believers in general, suffering and adversities are consistent with being followers of Jesus Christ. God does not exempt Christians from misfortunes.

In spite of suffering and their flaws and weaknesses, God's people can be more than victors—people who win total victory over their adversaries. No powers on earth or in heaven can divorce God's children from His love. Christ's lordship extends over all these powers and reveals God's absolute love and sovereignty.

LIFE APPLICATION

All that God has done and is doing in Christ leaves no doubt that we are under His favor and protection. We may be assaulted by opponents and powers of evil and our circumstances may be precarious, but we can enjoy overwhelming victory. The incredible gift of His Son for our salvation assures us that God will give us "all things" (*ta panta*, "the all"), perhaps meaning more than salvation (8:32). We are promised to be heirs "of the world" (4:13) and "joint heirs with Christ" (8:17).

Does this teach us that in the End Time we will have sovereignty over the world under the lordship of Christ? I think it does. What a message of assurance! Just imagine that regardless of whatever our circumstances may be—the loss of health, home, or loved ones; financial and marital problems; or human or demonic opponents,

> inciting persecution and conflict from within and from without the church—none of these can disqualify us from the glories of inheriting the world with Christ.
>
> God gives us no guarantee of exemption from misfortune and from having enemies, but living as disciples of Christ under the shadow of the cross, no matter the hardships in life, assures us of inheriting the world with our Savior.

REFLECTION—PART FOUR
Romans 6:1—8:39

1. What do you think about the teaching that a Christian should continue in sin to increase God's grace?

2. Compare and contrast *positional sanctification* and *practical sanctification*.

3. Christianity is not a one time spiritual experience, for it requires living out the experience every day. How would you relate the significance of water baptism to this truth?

4. What does the word *holiness* mean to you?

5. What are some of the practices that nurture our faith and holy living that have been helpful in your Christian life? (See Appendix (G) pages 430-433.)

6. How would you relate your experience to Paul's idea of two slaveries?

7. In Romans 7:14-25, Paul describes an inner, spiritual struggle. Do you think that such a struggle is characteristic of the Christian life? Does Paul's statement about dying to sin allow for any ongoing struggle with sin in the life of a Christian (6:11)?

8. Indicate at least three ways Paul uses the term *flesh*.

9. Compare life "according to the flesh" with life "according to the Spirit."

10. What is your understanding of the Roman background and the scriptural significance of adoption? How does the contemporary practice of adoption compare with the biblical doctrine of adoption?

11. What are some of the implications of the biblical teaching that the natural world is destined for redemption and restoration?

12. How should we relate the indwelling of the Holy Spirit in our hearts to the fact that we still experience suffering and troubles?

13. The Holy Spirit prays for believers. Have you ever experienced the intercessory ministry of the Spirit? If so, describe your experience and the results.

14. Briefly state your understanding of these terms: *foreknowledge*, *predestination*, *calling*, *justification*, and *glorification*.

15. What does Paul mean by the question, "If God is for us, who can be against us?" (8:31)?

16. In verses 31-39, Paul addresses the matter of suffering and troubles. What is the significance of his comments in light of his own personal hardships and the powers which cannot separate us from Christ's love?

Prayer

Our Father, we approach Your throne as people in need of Your grace and help—experiencing life's temptations, hardships, and problems. Please grant us daily the sanctifying grace of Your Spirit and His aid in prayer. May Your will be uppermost in our lives, and the depths of our hearts be filled with Your holiness. Amen.

PART FIVE—Romans 9:1—11:36

Salvation and Israel

- **Paul's Love for Israel**
  Romans 9:1-5
- **God's Sovereign Purposes and Choices**
  Romans 9:6-13
- **God's Sovereign Will and Mercy**
  Romans 9:14-29
- **Israel's Reliance on the Law, Rather Than on Faith**
  Romans 9:30-33
- **All People Invited to Salvation Through Faith**
  Romans 10:1-13
- **Revelations About Faith in Israel's Teachings**
  Romans 10:14-21
- **God's Salvation Plan for the Faithful of Israel**
  Romans 11:1-10
- **God's Salvation Plan for Non-Jews**
  Romans 11:11-24
- **Completion of God's Salvation Plan for Israel and the World**
  Romans 11:25-32
- **Paul's Praise to God**
  Romans 11:33-36

In chapters 1-8, Paul has shown how the gospel is "the power of God to salvation for everyone who believes, for the Jew first and also for the Greek [Gentile]" (1:16). He has discussed the doctrines of sin, justification, and sanctification and has also discussed God's purpose for the Jewish people. **He has explained that even though the Jewish people have certain important historical advantages and blessings, the Jewish people and the Gentiles are equal in God's sight.**

In his discussions, Paul has pointed out that while some Jewish people, like himself, had readily received the Good News of Christ as their Messiah, many Jews had not believed that Jesus was God's Son, sent by the Father. On the other hand, many Gentiles had become dedicated followers of Christ. No doubt, the Gentiles had outnumbered the Jews in the church by this time. **This development of the Gentiles' becoming followers of the Jewish Messiah raised a number of questions: Are the Jews not God's chosen people? Was the gospel not offered first to them? Has God been fair to Israel and faithful to His promises to them?**

Paul has explained in considerable detail the doctrine of salvation and has drawn attention to the spiritual need and a self-righteous attitude that he had observed among some of his own people. Although the Jews were God's chosen people and were committed to following God's law, they were not perfect and ended up disobeying it. Some even judged other people for the same weaknesses that they themselves had. **Though the Jews had the advantage of having the Scriptures, they, like all people, were guilty of sinning and must be saved by grace (2:12ff.).** However, until this point in chapter 9, Paul has not discussed fully his people's not believing that Jesus was their Deliverer. **In chapters 9-11, Paul discusses in greater depth the need for his people to turn to Christ.** These chapters form a distinct section in Romans. Some scholars have suggested that this section was inserted into the letter, but there is no manuscript evidence to support that idea. Moreover, the transition from chapter 8 to 9 and the transition from 11 to 12 are smooth and logical. **These middle chapters are best understood as Paul's recognition of the need to address the perplexing question of why God's own chosen people as a whole had not followed Jesus, whom the apostle Paul had proclaimed as being their Messiah and the Savior of the world.** So now, in chapters 9-11, Paul grapples with some End-Time events, particularly, the important matter of the spiritual destiny of Israel.

PAUL'S LOVE FOR ISRAEL
ROMANS 9:1-5

> 📖 ¹ I tell the truth in Christ, I am not lying, my conscience also bearing me witness in the Holy Spirit, ² that I have great sorrow and continual grief in my heart. ³ For I could wish that I myself were accursed from Christ for my brethren, my countrymen according to the flesh, ⁴ who are Israelites, to whom pertain the adoption, the glory, the covenants, the giving of the law, the service of God, and the promises; ⁵ of whom are the fathers and from whom, according to the flesh, Christ came, who is over all, the eternally blessed God. Amen.

Paul's Grief for His People

The tone of Paul's letter takes an abrupt change in chapters 9-11. At the end of chapter 8, he has celebrated the assurance that God's love in Christ gives to all believers. After taking his readers to the mountaintop, **Paul begins chapter 9 with a jarring shift— his deep lament because the majority of the Jewish people, whom he loved deeply, had chosen not to accept Jesus Christ as being their Messiah.** A factor that could have prompted Paul to write chapters 9-11 was a possible claim that he no longer loved his own people, that he only cared for the Gentiles now. Paul was grieved that the leaders of his own faith had stirred up some of the people against Jesus, inciting the Roman government to crucify Him.¹ The results were that the man whom Paul knew to be the

---

¹ At different points in history and in various Christian groups, Jewish people have been falsely accused of crucifying Jesus. It is very important for Christians to be accurate when we talk about Christ's death and not indiscriminately cast blame, contributing to negative attitudes toward the Jewish people.

The account of the Crucifixion recorded in the Gospels indicates that it was only a group of the Jewish leadership who plotted against Jesus, handed Him over to the Roman government, and instigated a mob to call for His execution. Jesus was a Jew himself and was loved by many of His people, so this group of Jewish leaders most likely felt that Jesus' popularity threatened their own power. It is important to note that

Son of God and the Jewish people's Messiah had died a criminal's death on a cross. Paul knew that God had promised the gospel beforehand through His prophets (1:2) to the very religious leaders who had tried to stop the spread of His message. It was Paul's heartfelt desire that his people would come to know the love, grace, and abundant life that Jesus Christ offered them.

God has never backed out on His promises to the nation of Israel. Paul's heartbreak was not due to any failure on God's part. God had not rejected Israel even though, except for a small minority, many in Israel had denied that God's Son was their Messiah. God had called Paul to teach and encourage the Gentiles to place their faith in God, but now Paul discloses his deep sorrow over the lack of faith among his own people.

In his opening remarks, Paul affirms under oath his anguish of heart. To prove his love for his people, he calls upon Christ, his conscience, and the Holy Spirit as his witnesses (9:1). Perhaps Paul had been accused of ignoring his people and devoting most of his energy to preaching the gospel to the Gentiles. He declares that, under the influence of the Holy Spirit, his conscience is clear and that his life is in Christ. Instead of being indifferent to his people, Paul has "great sorrow and continual grief" because of Israel's unbelief (v. 2). **The apostle Paul makes no charges against the Jewish people, nor does he criticize them for their inability to recognize that Jesus Christ is their promised Messiah.**

Similar to Moses' prayer on the occasion of Israel's making a golden calf (Ex. 32:31ff.), **Paul, in his anguish, states that if**

---

during the events leading up to Christ's death, most devout Jewish people would have been with their families making preparations and observing Passover, not participating in mob activity. The Roman government made the final decision and carried out the crucifixion of Jesus.

Through the cross of Christ, God has shown His profound love for all humankind, including those who had a hand in the execution of the Savior. The Christian church is called to love the Jewish people with the love of Jesus Christ. Who are we to accuse God's chosen people or anyone else? After all, each of us had a hand in Calvary, for it is our sins that made Christ's death on the cross necessary. Jesus Christ chose to die so that each of us could be set free from our bondage and enjoy life with Him forever.

Salvation and Israel

he himself could be "accursed" in order to save his people, he would desire it (Rom. 9:3). Paul loved his people so much that he was willing to sacrifice himself for their well-being. In the Bible, the word *accursed* (*anathema*) is used to refer to something or someone doomed for destruction. For example, Scripture records that whenever Israel captured a heathen city, the city was "accursed," meaning that it was to be destroyed, because everything in it was considered polluted by the sins of its people (Deut. 3:6; Josh. 6:17). Also, if a person tried to lead Israel into idolatry, that person was said to be "accursed," and would suffer dire consequences for his efforts to turn God's people away from their Lord (Deut. 13:6-11).

Paul's willingness to be separated from Christ shows his great love for his people. Such a separation would have meant abolishing his relationship with Christ and being excluded from the body of Christ. Paul was suggesting that if it would save his people, he was willing to go to hell. **Paul's lament is a cry of passion and love for his people and for all those who are lost and hurting in the world.**

God's Blessings for the People of Israel

The increasing number of Gentiles in the church, and so few Jews coming to Christ, made it appear that God's promises to Israel were not being fulfilled. The concern that Israel might now be living outside of God's blessings inspires Paul to remind his Gentile and Jewish readers of the many advantages and blessings that God had given them through the Jewish people. In Romans 9:4-5, Paul speaks of his people not as "Jews" (national origin), but as "Israelites," which indicates membership in the covenant community based on God's promises to Jacob. God changed Jacob's name to *Israel* (Gen. 32:28). **The Jews had enjoyed a privileged place in the plan of God.** At the beginning of Romans 3, Paul had asked if there was any advantage to being a Jew. His answer was that **the Jews had been entrusted with the inspired Scriptures (3:2).**

Blessings in Israel's Past (9:4-5)

Now, Paul looks at the past history of Israel and lists eight specific blessings:

1. ***Adoption*—God gave Israel the blessing of adoption.** God had adopted the Israelites into His family and conferred on them the status of being His children. He bestowed on them blessings during the exodus from Egypt: "Israel is My son, My firstborn" (Ex. 4:22). Again: "When Israel was a child, I loved him, and out of Egypt I called My son" (Hos. 11:1). It was evident that throughout her history, Israel had not fully accepted her adoption in the fullest sense, since many Israelites did not come to understand and embrace all the blessings that God had for them as His children. Many of them had worshiped idols.

Since Jesus Christ came to this world, all people have been given a direct invitation to receive the blessing of adoption into God's family. Those who accept Jesus Christ as their Savior, Lord, and Deliverer are receiving this blessing in its fullest sense. They can fully enjoy the grace and peace that come with their new familial standing.

2. ***Glory*—God gave Israel the blessing of glory.** When the Israelites had been set free from slavery in Egypt, during their attempt to cross the Red Sea, God manifested His glorious power by miraculously parting the sea for them (Ex. 15:6, 11). They also saw God's visible presence in the pillar of fire and cloud that He provided to guide them (16:10). From time to time, God's divine glory appeared at the Tabernacle where they worshiped. After the people reached the land promised to them, and they built the Temple, the glory of God filled it (1 Kings 8:1-13). Israel had seen the glory of God, but in spite of His miracles among them, they continued to become afraid and to doubt God's ability to take care of them. Instead of relying on God, they resorted to their own abilities to address their problems and fears. This self-reliance and self-interest resulted in their not accepting many of the blessings that God wanted to give them.

3. ***The Covenants*—God gave Israel the blessing of the covenants.** The covenants marked Israel as a special people. God had approached Israel and had entered into a special relationship with them. There were several covenants. Among them were the covenants with Noah, with Abraham, and with Moses. Although in these covenants God had promised to bless and save His people,

Salvation and Israel

still many Israelites at various times were unfaithful to those covenant commitments. Finally, God offered them a new covenant through Jesus Christ. Their response to this new covenant was essentially the same as to the earlier ones—many Israelites were skeptical and untrusting of God's grace and promises.

4. *The Law*—**God gave Israel the blessing of the Law.** Through the Law, God gave Israel a direct revelation of His will. The Law was given in written form so that the Israelites could read it and know what God required of them. As a result, whenever they sinned, they could not plead ignorance of God's will. God had urged Israel to be holy, for He was holy. The Law given at Mount Sinai was a clear guide for holy living.

5. *Worship*—**God gave Israel the blessing of approaching Him in service and worship.** The "service of God" in Romans 9:4 can be understood to refer to the worship of God. The Israelites' worship could occur in the their designated places of worship (the Tabernacle or Temple), as well as in any other place where the people chose to praise God. They were blessed in that they had abundant opportunities to approach God and truly have access to Him. They could worship the true God in the true way—worship being an integral part of their lives.

6. *Promises*—God gave Israel the blessing of special promises. Many of the prophecies recorded in the Old Testament that dealt with future events pertained to the Coming of Christ, the new covenant, and the ministry of the Holy Spirit. The prophets gave the people of Israel the assurance of a glorious future—Christ would come into this world through them, and great things would be in store for them.

7. *The Great Patriarchs*—**God gave Israel the "fathers," known as the "great patriarchs."** Men like Abraham, Moses, and David were the Israelites' ancestors. These men, as well as others, were people of faith and outstanding servants of God. They were people of whom Israel could be proud. Through them, Israel had a rich spiritual heritage.

8. *The Messiah*—**God gave Israel the Messiah, Jesus Christ, who was born into their nation.** By sending Jesus to earth as a Jewish child, God demonstrated His trust of Israel to nurture,

teach, and prepare Jesus for His ministry on earth. This last blessing of the gift of the Messiah was the greatest of all Israel's blessings. The other blessings had been leading up to the Coming of the Savior and should have prepared Israel to receive Christ; but when He arrived, many did not recognize Him and did not believe that He was sent by God.

Paul's Praise to the Lord

After listing Israel's blessings, **Paul breaks out in words of praise to God: "who is over all, the eternally blessed God. Amen" (v. 5).** The New King James Version connects these words to Christ and, therefore, identifies Christ as God. Though some translations connect this doxology to God the Father, there is no violation of Greek grammar to understand that here Paul is declaring the deity of Christ. This understanding is consistent with Paul's speaking of Christ as "Lord," which is used in the LXX (Septuagint, Greek translation of the Old Testament) and is equivalent to the Hebrew *Yahweh* (Jehovah) (see 10:9; 14:11; 1 Cor. 8:6; Eph. 4:4-6; Phil. 2:9-11; Col. 1:16; 2:9). **Paul's belief is that from the human side, Christ was a Jew, and from the divine side, Christ was and is in fact God (Barrett, 1991, 179). The New Testament as a whole teaches that Jesus was both human and divine.**

Now that the apostle Paul has laid bare his grief for his people's response to Christ and has recounted their blessings, he moves on to discuss the difficult matter of their unbelief.

ROMANS 9:1-5

KEYWORDS

Adoption (see p. 214)

Covenant (*diatheke*) (see p. 100)

Flesh (see p. 58)

Glory (see p. 86)

Israel
Chosen people—*Israel* became the covenant name for the descendants of Jacob, whom God chose to be His people. The name was applied collectively and nationally to the twelve tribes, identifying them as either the *children* or *sons* of Israel.

Salvation and Israel

Jews / Israelites / Hebrews (see p. 29)

The Law (*Torah*) (see p. 48)

Messiah
The Anointed One. In its early usage, *messiah* often referred to a high priest as God's anointed (Lev. 4:3, 5, 16) or to a king as the Lord's anointed (1 Sam. 26:11; Ps. 89:20). The Old Testament prophets spoke about a specially anointed One who was to come from the throne of David and who would have an eternal government in an unlimited rule (Isa. 9:2-7; Mic. 4:3; 5:2). The New Testament writers later declared that such prophecies were fulfilled in the First Coming of Jesus, the Messiah.

Patriarch / Father
Head or founder of a family or tribe. The term is used to describe Jewish ancestors prior to the time of Moses. The New Testament identifies Abraham, the twelve sons of Jacob, and David as patriarchs.

Promise (see p. 134)

Worship
The act of giving honor and deference to someone or something

SUMMARY

Paul was filled with sorrow because many of the Jewish people of his day did not believe that Jesus was the promised Messiah. He wanted his people to understand that God had lavished His promises and blessings on them. Paul's conscience and the Holy Spirit bore witness to Paul's love for the nation of Israel. He was even willing to be "accursed from Christ" if that could save Israel (Rom. 9:3).

In his grief, Paul explained that he and his people had been blessed. God in His sovereign grace had bestowed on them adoption, glory, covenants, the law, opportunities for worship, promises, and spiritual ancestors. God had also blessed them by sending His Son, the Messiah, Jesus Christ, to earth through them. The gospel itself had come to them first (1:16).

LIFE APPLICATION

Paul was deeply and sincerely sorrowful because many of his people did not believe that Jesus was their Messiah and Savior. The Jewish people had been the recipients of so many blessings from God, which had prepared them to welcome and receive the Messiah. Paul's deep desire was for them to experience the gifts of grace and freedom that only Jesus Christ can give.

Like many of the Jewish people of Paul's day, many people today engage in efforts to save themselves and, as a result, develop pride

> when they feel that they have done so. Do we love unbelievers and have a heartfelt desire to see them saved as Paul did his people? He loved them more than he loved his own personal salvation and was willing to be separated from Christ for their sake.

GOD'S SOVEREIGN PURPOSES AND CHOICES
ROMANS 9:6-13

> 📖 ⁶ But it is not that the word of God has taken no effect. For they are not all Israel who are of Israel, ⁷ nor are they all children because they are the seed of Abraham; but, *"In Isaac your seed shall be called."* ⁸ That is, those who are the children of the flesh, these are not the children of God; but the children of the promise are counted as the seed. ⁹ For this is the word of promise: *"At this time I will come and Sarah shall have a son."*
>
> ¹⁰ And not only this, but when Rebecca also had conceived by one man, even by our father Isaac ¹¹ (for the children not yet being born, nor having done any good or evil, that the purpose of God according to election might stand, not of works but of Him who calls), ¹² it was said to her, *"The older shall serve the younger."* ¹³ As it is written, *"Jacob I have loved, but Esau I have hated."*

God's Fulfillment of His Promises to Israel

Because of Paul's grief over many of the Jewish people's not accepting Jesus Christ as their promised Messiah, some might have concluded that God's plan for Israel had failed.

In verses 6-13, Paul makes two points:

First, God will remain faithful to His promises to Israel. Even though Israel, God's chosen people, had not (on the whole) recognized and followed God's Son, Jesus Christ, God would follow through on His promises to them. **The people of Israel's disbelief did not stop God from fulfilling His promises.**

Second, not all of the descendants of Israel (the man Jacob) are part of the true Israel (the nation God chose to bring the Messiah). God's special relationship (covenant) with the people of

Israel began with Abraham (Gen. 12:1-3). **God chose to transmit His covenant promises to Abraham and the people of Israel through Abraham's second-born son, Isaac, and Isaac's second-born son, Jacob.** In doing so, God went against the cultural norm of granting the greatest responsibility and position to the firstborn; God was passing over Abraham's firstborn son, Ishmael (born to Hagar), and Isaac's firstborn son, Esau. **God, in choosing Isaac and Jacob, selected men of lower cultural status to convey His plan of salvation and to bring about His plan for the world.**

God's Sovereignty and Salvation
God's Saving Purpose in the World

God's selection of the second-born descendants of Abraham and Isaac as the carriers and messengers of His blessings demonstrates that **God has sovereign freedom to select whomever He chooses to best accomplish His saving purpose in the world.**

God's Saving Work in Individual Lives

God, however, does not use His sovereignty to dictate personal salvation—that is, whom He will save and whom He will not save. He does not predetermine that some will be saved and others will be lost. As we have noted in our discussion of 8:28-30, the terms *foreknowledge* and *predestination* mean that God in eternity made provision for the salvation of all humans.

God's Criteria for Whom He Chooses to Accomplish His Saving Work

In the case of Isaac and Jacob, merit had nothing to do with God's choosing them. Both Isaac and Jacob were younger brothers, not firstborn as were Ishmael and Esau. In biblical times, the firstborn had authority over the family and a double share of the inheritance. Working through Isaac and Jacob, God chose to work through the weak and the helpless in carrying out His mission. **Personal merit and status over others do not influence God's decision regarding whom He will use. God's choice of the "least" ones, the excluded, disadvantaged, and oppressed demonstrates His love and power (Judg. 6:15; 1 Sam. 9:21; 17; Matt. 13:32; 25:40; Luke 9:48).**

God's decisions about whom He would choose were not for the purpose of excluding anyone from salvation. His intent has always been to reach all individuals and nations with the message of salvation. The fact that He chose not to work through Ishmael and Esau says nothing about their salvation or damnation. **God's selecting of individual people for particular spiritual responsibilities is not done in order to control those individuals' eternal destinies, but is done in order to accomplish God's plans for the world. Personal salvation always depends on one's own response to saving grace, regardless of that person's station in life.**

God's Sovereignty in Choosing Israel

Now we will turn to the details of the passage in Romans 9. Earlier, Paul has clarified the definition of a genuine Jew (2:28-29), and now he provides further clarification when he says, "They are not all Israel who are of Israel" (9:6). Grace and faith determine Israel, not "the flesh"—not by being a descendant of Abraham. His point is that his gospel is what has always been; it is not something "new." So Abraham is justified by faith, since grace and faith determine Israel, never race. To illustrate this, **Paul gives two examples from the Old Testament that show that just being a natural descendant of a blessed people does not make a person a child of God.**

    1. **Ishmael and Isaac.** Abraham had two sons, Ishmael and Isaac, who were half brothers. Ishmael was the son of the Egyptian servant Hagar, and Isaac the son of Sarah. The differences in Ishmael's and Isaac's religious heritage (serving many gods vs. serving the one true God), along with God's choosing Isaac to fulfill His plan, emphasize that only those who follow God in faith are of true Israel.

When Ishmael mocked his brother Isaac, Sarah, demanded of her husband Abraham that Ishmael and Hagar be sent away. Because Ishmael was Abraham's firstborn son whom he loved, this turn of events was very distressing. When Abraham sought God, He instructed Abraham to listen to Sarah and to send away Hagar and Ishmael. God comforted Abraham, indicating to him that he did not need to worry about Ishmael, because God would care for him and would bring a great nation through him. God also promised Abraham that in addition to the nation that would come from Ishmael, Abraham's name and his descendants would come through Isaac, his second-born son.

The Ishmaelites, while loved and provided for by God, were never identified as being God's chosen people through whom He planned to bring the Messiah to earth. Isaac was chosen by God to be the representative of the true Israel, that is, the children who had received God's promise and with whom God had a special covenant.

2. **Esau and Jacob.** Paul cites another example. When Rebecca, the wife of Isaac, was carrying Esau and Jacob in her womb, God told her that the two sons would be fathers of nations and the older would serve the younger (Gen. 25:23). Esau was just as much a son of Isaac as was Jacob. Despite this fact, the Edomites, of which Esau was the father, were never recognized as God's chosen people.

God's choosing of Isaac and Jacob and His passing over of Ishmael and Esau for particular purposes had nothing to do with their works or merit, on which many Jews had relied for their salvation. God had distinguished between Ishmael and Isaac, and between the twins Esau and Jacob before they were born—before they had a chance of doing any good or evil (Rom. 9:11). **God's decisions regarding Ishmael and Isaac as well as Esau and Jacob were not due to any lack of love for them or to any particular individual's or nation's actions. Although we cannot know God's full intent in His choices, we can conclude that God chose Isaac and Jacob in part to accomplish His plan for bringing the Messiah to earth.** As already noted, Isaac was the representative head of true Israel, the line of people through which God determined to accomplish His plan. Likewise, the focus of Genesis 25:23 is not on Esau and Jacob as individuals, but as fathers of two nations. Neither Genesis nor Romans refers to the eternal destiny of the twins.

Observations About God's Choices

Five concluding observations are in order regarding God's decisions about whom He will call to do particular work and through whom He will accomplish His plans.

1. **God has absolute freedom to choose individuals to advance His work in the world.** Nevertheless, Paul makes a striking statement: "Jacob I have loved, but Esau I have hated" (Rom. 9:13; cf. Mal. 1:2-3). Among the Hebrews, this was a way of saying, "I preferred Jacob to Esau." Genesis 25:23 states that Esau would serve Jacob, but he actually never did. However, the Edomites did serve the Israelites. The statement "I have loved Jacob, but I have hated Esau" does not express God's intent to save one and damn the other, or His lack of care. It simply means that Jacob and the people of Israel would have a significant role to play in God's plan of salvation for the world, and that Esau and the people of Edom would not play that particular role.

God loved both Esau and Jacob, but He did not love Esau's response of unbelief. In Paul's day, the majority of the Jewish people had followed the pattern of Esau—that of unbelief. God preferred the response of Jacob—that of belief. Of course, should Jacob have become arrogant and unbelieving, God in His sovereignty could have chosen to no longer use Jacob to carry out His plans. **God will always accomplish His holy plans, regardless of particular human beings' actions.**

2. **God chose Abraham, Isaac, and Jacob—not to exclude anyone from salvation, but to advance His plan of salvation and to reach all nations and people with the gospel. When the gospel reaches people, it tears down the walls that separate them and makes salvation available to all (Eph. 2:14).** God's love and mercy toward all people are made evident in Jesus Christ. **God has always loved all people equally**—that included Ishmael and Esau.

3. **Ancestry alone is insufficient to define who God's people are.** Esau and Jacob had the same mother and father and were twins. This fact warned the Israelites against assuming that just because they were descendants of Abraham, they had the right to think of themselves as privileged children of God. **The Israelites' salvation, like ours, rested and continues to rest on grace and faith alone.**

The thought that "Israel" as described in the Bible is based on racial or national factors is inaccurate. Only those Jewish people who do not rely on being part of a particular race for determining their spiritual status, but instead put their trust in God, are and have always been "Israel." It was to this Israel of faith that God made His promises.

4. **The blessings bestowed on Israel continue to have significance today.** Paul includes adoption as one of Israel's blessings. Being adopted is the status of all those who are in Christ (8:13-17, 23). **God's adoption of Israel into His family still has relevance, meaning that the people of Israel are still God's chosen people, and are important in God's plan for the world.** Nothing in Romans supports the argument that the church has replaced Israel, the nation through which God chose to bring His Son into this world (see Ex. 4:22-23; Deut. 14:1-2). Paul does clarify a Jew as being a person who is not only a Jew by birth, but one who has a relationship with God (Rom. 2:25-29), but we should avoid using his clarification as a pretext for substituting the church for Israel. **The Christian church is not a replacement for Israel.** Romans 9:1-3 is a lament over the nation of Israel's response to the gospel, but Paul still sees the nation of Israel as a chosen people having a place in God's plan. **In short, God's complete plan for His chosen people has not yet been fulfilled (ch. 11).**

The body of Christ is the place to receive atoning grace. This important responsibility of the church could be considered to be a continuation of one of the spiritual responsibilities that God gave the nation of Israel—that of pointing people to the Messiah and His grace. Some might describe this role of the church as "replacing" the role that Israel once had, since Israel's role for pointing the world to the Messiah was completed when the Messiah, Jesus Christ, arrived on earth. Now it is the church (a body comprised of both Jewish and Gentile followers of Christ) who is to point to Jesus Christ and to be the instrument of God's grace and redemptive presence in the world. Since God continues to love Israel and continues to have a plan and purpose for His chosen people, in this respect the church has not "replaced" Israel.

5. **God's mercy is offered to all people, but God often prefers to use the lowly—those lacking status, power, and position—**

to carry forward His mission to the world. In God's plan to work through the people of Israel in order to carry out His purposes, He had a preference for Isaac and Jacob—not for Ishmael and Esau, who both were firstborn and had more status than their younger brothers. **Acting contrary to culture's way of doing things and working through the weak has often been God's way of doing things.** When choosing a nation, He often has turned to a small, insignificant people. **In their beginnings, the people of Israel were wanderers and slaves in Egypt; but even so, God called Israel to a worldwide service and worked through them. God worked through both Israel's successes and failures.** God's choice to value and use people whom the world might think as being "lowly" (like the Israelites who were slaves in Egypt) is typical of His divine, compassionate mode of operation.

Jesus Christ is the best example of the way God works—Jesus was one of the poor, having no place to lay His head. He had no comfortable home immediately following His birth, nor any permanent home as an adult while He traveled and ministered. Many of Jesus Christ's own people did not believe He was of God and rejected His message. Also, by society's definition, **Jesus suffered the most shameful of deaths—execution on a cross by the Roman government. Through Christ and His profound suffering, God demonstrated His love for all people.**

Paul says it so well when he writes, **"God chose what is foolish in the world to shame the wise, God chose what is weak in the world to shame the strong, God chose what is low and despised in the world, even things that are not, to bring to nothing things that are, so that no human being might boast in the presence of God" (1 Cor. 1:27-29 RSV).**

Paul's use of the stories of Esau and Pharaoh demonstrates that unbelief or insensitivity by individuals or nations will not stop the redemptive plan of the Lord. These stories show that God extends His grace to and uses those whom society may consider to be "second choices" or "unacceptable." Since God uses people in a variety of circumstances who may make desirable or undesirable choices, we can conclude that even though there was unbelief among Israel, while this was not behavior

Salvation and Israel

pleasing to God, Israel was still used by the Lord to accomplish His plan to extend His grace to the Gentiles. **God in His sovereignty uses both belief and unbelief to expand His grace and accomplish His plans in ways that are outside culturally accepted boundaries.**

ROMANS 9:6-13
KEYWORDS **Children of God/Sons of God** (see p. 214) **Chosen by God** (see p. 105) **Elect of God** (see p. 238) **Flesh** (see p. 58) **Promise** (see p. 134) **Salvation** (see p. 23) **Sovereignty of God** God's control of every area of His creation **True Israel** Those people who were descendants of Abraham, with whom God made a special covenant, promising that He would bless them and bring the Messiah to the earth through them. Those Israelites who continued to be faithful and *true* to God and put their hope in the promises He made to them are often referred to by scholars as "true Israel."
SUMMARY God had chosen Israel to be a light to the rest of the world and to bring His Messiah into that world. Not all people descended from Abraham (Israel) were considered to be those who were chosen for this special work. For example, both Ishmael and Isaac descended from Abraham, and both Esau and Jacob descended from Isaac; but God chose only Isaac and Jacob through whom to work. Neither Isaac nor Jacob was a firstborn son. God chose them despite that in their culture due to their position in their families, they were considered to have a lower, less privileged status. God is sovereign and He has the right and power to choose individuals through whom He will accomplish His plan of salvation. God has the freedom to choose whomever He desires to advance His work. His selection does not indicate His love for one person over another. What He does always rests on His mercy and compassion (9:15).

LIFE APPLICATION

Down through history, there were those Jewish people who remained faithful to God, the true Israel. In Paul's day, some of the Jewish people believed the gospel, while others did not. Questions for us today are these: Are we being faithful to God? Are we being the true Christian church? Are we seeking God, so that we can recognize His voice and follow Him in faith, no matter how unexpected the paths on which He leads us?

As the accounts of God's decisions regarding Ishmael and Isaac as well as Esau and Jacob indicate, salvation is solely a matter of grace and does not depend on human merit, works, or virtue. The grounds for being a true child of God are not who our father or mother is, what our status in society is, or our personal achievements. The only way we Christians can be true to God is by embracing God's promises in the gospel and remaining faithful to Christ.

GOD'S SOVEREIGN WILL AND MERCY
ROMANS 9:14-29

[14] What shall we say then? Is there unrighteousness with God? Certainly not! [15] For He says to Moses, "*I will have mercy on whomever I will have mercy, and I will have compassion on whomever I will have compassion.*" [16] So then it is not of him who wills, nor of him who runs, but of God who shows mercy. [17] For the Scripture says to the Pharaoh, "*For this very purpose I have raised you up, that I may show My power in you, and that My name may be declared in all the earth.*" [18] Therefore He has mercy on whom He wills, and whom He wills He hardens.

[19] You will say to me then, "Why does He still find fault? For who has resisted His will?" [20] But indeed, O man, who are you to reply against God? Will the thing formed say to him who formed it, "Why have you made me like this?" [21] Does not the potter have power over the clay, from the same lump to make one vessel for honor and another for dishonor?

[22] What if God, wanting to show His wrath and to make His power known, endured with much longsuffering the vessels of wrath prepared for destruction, [23] and that He might make known the riches of His glory on the vessels of mercy, which He had prepared beforehand for glory, [24] even us whom He called, not of the Jews only, but also of the Gentiles?

> ²⁵ As He says also in Hosea:
>
>> "I will call them My people, who were not My people,
>> And her beloved, who was not beloved."
>> ²⁶ "And it shall come to pass in the place where it was said to them,
>> 'You are not My people,'
>> There they shall be called sons of the living God."
>
> ²⁷ Isaiah also cries out concerning Israel:
>
>> "Though the number of the children of Israel be as the sand of the sea,
>> The remnant will be saved.
>> ²⁸ For He will finish the work and cut it short in righteousness,
>> Because the Lord will make a short work upon the earth."
>
> ²⁹ And as Isaiah said before:
>
>> "Unless the Lord of Sabaoth had left us a seed,
>> We would have become like Sodom,
>> And we would have been made like Gomorrah."

Predestination and God's Work Through People

Again the emphasis in verses 14-20 is God's freedom to work through particular individuals in order to accomplish His good pleasure. In light of this focus, it needs to be stressed that God's rule does not include His manipulating an individual's choices regarding that person's salvation. That is to say, God does not predestinate who will be saved and who will be lost.

God's calling Paul to the special mission of preaching the gospel shows that individuals are predestined for particular service, but it does not show that individuals are predestined to make a particular salvation decision (Acts 9:15; Gal. 1:15; cf. Jer. 1:5). There are no statements in Scripture that indicate the eternal destiny (salvation or damnation) of Ishmael, Isaac, Esau, Jacob, or even Pharaoh. Likewise, Paul, in his account of Moses and Pharaoh in this passage of Scripture, makes no mention of Pharaoh's final destiny. Paul does indicate that God used Pharaoh to advance His purpose for the world by the deliverance of the Israelites from Egypt.

The way God treated Pharaoh has raised questions as to whether God has been unjust to certain people (v. 14). God

did harden Pharaoh's heart (vv. 17-18), but not arbitrarily because Pharaoh had hardened his own heart (Ex. 8:15, 32; 9:34). The account of Pharaoh demonstrates God's freedom to use a pagan king (Isa. 45:1-13), as well as His own followers, like Isaac and Jacob, as instruments to accomplish His will and purpose.

God is able to use negative elements and uncooperative people to work full redemption in the life of believers (Rom. 8:28) and to expand His redemptive hand in the world (as in the cases of Ishmael, Esau, and Pharaoh, as well as Israel during different points of their history). **God has a clear purpose when He uses individuals to assert His power and presence in human affairs.**

God's Work Through Moses and Pharaoh

The accounts of Moses and Pharaoh are good examples of how God may use people to accomplish His will.

- **Moses—an example of God's mercy for those who will accept His love**

    Moses asked God for proof that He was with the children of Israel (Ex. 33:14-19). In response to Moses' request, **God told him that He would have mercy on whom He wanted to have mercy.** As Paul explains, "So then it is not of him who wills, nor of him who runs, but of God who shows mercy" (Rom. 9:16). Again, God's *freedom* is being affirmed. No one can dictate or control how God dispenses mercy and grace. Jewish people cannot rightfully say to God that Gentiles cannot receive mercy and compassion, nor can Gentiles rightfully claim that they are to be the sole recipients of God's mercy. God's mercy is for all people, and only God chooses how and when He will show His mercy.

    Mercy does not depend on justice (in the sense of what one accomplishes or deserves), but on the grace of God. God set the terms under which He will extend His mercy and compassion, and grants mercy and compassion to those who accept His terms—faith in Jesus Christ. The words of

Romans 8:28, "those who love God," are useful for understanding the concept of love in chapter 9. Our love derives from God's love, which is poured out in our hearts through the Holy Spirit (5:5). In believers, the Holy Spirit evokes profound expression of God's love, inspiring their acceptance of all of God's children. Nevertheless, God is in control, but humans have the freedom to accept or reject the gospel. The emphasis in 9:16 falls on God's mercy, not on His freedom; but "His will" should be taken into consideration when attempting to understand His mercy.

What moves God is the acceptance of the grace that He offers us. God's mercy and compassion do not depend on human merit, status, or greatness. **God's purpose is to be merciful to all (11:32).** As Christians we already have His mercy in Christ. God's mercy calls for us to be what we are in Christ and to reflect in our daily living that we are His children.

- **Pharaoh—an example of God's sovereign freedom to use anyone to fulfill His purposes, regardless of that person's faith**

Now in 9:17-18, Paul presses his point about God's sovereign freedom to accomplish His saving purpose. He uses the deliverance of the Israelites from Egypt as an example (Ex. 9:16). Pharaoh thought he was the master of the situation in Egypt, but he was not. **God had raised up and placed Pharaoh in his leadership position for two reasons: (1) in order that God's power would be manifested and (2) in order that God's power might be proclaimed throughout the whole earth.** God used the pagan king to serve His saving purpose. The results of God's acting through Pharaoh were that the Egyptian magicians who served Pharaoh came to recognize that God existed (Ex. 8:19). Also, because of the plagues that God sent in response to Pharaoh's stubbornness, the Philistine people heard about the power of God (1 Sam. 4:8). God used Pharaoh's resistance to expand redemption. God delivered the people of Israel, making God's power evident to all the people.

God did harden the king's heart, but not unjustly. This pagan king had already hardened his own heart repeatedly and had been stubborn and cruel. So, rather than contradicting Pharaoh's will, God actually enhanced Pharaoh's will. God, however, tempered His hardening of Pharaoh by being long-suffering with the king and restraining Pharaoh's freedom, instead of immediately punishing him (Rom. 9:18, 22; Ex. 5:1ff.). **God can always be relied upon to act consistently with His character. He cannot treat anyone unjustly, because that would be contrary to His nature.** What God did in Egypt brought glory to His name and deliverance to His people. In accomplishing His purposes, God used the most unlikely person. **However, in using the pagan king, there was no hint that God determined Pharaoh's final destiny.** Nevertheless, God does set the conditions for His mercy and compassion, which He has revealed supremely in Jesus Christ. Those who reject His mercy, which He has demonstrated through Christ, are not numbered among His children until they decide to call on the Lord and accept His mercy.

God's Justice and Mercy

In Romans 9:19-29, the apostle Paul anticipates that his opponents will challenge his comments about God's mercy and sovereignty. He expects that to them it will appear that he has represented God as being unjust, and has claimed that the way that God governs the world is not right, since a just God would have no business condemning sinners whom He has hardened. **He expects them to ask: If God makes people the way they are, why would He find fault with them (v. 19)? Paul replies by explaining that no person is in a position to question God's dealings with him or her, because none of us is God—we are simply creations of God.**

Paul states that no one can ever be anything but a creature of God (v. 20). **To illustrate his point, he introduces the parable of the potter and the clay (v. 21; Isa. 29:16; 45:9-13; Jer. 18:1-6).**

What does this parable teach? **The potter (God) has the right to fashion each vessel for a function and to use it for that purpose.** The vessel does not question the potter. Therefore, since God has created the human race, the wisest course for humans is not to pass judgment on the Creator, but to accept their position in humility. All people are created beings, and we do not have the full understanding that God has.

Because the people whom God created have become sinners, God must deal with them as sinners, as people who need His instruction and mercy. Paul does not suggest that God deals with people in an arbitrary, unreasonable way, but rather in a merciful and compassionate manner, giving them many opportunities to repent and accept His love. God's dealing with humans in mercy and compassion shows that what He does is grounded in His character, not in some mysterious, arbitrary decision distinct from His will.

Meaning of the Phrase "The Vessels of Wrath"

No one can rightly accuse God of being unjust, because He has been long-suffering. Although many people of Israel did not accept Christ and His teachings and continued to live very self-focused lives, God was patient with them and did not destroy "the vessels of wrath prepared [preparing themselves] for destruction" (v. 22). **Like a potter, God may create vessels (individuals) for a wide range of purposes—for more honorable uses to more common uses—but He does not create any for destruction.**

In Paul's time, many Jews and Gentiles were "vessels of wrath," objects of His displeasure due to their disobedience, but those who had repented had become "vessels of mercy" (vv. 22-23). In the context of Romans 9, the vessels of wrath were those Jewish people of Paul's day who persisted in unbelief and rejected God's saving grace available through Jesus Christ.

Two Translations of the Verb "Prepared" (*katertismena*) (v. 22)

"Prepared for destruction" (v. 22) refers to those Jews who insisted on continuing in their lifestyles of religiosity, rather than pursuing a more spiritual way of living anchored in God's

mercy, grace, and love. Their choice for religion over a trusting relationship with God, which led them down a negative path, raises a question: Did God prepare them for destruction (*apoleia*)?

In the Greek, the word *prepared* (*katertismena*) can be either perfect passive or middle participle. If it is taken as passive, then God prepared the vessels of wrath for destruction. However, if it is understood to be middle, then the people are doing the preparing.

1. **Translation in some Bible versions: "prepared" [by God]; passive verb—God is doing the preparing.**

Although a number of English versions, including the *New King James Version*, assume that the form is passive—that God did the preparing of the "vessels of wrath," if one considers the usage of the verb *prepared* in the context of the entire letter to the Romans, a more logical translation would be to understand the verb as being middle (people doing the preparing), rather than passive (God doing the preparing). The rationale for not understanding the verb to be passive is Paul's understanding of God's wrath. As Paul stated earlier in Romans 1:18, **God does express His wrath (or holy displeasure) to people who have suppressed the truth, which they have demonstrated by their ungodliness and unrighteousness. However, God does not set out to prepare particular people to be destroyed and to receive eternal punishment.**

Paul's people were experiencing the wrath of God only *after* God had called them to repent. But there was no final wrath, no final judgment of these people who had rejected Christ. ***Destruction* (*apoleia*) means final judgment. As long as people are still on earth, they may repent and avoid final judgment. God does not prepare them for a final judgment of eternal punishment.** Throughout the Jewish people's history, God had patiently tolerated their indecisiveness and acts of disobedience, and He continued to do so. However, because of their unbelief in God's promises, the Jewish people (like all of us when we fail to follow God's leading) deserved God's judgment. God's patience toward the Jewish people was an indication of His love for them and demonstrated that He had not "prepared" them for destruction.

2. **Preferred translation: "preparing themselves"; middle (reflexive) verb—people are doing the preparing.**
It is better to translate the term prepared (*katertismena*) to be a middle reflexive form, expressing personal action by humans. Using the middle reflexive form, the translation in 9:22 is "God endured with much longsuffering the vessels of wrath [people who were living disrespectfully, displeasing God] *preparing themselves* for destruction." Some Jewish people (who were like many of us today) persisted in unbelief and refused to repent of their wrongdoings, setting themselves up for God's judgment. God in His mercy dealt with them (as He does us) in patience, giving them opportunity to repent and accept Jesus Christ as their Savior (2 Peter 3:9). **When people repent of their sins and turn to God, whether they are Jews or Gentiles, they are choosing not to be "vessels of wrath" any longer, but to become "vessels of mercy."** God honors the freedom of all people and pursues their salvation with great patience.

God's Mercy for Both Jews and Gentiles

According to Romans 9:23 and 24, God's purpose was to create a people—vessels of mercy—from both the Jews and Gentiles. He never wanted to spurn either the Jews or Gentiles, so beforehand He had made provision for their salvation. In His mercy, God had endured the stubbornness of Pharaoh and the times that Israel was unfaithful. Through His encounters with Pharaoh and Israel, God had revealed His wrath (His displeasure) for their wrongdoings and rebellion, but also had demonstrated His saving power, showing His mercy to both Jews and Gentiles. **God's goal was that all people would experience the riches of His salvation and become vessels of mercy.**

Mercy for Non-Jews

Long ago, the prophets had predicted that God would give **His mercy to non-Jews by extending an invitation of adoption into His family.** He would also honor the wishes of Jewish individuals who did not want to follow Him by allowing them to go their own way (vv. 25-29). God was creating a new people, consisting of Jews and non-Jews. These actions were in agreement with the prophecies recorded in the Old Testament Scriptures.

- **Prophecy Regarding the Gentiles**

  At this point in verses 25-29, Paul reverses the usual order of his discussion and begins by mentioning the Gentiles first. He begins by citing the words of Hosea (Rom. 9:25 and Hos. 2:23; Rom. 9:26 and Hos. 1:10). **The prophet Hosea had directed his message to the northern tribes of Israel, who were guilty of apostasy and idolatry. To the northern tribes' displeasure, the prophet Hosea had predicted that the Gentiles would be converted and would become God's people.** Hosea foresaw that God would gather a people who were not yet His people.

- **Prophecy Regarding the Jewish People**

  Isaiah predicted that not all members of the nation of Israel would choose to be faithful to God, but only a portion (a *remnant*). God would release them to go their own way, which would naturally result in their becoming broken off. God's provision of salvation was and is today for individuals who want to follow God and be a part of His family (Rom. 9:27-28; Isa. 10:22-23). **Due to His mercy, God never abandoned the Jewish nation then or today, nor has He abandoned us during our times of weakness. God continues to offer mercy and forgiveness to anyone who desires a relationship with Him.**

  An example of God's mercy is His act of saving Lot and two members of his family during the destruction of Sodom and Gomorrah. Although God destroyed those cities due to their rebellion against Him, He extended His mercy to those members of the Jewish people in Sodom who still desired to be a part of God's family and follow His ways (Gen. 19). "The Lord of Sabaoth" (Rom. 9:29)—(*The Lord of Hosts*)—continues to save the faithful, although small in number, as He saved the few who lived in Sodom, for He is a God of mercy.

Concluding Observations

From what Paul has told us in 9:14-29, we can draw a few concluding observations:

Salvation and Israel

1. **God knows what He is doing, just as He did in delivering Israel from Egypt; but He works in mysterious ways that we often do not understand until the goal is reached.**

2. **God the Creator is sovereign and free to manifest His presence and power in human affairs and to use unlikely individuals and groups, such as Pharaoh and the Egyptians, to advance His plan of salvation.**

3. **Humans, even in a fallen condition, have a range of personal freedom and responsibility.** No one can be saved apart from grace, and God established faith as the means by which His mercy is received in Jesus Christ.

4. **God is long-suffering and merciful, but by no means is He powerless.** God, however, in the truest sense is a waiting God. His long-suffering and patience speak of His great grace and mercy.

ROMANS 9:14-29

KEYWORDS

Final Judgment (see p. 84)

The Lord of Sabaoth
Lord of Hosts; God of all beings and forces, which He created and maintains

Mercy of God
A characteristic or attribute of God that expresses God's love and compassion to those who are in trouble and victims of sin. The supreme expression of God's mercy was God's provision of salvation at Calvary.

Prophecy
A message from the Holy Spirit given directly to a prophet

The Remnant
In the Old Testament—the portion of the Jewish community who truly believed in God and were faithful; *in the New Testament*—in the first century, a minority of Christian believers among the Jewish people.

Sovereignty of God (see p. 259)

Vessels of Wrath/Vessels of Mercy

Analogy that distinguishes between those who embrace a real relationship with God (true Israel), as demonstrated through Jesus Christ's gift of grace and forgiveness (the gospel), and those who do not desire a relationship with God. God's desire is to change the "vessels of wrath" into "vessels of mercy" through the power of the gospel. Paul's explanation indicates the predominance of divine mercy over divine wrath (v. 23; cf. 11:26-32) and reconciles the roles of human responsibility and God's sovereign power in salvation.

Will of God

God's eternal plan and sovereign purpose

Wrath of God (see p. 75)

SUMMARY

God's Requirements

God in His sovereignty has the right and power to determine the terms through which people come into relationship with Him. Many people of Israel did not believe that Jesus could be the Messiah and that they could be forgiven and receive eternal life without working for it. For those people who chose not to listen to the voice of God, not accepting His invitation of grace and forgiveness through Christ, God was fair in His displeasure and His releasing them to go their own way.

God's Mercy

God is a merciful God. To give an example of God's mercy for both Israel and the Gentiles, Paul refers to Moses and Pharaoh:

Paul reminds his readers that even though God had set the Israelites free from slavery in Egypt, at Mount Sinai, they had built a golden calf and had worshiped it, instead of worshiping the one true God. Moses, in his distress over their actions, had requested proof from God that He would still remain with Israel. God's response was that He was merciful. Divine mercy is not based on what a person deserves, but on grace—the undeserved favor of God.

Pharaoh himself is an illustration of how God uses people's decisions and events to accomplish His purposes. This king had opposed God, but God used Pharaoh's arrogance for accomplishing His purpose and for His own glory. In His deliverance of Israel from Egypt, God was the master of the situation.

God sets the terms of His mercy, and as God, He does not have to answer to people for anything. Just as the potter is not answerable to the clay, God is the master of His work and does not have to give an account of what He does.

Throughout Israel's history in making His power known, God had been patient and merciful with Israel ("vessels of wrath"—people who had set themselves up to be possible recipients of God's wrath). Instead of destroying those who rebelled against Him, God gave them the opportunity to repent, although they did not deserve it. Both the Jews and Gentiles who followed His way became God's "vessels of mercy." God granted to them His glorious salvation, just as prophesied by the prophets.

LIFE APPLICATION

Is God faithful to His people? Has He been fair to Israel and to others? Paul's conclusion is yes. He has been faithful and fair to all—both to the Jews and the Gentiles. How then can anyone charge God with being unjust when everything He has done has been directed toward the good of all? As with Pharaoh, as well as with unbelievers in general, there comes a point when the Holy Spirit may no longer strive with individuals and they become completely indifferent to their spiritual condition and, as a result, to the gospel invitation to relationship with God.

God has a definite purpose for each individual. His will can be resisted despite everything God does toward giving us time to repent and be saved. Some Jews said *yes* to the gospel, becoming "vessels of mercy." Others said *no* to the gospel, remaining "vessels of wrath." We, too, are free to accept or reject God's saving grace in Christ. Whether we are Jews or Gentiles, if we trust in Christ, indeed we are "vessels of mercy" to whom God makes "known the riches of His glory" (v. 23). If we have received the benefits from God's faithfulness, we have a responsibility to remain faithful to Him.

ISRAEL'S RELIANCE ON THE LAW, RATHER THAN ON FAITH
ROMANS 9:30-33

³⁰ What shall we say then? That Gentiles, who did not pursue righteousness, have attained to righteousness, even the righteousness of faith; ³¹ but Israel, pursuing the law of righteousness, has not attained to the law of righteousness. ³² Why? Because they did not seek it by faith, but as it were, by the works of the law. For they stumbled at that stumbling stone. ³³ As it is written:

"*Behold, I lay in Zion a stumbling stone and rock of offense,
And whoever believes on Him will not be put to shame.*"

The apostle now summarizes his thoughts, beginning with the question "What shall we say then?" (v. 30). **In Paul's time, many of the people of Israel had chosen not to follow Jesus Christ, while large numbers of Gentiles had chosen to follow Him. The differing responses of the Jews and Gentiles called for some explanation.**

Responsibility for Spiritual Choices

It might appear that previously Paul has said that individuals have nothing to do with their relationship with God and that it depends solely on God's sovereign choice. If this were true, then God would have removed all responsibility from the Jewish nation, and its individual members would not have had any responsibility in their relationship with God. There would have been no reason for Paul's heartbreak over his people's refusal of Christ (v. 2). **In God's plan, all individuals have responsibility for entering and continuing in their relationship with God.** If individuals did not have any responsibility for their relationship with God and their own destiny, then the inevitable conclusions would be that the gospel is not for all people and that a Messiah for the Jewish people was not necessary. Paul could not accept such conclusions.

To emphasize that the Jewish people were in need of a Messiah who would offer them grace, and that this Good News that the Messiah would bring was for all people, Paul addresses two possible questions:

First, Why did many of Paul's own people not believe in Jesus Christ as the Messiah?

Many of the Jewish people had not believed that Christ could be their Messiah and their path to becoming right with God. Christ was offering free salvation, but many of them believed that the only way salvation could be obtained was through obedience to the law and doing good deeds. True righteousness—not ethical virtue, but a right relationship with God as explained earlier in Romans—can only be obtained by faith in Christ (2:17-29; 3:21-24). Despite the Jewish people's unparalleled blessings (9:4-5), many of them looked not to God but to the Mosaic law, where salvation cannot not be found. An

Salvation and Israel

opinion common among the Jewish people was that it was impossible for the Gentiles to be God's people, because they did not follow the rules laid out in the law. However, the truth was and is that mere observance of the law without a relationship with God cannot justify either Gentiles or Jews.

Under the Mosaic law, for one's obedience to be genuine, that person must trust in God. Even so, many tried to put themselves in a right relationship with God through doing certain deeds required by the law without relying on faith in God. It was Israel's own choices that prevented them from achieving their goal of righteousness. **Seeking righteousness through observing the law may produce a human righteousness, but not a God righteousness** (Barrett, 1991, 193).

Second, Why did many of the Gentiles believe?

Paul had not encountered the resistance to his preaching from the Gentiles, as he did from his own people (v. 30). Even though many Gentiles had looked for salvation in other places (pagan religions, etc.), **the Gentiles had an advantage in that they had not been taught that the main requirement for salvation was to follow a set of laws perfectly**—a mode of thinking that would need to be challenged before they would be able to accept a God of relationship. God had not given the Gentiles the Mosaic law, and they had no real interest in adhering to its requirements except perhaps some Gentile God-worshipers (Luke 7:5; Acts 8:27; 10:1ff.). **Large numbers of Gentiles had received Christ and salvation through faith, not by trying to perform deeds required by the law.** What saved the Gentiles was their accepting the gospel and allowing God's grace to reshape their lives, a response which stood in contrast to many Jews' response of distrust in the gospel and its promises of a new grace-filled life. **While many of the Jews worked for salvation, many of the Gentiles received it simply by casting themselves on the mercy of God in Jesus Christ.**

Salvation Through the Cross

On the basis of Scripture, Paul explains the baffling circumstances of his people. He cites the prophecies of Isaiah 8:14 and 28:16, which had been fulfilled in Christ (Rom. 9:33). **Paul's** opinion was that his people, the Jews, had stumbled over the foundation stone (Christ), which had been laid down by God in Zion (Jerusalem), instead of continuing to build upon "the stone which the builders rejected" (Ps. 118:22; Matt. 21:42; Mark 12:10; Luke 20:17; Acts 4:11; 1 Peter 2:7). Christ was the very foundation of spiritual Israel, but as the foundation stone, He had become a stone of stumbling for God's chosen people. **The foundation stone brought a righteousness that can only be received through faith. Many Jews stumbled over Christ because they sought righteousness through their works. By focusing on works, they fell off the path that led to true righteousness.**

The result was that the foundation stone became a stumbling stone; it also became "a rock of offense" (1 Peter 2:8). Christ had offended the Jews through His claims to be their Messiah. They could not believe that Jesus was the Son of God. He was born in the obscure town of Nazareth, did not receive a rabbinic education, had not observed the details of the law, and had died a shameful death on a cross. Even so, Christ had a double effect. Some were deeply offended by Him, but others were profoundly attracted to Him. **Those Jews who had set ideas about the way God does things could not imagine that God's eternal Son could die on a cross at Calvary. To the Jews who were interested in miracles and to the Greeks who sought wisdom, a Messiah's death on a cross did not make sense and was offensive (1 Cor. 1:18ff.).** God on a cross was unthinkable to them then, just as the idea of God being executed in such a gruesome manner is still an offence to many today, and staggers the human mind.

It was hard for both the Jews and the Greeks to believe in Christ, but "whoever believes on Him will not be put to shame" (Rom. 10:11). **The foundation of our salvation was laid down by God through the cross-death of His Son. All who believe in Jesus Christ will never be disappointed—"will not be put to shame" (cf. 1:16).** For those who believe, nothing is more precious than the cross.

ROMANS 9:30-33

KEYWORDS
Believe (see p. 119)

Salvation and Israel

The Cross (see p. 122)

Faith (see p. 23)

Israel (see p. 250)

The Law (*Torah*) (see p. 48)

Righteousness for Believers/Righteousness of Faith
The state of being in right relationship and standing with God, which is a gift from God to all believers.

SUMMARY

From Paul's earlier discussion about God's sovereignty, his readers might have concluded that the nation of Israel and its people bore no responsibility for their own spiritual condition and that their choices regarding faith in God's Son Jesus, their Messiah, were out of their power. To avoid this misunderstanding, Paul explains that many Jews had not been able to believe in a Savior of grace because of their belief that the only way to attain righteousness was through doing good works and following the law.

Because of the Jewish peoples' presuppositions, Christ had become their "stumbling stone" to understanding the true message of salvation (9:32-33; 1 Cor. 1:18ff.). The result was that many Jewish people trusted themselves more than they trusted the unusual circumstances of Jesus Christ's appearance, life, and death. They could not imagine that Jesus, with His humble life and message of faith and grace, could possibly be God's Son, the promised Messiah. God did not cause the people whom He loved so dearly to respond in disbelief to His plan. The cause of their doubt was their inclination to rely on their own efforts to make themselves acceptable to a demanding God, rather than responding with trust to a God of grace and mysterious ways.

LIFE APPLICATION

No one has ever been saved on the basis of good works. Ever since Adam was expelled from the Garden of Eden, the only way of salvation has been to trust in God. As worthwhile as living a moral life, serving humankind, and excelling in church work may be, none of these will save our souls. Personal merit, efforts to save ourselves, or endeavors to establish our own righteousness will not bring about salvation and eternal life. Where we all must start is with faith in Jesus Christ. Otherwise, the tragic result is the same for us as it was for some of the Jewish people in Paul's day, who tried to do good works to win God's favor, rather than entering into a relationship with God.

> Without a relationship with God's Son, Jesus Christ, we can merely stumble *over* Christ, rather than experiencing the grace and forgiveness that we are meant to experience *through* Him. The wonderful Good News is that there is no need to stumble over Jesus. Trust in Christ always places us in right standing with God and brings us great joy.

ALL PEOPLE INVITED TO SALVATION THROUGH FAITH
ROMANS 10:1-13

> 1 Brethren, my heart's desire and prayer to God for Israel is that they may be saved. 2 For I bear them witness that they have a zeal for God, but not according to knowledge. 3 For they being ignorant of God's righteousness, and seeking to establish their own righteousness, have not submitted to the righteousness of God. 4 For Christ is the end of the law for righteousness to everyone who believes.
>
> 5 For Moses writes about the righteousness which is of the law, "*The man who does those things shall live by them.*" 6 But the righteousness of faith speaks in this way, "*Do not say in your heart, 'Who will ascend into heaven?'*" (that is, to bring Christ down *from* above) 7 or, "'*Who will descend into the abyss?*'" (that is, to bring Christ up from the dead). 8 But what does it say? "*The word is near you, in your mouth and in your heart*" (that is, the word of faith which we preach): 9 that if you confess with your mouth the Lord Jesus and believe in your heart that God has raised Him from the dead, you will be saved. 10 For with the heart one believes unto righteousness, and with the mouth confession is made unto salvation. 11 For the Scripture says, "*Whoever believes on Him will not be put to shame.*" 12 For there is no distinction between Jew and Greek, for the same Lord over all is rich to all who call upon Him. 13 For "*whoever calls on the name of the Lord shall be saved.*"

In chapter 9, Paul has discussed the spiritual condition of his people, the Jews. While expressing his concerns for them, Paul has painted a picture that would seem dark, but he continues to have hope and to pray for his people. His prayers should be a good example for us to continue to pray that those whom we love will come to know the love and grace of Christ.

Now in chapter 10, Paul addresses all the people in the church in Rome. He calls them "brethren," just as he referred to the Jewish people earlier (9:3). In 10:1-3, he uses the words *they*, *them*, and *their* to refer to the Jewish people, identifying them as distinct from himself.

Zeal for the Law

Paul tells the church that he is continuing to pray for the Jewish people and their salvation, indicating that he continues to have hope that they will come to know the love and grace of Christ. Paul also acknowledges that the Jewish people take their religion seriously: "they have a zeal for God, but not according to knowledge" (v. 2). The apostle Paul could relate easily to his people's way of thinking, because their mind-set was characteristic of him before he met Christ on the road to Damascus. His zeal had prompted him to outdo his contemporaries in devotion to his religion and motivated him to persecute members of the early Christian church (Gal. 1:13-14; Phil. 3:4-6). **Like Paul before his conversion, many Jews had a real zeal for their religion, but for some, this zeal was not based on the complete truth of God.** Lacking true and adequate knowledge, many of them established their own righteousness and became disobedient to God rather than submitting themselves to God's righteousness. The law revealed that there is a saving righteousness of God to which both the Law and the Prophets point. **Some Jews sought to earn for themselves salvation, and as a result trusted their religion rather than God's righteousness (Rom. 3:20-22).** Paul indicates that they were responsible for their current spiritual condition, which had resulted from their not relying on God. Only God's righteousness (His saving action in Christ) could bring them to salvation.

Christ, the End (The Goal) of the Law

What led to many of the Jews' skeptical response to Jesus Christ was that they did not understand that He was "the end of the law" (v. 4). Scholars have debated the meaning of the word *end* (*telos*)—whether it means end in the sense of goal or end in the sense of *termination*. Very likely Paul intends both meanings. There can be little doubt that Paul holds the law in high regard, and even Jesus himself during His time on earth had affirmed aspects of the law by broadening and deepening its meaning.

We know that Christ was the goal of the law because (1) He fulfilled the ceremonial law through His death on the cross (3:25; 1 Cor. 5:7), and (2) He embodied in His own character and life the perfect moral fulfillment of the law. Not only did Christ reveal the will of God, but He also lived in perfect obedience to it. **The moral aspects of the law, which are summed up in Christ's commandments to love God and one's neighbor, still have relevance today (Lev. 19:18).** The Mosaic law reached its goal in Jesus Christ, since it had looked forward to and anticipated His coming.

Christ was the termination of legalism as far as its being a means of obtaining salvation. Jesus Christ brought an end to the old order of relations between God and humans and introduced a new order in which the Spirit enables believers to do God's will (Rom. 8:4). Without Christ, the believer would be left with the daunting task of trying to keep perfectly the letter of the law (2:27-29). But to have Christ is to have the Spirit (8:9). **Christ through the ministry of the Spirit brought about the end of legalistic efforts to earn salvation. During His time on earth, Christ preached salvation through faith as always having been the real means by which people are saved.** For every believer, Christ puts an end to the establishing of one's own righteousness. **Since Christ is the goal and the end of the law, salvation belongs to every believer.**

Salvation Through Faith

As Paul clearly sees it, no one has to earn God's favor in order to receive forgiveness and eternal life. God has made salvation readily available to everyone. The only requirement is to receive God's offer through Jesus Christ. For scriptural support, Paul refers to two passages from the Old Testament (vv. 5-8).

Human Striving

Romans 10:5
For Moses writes about the righteousness which is of the law, "*The man who does those things shall live by them.*"

Leviticus 18:5
You shall therefore keep My statutes and My judgments, which if a man does, he shall live by them: I am the Lord.

The person who keeps the law will find life (Lev. 18:5). God never intended the law to save, but rather to be a guide for holy living. The law was for those who were already saved by grace. Securing of salvation by the keeping of the law would require the perfect keeping of every commandment. But humans, with their imperfections, can never measure up to God's perfections. Should one keep every single commandment, then he could talk about creating life, but not before.

Divine Grace

Romans 10:6-8
⁶ But the righteousness of faith speaks in this way, "*Do not say in your heart, 'Who will ascend into heaven?'*" (that is, to bring Christ down from above) ⁷ or, "'*Who will descend into the abyss?*'" (that is, to bring Christ up from the dead). ⁸ But what does it say? "*The word is near you, in your mouth and in your heart*" (that is, the word of faith which we preach).

Deuteronomy 30:12-14
¹² It is not in heaven, that you should say, 'Who will ascend into heaven for us and bring it to us, that we may hear it and do it?' ¹³ Nor is it beyond the sea, that you should say, 'Who will go over the sea for us and bring it to us, that we may hear it and do it?' ¹⁴ But the word is very near you, in your mouth and in your heart, that you may do it.

Righteousness (salvation) is through faith (Deut. 30:12-14; Rom. 3:17—4:8). The requirement is not works or performance. The way to life is simple. **God has already provided salvation in Christ. So it is not a matter of who will go into heaven and bring Christ down to the earth. And, too, it is not a question of who will descend into the grave and raise Christ from the dead.** All this has already happened. Christ has come to earth, died on a cross, and arisen from the dead. God has done in Christ all that is necessary for salvation. Again, human might and works are of no consequence for salvation. **The only thing we have to do is accept what God has done for us through trusting Him.** "The word" (the gospel, the Good News) is available to everyone; it is "near you, [even] in your mouth and in your heart" (10:8).

In Paul's day, the gospel was news that was not difficult to get. It had been preached by Paul and many others in many places. One did not have to leave or transcend this world in order to discover the truth and to be transformed. God had already put into the hearts of those who were hearing the preaching of the gospel the proper response to it. The gospel, appropriately described as "the word of faith" (v. 8), would justify, declaring one to be righteous, through God's grace and that person's faith. **Faith was, and is, God's way of saving humankind in the Old Testament, the New Testament, and today.**

How We Put Our Trust in God

How do we rely on what God has done for us in Christ? To answer this question, Paul brings forward the ideas **"in your mouth and in your heart" (Deut. 30:14; Rom. 10:8),** and says that salvation rests on two conditions:

First, we must confess with our mouths that Jesus is Lord, which the *New King James Version* renders "the Lord Jesus" (10:9). The preferred translation is "Jesus is Lord" (NIV), emphasizing the deity of Christ. In the Old Testament, *Lord* is a title given to God himself. "Jesus is Lord" reflects the oldest Christian belief that Jesus is God. The early Christians confessed Him to be God. Since the modern usage of the word *confess* usually implies admitting some wrong, it is better to substitute the term *testify* or *acknowledge*. Jesus is not a lord among many (Barrett, 1991, 201), but uniquely the divine Lord and Savior (1 Cor. 8:5-6). **Real conviction that Jesus is Lord will shape and fashion our lives so that we live to the glory of God and under His rule.**

Second, we must believe in our hearts that God raised Jesus from the dead. Belief in the Resurrection is a major emphasis throughout Paul's letter to the Romans (1:4; 4:24; 5:9-10; 6:4-5; 8:11). Christ's triumph over death assures believers that the Coming

Age has begun. An essential belief of the Christian faith is that Jesus arose from the dead. Christians must not only believe that Christ came and died on a cross, but that He also conquered death. The emphasis on His resurrection does not ignore the cross, but it does call attention to the event that completed our salvation. **Christ was raised for our justification (4:25). In raising His Son, God confirmed the saving value of the cross.** Christ was a historical person, but His resurrection showed that He is a living presence. **All who are joined to Christ through faith can have the assurance that they will conquer death and live with Him forever.**

Equality of Jews and Gentiles

In verses 11-13, Paul returns to a major theme: Jews and Gentiles are on equal footing. There is no distinction between them as far as opportunity for salvation, since "the same Lord over all is rich to all who call upon Him" (v. 12). Christ becomes the Lord and Savior of Jews and Gentiles by their calling on Him for salvation.

In Old Testament times, two prophets had predicted that the gospel would be for everyone:
- **According to the prophet Isaiah—"*Whoever* believes on Him will not be put to shame" (Rom. 10:11; Isa. 28:16).** Isaiah says nothing about works or any kind of performance. His prophecy indicates that salvation is simply a matter of faith for everyone—that is, a matter of the mind and heart—nothing more. When people put their life in the hands of Christ, they will not leave disappointed.
- **According to the prophet Joel—"*Whoever* calls on the name of the Lord shall be saved" (Joel 2:32; Rom. 10:13).** There is no limitation. **Anyone who calls in faith on the Lord for salvation will receive a true relationship with Christ and the salvation that he or she seeks.**

The Need for Knowledge-Based Zeal and for Testimony of Faith

Now return to a couple of truths to which Paul has called attention in this passage.

1. **Zeal for God is commendable if it is based on knowledge.** Israel had a courageous and devoted religious zeal, but it

was not fully enlightened and was in part misdirected. Enthusiasm uninformed by correct knowledge often has detrimental consequences, as it did for Israel and Paul. From time to time we hear the faulty statement, "It makes no difference what you believe as long as you are sincere in believing it." It does make a difference. What Israel believed led them to seek their own righteousness rather than God's righteousness. This overzealous desire to be righteous is what led Paul earlier in his life to persecute and murder followers of Christ in order to purge the world of people he thought to be in error. Paul's and Israel's religious zeal was not enlightened by the truth. In spite of their sincerity, they were wrong in some of their responses to that zeal. **Zeal informed by God's Word and His Spirit and energized by His love and mercy is the right prescription for belief and living.** The Pharisees knew the Word in a literal sense, but were devoid of enlightenment of the Spirit.

2. **Salvation rests in the lordship and resurrection of Christ and requires faith, which results in public acknowledgment of that faith (vv. 9-10).** Paul indicates that public acknowledgment or confession of our faith in Christ as Savior is a necessary response to believing in our heart. What is received by the heart is to be proclaimed by the mouth. On this basis, there is no such thing as "secret Christians." Those who are saved should publicly confess and openly acknowledge Jesus as their Lord and Savior.

Confessing our faith with our mouths helps to join us with other believers who have received eternal life. **God knows and understands our limitations.** Persons who are verbally impaired are joined with other believers through whatever communication gifts God has given them. Sometimes that may mean simply being who God created that person to be. Under certain circumstances, surely a nonverbal way of affirming our faith is sufficient. For example, the gospel is preached and taught in countries where the Christians and the church are persecuted. Therefore, there are times to talk about one's faith and times to keep silent. This concept may also be applied to sharing our faith in the workplace.

Effectively communicating (confessing) our faith involves carefully listening to the Holy Spirit for guidance regarding

when to speak and when to act, then using the talents and opportunities that the Lord has given us to communicate His love and hope to others.

ROMANS 10:1-13

KEYWORDS

Believe (see p. 119)

Brethren (see p. 63)

Confess
Meaning "to testify, acknowledge, declare." In certain contexts this term may mean "to admit," such as the confessing of sin and asking God to forgive us of wrongdoing and to change us.

Faith (see p. 23)

Grace (*charis*) (see p. 23)

Jesus Christ (see p. 59)

The Law (*Torah*) (see p. 48)

Lord
A term that expresses the nature of deity as the Sovereign of heaven and earth

Righteousness (*dikaiosune*) (see p. 48)

Salvation (see p. 23)

SUMMARY

Again Paul affirms his love for Israel and wishes good for his people. He recognizes that many Jews have had a religious zeal, but have had a lack of understanding about who Jesus Christ was and His relevance for their lives. Paul indicates that more than a lack of knowledge has been involved in his peoples' hesitancy to follow Christ. Many of them believed that they could establish their own righteousness by trusting in their own obedience to the law and determined to do so. As a result, they rejected the idea that faith could be a possible means for receiving salvation, and so did not respond to the way of faith, when it was presented to them through the Good News about Christ.

God's way of salvation is faith in Jesus Christ. Christ is the goal and the end of the law for everyone who believes. The Old Testament had announced salvation as being based on faith, and the New Testament tells us that salvation is immediately available to all who believe in Christ and profess their faith in Him.

LIFE APPLICATION

Zeal for God can be marred by a lack of knowledge (*epignosis*) of Him. In Paul's time, the Jewish people had a genuine zeal for God, but for some, their passionate devotion was misplaced because of inadequate knowledge. Some Jewish people misconstrued what God's will was and became legalistic, trying to establish their own righteousness, rather than relying on Christ to place them in right standing with God and help them do God's will. The moral law was a good guide to holy living for the Jewish people, like it is for us today, but it never is the means for receiving salvation.

The only thing required to receive forgiveness of sins is simply faith in the gospel—a faith, of course, that evidences itself in holy living. The gospel fulfilled God's promises recorded in the Old Testament. Christ came down from heaven, died on the cross, and rose from the dead for all peoples' benefit. Now it is only a matter of our accepting Christ's free gift of forgiveness of sin and newness of life. The gospel of salvation is already "near you, even in your mouth and in your heart" (Rom. 10:8).To enter into a relationship with Christ, all we have to do is trust in Jesus and confess Him as our Savior: "Whoever calls on the name of the Lord shall be saved" (v. 13).

REVELATIONS ABOUT FAITH IN ISRAEL'S TEACHINGS
ROMANS 10:14-21

¹⁴ How then shall they call on Him in whom they have not believed? And how shall they believe in Him of whom they have not heard? And how shall they hear without a preacher? ¹⁵ And how shall they preach unless they are sent? As it is written:

"*How beautiful are the feet of those who preach the gospel of peace,
Who bring glad tidings of good things!*"

¹⁶ But they have not all obeyed the gospel. For Isaiah says, "Lord, *who has believed our report*?" ¹⁷ So then faith comes by hearing, and hearing by the word of God.

> ¹⁸ But I say, have they not heard? Yes indeed:
>
> *"Their sound has gone out to all the earth,
> And their words to the ends of the world."*
>
> ¹⁹ But I say, did Israel not know? First Moses says:
>
> *"I will provoke you to jealousy by those who are not a nation,
> I will move you to anger by a foolish nation."*
>
> ²⁰ But Isaiah is very bold and says:
>
> *"I was found by those who did not seek Me;
> I was made manifest to those who did not ask for Me."*
>
> ²¹ But to Israel he says:
>
> *"All day long I have stretched out My hands
> To a disobedient and contrary people."*

The best way to understand verses 14-21 is to realize that in this passage, Paul is returning to his earlier discussion about why many Jewish people did not accept the gospel as being true (9:31-32). The apostle Paul has stated in the previous passage, "Whoever calls on the name of the Lord shall be saved" (10:13). In response to this statement, the question arises concerning how one can possibly go about calling on the Lord Jesus Christ if he or she has not heard the Good News. The Jews scattered throughout the world in Paul's time could have claimed that they had not had opportunity to hear and believe the news about Jesus Christ. Before answering this assertion, Paul traces the steps that are involved in the process of calling on the Lord Jesus (vv. 14-15).

Calling on the Lord Jesus for Help and Salvation
- **Before calling, one must believe:**
  "How then shall they call on Him in whom they have not believed?" (v. 14)

  The only way anyone can receive forgiveness through grace, which results in salvation, is by calling on the Lord. Logically speaking, calling on Jesus and asking Him for help and salvation require that one has already believed in Him. The majority of the Jewish people who had heard of Jesus considered His claims to be the Son of God to be untrue and thought of Him as an impostor, similar to many false prophets of His day. The apostle Paul also had the same opinion before he came to believe in Christ on the road to Damascus. For Jews to call on the Lord Jesus, they would have had to believe that Jesus of Nazareth was the Son of God and the Messiah of Israel. It also meant that they would have had to believe in Christ's death, resurrection, and lordship (vv. 9-10).

Calling on the Lord Jesus Christ has always and continues to require belief, and involves more than repeating a set confession, such as this: "You repeat after me and you will be saved." **Calling on the Lord means trusting in Jesus Christ for salvation.** No one can be saved without faith in Him.

- **Before believing, one must hear:**
"How shall they believe in Him of whom they have not heard?" (v. 14)

    The better translation here is *whom*, not *of whom*. The Greek does not include the word *of*. The implication is clear. When genuine preaching has occurred, the listeners of the sermons have heard either Christ speaking for Himself directly to them, or Christ speaking through His preachers, who proclaim His Word.

    Both the Jews and Gentiles of Paul's day, as well as all of us living today, not only have needed to hear about Christ, but **they (and we) have needed to hear Christ speaking directly to them (and us). No one can truly believe in a person and his or her message without hearing that person's own beliefs communicated in some way.** Hearing other peoples' personal impressions about a person are not the same as hearing or reading a person's words for oneself. Let the preachers and all the people of God remember that this biblical preaching must be Spirit-empowered if Christ is to be heard. Otherwise, a person is just making a speech, and anyone can do that—even someone who is not called.

- **Before hearing, someone must preach:**
"How shall they hear without a preacher?" (v. 14)

Men and women hear the gospel when others preach it. The preaching of the gospel is absolutely essential to the life of the church; the church cannot live without it. This is not to imply that the church does not exist unless there are weekly sermons of a specified structure and length, delivered on particular days, at particular times in a church building. In countries where Christians are persecuted, observing rigid requirements for public worship can sometimes be impossible. **The proclamation of God's Word can occur anywhere and anytime God's people are together, which implies that two people could proclaim God's Word.** It may occur in our pulpits, in our cars, or on the street as we walk and talk with each other. **Biblical preaching occurs wherever the Word of God is proclaimed by anyone whom God calls to speak His Word.**

Genuine, Spirit-anointed preaching is fundamental to the life of the church. Men and women are saved through it, and they are also strengthened and sustained in their walk with the Lord by it. **According to the New Testament, biblical preaching can take place in many forms and when and where it pleases God (Barrett, 1977, 56-57) (see Acts 2:22ff.; 4:5ff.; 7:2ff.; 17:22ff.).**

- Before preaching, someone must be sent to preach: "How shall they preach unless they are sent?" (v. 15)

Words become preaching when the one delivering them is *sent* (called) by the Lord to proclaim the Word of the Lord. Simply standing up and delivering a discourse is not necessarily preaching, unless that person has been called of God to do so and the words spoken are in agreement with God's Word as recorded in Scripture. Preaching is not a matter of personal choice or done on the basis of one's own authority. The verb *sent* (*apostolosin*) is derived from the same root as *apostle* (*apostolos*)—one commissioned by the Lord or the church. Preachers of the gospel, therefore, proclaim the Word of God under and with the authority of the One who sent them. There are no true messengers unless the Lord sends them. God is completely free to choose and send whom He wills.

The church's responsibility is to examine and support those whom the Lord sends. The need is for the church's sending to coincide with the Lord's sending, but sometimes the church may make mistakes. In the Old Testament, Israel made mistakes in regard to its prophets and kings (see 1 Sam. 19:1ff.; 1 Kings 13:1ff.; 14:1ff.; 2 Chron. 24:22-24; Jer. 26:20-24; Amos 7:10-17). In order to avoid making such mistakes, the church must be diligent in determining those who have a divine call to ministerial leadership. The church has an inescapable obligation to communicate the Good News of God's love for all people and to tell about the freedom and life that we all can enjoy in Christ. In order to do so, the church must prayerfully seek God's guidance and send those whom the Lord has called.

A Summary of the Steps for Calling on the Lord

Through his questions, Paul has described in reverse order the steps involved in calling on the name of the Lord. These steps are as follows: Someone is sent by God. → That person preaches. → Listeners hear the words from the Lord delivered through the preacher. → Listeners believe. → Listeners call on the Lord. → God then calls some of those who have called on the Lord to preach. The process repeats with more people coming to Christ and those people spreading the Good News. In one's own life, this process would begin with the Lord (calling on the Lord as the result of one's faith), then ultimately conclude with the Lord (preaching because of being sent by God).

Israel's Opportunities to Hear the Good News

The four questions that Paul raises in verses 14-15 have strong implications about what it means *to be called* or *to hear Jesus speak*. These questions are applicable to more situations than just for the purpose of putting together sermons or discussing how to preach. These questions are really a starting point for understanding Christian preaching, which must always be biblical—Christ-centered and Spirit-anointed in order to measure up to the apostolic, Pentecostal preaching of the first century.

> **Paul's Questions:**
> - *How . . . shall they call on Him in whom they have not believed?*
> - *How shall they believe in Him in whom they have not heard?*
> - *How shall they hear without a preacher?*
> - *How shall they preach unless they are sent?*
>
> (Rom. 10:14-15)

Paul responds to these four questions by quoting Isaiah 52:7—"How beautiful are the feet of those who preach the gospel of peace, who bring glad tidings of good things!" (Rom. 10:15). By using this quote from Isaiah, Paul is saying that more than eight hundred years earlier, the prophet Isaiah recognized that he and others were preaching the gospel (the Good News about the coming Messiah). By saying "How beautiful are the feet of those who preach," Isaiah had characterized in a poetic manner the messengers as being the fairest people who had trod the earth.

According to Paul, if Israel had not had their prophets (preachers) who shared many revelations about the coming Messiah, then there would not have been the expectation that Israel would be able to recognize the Messiah when He came. In Israel, there was not a lack of opportunity for the Jewish people to hear the truth. All devout Jews had grown up hearing the revelations of the prophets, which included descriptions of their coming Messiah and His purpose. This Good News was proclaimed in the teachings of their prophets and was taught to them in their synagogues and homes.

For many Jewish people, their hindrance to accepting a new way was that they (like many of us today) were comfortable within their existing religious practices. Their religious tradition called for them to follow a law code to the letter in order to win favor with God, and they could not fathom a

God of power and love who would come to them in a humble form, offering free grace and forgiveness.

Paul, once again in order to explain to his people that this Good News of free grace and life through faith was embedded in their teachings, appeals to Scripture, quoting Psalm 19:4: "Their sound has gone out to all the earth, and their words to the ends of the world" (Rom. 10:18). The message about the Messiah had gone throughout the world. God's people could not accurately plea that they had never heard the gospel, for it had been revealed through the teachings of their prophets, and then later had been preached far and wide in the Roman Empire. They had heard the Good News, but **the only way that God can have a true personal relationship with a person is if that person listens and really hears God's words of invitation, and responds with trust and obedience.** Paul sums up the situation in verse 17: "So then faith comes by hearing, and hearing by the word of God."

Israel's Understanding and Response to the Good News

"Did Israel not know?" (v. 19). That is, was the message too difficult, too profound, or too obscure for the people of Israel to grasp? Paul's response in verses 19-20 was that many of the Gentiles had understood God's grace even though, prior to the preaching of the gospel to them, they only had God's revelation provided through the Creation (1:20). God had given many additional advantages to the Israelites, His chosen people, in order to prepare them to welcome and nurture the world's Messiah when He arrived. On the other hand, the Gentiles who accepted God's grace had not had the added benefits of the law, the prophets, and other innumerable blessings like Israel, but they were still able to grasp the love and forgiveness that God had for them (9:4-5).

Israel's inattention to all of the spiritual truths contained in their teachings is representative of many people who over the centuries have heard God's voice, but either have not recognized it as the voice of God or, due to discomfort or fear, have not readily responded. Israel, like many individuals and nations since then, had a long history of struggles with God. Long

Salvation and Israel

ago, Isaiah had said, "[Lord], who has believed our report?" (53:1; Rom. 10:16). Such passages from Israel's own Scriptures indicate that the people of Israel had opportunities to hear and learn about God's salvation plan of grace and faith. Their failure to perceive the message and to respond positively should be a warning to the church today. **Like Israel, we have a rich spiritual heritage and tradition as well as tremendous opportunities and blessings, to which we need to be attentive and grateful, and to respond to God with faith and commitment.**

God's Foreknowledge Regarding Israel's Response

God had foreseen that many people of Israel would not grasp and respond in faith to the gospel. To demonstrate this point, Paul cites two passages from the Old Testament, the first from the Law and the second from the Prophets:

From the Law (Moses)

Romans 10:19
"I will provoke you to jealousy by those who are not a nation, I will move you to anger by a foolish nation."

Deuteronomy 32:21
"They have provoked Me to jealousy by what is not God; they have moved Me to anger by their foolish idols. But I will provoke them to jealousy by those who are not a nation; I will move them to anger by a foolish nation."

In this passage from Deuteronomy, Moses declared that the Gentiles would share in the blessings of God and that their inclusion would provoke anger and jealousy among God's people. **Moses had prophesied that the Gentiles' grace-filled relationship with God would provoke envy among the Jewish people—for the Jewish people, like all people, in their innermost being, desired to be forgiven and to have an intimate relationship with God.** (This theme will be developed more in our discussion about Romans 11.)

From the Prophets (Isaiah)

Romans 10:20
"I was found by those who did not seek Me; I was made manifest to those who did not ask for Me."

Isaiah 65:1
"I was sought by those who did not ask for Me; I was found by those who did not seek Me. I said, 'Here I am, here I am,' to a nation that was not called by My name."

Isaiah had prophesied that "a nation that was not called by My name" (aliens, Gentiles, non-covenant people) would be included in God's family (65:1). Later in history, Paul himself had also pleaded with his people to seek God in matters of revelation and truth, but he had received little more from them than skepticism and rebuff. The Book of Acts shows that in the initial period of his missionary work, Paul taught his own people in Jewish synagogues in cities to which he traveled. It was not until after his own people did not respond to his message of grace and faith that Paul shifted his work to ministering predominantly to Gentiles (Acts 13:44-46; 18:5-6; 19:8-10). **As Moses and Isaiah had predicted, in response to Israel's skepticism about God's mysterious salvation plan, God no longer focused His efforts primarily on them—the people whom He had chosen to bring the Messiah into the world. God was calling new messengers, such as Paul, to spread the Good News to the rest of the world.** The results were that many of the Gentiles understood and received the gospel, even though they had not had some of the advantages that Israel had.

Lessons for Christian Ministry Today

The truths that Paul communicates in Romans 10:14-21 apply not only to the church and Jewish people of Paul's day but also to those of us in the Christian church and to our friends in the broader world today. **The world in which we live needs to hear the proclamation of the gospel. People are in need of God's love and forgiveness that is available through a life-giving relationship with Christ.** As Christians, we are not only to be servants of Christ but also heralds of this message of salvation. **Receiving the message of the gospel is the *basis* of our Christian life, and the *fruit* of that new life is our sharing of the gospel with others.**

Living the Christian life is important, for it is the expression of our love for Christ. It also demonstrates the reality of our message and will help others to receive Christ; but it does not take the place of the preaching of the gospel—also telling others our Good News. The lifestyle of the most devoted Christian cannot bring the assurance of the forgiveness of sins that is so desperately needed. Only the message of salvation through the blood of Christ can bring forgiveness. **Directly telling others the Good News about Jesus Christ—about His grace and forgiveness, and the eternal life that He offers—is the primary means of introducing people to the Savior.** The truth that God has revealed in His Son must be proclaimed. The Christian lifestyle complements the preaching of the Word, but does not replace it. **Both the Word *and* godly living are vital to the life of the church; but without the Word of God, the faith that has prompted us to love and serve others will dry up and wither away. The life of faith and love flows from the Word of God.**

In Paul's day, God's chosen people were part of a religious system that focused on following rules rather than building relationships with God. The church in the twenty-first century sits within a modern, secular culture that is often more focused on acquiring knowledge and skills and tending to matters of finance and success, rather than tending to the soul. **The church's commitment to preaching the life-giving gospel and living the Christian life has never been more urgent. The church must give an understandable, compelling witness to a world that is groping in darkness and gripped by sin, anxiety, and fear.** The faithful must be filled and empowered by the Spirit to bear witness to Christ and His saving work. **Indispensable to the witness of the church is that people not simply hear about Christ but that they hear Christ speaking directly to their minds and hearts through the Holy Spirit's use of our words and actions.** This is the urgent need today—that all of us hear Christ himself speaking to us.

ROMANS 10:14-21

KEYWORDS

Believe (see p. 119)

Called by God (see p. 228)

Faith (see p. 23)

Forgiveness (see p. 47)

Obedience to the Gospel/Obedience of Faith (see p. 185)

Preach
To proclaim God's Word. True preaching is done by a person who has received his or her assignment and message from God.

Revealed (see p. 68)

SUMMARY

Throughout Israel's history, God had revealed and communicated His Good News about the coming Messiah and His message of forgiveness through the teachings of Israel's prophets. God had blessed the people of Israel with extraordinary opportunities to learn and to receive His grace and blessings in all their fullness. In the teachings of their prophets, the Jewish people had the information that they needed to recognize the Lord's presence when He arrived among them and to call on Him for help and salvation.

In Romans 10:14-21, in order to explain the chain of events necessary for a person to be saved, Paul raises a number of questions that come directly from his people's own Scriptures. Although the prophecies to which Paul refers in his questions had already come to pass, Paul indicates that his people still had not come to a realization that the prophecies had been fulfilled. Paul and fellow believers had taught about Jesus the Messiah throughout the Roman Empire where the Jewish people lived, but many of them still did not grasp this message of Good News. At the same time, many Gentiles who had not been privileged to hear about the Messiah through revelations and prophecies throughout their lives had readily understood and embraced the message of Good News when they heard it. Paul's implication in this passage is that because his people had had such rich instruction in their religious teachings, they were responsible for responding to this God of love who had revealed Himself to them in such a miraculous manner through Jesus the Messiah.

LIFE APPLICATION

Like the Jewish people, God has given us many blessings, and we have many reasons for accepting God's redeeming love in Christ. Through our reading of the Book of Romans, God has been revealing Himself to us and has been placing the transforming power of the gospel within our easy reach. God is using the words of the apostle Paul to invite us into relationship with Himself. Like the Jewish people, in order to enter into a true relationship with God, we must make the decision to respond to God's blessings and invitation. Will we accept His grace and forgiveness, and His invitation to a relationship with Himself through Jesus Christ? Will we accept the peace that God has promised us through His Holy Spirit?

For those of us who have accepted God's gift of grace, we must now share that Good News with others. The preaching of the gospel is so important because it stirs up faith and invites others to receive Christ as their Savior and challenges them to express their faith in Christ through holy living.

God calls and sends preachers to carry out the Great Commission, their task being to herald the message of God's redeeming love. The results for those who hear and accept this message are the freedom that salvation offers and eternal life with God. Since there is no greater message, Paul describes the feet of the messengers as beautiful. It is so urgent that this message of Jesus Christ is to be spread to the ends of the earth!. Let us—the church, God's people—be God's instruments of grace for the world. God's Good News can save you and me—in fact, all of humankind.

GOD'S SALVATION PLAN FOR THE FAITHFUL OF ISRAEL
ROMANS 11:1-10

¹ I say then, has God cast away His people? Certainly not! For I also am an Israelite, of the seed of Abraham, of the tribe of Benjamin. ² God has not cast away His people whom He foreknew. Or do you not know what the Scripture says of Elijah, how he pleads with God against Israel, saying, ³ *"Lord, they have killed Your prophets and torn down Your altars, and I alone am left, and they seek my life"*? ⁴ But what does the divine response say to him? *"I have reserved for Myself seven thousand men who have not bowed the knee to Baal."* ⁵ Even so then, at this present time there is a remnant according to the election of grace. ⁶ And if by grace, then it is no longer of works; otherwise grace is no longer grace. But if it is of works, it is no longer grace; otherwise work is no longer work.

⁷ What then? Israel has not obtained what it seeks; but the elect have obtained it, and the rest were blinded. ⁸ Just as it is written:

"God has given them a spirit of stupor,
Eyes that they should not see

> And ears that they should not hear,
> To this very day."
>
> ⁹ And David says:
>
> "Let their table become a snare and a trap,
> A stumbling block and a recompense to them.
> ¹⁰ Let their eyes be darkened, so that they do not see,
> And bow down their back always."

God's Ongoing Love for the Jewish People

Since many of God's chosen people had not been attentive to all the details in the revelations found in their teachings, they did not recognize and embrace the Messiah when He came. Would God then reject them because they had not done so? **In spite of the people of Israel's disbelief that Jesus could be their Messiah, Paul has continued to assert that God's promises to Israel have not failed. Even so, Paul still anticipates that some critics will ask, "Has God cast away His people?" (v. 1). In response to this possible question, the apostle Paul strongly objects, "Certainly not!"**

Down through the centuries, people have erroneously claimed on the basis of Paul's warnings that God has disowned the Jewish people, because He has considered them to be a rebellious nation. Sadly, such misinterpretations of Paul's words have even been used to justify anti-Semitic attitudes and persecution of the Jews. The idea that God would disown His chosen and beloved people is an unthinkable idea to Paul. God had by no means washed His hands of His people. **God has always loved and continues to love the Jewish people. Though many people of Israel did not fully comprehend who Christ was and, as a result, did not follow Him, Israel always had and will continue to have an important place in the plan and purpose of God.** Why?

Paul's position is that Israel will continue to be a beneficiary of God's love and a portion of His blessings, because there will always be Jewish people who respond in faith and obedience. Paul mentions again the *doctrine of the remnant* **(see 9:27),** which had appeared in a number of the Old Testament teachings,

Salvation and Israel

especially the prophecies of Isaiah (8:18; 10:21). **The *doctrine of the remnant* refers to the portion of Jewish people who remained faithful to God, both in Old Testament times and in Paul's day.**

The apostle Paul was a Jew, a descendant of Abraham and from the family of Benjamin, and he was also a part of the remnant, a minority in Israel who had remained faithful. **As a part of the remnant, Paul was among those who had come to be the hope of Israel (Rom. 9:27-29).** In no way had God rejected Paul just because he was part of a larger group of people who, at different points in their history, had not been faithful. It was ludicrous to suggest that. Paul was both a Jew and a Christian whose life had been radically changed by the grace of God. Besides *not* being rejected, but he had become a committed follower of the risen Christ and had received additional blessings. The implication here is that **God, out of respect for the remnant and His love for His chosen people, will continue to reach out in invitation to Israel, inviting them to a full life of grace and faith through their Messiah, Jesus Christ.**

A few months after writing this letter to the Christians in Rome, Paul told the Jerusalem church that many thousands of Jews had believed on the Lord (Acts 20:21). God had not repudiated the faithful remnant which He foreknew as His people (Rom. 11:2). **Paul and others were living proof that God was not finished with His remarkable plan for the Jews.**

The Remnant in Old Testament Times
Elijah and the Remnant

A good example of the faithful remnant existed in Elijah's time. During that time, the nation of Israel as a whole had become apostate; that is, the majority of the people were being disloyal to God. **Recognizing the spiritual condition of his people, Elijah falsely assumed that he was the only one who was remaining faithful to God. As a result, he was overwhelmed with despair.** He exclaimed, "Lord, they have killed Your prophets and torn down Your altars, and I alone am left, and they seek my life" (Rom. 11:3; 1 Kings 19:10, 14). Indeed, Elijah's state of mind is a classic example of how deep despair can result from our making assumptions based on the partial information that we have as limited human beings. **A divine oracle—a revelation from God—informed the prophet that there were seven thousand in Israel who had not bowed to Baal (1 Kings 19:18; Rom. 11:4). The oracle gave Elijah assurance that God had not abandoned His people.** Elijah was only one among a number of faithful souls. The presence of a faithful remnant was a reminder of the tension between belief and apostasy—a tension that ran throughout Israel's history. The existence of this faithful minority can also be an encouragement to us today when we face difficult times, reminding us that we are not alone. **God does not abandon His people, and it is good for us to pray for others who may also feel isolated and alone.**

Characteristics of the Remnant

Whether the whole people or just a minority, God's people are always defined by grace and faith, not by works and performance (Rom. 11:5-6). The remnant did not create itself through being good; God's grace and love brought it into existence. **This reality of God's grace should free us all from arrogance and the illusion that we can save ourselves. God's grace must be accepted and received, and then it motivates people of faith to do good works and to live humble, holy lives. As a result, we will reach out with love to all peoples, inviting them, as God has, to a relationship of grace and healing in Jesus Christ.**

The Prophets and the Remnant

Throughout Israel's history a small minority of the people were consistently faithful souls. **Among Israel's faithful were the prophets, who prophesied about the Jewish people's present and future faithfulness to God and their future response to the coming Messiah.** Despite the prophets' revelations, many people were unable to recognize Jesus Christ as being their Messiah, and some even thought that He was an impostor and blasphemer. There was, however, a remnant, a minority, who believed that Jesus was their promised Savior, and upon accepting Jesus, they bowed before Him as their Lord.

Prominent among the Old Testament prophets who prophesied about the coming Messiah were Micah and Isaiah.

- **Micah**—Micah was one of the prophets who had spoken about the future of the Jewish remnant. **He related his vision of God's gathering the remnant (Mic. 2:12; 5:3).** As a shepherd gathers his sheep and leads them back to their home pasture, the prophet expected God to restore a faithful remnant of His people to Jerusalem from their exile.
- **Isaiah**—**Throughout the Book of Isaiah, the doctrine of the remnant had great prominence (see 6:1-13; 20:6), indicating that there would always be a group of Jewish people who would remain faithful.** In fact, Isaiah called his son *Shear-Jashub*, which means "salvation of the remnant" or "the remnant shall return" (see 7:3). Although the theology of the remnant does draw a distinction within Israel between the obedient and the disobedient, God has always been at work among those who are being disobedient, as well as those who are being obedient, offering and working out His saving mercy and grace (Rom. 11:5-10).

Prophecies About God's Response to Israel

God extended His ongoing grace to the true Israel (those who remained faithful) while allowing those who were pursuing their own self-interests and not seeking God to go their own way. Their choices ultimately resulted in their becoming indifferent and being unable to see and hear what God was doing (vv. 7-8). This alienation is God's response (often referred to as *judgment* or *wrath*), which was and continues to be the natural outcome of going one's own way, instead of making the Lord the priority of one's life.

Paul puts together a number of Old Testament scriptures showing that God had foreseen Israel's response to God and the resulting outcome (v. 7). He quotes Psalm 69:22, "Let their table become a snare and a trap" (Rom. 11:9). This statement refers to people who are comfortably seated at a banquet table feasting, and depicts a common attitude that Paul saw among his people. **Because Israel had been chosen by God to bring His Messiah into the world, some of the Israelites had**

become overly confident in and reliant on their special status and calling, which eventually led to their becoming prideful. It was this pride that had become a hindrance in their relationship with God.**

Continuing, Paul cites additional Old Testament scriptures indicating that whenever the people of Israel had been unfaithful, God had responded to their desire to be free of His authority by allowing their hearts to become hard, as in the case of Pharaoh. **During the times when Israel was guilty of abandoning the ways of God, their absence from Him resulted in a spiritual sleep coming upon them. They were no longer able to hear God's voice, and they became spiritually blind (Deut. 29:4; Isa. 6:9-10; 29:10).** Because of their disobedience and desire to go their own way, out of respect for their choices, God withdrew His Spirit and left them to their willful ways. Hardness of heart, spiritual blindness, and spiritual sleep indicated that they were out of touch with God. **This hardening of hearts, which is the natural result of withdrawal from God, should be understood to have been occurring while God's children were being disobedient to the Lord, and that the hardening was only temporary (cf. Rom. 11:11ff.).**

The Remnant of Israel and the Christian Church Today

The theology of the remnant has identified a distinction between the faithful and the unfaithful among the people of Israel. **The presence of a smaller faithful group within the chosen people of God that existed during Paul's day has at least three implications for the church today.**

1. **The existence of the remnant today, as in biblical times, gives assurance that God is continually present with those who seek Him, and that He has not abandoned the nation of Israel.** At first glance, some of Paul's statements might appear to imply that the gates of heaven are closed to Israel, except for the remnant of Israel. God has not withdrawn His promises to Israel, nor has He renegotiated those promises to include only a faithful few. Neither has God allowed some of His chosen people to move away from communion with Him so that a "new Israel"

(the Christian church) could replace them—the Christian church has not replaced and will not replace Israel.

2. **In light of Israel's disobedience at different points in their history and their failure to recognize their Messiah, they, like us (when we fail to understand and live according to God's plan for us), can never be truly deserving of God's grace.** What person or nation does deserve God's grace? **God's mercy and grace are far more abundant than any person or nation deserves.** Paul anticipates that before the end of history, God will focus once again on Israel, reaching out to them, and large numbers will turn to Christ as their Messiah (Rom. 11:26-27). As Christians, we do well to pray for the Jewish people and look forward with anticipation to the day when all God's people, Jews and Gentiles, will join together celebrating God's saving grace in Christ.

3. **God had entered into a special covenant relationship with the nation of Israel, but this did not guarantee that the entire nation would seek Him and would be saved.** From the days of Moses until Paul's time, at no time in their history had the entire nation of Israel been faithful to the Lord. **Only those people who believed in God (as Abraham did) and kept their covenant commitments had a true relationship with God and were saved.** God made a distinction between Abraham's spiritual children and his natural children (2:25-29). In reality, the nation as a whole was never the people of God, but there was always a faithful remnant who truly trusted in God and submitted themselves to Him. **The remnant in Israel teaches us that God does not save a nation, a race, or a denomination. Salvation is a matter of a personal relationship with God.** Belonging to a certain race or denomination will not make us right with God. During different points in their history, the Israelites as a whole became unobservant and unmindful about spiritual matters, forgetting God's extraordinary blessings. It was only a minority of them who remained faithful and trusted in the Lord. This remnant consisted of the dedicated and faithful men and women within the nation. There is a remnant in the church today. They are bound to their Savior by faith and they live in obedience to Him.

The Greatest Letter Ever Written

ROMANS 11:1-10

KEYWORDS

Chosen by God (see p. 105)

Elect of God (see p. 238)

Foreknowledge (see p. 228)

Grace (*charis*) (see p. 23)

Jews/Israelites/Hebrews (see p. 29)

The Remnant (see p. 269)

Salvation (see p. 23)

SUMMARY

Among the Jewish people was a minority (a remnant), who believed that Jesus was their promised Messiah. This group of people had accepted Jesus Christ's invitation to a life of grace and freedom and had come to rely on God's grace and faith as the basis for eternal life, rather than relying on their own good works.

Paul's own conversion from a religion of constantly striving to be good in order to please God to accepting a life of grace and freedom in Christ is an indication that God had not rejected Israel. God was continuing to call His chosen people, inviting them into relationship, just as He had done for Paul.

In Paul's day, there continued to be a faithful remnant, just as there had been during the days of Elijah. During the days of Elijah, many of God's own people had not remained faithful to Him. Only a few had heeded Elijah's message, and later the response to Jesus and His apostles had been the same. Throughout history, for those who have not wished to follow God's plan and to include Him in their lives, God has respected their choices and has sorrowfully withdrawn His Spirit from them, leaving them to their willful ways.

God continues to reach out and call all people. He offers grace that will save anyone who is willing to receive the gospel. Although there may be only a minority who respond, this minority, as in the days of Elijah and Paul, benefits from a personal relationship with God and free salvation.

LIFE APPLICATION

God has always loved the Jewish people, never closing the door of privilege and opportunity to salvation to them. The blessings of the glorious gospel, which were promised through the prophets, continue to be available to all Jewish people. The Good News of Christ invites each Jewish person into a relationship with the Savior and into the church (the body of Christ).

As Christians we have a responsibility to the Jewish people—to be grateful to God for them, respect and interact with them in friendship, and take any opportunity we may have to share with them the Good News of grace, forgiveness, and freedom of Jesus the Messiah. We owe no people as much as we do the Jews. After all, our Savior was a Jew and our Christian faith is rooted in the Jewish faith.

Today among the Jewish people, there is a remnant of those who believe in and follow Jesus as their Messiah. At a future time, Jesus Christ will return and then the majority of God's chosen people will believe in Him as their Messiah and be saved (11:25-31).

One has to wonder if there is not a great deal of similarity between present-day Christians and the majority of the Jews in Elijah's and Paul's day. Could there be only a remnant of true Christians (those who truly trust in God) in the present-day church? Let us examine our souls and submit our lives in humility to God, allowing Him to forgive and transform us and bring us all into a true relationship with Himself.

GOD'S SALVATION PLAN FOR NON-JEWS
ROMANS 11:11-24

¹¹ I say then, have they stumbled that they should fall? Certainly not! But through their fall, to provoke them to jealousy, salvation has come to the Gentiles. ¹² Now if their fall is riches for the world, and their failure riches for the Gentiles, how much more their fullness! ¹³ For I speak to you Gentiles; inasmuch as I am an apostle to the Gentiles, I magnify my ministry, ¹⁴ if by any means I may provoke to jealousy those who are my flesh and save some of them. ¹⁵ For if their being cast away is the reconciling of the world, what will their acceptance be but life from the dead?

¹⁶ For if the firstfruit is holy, the lump is also holy; and if the root is holy, so are the branches. ¹⁷ And if some of the branches were broken off, and you, being a wild olive tree, were grafted in among

> them, and with them became a partaker of the root and fatness of the olive tree, [18] do not boast against the branches. But if you do boast, remember that you do not support the root, but the root supports you.
>
> [19] You will say then, "Branches were broken off that I might be grafted in." [20] Well said. Because of unbelief they were broken off, and you stand by faith. Do not be haughty, but fear. [21] For if God did not spare the natural branches, He may not spare you either. [22] Therefore consider the goodness and severity of God: on those who fell, severity; but toward you, goodness, if you continue in His goodness. Otherwise you also will be cut off. [23] And they also, if they do not continue in unbelief, will be grafted in, for God is able to graft them in again. [24] For if you were cut out of the olive tree which is wild by nature, and were grafted contrary to nature into a cultivated olive tree, how much more will these, who are natural branches, be grafted into their own olive tree?

After speaking to Jews and Gentiles in the church in Rome, Paul turns to speak primarily to the Gentiles in verses 11-24. Although he has been speaking to them since 9:1, "to you Gentiles" (11:13) indicates that Paul wants the Gentile Christians to pay special attention to what he is going to say. This does not indicate a change in audience, for the church in Rome was comprised primarily of Gentile Christians. **The Gentile presence in the church had been growing, creating a situation where the Jewish Christians were now in the minority.**

God's Outreach to the Gentiles

Paul begins this passage by posing questions for thought to the Gentile Christians. Since Israel had stumbled (did not recognize their Messiah when He had come), had they stumbled into utter destruction? Paul's answer is, "Certainly not!" (v. 11). Paul's next comment in the second part of verse 11 is the main theme of chapter 11. The Jewish people's stumbling in regards to their Messiah opened the door to the Gentiles. As a result, many Gentiles came to follow Christ, and the Jewish people who observed the Gentiles' grace-filled lives became envious and desired these blessings also.

The immediate result of the Jewish people's lack of favorable response to the gospel was that the Good News was sent to the

Gentiles. As the Book of Acts indicates, Paul himself had witnessed the effect that the inclusion of the Gentiles had on the Jews (13:46-50; 18:6-17). **God in His wisdom used the Jewish people's response toward fulfilling His own plan of offering free salvation to all peoples. Although God did not cause the Jewish people to stumble, He did use their mistakes for the good of the whole world.**

Israel had erred, but out of their error had come a gracious, far-reaching result—the preaching of the gospel to the Gentile world. Twice in Romans 11:12, Paul describes the gospel as Gentiles' "riches." Israel's discomfort with the Good News opened up a way for the news to be directly offered to a people who would accept it. The Jewish people's misunderstandings about the gospel actually enriched the Gentiles and brought the world many blessings. Through the stumbling of Israel, God offered the gospel to the world and good, not evil, has come out of it. Part of the good outcome was Paul's calling by God to be the "apostle to the Gentiles" (v. 13). This, too, was serving the plan of salvation.

Paul's Hope for the Jewish People

As Paul increased his ministry among the Gentiles, he hoped it would arouse the consciences of the Jews so that they would rethink their understanding of Jesus and would turn to Him for forgiveness and salvation. In fact, Paul implies that his concern for the Jews was one of the major reasons that he worked so hard (v. 14). His ministry, therefore, was not only for the benefit of the Gentiles, but for the Jews as well.

Paul's thinking is that his people's acceptance of the gospel will be nothing short of "life from the dead"—that is, resurrection (v. 15). **One day, when many Jews ultimately accept Christ as being Lord, their change of heart will have a major positive impact on the world (cf. v. 12). This reigniting of Israel's fervor for God (a spiritual resurrection) and the resulting deeper unity with other believers will occur at the time of the Second Coming of Christ, and will bring about great blessings to the whole body of Christ.** At that time, the Old Age of this current world in which we live will give way completely to a New Age in the world to come. Israel will fulfill its appointed destiny to bring blessings to the nations (Gen. 12:3).

The stumbling of the Jews in the past has brought the great wealth of the gospel to the Gentile world, and this turn of events will work out indirectly to turn the Jews to the gospel. God, in His infinite mercy, handled the Jewish peoples' initial turning down of His offer of salvation, so that their actions served His inclusive plan of salvation for the whole world. **The end result will be that many of the Jewish people, along with the Gentiles, will experience the fullness of God's grace and forgiveness through Christ. Both Jews and Gentiles are and will continue to be debtors to the loving, forgiving God.**

Paul's Illustrations of Firstfruit and the Olive Tree

In verses 16-24, Paul uses two illustrations—*firstfruit* and *the olive tree*—to demonstrate that the separation of God's chosen people is not permanent and final, and that Israel has a future in the plan of God.

1. **Firstfruit:**

   "For if the firstfruit is holy, the lump is also holy . . ." (v. 16).

The implication of Paul's comment about firstfruits is that if the first part of something is dedicated to God, then the whole of that something becomes holy and belongs to God. According to Judaic law, a portion of the first batch of bread dough was to be baked and presented as an offering to God (Num. 15:17-21). Presenting this first part sanctified the whole. When a small seed was planted and dedicated to God, the branches that later grew were consecrated. Thus the offering part of something assured blessing on the whole and relates to the following tree-root illustration.

2. **The Olive Tree**
   —The Root:

   ". . . and if the root is holy, so are the branches" (v. 16).

By deduction, Paul concludes that Israel is holy because the patriarchs (the root), from whom the nation sprang, were

holy. So men like Abraham, Isaac, and Jacob consecrated the whole nation of Israel. The point is the relation between the part and the whole.

Paul is not teaching that righteousness is inherited or that there is a natural holiness, but what has been consecrated to God belongs to Him. **The full spiritual potential is in Israel, and eventually this potential will come into reality for the large numbers of Jews who turn to Christ.** This does not mean that every Jewish person irregardless of his or her spiritual choices will be saved. The path to salvation is the same for Jewish people as for Gentiles, requiring that each person make a personal decision to call on the Lord.

—**The Grafted Branches:**

> "And if some of the branches were broken off, and you, being a wild olive tree, were grafted in among them, and with them became a partaker of the root and fatness of the olive tree, do not boast against the branches. But if you do boast, remember that you do not support the root, but the root supports you" (vv. 17-18).

A number of the prophets had referred to Israel as the *olive tree of God* (e.g., Jer. 11:16; Hos. 14:6). In this example in Romans 11:17-18, Paul has in mind two kinds of olive branches. **The original branches represent the Jews. Many of them had become broken off (alienated) due to their movement away from faithfulness and belief. By drifting away from a relationship with God, they had become separated from the rest of the olive tree, a state in which they were no longer receiving the spiritual nourishment that they needed.**

On the other hand, the branches from the wild olive represent the believing Gentiles, who have been grafted into the garden olive and were now taking their nourishment from the root (the rich spiritual heritage of the Jewish people).

Some scholars have felt that this illustration indicates that Paul was ignorant of horticulture and reflects that he was a man of the city. Paul admits that the illustration runs "contrary to nature"—that one would not normally be able to graft branches taken from a tree from the wild into a cultivated tree (v. 24). The theological point is that the acceptance of the Gentiles and the breaking off of the Jews were as unnatural as grafting wild branches into a garden olive.

Paul reminds the Gentiles that Israel is the root and that the root supports them (v. 18). Therefore, the Gentile Christians are privileged to enjoy the rich benefits and supernatural life of God's people, the Jews (v. 17; Barrett, 1991, 217). **God is God, and He has the power to perform miracles, bring about life, and create unity where it seems impossible.**

Applications for the Olive Tree Illustration

From the olive tree illustration, Paul makes two applications:
- *A Warning to the Gentiles* **(v. 18). Paul offers a word of warning to the Gentile Christians about becoming arrogant. Probably this warning was prompted because the Gentile believers, comprising the larger group in the church of Rome, were developing a superior attitude toward the Jewish believers and pushing them to the periphery of the church.** The danger was that the Gentile Christians would fall into the sin of spiritual pride as some of the Jews had done (2:17).

    Paul warns the Gentiles that even though some of the Jews were broken off the garden olive tree, the Gentile Christians were to "stand by faith" and not to be "haughty" but to "fear" God (11:20). He cautions that since Gentiles have become part of God's people through faith, they should not become conceited. As God's children, they are to live in "fear," which refers to their having a reverential awe for God, not a sense of terror that God might punish them (cf. 8:15). It would be less drastic to cut off the branches that had been grafted in than the natural branches. **Since it is possible that any of the grafted branches (the Gentile believers), who engage in self-righteousness could become alienated from God, Paul urges them to be humble and not to have a superior attitude toward the Jews.** "If God did not spare the natural branches [Jews], He may not spare you [Gentile believers] either" (11.21).

The Gentile branches were still subject to being cut off from the garden olive into which they were grafted. Their protection against such an outcome was faith and humility.

Faith is expressed by responding to God's goodness (grace), but Israel had come under the severity of God because of unbelief. If the Gentile believers were not to continue in God's goodness, they too would become cut off. At every point, Paul rejects the rigid doctrine that teaches that God has predetermined who will be saved and who will be lost. **The point of Paul's illustration of the olive tree is to describe what determines whether men and women, or Jews and Gentiles, are saved. Only continuing in faith assures anyone of salvation.** The Scripture says that many in Israel were "broken off" because of unbelief (v. 20), but Christians can be broken off, too, unless they continue to stand by faith (vv. 20-21).

- *Hope for Israel* (vv. 23-24). **In verses 23-24, Paul is looking forward in hope to the day when many Jews will recognize and believe in Jesus as their Messiah, and be welcomed back and united with all those who serve the Lord.** Paul proposes that if it is possible for wild olive branches to be grafted into a cultivated olive tree, certainly it is possible for the cultivated tree's own branches to be grafted back in after becoming broken off. **With his illustration of the olive tree, Paul is indicating that when those Jewish people who have been unfaithful believe and call on the Lord, they will be restored to the garden olive.**

ROMANS 11:11-24
KEYWORDS
Firstfruit (see p. 220)
Flesh (see p. 58)
Gentiles (see p. 29)
Holy (see p. 59)

Jews/Israelites/Hebrews (see p. 29)

The Olive Tree

A metaphor for Israel. This tree, including root and branches, represents Israel. Israel's existence provided the vehicle by which the Christian church came into existence. In the olive tree metaphor, some of the natural branches of the garden olive became broken off (those Jewish people who did not accept Jesus as their Messiah), and wild branches (Gentiles who followed Christ) were miraculously grafted in. Extraordinary benefits have come to the Christian church because of its connection to and participation with Israel. God's ultimate plan is to one day reunite all of His people who believe (both Jews and Gentiles). The Jews will be restored alongside Gentile believers to the holy olive tree. Through His power, God is able to transform both Jews and Gentiles by the miracle of grace.

Reconciliation (*katallage*)

A restoration of personal relationship between God and human beings or between human beings

Salvation (see p. 23)

SUMMARY

Although the Jews stumbled by not realizing that Jesus was their promised Messiah, it has not brought about their utter destruction. Their stumbling has brought blessing to the whole world. God did not cause their stumbling, but in His wisdom and mercy, He certainly used it to offer salvation to the Gentiles. Israel's disbelief that Jesus could be their Messiah enabled Paul and his coworkers to turn more readily to the Gentile world.

The conversion of the Gentiles from following pagan gods to accepting the message of Christ and following the One God caused the Jewish people to take notice. Many became envious as they saw the joy and freedom the Gentiles experienced in their relationship with God, which was based on grace, not works.

Paul warns the Gentile Christians against becoming arrogant and thinking that they are superior to the Jewish people who did not believe just as they did. He reminds them that they have been grafted into the Jewish tree. He cautions that they, like the Jewish people, could find themselves alienated from God due to their lack of faithfulness and respect for God's ways. The desired attitude for the Gentiles of Paul's day, as well as for all of us today, is to have humble respect, gratitude, and hope—*respect* for God and the Jewish people, *gratitude* for our inclusion in God's family and the rich spiritual heritage received from the Jewish people, and *hope* that Israel and all people will come to know the grace of Christ and be united with each other in service to God.

> **LIFE APPLICATION**
>
> Today we benefit greatly from our Jewish heritage. God has reached out to us in a way that we can understand through the Messiah, Jesus, whom He brought into this world through His chosen people, the Jews. We have also benefited from the deep faith of the Jewish people throughout their history, as well as their mistakes, which God has used to teach us great lessons about forgiveness, grace, and humility and to guide us in our walk with Him. We are indebted to God for opening the door to those of us who are not Jews and embracing us as part of His family.
>
> As believers, we look forward to the day when we and the Jewish people will be united in praise to Jesus Christ the Messiah, our Savior. We understand that when Israel comes to an understanding that Jesus is also their Messiah, revival will sweep the world and will revitalize all of us in our faith within the body of Christ. As we are all united as one—the olive root and branches, we will have new life and fruitfulness through Jesus Christ. The Jewish people will receive God's grace, mercy, and restoration, and the body of Christ will be whole.
>
> Until that day of restoration and unity, we are to love our Jewish friends and neighbors here and throughout the world. We are to realize that all the spiritual benefits we have experienced are truly a result of God's grace and not of our making. We are to be humble in our view of ourselves and to be understanding and compassionate in our view and treatment of others. If we become prideful, we place ourselves in danger of becoming alienated from God.
>
> Today, let us pray in humility and gratitude for our friends the Jewish people, for God to bless them in their lives, and for God's guidance in our relationships with them.

COMPLETION OF GOD'S SALVATION PLAN FOR ISRAEL AND THE WORLD
ROMANS 11:25-32

> 25 For I do not desire, brethren, that you should be ignorant of this mystery, lest you should be wise in your own opinion, that blindness in part has happened to Israel until the fullness of the Gentiles has come in. 26 And so all Israel will be saved, as it is written:
>
> *"The Deliverer will come out of Zion,*
> *And He will turn away ungodliness from Jacob;*

> *²⁷ For this is My covenant with them, When I take away their sins."*
>
> ²⁸ Concerning the gospel they are enemies for your sake, but concerning the election they are beloved for the sake of the fathers. ²⁹ For the gifts and the calling of God are irrevocable. ³⁰ For as you were once disobedient to God, yet have now obtained mercy through their disobedience, ³¹ even so these also have now been disobedient, that through the mercy shown you they also may obtain mercy. ³² For God has committed them all to disobedience, that He might have mercy on all.

The Importance of Israel's Role in God's Plan

In verses 25-32, the apostle Paul leaves his illustration of the olive tree, but continues his discussion of the concept that all Israel who believe in Christ will eventually be saved. **The conversion of Israel is an essential part of the end of history of the Current Age. The beginning of the story of salvation focused on Israel, and Israel will also play a great role in the conclusion of this story.**

Gentiles' Blessings and Israel's Hope

Gentile Christians should take into account that God has not completed His work with the nation of Israel. **The fact that many Jews will come to Christ and receive grace and salvation was divinely disclosed to Paul. He describes it as a mystery; that is, it had been a secret, but God has now revealed to him that there is a set time limit on the "blindness" that has occurred among part of the Jews (v. 25).** Paul's probable intent in explaining to the Gentiles that this mystery has been demystified is so they would be less likely to succumb to the temptation to be conceited and filled with pride. **The time limit on the partial blindness among the Jews is "until the fullness of the Gentiles has come in" (v. 25).** "The fullness of the Gentiles" should be understood as referring to "a great mass of Gentiles" (Weymouth 1946, 374) rather than a specific predestined number.

A large part of Israel had become blind to the full truth and to what God was doing among them. In relation to this situation, Paul reports that he received a revelation that the purpose of God's releasing the Israelites to pursue their own way was, in part, for the sake of non-Jewish people. **Israel's distrust in God's offer of salvation through grace and faith, therefore, enabled the Gentiles to receive the gospel and to be reconciled to God (v. 28). Nevertheless, when the appropriate time arrives, "all Israel will be saved" (v. 26).** This End-Time miracle will result in the conversion of a large number of Jews coming to faith in Christ.

The expression "fullness of the Gentiles" in verse 25 does not refer to every Gentile. Neither does the statement, "all Israel will be saved" include all Jews who have died, nor all Jews living during the time of the salvation of believing Israel. Rather than the sum total of all individual Jews, Paul has in mind the large number of Jews who will believe on Jesus Christ as their Messiah when He returns in His Second Coming. **Israel's Redeemer will appear to them, and many Jewish people will turn to God and accept Christ as their Savior.**

To prove that the alienation from God that many Jews have experienced is only temporary, Paul (in vv. 26-27) cites a combination of Isaiah 27:9 and 59:20-21. **However, the Jewish people's Deliverer will come out of Zion (heaven or heavenly sanctuary), and, among other blessings, He will take away and forgive their sins and will secure for them the new covenant of grace. The hope of Israel is in Christ and His return.**

God's Covenant to Bless Israel

Some people in Paul's day, as well as others living in different eras of history, considered the Jewish people to be enemies of God, since many of them had not embraced Christ as being their Messiah. **The Jewish people are still beloved, because God chose them and made covenants with their faithful ancestors—the patriarchs Abraham, Isaac, and Jacob (Rom. 11:28).** Essential goodness of people is not ever God's motivation for loving them; He loves them because He is a merciful and compassionate God. Also, God is just, meaning that He does not show favoritism to any group people (Acts 10:34; Gal. 3:28). The people of Israel, like all people, come far short in that regard. Like us, they are normal human beings who have sinned, and so do not merit God's blessings. Even so, God loves them and wants to bless them. Israel will reap the benefits of God's promises to their forefathers.

God's faithfulness to His Word is the basis for Paul's declaring "the gifts and the calling of God are irrevocable" (v. 29). God does not withdraw His offers or take back His gifts. God still has blessings in store for the Jewish nation, and upon their repenting, He will restore them when the appropriate time comes. **The covenant God made with Israel is secure.** He has made an irrevocable call to Israel and has offered them gifts (privileges) of the covenant (9:4-5).

God's Gift of Choice to All People

God's plan for Israel, as well as for the Gentiles, includes a response of faith before it can be fulfilled. The responses of humans are not decisions programmed by God long ago. **God gives humankind the freedom to accept or reject God's plan of salvation.** As with Israel, God does not give up on us. His patience with us and our responsibility to respond to Him cannot be magnified more than they are in Romans 2:4-10:

> [4] Or do you despise the riches of His goodness, forbearance, and longsuffering, not knowing that the goodness of God leads you to repentance? [5] But in accordance with your hardness and your impenitent heart you are treasuring up for yourself wrath in the day of wrath and revelation of the righteous judgment of God, [6] who *"will render to each one according to his deeds"*: [7] eternal life to those who by patient continuance in doing good seek for glory, honor, and immortality; [8] but to those who are self-seeking and do not obey the truth, but obey unrighteousness—indignation and wrath, [9] tribulation and anguish, on every soul of man who does evil, of the Jew first and also of the Greek; [10] but glory, honor, and peace to everyone who works what is good, to the Jew first and also to the Greek.

The Need to Persevere in Faith

Paul clearly warns against our failing to continue in God's saving grace (11:22). God's initiative in salvation and our need for perseverance are placed side by side. Earlier in his letter, the apostle Paul had informed the Gentiles of their being grafted in, but he also told them to take heed and remain faithful, so that they did not risk becoming cut off as many of the Jewish people had become (8:4; 11:20). Should the Gentiles cease to rely on faith and become filled with pride, considering themselves better than the Jews, the natural result would be that they would become spiritually bankrupt and would break off. This separation of the Gentiles from the body of Christ due to their pride would not be any less drastic than the breaking off of the Jews due to their unbelief. **Unbelief and disobedience bring about separation from God and force us to become disconnected from the life of God (11:13-22).** Our freedom provides the basis of our responsibility before God (Arrington, 2005, 105-06).

God's Mercy for All People

In verses 30-32, Paul once again emphasizes human disobedience and divine mercy. God's mercy stands behind everything that He does in carrying out His plan of salvation. **God has only one way of dealing with humankind, whether Jew or Gentile, and that is in mercy.** No matter who we are—outright sinner or devout Christian, rich or poor, blue-collar worker or professional person, an untaught child or a scholar, a busy church worker or a passive church member, free or oppressed person—if we know God, whoever we may be, we know Him as the merciful God. **God's plan and purpose are merciful.**

According to Paul, "God has committed them all [all humankind] to disobedience, [so] that He might have mercy on all" (v. 32). We should not press this statement to teach universalism, which denies that there is a hell and insists that everybody will eventually be saved. It also does not mean that God makes people sin. **God, however, has declared that all people are disobedient (3:23). His declaration of the truth that peoples' sins have made them prisoners allows God to show mercy and to set us free. As Paul sees it, God shapes human history by His exercise of mercy.**

God's dealings with the Jewish people are a prime example of God's mercy. Like all people, the Jews have been involved in disobedience, and as a result, when salvation comes, they will be aware that their salvation is altogether due to God's grace and mercy, and not because of their own merit.

God has also been merciful to the Gentiles. Because of Israel's failure to recognize the Messiah when He came and their reluctance to embrace the salvation through faith that Christ offered them, missionaries were called to actively offer salvation to the Gentiles—both to those who lived in Rome and elsewhere. **One day, the mercy that God has shown to the Gentiles will lead to Israel's coming to a better understanding of God's grace and mercy, and their repentance for not following the Messiah.**

God's mercy toward all people is made evident in Jesus Christ, and it reaches to all nations and individuals. Through His mercy, God through Jesus Christ has established a new plan and order for all of humanity. In His plan, God desires all humans to be united with Him and with each other in peace and friendship.

ROMANS 11:25-32

KEYWORDS

Covenant (*diatheke*) (see p. 100)

Elect of God (see p. 238)

Gentiles (see p. 29)

Gospel (see p. 23)

Israel (see p. 250)

Mercy of God (see p. 269)

Patriarch/Father (see p. 251)

Salvation (see p. 23)

Sin (see p. 48)

Ungodliness (see p. 75)

SUMMARY

Paul reveals the mystery of God's plan for Israel's future. Up to this point, he has only hinted at the future salvation of the Jews. Now Paul explains that when the full number of Gentiles have turned to Christ for salvation, many Jewish people will also accept Christ as their Savior, and God will keep His promises to them.

God's chosen people remain dear to Him, and He has not and will not withdraw His call and blessings from them. Israel's disbelief that

Salvation and Israel

Jesus was the Messiah, who had come to bring them forgiveness and salvation through grace, has ultimately benefited the Gentiles. It has opened the door to non-Jews' being directly invited to receive God's blessings.

Paul warned the Gentile believers that they should keep in mind the blessings that they had received from the Jewish people and avoid developing an attitude of superiority toward them. All people (both Gentiles and Jews) have been disobedient and have received salvation only because of God's mercy.

God continues to love His chosen people. Scripture teaches that although God's promise for Israel's salvation has not yet been fulfilled, it will be one day, and it could happen any day.

LIFE APPLICATION

Paul has urged that honor and respect should be shown to the Jewish people and has envisioned that many of them living at the return of Christ will repent and turn to Christ in the latter-day revival. They will join all Gentile Christians in the body of Christ. The reconciling power of the gospel will have accomplished its goal of uniting all people. Both Jewish and Gentile believers will be joined together in the garden olive to bear fruit to God.

It is hard to anticipate the joy on the earth and in heaven at the conversion of God's chosen people. The grace that God has shown each of us will be lavished on the Jewish people. God's faithfulness and mercy are moving human history toward the fulfillment of His plan of salvation. Even though today many of God's chosen people may not understand that Jesus is their Messiah, they still remain very dear to God. In the meantime, the Holy Spirit continues to gather Gentile believers into the family of God. When most of the Gentiles who are going to come to Christ have done so, God will bring about a revival in which many Jewish people will come to see who Jesus Christ truly is. Until that day, God's invitation of grace is available through Jesus to all people, whether they are Jews or Gentiles.

PAUL'S PRAISE TO GOD
ROMANS 11:33-36

33 Oh, the depth of the riches both of the wisdom and knowledge of God! How unsearchable are His judgments and His ways past finding out!

> ³⁴ *"For who has known the mind of the Lord?*
> *Or who has become His counselor?"*
> ³⁵ *"Or who has first given to Him*
> *And it shall be repaid to him?"*
>
> ³⁶ For of Him and through Him and to Him are all things, to whom be glory forever. Amen.

Praise for a Merciful God

Having discussed God's merciful plan for Jews and Gentiles, Paul now takes the stance of a worshiper and stands almost speechless before the merciful wisdom of God. Amazed that God makes no distinction among people and that His mercy is available to all, Paul can go no further without giving way to the admiration of divine wisdom and knowledge and to the worship of God. What can be more fitting than to end chapter 11 with words of praise, recognizing that the divine plan surpasses all human understanding?

Gratitude for Mercy in Salvation

For eleven chapters, Paul has given a wonderful account of the gospel and has described salvation at length, recognizing that God remains in control of the total process of salvation. **Paul's discussion of God's salvation plan has included these three truths:**

1. **When God's people are finally redeemed, God will deliver creation itself from the corrupting influence of Adam's sin (8:19-21).**

2. **God causes all things to work together for good to those who love Him (8:28).**

3. **God has allowed people in their disobedience to experience unpleasant consequences, so that He can show them mercy and set them free (11:32). The only door that will permit them to leave their prison of disobedience is the mercy of God in Christ.**

Contemplation of how merciful God is leads Paul to break out in praise in this hymn. In considering God's blessings of salvation, Paul finds himself unable to express fully the wonders

Salvation and Israel

of God, **as he looks forward to the great day when Israel will be saved through their faith in their Deliverer.** He knows that the story of salvation begins with Israel, and it will conclude with them. **His gratitude comes from the assurance that salvation is for all people (both Jews and Gentiles) and can be received through faith in Jesus Christ.**

Gratitude for God's Wisdom and Knowledge

Paul's hymn of praise opens with the exclamation "Oh," a passionate assertion of awe and reverence. **Paul's gratitude and worship is stimulated by his consideration of "the depth of the riches both of the wisdom and knowledge of God" (v. 33; Moo, 1996, 741). God's profound knowledge and wisdom enables Him to have a clear and infallible view of all things that were and are and shall be.** Nothing is hidden from Him—this is His knowledge. **God rules and orders all things.** He directs and disposes of all things and brings about His purposes and counsels for His own glory. The inexhaustible magnitude of God's knowledge and wisdom are evident in "His judgments" (*krimata*) and "ways." Who would have thought His judgments could be described as merciful? Who would have thought that since God's ways are beyond human understanding, He would freely and graciously reveal Himself and His ways in Jesus Christ?

Our Admiration of God
Paul's Questions

In biblical terms, Paul expresses his admiration for God by raising three questions (vv. 34-35; cf. Isa. 40:13; Job 41:11). Each question expects the answer "Nobody but God."

1. **"Who has known the mind of the Lord?"** This question stresses how profound and inexplicable are God's decisions.

2. **"Who has become His counselor?"** No one has ever served as God's adviser, directing Him in His ways. What God is doing in the world is beyond human understanding.

3. **"Who has first given to Him and it shall be repaid to him?"** This question focuses on divine grace. Only because of

God's grace can we experience the depth of the riches of His plan of salvation. No one is ahead of God in giving. From its beginning to its end, salvation lies in His grace. How absurd it is for us to speak of the merit of our good works. None of us can bring God under obligation.

Humility and Praise

We are to approach and reverence God with humility and praise. We can never switch roles with God. Such an attempt would be motivated by the desire to humanize God and deify ourselves. No grounds can be found for us to claim glory for ourselves instead of for God, since He created us and now sustains us. How unreasonable it is for us to live for any purpose other than to make known the glory of Him who formed and prolongs our existence (v. 36). **When we try to understand our Creator, Redeemer, and Sustainer, the best thing we can do is turn our understanding and questions into adoration and praise of God.** My deepest and most profound understanding of God's Word and the mysteries of redemption have come to me on those occasions of Pentecostal worship when the Holy Spirit moved in special ways, a holy hush settled over the congregation, and everything was laid aside except the praise and worship of Almighty God.

In these final words of praise of chapter 11, Paul expresses that **the way God deals with His people, both Jews and Gentiles, cannot be fully grasped by the human mind. We all must give glory to God and adore and praise God without fully understanding.** Chapters 12-16 will tell us how we can give glory to God and worship and serve Him.

ROMANS 11:33-36

KEYWORDS

Glory (see p. 86)

Mercy of God (see p. 269)

SUMMARY

The apostle Paul stands amazed at God's plan of salvation. Because God's plan surpasses all human understanding, Paul breaks out in praise for the grace, goodness, and mercy of God. No human being has known the mind of the Lord; no one has served as His adviser; no one ultimately gives God anything. Since all things are from God, through God and to God, God deserves all glory to the uttermost depths of eternity.

LIFE APPLICATION

The Scriptures teach us that we need divine assistance to be able to grasp "the deep things of God" (1 Cor. 2:10). In Romans 1-11, Paul has explained the merciful wisdom and knowledge of God. Nevertheless, it is difficult for us to understand fully the mysterious ways of God, even though they have been demonstrated to us through Jesus Christ. What can we do but stand in amazement and join Paul in praising The Almighty God?

God's unlimited wisdom is evident in the providence with which He has guided human history and in His provision for the salvation of both Jews and Gentiles. No one can completely fathom God's ways, accurately analyze His judgments, or fully understand His righteousness and mercy in Christ.

All that God is and has done for us call us to be humble-minded and to exalt and give Him praise as God, the Father of our Lord Jesus Christ. God is the Creator, from whom all things come and who is their end and purpose. From Him flows everything—all material and spiritual benefits—that give meaning to our life. Let us join the chorus and forever ascribe all glory and praise to the God of our salvation!

REFLECTION—PART FIVE
Romans 9:1—11:36

1. What is the main topic that Paul deals with in chapters 9-11? How can we as Christians be encouraged in our own lives from learning about God's care and plans for the Jewish people?

2. Compare and contrast Israel's blessings with our blessings as Christians.

3. How would you explain to someone why God chose Isaac and Jacob, rather than Ishmael and Esau, through whom to transmit the promise of salvation? Did God's choice for their roles in history determine whether or not they would be saved and have eternal life with Him?

4. Explain this statement: "Jacob I have loved; but Esau I have hated" (Mal. 1:2-3; Rom. 9:13).

5. If you believe that each of us is free to receive or reject the gospel, how would you explain "the vessels of wrath prepared for destruction" (9:22)?

6. Paul speaks of the Jewish people of his day as having religious zeal, but it was not based on full knowledge (10:1-3). What is your understanding of this statement? Have you ever encountered people who were passionate about their religion or spiritual experience, but were not fully knowledgeable about the scriptures they quoted—maybe someone who visited your home to give you literature?

7. Interpret Paul's statement: "Christ is the end of the law for righteousness to everyone who believes" (10:4).

8. Paul says that salvation depends on two conditions: confessing with the mouth that Jesus is Lord and believing in one's heart that God raised Him from the dead (v. 9). How would you explain the significance of these conditions to a person who is not a follower of Christ?

9. Explain why Paul concludes that Jews and Gentiles (all people) are on equal footing before God.

10. Paul traces the steps that are involved in calling on the Lord's name. In light of these steps, why is preaching the gospel so important?

11. What is your understanding of the salvation of the remnant? Describe what the *theology (or doctrine) of the remnant* is, and the implications that this teaching has for the church today.

12. The Jews' disbelief in the gospel turned out to be a blessing to the Gentiles. Explain why. Does this tell us anything about God?

13. What is the significance of the illustration of the olive tree?

14. The beginning and the end of the story of salvation are determined by the future destiny of Israel. What does that fact

tell us about God's completion of His plan of salvation and about its significance for the nation of Israel?

15. Explain how divine sovereignty and human freedom can be reconciled.

16. What are some practical ways we as Christians can show our gratitude and express our love to our Jewish friends and neighbors who live in our communities, and to our Jewish friends and neighbors who live in other parts of the world?

Prayer

Our Father, we need a deeper hunger for a Spirit-born revival and a greater burden for sharing the Good News of Christ with the world. We ask You for direction, guidance, and strength, and for an outpouring of Your Spirit in the world.

In our vision for salvation of the world, (1) help us not to forget to pray for Israel, and (2) help us to reflect and express Your love to the Jewish people with whom we work and live, as well as to those living in other nations.

We look forward to the day when all Your people, Jews and Gentiles, will join together in celebrating Your saving grace in Christ. Amen.

PART SIX—Romans 12:1—15:13

The Christian Life

- **True Worship in Changed Lives**
  Romans 12:1-2
- **Service Within the Fellowship**
  Romans 12:3-8
- **Standards for Daily Living**
  Romans 12:9-13
- **Christians' Response to Non-Christians**
  Romans 12:14-21
- **Christians and Civil Government**
  Romans 13:1-7
- **Love Fulfills the Law**
  Romans 13:8-10
- **End-Time Urgency**
  Romans 13:11-14
- **Personal Freedom and Respect for Others**
  Romans 14:1-12
- **Acting in Love Toward One Another**
  Romans 14:13-23
- **Characteristics of Christian Fellowship**
  Romans 15:1-13

Chapter 11 ended with Paul taking the stance of a worshiper, praising God and celebrating God's wealth, knowledge, and wisdom. **In 12:1—15:13, Paul talks about the Christian life that is made possible by the death and resurrection of Jesus Christ.** The concluding chapters of Paul's letter to the Romans are an indispensable part of his letter. Without these chapters, we would not have Paul's full message. They help us to discern and encourage integrity in living the Christian life. As believers, our life and motivations are to be shaped by the life of Christ. Along with earlier admonitions (6:11-14; 8:12-14), the five remaining chapters urge us to bring our motives and behaviors in line with the righteousness of faith.

So far in Romans, we have read about . . .
- The universal sinfulness of humankind
- God's unlimited grace
- Justification by faith
- Sanctification
- Christ's dying for our sins

- The Spirit's power to bring life out of death
- God's provision for salvation of all people
- God's divine mercy.

Nevertheless, the apostle Paul still has more to tell us about how God's saving grace affects our daily lives.

Sanctification and Practical Application

As we move on to chapter 12, there is an obvious shift from Paul's discussion of God's dealings with Jews and Gentiles (chs. 9-11) to the doctrine of sanctification, which Paul has already discussed (chs. 6-8). **As Paul discusses sanctification this time, he deals particularly with its practical application.** "Hence Paul repeatedly follows up an exposition of doctrine with ethical exhortations ..." (Bruce, 1963, 225), so that what the Bible teaches is not to be simply known, but also to be applied and experienced in daily living.

As Paul has made clear, neither human achievement nor good works will save anyone. Faith and good works are only mutually exclusive in regards to our receiving salvation, not to our living the Christian life. In 1 Thessalonians 1:3, the apostle speaks of the "work of faith," meaning work that is "produced by faith" (NIV). In the same passage, he mentions "labor of love" and "patience of hope."

The reality of saving faith is demonstrated through the practical effect it has on a believer. Faith that is real and justifies apart from works of the law is faith from which flows good works. As Paul works out the practical implications of God's saving mercies in the remaining chapters of Romans, it will become clear that **holy living, which always includes good works, is inseparable from faith and indispensable to the demonstration and maintenance of faith.**

TRUE WORSHIP IN CHANGED LIVES
ROMANS 12:1-2

> ¹ I beseech you therefore, brethren, by the mercies of God, that you present your bodies a living sacrifice, holy, acceptable to God,

> which is your reasonable service. ² And do not be conformed to this world, but be transformed by the renewing of your mind, that you may prove what is that good and acceptable and perfect will of God.

At the beginning of chapter 12, the phrases "therefore" and "mercies of God" (v. 1) refer back to Paul's discussion in 1:18—11:36, and also connect the reader to Paul's comments that are to come. **The focus of the first eleven chapters has been the mercy of God expressed through Jesus Christ. The apostle Paul has spoken about God's mercy as being present in His grace, faith, forgiveness, and resurrection, all of which are means through which God relates to both Jews and Gentiles.** Believers may pray for God's mercy, but we already have His mercy in Christ. Paul makes his appeal "by [*dia*, through] the mercies of God." **What God has done in Christ should move Christians to give themselves entirely to God.** There is no coercion here; Paul simply makes an appeal to his readers: "I beseech you" ("I urge you," v. 1 NIV).

The Christian Life, a Life of Sacrifice

Sacrificial language is used by Paul to describe the Christian life. The essential idea behind ancient sacrifices was that offerings belong to God. **In their worship, the Jews often presented animal sacrifices, but in the new order introduced by Christ, people are called to make a different kind of sacrifice—"a living sacrifice," which is a life lived in such a way that it belongs entirely to God (v. 1). To offer this kind of sacrifice calls for us to present our bodies (*somata*), meaning to offer *ourselves* (our whole being) to God.** In 1:24, it is striking that God allows sinners to dishonor their bodies (*somata*). However, in chapter 6, the Greek word for the verb *present* (*paristemi*) occurs five times, and we are urged to present ourselves to God in obedience, for righteousness and sanctification (vv. 13, 16, 19). So Paul's solemn appeal for us to give our whole being as a living sacrifice reemphasizes our responsibility as Christians.

This sacrificial life in Christ is the transforming life that God has given us, and our dedication to that life is demonstrated by doing what is "holy, acceptable to God," which the NKJV defines as being "reasonable service" (*logike latreia*), but is better translated as "spiritual worship" (v. 1).

"Reasonable service" (spiritual worship) is not restricted to what we do at church, for it encompasses far more than our churchgoing, singing, and praying. **A living offering (spiritual worship) calls for a lifestyle that pleases the Lord who loved us and gave Himself for us.** This sacrificial way of life includes obedience to God expressed through our actions, our speech, and our attitudes. It calls for deep repentance, determined praise, and willingness to serve God. As an offering, a life of spiritual worship places us on God's altar. **All of life is indeed to be an act of worship.**

Renewal of Our Minds

In verse 2, Paul now moves from discussing the dedication of our whole beings to discussing the renewing of our minds. Spiritual worship is appropriate for those who live in the Spirit. Jewish worship required worshipers to offer animal sacrifices at the Temple, but living in the Spirit requires that we offer ourselves to God and allow Him to change and renew the way we think.

Paul began his discussion of the sacrificial sanctification concept (*paristemi*) in chapter 6 and continues it in chapter 12. His phrases "present your members"/"present yourselves" (6:13-19) and "present your bodies" (12:1) communicate a strong formation/conformation element. The phrases "conformed to the image of His Son" (8:29) and being "transformed" (12:2) also refer to this formation process. All of these phrases reflect the developmental process of sanctification, which results in changed thinking and living. **Transformation that results in a revolution in our thinking enables us to live a dedicated life day in and day out.**

Nevertheless, Paul recognizes that intelligent, consecrated service to God has its challenges because the Christian still lives in "this [present evil] world" (*aion*, age) (v. 2). Behind this idea is the way Paul and the Jewish people thought of time. They divided time into two parts: This Age and the Coming Age. *This Age* is the time in which sin and evil, and suffering and death prevail. In contrast, the *Coming Age* is the time when God will put an end to sin and death, and He will exercise His authority and power over all things. The Coming Age dawned during the first coming of Christ, but the Present Evil Age will not be completely put out of operation until the Second Coming of Christ. **Since we live in a world where evil is pressing in from all sides, and practices contrary to the gospel are common, our minds need ongoing renewal and strengthening by the Spirit in order for us to continue to live according to the ways of God and to bring hope to a world in pain.** It is easy for our attitudes, behavior, and values to be shaped by this age of sin and death. Over time, the world seeks to squeeze us into its own mold. For transformation to take place consistently and completely, we must totally surrender to Christ both our ethical decisions and life choices each moment of every day.

Paul's Advice for Living in the World

To guard against the danger of becoming conformed to the world's ways, Paul focuses on two essential aspects of resisting the pressures of This Age and living in accord with the values of the gospel.

- **Paul's warning: "Do not be conformed to this world" (12:2a).** The Greek (*me*, with the present imperative) suggests the stopping of the tendency to conform one's life to the values of This Age. Values, trends, fashions, customs, and other cultural practices that are inconsistent with the gospel are not to regulate the lives of us who have died and been raised with Christ. The gospel requires that we distance ourselves from sinful patterns, priorities, and harmful stimulations of our society, but it does not summon us to total separation from the world. As Paul explains in Romans 12:2 and 1 Corinthians 5:10-11, although we are to be in this world—living and serving—we are not to be conformed to the world's ways. We must engage in worthwhile causes in the world and be concerned about people who are lost, hungry, and helpless. At the same time, we must take a stand against the spirit of sin and idolatry in the world. **Our calling is for both separation from the sin and evil of the world and for active involvement in the world by living a life of service that reflects**

Christ and by telling others about His transforming love. To live under the cross is to "shine as lights in the world" (Phil. 2:15).** We are to live responsible and sober lives in the world.
- **Paul's exhortation: "Be transformed by the renewing of your mind" (12:2b).** The word *transform* (*metamorphoo*) here is also used to describe Christ's transfiguration. To be *transformed* means that the inward person must undergo change. Obviously, such transformation has to be done by God. **Transformation is something that God does within us in response to our faith.** Titus 3:5 says that transformation is the work of the Holy Spirit (cf. 2 Cor. 3:18). The manifestation or evidence of this work of the Holy Spirit is that the mind is being renewed. **The present progressive tense of the verb *transform* (*being transformed*) indicates that this change is a daily, ongoing process.** The renewing process begins at our conversion and continues throughout our life.

Spiritual renewal and transformation give us the capacity to discern the will of God and to distinguish between good and evil, and truth and error, anchoring us in the same biblical faith that was once delivered to the saints (Jude 3). Such a revolution in thinking imparts new moral and spiritual sensitivities needed to meet the daily and the hourly needs of the soul. **Only the renewed mind can "prove what is that good and acceptable and perfect will of God" (Rom. 12:2). The word *prove* (*dokimazo*) means more than just testing, discerning, and finding out God's will; it also means doing God's will.** More is required than contemplating and appreciating God's will, for we are to live according to it. Our minds are to be daily renewed by the Holy Spirit and God's Word, becoming more and more of what we are in Christ. This is similar to being "conformed to the image of His Son" in Rom. 8:29. Mature judgment of God's will calls for action. As Christians we, therefore, stand in need, not so much of reconversion, but of deeper conversion (Bloesch, 1968, 86-87). There is an essential relationship between conversion and obedience to the will of God. Doing God's will is the result of a heartfelt devotion to Him, and it constantly gives practical expression to our faith.

Ongoing spiritual renewal should reach beyond the individual Christian to the body of Christ, the church. The body of Christ not only has a mission to the world, but also a mission to itself. It has a call to constant self-renewal and reform in order to guard against conforming to the world and seeking glory from humankind. The body of Christ makes itself credible through its faithfulness to the gospel. Otherwise, the church's message becomes little more than "sounding brass or a clanging cymbal" (1 Cor. 13:1). In short, **holiness is not only possible, but it is mandatory for the integrity of the individual Christian and for the church.**

ROMANS 12:1-2

KEYWORDS

Holy Living (see p. 170)

Holy Spirit/The Spirit (see p. 25)

Living Sacrifice
The placing of one's life on God's altar in daily life—that is, living one's whole life for God

Mercy of God (see p. 269)

This Age/The Coming Age (The Two Ages) (see p. 48)

Transformation
The process of God's changing and renewing a believer's mind, enabling that person to live a holy life, dedicated to God

Will of God (see p. 270)

SUMMARY

Romans 12:1-2 indicates an appropriate response to God's grace and introduces Paul's discussion about Christian living in 12:3—15:13. The first two introductory verses of chapter 12 sum up what it means to live in a way that pleases God.

Christians are to give themselves entirely to God. Paul uses sacrificial language from the Old Testament system, under which live sacrifices were put to death. In contrast, Christ has introduced a new order in which Christians are living sacrifices. We have died with Christ in His death and have been raised to new life with Him.

Our sacrifice (spiritual worship) includes presenting ourselves daily to God. However, since this Present Evil Age still threatens who we are in Christ, we must resist its pressures and values by being daily renewed by the Holy Spirit. In doing so, we will be better able to discern God's will and to live as a daily sacrifice to God, exercising responsible freedom as we are transformed into the likeness of Christ.

LIFE APPLICATION

The failure of humankind to worship God leads to our downfall (1:20-25). True worship of God is vital to our relationship with Him. We have experienced His mercies through faith in Christ's work at Calvary. Since we have been redeemed, our responsibility is to submit ourselves daily as living sacrifices—our whole body, soul, mind, and spirit—to God. This stands in contrast to the lifeless sacrifices of the Old Testament.

Giving ourselves and our daily life to God is our spiritual worship. Every Christian has the opportunity to worship God each day by praying, praising, and serving Him. We have greater access and a closer relationship with God than did the Old Testament priests. Day in and day out, we can stand in His presence and enjoy His wonderful grace.

Such worship places our lives on the altar and is truly transforming. This transformation requires us to surrender to God's will and is marked by the renewal of our thought processes and attitudes toward life and others. The discerning of God's will and following through on what we know grow out of the sanctifying work of the Holy Spirit. The fruit of such heartfelt devotion is the evidence of true worship of God. True worship changes our relationship with the world and enables us to live our faith in the world.

* For a list of *Practices That Nurture Our Faith and Holy Living*, see Appendix G on pages 430-433.

SERVICE WITHIN THE FELLOWSHIP
ROMANS 12:3-8

³ For I say, through the grace given to me, to everyone who is among you, not to think of himself more highly than he ought to

> think, but to think soberly, as God has dealt to each one a measure of faith. ⁴ For as we have many members in one body, but all the members do not have the same function, ⁵ so we, being many, are one body in Christ, and individually members of one another. ⁶ Having then gifts differing according to the grace that is given to us, let us use them: if prophecy, *let us prophesy* in proportion to our faith; ⁷ or ministry, *let us use it* in our ministering; he who teaches, in teaching; ⁸ he who exhorts, in exhortation; he who gives, with liberality; he who leads, with diligence; he who shows mercy, with cheerfulness.
> [*emphasis added*]

The Body of Christ, the Church

In most of Paul's letter to the church in Rome, he uses the word *body* to refer to the Christian community. He only uses the term *church* (*ekklesia*) in his closing remarks, which are recorded in the final chapter of Romans. **According to Paul, the church, like the human body, is characterized by diversity and unity, both of which are indications of God's grace (cf. 1 Cor. 12:12-31).** God has called all men and women, inviting them to come into relationship with Him and to become part of the *body*. This call includes everyone regardless of his or her background, temperament, human talent, status in life, and personal or economic need.

Whenever people become followers of Christ, God bestows a variety of spiritual gifts on them. Whatever their backgrounds and gifts may be, God calls them to serve and worship together for the common good of the local body of believers. Paul's use of the term *body*, therefore, emphasizes the positive results of unity within a fellowship of believers and the dreadful consequences that result when there is a lack of unity. **Each member of Christ's body has his or her function just as each member of the human body has its particular function.** As each member of the church performs his or her service, only then does the church function as it ought. A real problem in the church is that its members have not learned to live and function as a body.

Unity in the Body

Paul first warns the Christian "not to think of himself more highly than he ought to think" (Rom. 12:3). This mind-set creates strife and destroys the peace and unity of the church. Each believer needs to be realistic and give sober assessment "as God has dealt to each one a measure of faith" (vv. 3). **The only way we can understand who we are as a body is by realizing what God has done for every one of us—that He has given each of us grace and faith, and we are all equal in His sight.**

All believers, like Paul himself, have been beneficiaries of God's grace, which has produced different spiritual gifts (vv. 3, 6) and has given rise to a variety of ministries. **God has given to each believer a measure of faith through His gifts of the Spirit (cf. 1 Cor. 12:7-10). Each believer has the responsibility of using his or her gift(s) and avoiding comparisons with the gifts of others.** What Paul calls for is not false humility, but an honest estimation of our gifts as being gifts from God that come with responsibilities. **The absence of false modesty and conceit will go a long way in removing disharmony and maintaining unity in the body.** There is no place in the church for attitudes of superiority or inferiority.

Spiritual Gifts in the Body

Gifts of the Spirit occurred among God's people in Old Testament times (Ex. 28:2-3; 35:30-31; Judges 6:34; 2 Kings 2:9-10; 2 Chron. 24:20) and during the ministry of Christ on the earth (Matt. 17:20; 21:21; Luke 9:1-2; 20:23). Following the outpouring of the Holy Spirit on the Day of Pentecost, the gifts began to flourish. Spiritual gifts are manifested more freely among those who have experienced the fullness of the Spirit. **Whatever spiritual gift(s) a believer may have comes from God (Rom. 12:6). Each believer is to recognize the source of his or her gift(s) and to use those gifts with great care, considering them to be a sacred trust.** In verse 6, the Greek word for *gift* is *charisma* (the singular for the plural *charismata*). In Paul's letters, the term has a variety of meanings. For example, in Romans 6:23, *charisma* refers to the gift of salvation, and in 11:29 the term in its plural form refers to the blessings that God bestowed on Israel as His chosen people. So in a broader sense, the term *charismata* means the blessing of salvation or other blessings; but in its more restricted meaning, *charismata* refers to specific spiritual gifts given by the Holy Spirit to believers for Christian service. Some gifts are more remarkable and striking in their manifestation than others, but **all of the gifts are needed for the health of the church as are all the members of the human body vital to its health.**

In Romans 1:11, Paul writes, "I long to see you, that I may impart to you some spiritual gift . . . ." Though he does not tell us what is meant by "some spiritual gift," we get a good idea from the lists in 12:6-8 and 1 Corinthians 12:28-31. The term *charisma* does not in itself signify spiritual gift, but it has come to mean that today. It is more accurately rendered "grace-gift." **Spiritual gifts are gifts of grace. They are concrete, practical manifestations of divine grace (*charis*) in the lives of believers.** As a result, they are described as "gifts differing according to the grace that is given to us . . ." (Rom. 12:6). Gifts of the Spirit are not something given because of spiritual merit or on the basis of gender, education, or position. Even though they are an addition to our natural abilities, they may blend with our talents.

Examples of Spiritual Gifts in the Body of Christ

Paul mentions gifts in 1 Corinthians 12:4-10, 28-30, and Ephesians 4:8-12. In Romans 12:6-8, Paul lists seven kinds of ministry. While not exhaustive of all the gifts of the Spirit, this list points out to his readers ways in which the Spirit may be working among them.

1. **The gift of prophecy.** The importance of the gift of prophecy is emphasized by the apostle Paul in 1 Corinthians 14:1. **When the Holy Spirit uses the gift of prophecy to minister to people, a person receives a message directly from the Lord. That person then speaks the words inspired by the Holy Spirit, giving a divine revelation.** Normally, the message is not about the future, but about a more immediate concern and is for the edification, exhortation, and comfort of the congregation of believers (v. 3). Such an inspired message speaks to people's needs and offers comfort, encouragement, and insight (1 Thess. 4:13-18). A prophetic message can also take the form of exhortation, warning, or rebuke for carnal and divisive activities that may be occurring in the church (1 Cor. 1:10; Phil. 4:2).

Spirit-inspired prophecies have great value for the church, but they must be evaluated before they are accepted as true. Paul instructs believers to test all things (cf. 1 John 4:1) and to hold fast to the good (1 Thess. 5:20-21). The apostle avoids assigning the same level of authority to prophecy as he does to Scripture. In 1 Corinthians, Paul indicates that the prophets in Corinth were to be subordinate to Scripture and that their prophecies were to be evaluated (1 Cor. 14:29-33). A prophet may knowingly or unknowingly include his own thoughts. Recognizing this danger, Paul urges the prophets to "prophesy in proportion to [their] faith" (Rom. 12:6), which is the same type of faith mentioned in verse 3 and refers to spiritual gifts, not to saving faith. In the earlier part of Romans, Paul spoke about faith as being the means through which one enters into salvation. Doctrinal errors can be introduced through what is presented as inspired prophecy. **It is important for prophecy to be tested in light of the written Word of God as recorded in the Scriptures (1 John 4:1-6).**

2. **The gift of ministry (*diakonia, service*).** *Diakonia* is the gift of practical service and includes various kinds of spiritual service, such as ministry to the poor, preparing meals, assisting the disabled, and providing other practical services as opportunities present themselves. According to Paul, the one who has this gift is to use it by ministering, or serving (Rom.12:7). **Believers with the gift of service are to function in the community of faith by serving, just as a gifted teacher does by teaching.** Some believers do not have gifts for prophesying, preaching, or scholarship, but they may have the spiritual capacity for providing practical assistance, which enables them to show the love of Christ through deeds of service. Those gifted people touch the lives of so many with the gospel and serve their Lord magnificently.

3. **The gift of teaching.** Among the gifts of the Spirit, Paul ranks teachers third, placing them only after apostles and prophets, which indicates that their role is extremely valuable to the foundation of the church (1 Cor. 12:28).**Those who have the God-given gift of teaching exercise leadership in the church (see 1 Thess. 5:12-13) and are able to explain, expound, and proclaim the Word of God with power for the purpose of enlightening and building up the fellowship of believers (Eph. 4:12).** Endowed

The Christian Life

with special insight into spiritual truth, they are able to relate the Scripture to the immediate needs of the congregation. Briefly stated, their gifted ministry is to teach doctrine and to explain the Word of God, so that God's people will be strengthened in their faith and grounded in the truth.

Never have gifted teachers been needed more to teach and guide the church. Challenging issues and religious teachings prevalent during our time call for godly men and women equipped by the Spirit to teach and defend the truth against error and to build up the church. **Not only is there a need for the gospel to be proclaimed, there is a real need for it to be explained.**

4. **The gift of exhortation (*paraklesis*).** A function of the gift of prophecy is exhortation (1 Cor. 14:3), but Paul identifies *exhortation* as a distinct gift of the Spirit (Rom. 12:8). **This gift is a special ability given by the Spirit to certain believers that enables them to minister words of encouragement and comfort to others.** Those who have this God-given gift are able to speak wisely to the discouraged, the lonely, and the weak.

No doubt, the gift of exhortation was greatly needed in the early church. Many of the believers probably lived a difficult and stressful life, tested and tried by Satan and the world. Some might not have found Christianity to be all that they expected it to be. As a result, they were in need of a gifted person to give wise counsel and to speak words of comfort and assurance. Today many are lonely, hurting, and discouraged, and have the same need to be encouraged to be faithful to God. The Holy Spirit is able to break into situations and bring a comforting message that strengthens believers in their faith.

5. **The gift of giving.** This gift suggests a God-given capacity to share with others one's personal possessions. Often people connect *giving* to *goodness*, which does imply generosity. The close link of this gift with the fruit of the Spirit probably warns us against making too hard-and-fast distinction between the gifts and the fruit of the Spirit. **The gift of giving includes sharing money and other possessions such as food, clothing, and shelter for the benefit of others.** The proper way to exercise this gift is "with liberality" (*aplotes*) (v. 8)—that is, generously and sincerely, without any motive of personal gain. **The word *giving* refers to**

the kind of sharing that is "open-handed and open-hearted, giving out of compassion and singleness of purpose, not from ambition" (Rienecker, 1980, 2:30). So often God provides things we need in order that we may be generous toward others.

6. **The gift of leadership.** The Greek verb for *leads* (*proistemi*) has two meanings. **The first meaning of *lead* is "to set before," "to set," "to manage," or "to lead" and points to those who provide leadership.** Paul speaks of those who "are over you in the Lord" (1 Thess. 5:12). Still another example: "Let the elders who rule well be counted worthy of double honor" (1 Tim. 5:17). Obviously, the term *lead* refers to those who serve as leaders in the church. **The second meaning of *to lead* is "to care for" or "to give aid."** It is unnecessary to choose between the two meanings; they are not mutually exclusive, especially when thinking of the responsibility leaders assume for the care of those they supervise. **Church leaders lead and inspire the church in its relationship with God and its service to God, as well as give spiritual care and assistance to individuals in the Christian community and the world.** These tasks are part of their leadership responsibilities. According to Paul, leadership is a gift that is to be exercised with diligence.

7. **The gift of mercy.** It seem that "he who gives" and "he who shows mercy" are closely related, but Paul must have had something more specific in mind in his reference to showing mercy. **In the Old Testament, *mercy* expressed God's goodness, especially to those who were in trouble (Gen. 43:14; Ex. 34:6).** The gift of mercy can take a number of concrete forms, such as giving to the homeless; visiting shut-ins and prisoners; caring for the sick, the aged, and disabled; and showing kindness to the orphans and disadvantaged. **It takes the gift of mercy to minister to people when they have serious needs. Merciful kindness and concern are to be shown in cheerfulness. Service done with mercy is not a duty, but a joy and delight.**

Using Spiritual Gifts

Local churches have various needs, and Paul's primary desire is to motivate his readers to use their gifts to meet these needs. **Christians are to give themselves wholeheartedly to whatever**

ministry God has given them. In Paul's day, as well as in our time, God has bestowed on each believer a spiritual gift(s). As stewards of God's manifold grace, we are held accountable to use our gift to serve others (1 Peter 4:10). **God has called each of us to serve and has given us gifts of grace so that we can.** Spiritual gifts are all about serving—not for personal glory, but for God's glory. A proper appreciation of our gifts brings about greater humility and protects us against pride and feelings of superiority. After all, all gifts are gifts of grace, and are divine provisions for serving the body of Christ. The gifts of the Spirit are to be used in love; and when they are, the church is strengthened spiritually and numerically.

ROMANS 12:3-8

KEYWORDS

Called by God (see p. 228)

Church—The Body of Christ/One Body in Christ
The whole redeemed fellowship in heaven and earth (Matt. 16:18; Eph. 1:22-23). This theological term pictures the church as a fellowship similar to the human body. The members of the church are members of one another (Rom. 12:5).

Exhortation, Gift of (*paraklesis*)
A particular ministry of pastors and others to comfort, strengthen, and encourage fellow believers

Gift of the Spirit (see p. 64)

Giving, Gift of
A gift of the Spirit that enables a believer to share his or her resources for the benefit of others, whether food, clothing, money or possessions

Grace (*charis*) (see p. 23)

Leadership, Gift of (verb–lead, *proistemi*)
A gift of the Holy Spirit which gives one the authority to lead and to provide guidance in the church (v. 8)

Measure of Faith
A standard by which a Christian is to estimate himself/herself. A realistic appraisal of ourselves prevents us from thinking too highly or lowly of ourselves.

Mercy, Gift of
A Spirit-given capacity to express empathy in concrete ways to those who are in need, such as caring for the sick, providing for the poor, and tending to the elderly and those with disabilities

Prophecy, Gift of
A spiritual gift that enables a believer to speak words inspired by the Holy Spirit. A prophetic message may be predictive, referring to future events, or it may speak to a need or situation in the church at the time.

Service
1. **Christian Service (by all believers) (*diakonia*)**—Actions and work through which followers of Christ express God's love, peace, and joy, benefiting others and the world God created.
2. **Service/Ministry, Gift of (*diakonia*)**—A spiritual gift that enables one to do deeds of service (Rom. 12:7).
3. **Service/Ministry in Leadership, Gift of (*diakonia*)**—A spiritual gift that enables one to give leadership in the church (v. 8). Paul speaks of those who "are over you in the Lord" (1 Thess. 5:12). In Romans 12:8, the word translated **"he who leads"** (*proistemi*) may also suggest the idea of "to care for or "to give aid."
4. **Service/Helps, Gift of (*antilepseis*)**—A Spirit-given capacity to be helpers (1 Cor. 12:28).

Teaching, Gift of
The Spirit-given ability to instruct others in the Christian faith

SUMMARY

Let each one "not . . . think of himself more highly than he ought to think, but to think soberly" (Rom. 12:3). Harmony in the church depends on humility. Like the human body, the church has many members; and to the members of the church, God has given a variety of spiritual gifts. The utilization of these gifts is necessary for the body of Christ to fulfill its purpose. Each believer should be careful to use his or her spiritual gift(s) for the benefit of the church.

LIFE APPLICATION

A temptation that many Christians face is the attitude of superiority. This attitude tempts us to look down on others who are less favored than we are. As children of God, we are to be sober-minded and have a realistic and healthy attitude toward ourselves and avoid a depreciating view of others.

> **LIFE APPLICATION**
>
> Our recognition that we need each other is important to appreciating how valuable all our brothers and sisters in Christ are. Each believer has a spiritual gift (1 Cor. 12:7; 1 Peter 4:10). No matter how humble our status in life may be, we and our fellow Christians have important functions and ministries in the body of Christ.
>
> An honest estimation of our gifts and of the gifts of others is crucial to maintaining unity in the Christian community. In large measure, harmony in the church rests on our living within our own limits and showing respect to others and recognizing their value to the fellowship of believers.

STANDARDS FOR DAILY LIVING
ROMANS 12:9-13

> ⁹ Let love be without hypocrisy. Abhor what is evil. Cling to what is good. ¹⁰ Be kindly affectionate to one another with brotherly love, in honor giving preference to one another; ¹¹ not lagging in diligence, fervent in spirit, serving the Lord; ¹² rejoicing in hope, patient in tribulation, continuing steadfastly in prayer; ¹³ distributing to the needs of the saints, given to hospitality.

Love and Spiritual Gifts

Paul has stressed the importance of spiritual gifts and their proper use, and now he discusses the fruit of the Spirit, especially focusing on the main fruit—love. In order to understand Paul's comments about spiritual gifts, it is helpful to know that Paul wrote his letter to the Romans from the city of Corinth. In 1 Corinthians, Paul addresses the Corinthian believers' abuse of spiritual gifts and insists that **love should accompany the use of all spiritual gifts in order for them to be effective in strengthening the church (chs. 12-14).** So it is no accident that Paul's discussion about the fruit of the Spirit follows his discussion of spiritual gifts.

The fruit of the Spirit are the normal outcome of Christian growth and maturity. In a broad sense, love (*agape*) may be thought of as a gift of God (1 John 4:19), but it is never described in the New Testament as a gift of the Spirit (*charisma*). **Gifts of the Spirit define what Christians do, and the fruit of the Spirit define what Christians are.** Fruit of the Spirit are essential to the effective operation of spiritual gifts.

According to 1 Corinthians 13:2, if I use a spiritual gift without love, "I am nothing"; that is, my actions are ineffective and unprofitable for others or for me. **Without love (*agape*), gifts of the Spirit lose their authority, power, and effectiveness, and the value of all acts of service becomes diminished.** The Corinthians had a good mix of spiritual gifts (1 Cor. 1:7), but they had failed to use them in love. To avoid the separation of spiritual gifts from the fruit of the Spirit, Paul explores the life of love and relationships in the body of Christ in Romans 12:9-13.

Authentic Love in the Body

- **Loving without hypocrisy (v. 9a).** When sincerity is absent from one's "loving" actions, "love" is not really love at all. Genuine love is free of pretense and selfishness. There is a love that claims to give much, but it is not love because the real aim is to get more than it gives. **A sincere attitude and the absence of phoniness and manipulation are essential to genuine love.**
- **Abhoring evil and clinging to the good (v. 9b).** The word *abhor* (*apostugeo*) means "to hate," expressing extreme dislike. The term *cling* (*kollao*) means "to hold fast," like something has been cemented or glued together. Both words are in the present tense and, therefore, Paul urges believers to keep on viewing evil with horror and holding tenaciously to the good. **This practice is the sure way to real goodness and escaping temptation that may lead us to fall into sin.**
- **Being kindly affectionate toward each other (v. 10a).** Here a strong emphasis is placed on the Christian community as a family. "Kindly affectionate" (*philostorgos*) is the word for

family love, especially signifying the kind of love a parent has for a child. This indicates that Christians have close family ties and should love one another as parents love their own children. The phrase "with brotherly love" (*philadelphia*) stresses the need for strong family bonds. **Christians should love one another and have each other's best interest at heart because they belong to the same family.**
- **Honoring our brothers and sisters in Christ by giving them preference (v. 10b).** "Giving preference" (*proegeo*) literally means "go before as a leader" to show the way. The idea is to show respect rather than to demand one's rights and special honor. For Christians to prefer others to themselves would create an ideal situation in the church, in that the giving of special recognition or honor would not create personal resentment, tensions, or trouble. **It takes a real spirit of humility to be pleased when others are honored. Leading the way in showing honor marks a great Christian.**
- **Being fervent in Spirit, not sluggish, but diligent in serving the Lord (v. 11).** Loving acts must be done with the fire of the Holy Spirit. The *New King James Version* assumes that *spirit* (*pneuma*) refers to the human spirit, but here the context strongly suggests that the term *pneuma* refers to the Divine Spirit (cf. Acts 18:25). **Being filled with the Holy Spirit, we are to experience daily the fire and inspiration of the Spirit.** When this is a reality, our tasks, jobs, and professions are transformed into ministries for the Lord. Of course, this requires a combination of personal discipline (diligence, earnestness) and the power of the Holy Spirit (Acts 1:8; 1 Thess. 5:19).
- **Rejoicing in hope (v. 12a).** Christians are called upon to be optimistic. There is a better day coming—not only is it coming but it has already dawned in Jesus Christ, and we rejoice in it now. Because of what God has done in Christ, we know that His grace is sufficient regardless of the circumstances. **Our hope for eternal life in heaven with Christ**

provides us with confidence and the strength to persevere even in the midst of troubles and afflictions.
- **Being patient in tribulation, continuing to persevere in prayer (v. 12b).** We can endure adversities because of hope. Steadfastness during times of trouble is not without pain, but steadfastness in hope enables us to endure adversity. **Because of hope, we look to what God can do, and we persist in prayer in the face of inevitable storms and troubles of life.** As the storms blow and troubles mount, living prayerfully every day is imperative.
- **Giving to the saints in need (v. 13a).** Christians have an obligation to help others, especially fellow believers in need. **As the Holy Spirit works in our lives, we see our abundance, jobs, and businesses as opportunities to bless believers and others in need.**
- **Practicing hospitality (*philoxenia*, love of strangers) (v. 13b).** The practice of hospitality was recognized as being important for the early Christians. Traveling evangelists, missionaries, and other believers could not afford places of lodging. Many of the inns had bad reputations. As believers traveled, it was necessary for them to depend on fellow believers for lodging. Providing traveling Christians with a place to stay was a way of blessing them.

Even today, the Holy Spirit may direct us to see our homes differently—as centers of hospitality and spiritual blessings to others. **Whether or not we are able to host friends and strangers in our home, we are to find ways to be hospitable and kind to those with whom we come in contact each day, providing them comfort, encouragement, and friendship.**

Love as Our Foundation

It is necessary for the bond of love to be active and evident among believers. Love helps us to overlook the inadequacies of others, while complimenting them for their strengths. This takes some effort on our part and the help of the Holy Spirit. Fellow believers can irritate us, hurt our feelings, and cause us to feel isolated and rejected. Even so, we cannot separate ourselves from

The Christian Life

our brothers and sisters in Christ. Resentful and disrespectful attitudes toward church leaders and pastors, as well as tensions and conflict among church members, have a negative effect on the quality of worship and the effectiveness of ministry.

Love (agape) enables spiritual gifts to function on a sound basis and enables us to see that our brothers and sisters in Christ are more important than our personal ideas, egos, or resentments. **Love is the supreme character trait produced by the Holy Spirit, and our practice of love reflects the process of our taking on the mind and likeness of Jesus Christ.**

ROMANS 12:9-13

KEYWORDS

Evil (see p. 80)

Fruit of the Spirit
A cluster of gracious virtues produced by the Holy Spirit in the life of the Christian (Gal. 5:22-23; Eph. 5:9). The result is a Christlike life evident in one's words and deeds, including one's loving treatment of others.

Holy Spirit/The Spirit (see p. 25)

Hope (see p. 137)

Hospitality (*philoxenia*)
Compassion and generosity expressed toward others. In the biblical world, hospitality was focused primarily toward aliens, travelers, strangers, and those in need.

Love (*agape*) (see p. 144)

Love (*philadelphia*)
Love of believers for one another. Initially, *philadelphia* referred to familial love, but in the New Testament it extends beyond the family to include fellow believers (1 Thess. 4:9-10). This affectionate reality is to stand in opposition to cliques among members of a Christian congregation.

Pray/Prayer (see p. 61)

Saints (*hagioi*) (see p. 345)

Tribulation (see p. 87)

SUMMARY

Having discussed briefly the gifts of the Spirit, Paul turns to the fruit of the Spirit. It is not surprising that love heads the list. While believers are justified by faith, living the Christian life is an expression of true faith. The church must back up its preaching and teaching with genuine love, holding to the good, selflessly serving one another and showing preference for others over ourselves, fervently seeking the Spirit, maintaining hope, praying continually, and being generous toward people who are in need.

LIFE APPLICATION

Christians are saved through faith, then the fruit of that saving faith are good works, making faith and good works inseparable. Likewise the fruit of the Spirit and the gifts of the Spirit are intimately connected. The fruit of the Spirit, especially love (*agape*), ensures that the gifts of the Spirit operate properly. This kind of love is uniquely divine and comes from the Holy Spirit, who pours it out in our hearts (Rom. 5:5). Such love can be quenched and mingled with self-seeking, but by nature it is free of pretence and is spontaneous and extremely generous, not seeking position and status.

Christian love requires us to be committed to honesty, to abhor all evil, to passionately cling to good works, to show genuine interest in fellow believers, to seek greater honor for others, to give of ourselves to the Lord's work through the power of the Holy Spirit, to be patient and hold firmly to Christian hope, and to be generous and hospitable toward others.

Love is to govern all in the Christian community. It is the unfailing sign of discipleship (John 13:34-35) and the life we have in Christ (1 John 3:14).

CHRISTIANS' RESPONSE TO NON-CHRISTIANS
ROMANS 12:14-21

[14] Bless those who persecute you; bless and do not curse. [15] Rejoice with those who rejoice, and weep with those who weep. [16] Be of the same mind toward one another. Do not set your mind on high things, but associate with the humble. Do not be wise in your own opinion.

> ¹⁷ Repay no one evil for evil. Have regard for good things in the sight of all men. ¹⁸ If it is possible, as much as depends on you, live peaceably with all men. ¹⁹ Beloved, do not avenge yourselves, but rather give place to wrath; for it is written, *"Vengeance is Mine, I will repay,"* says the Lord. ²⁰ Therefore
>
> > *"If your enemy is hungry, feed him;*
> > *If he is thirsty, give him a drink;*
> > *For in so doing you will heap coals of fire on his head."*
>
> ²¹ Do not be overcome by evil, but overcome evil with good.

In this section of Romans, the apostle Paul draws on certain teachings of Jesus from His Sermon on the Mount (Matt. 5:1ff.) and His Sermon on the Plain (Luke 6:17ff.). **Paul applies Jesus' teachings to the Christians in Rome, particularly addressing their relationships with people who were not followers of Christ.**

Most likely, as Paul discusses these matters of relationship, he is aware that the Romans had expelled the Jews from the city around ten years earlier (in AD 49, during the reign of Claudius as emperor; (cf. Acts 18:1-3). Also, Paul must have considered that, at some point, the church in Rome might be perceived as a threat to Imperial Rome, and Christians would receive no better treatment than the Jewish people had received in AD 49. In spite of possible hostilities toward the church, Paul urges Christians to love and show compassion toward everyone, including those who are not followers of Christ.

Christian Compassion

- **Ask God to bless people who curse you, instead of cursing them in return (Rom. 12:14; Matt. 5:44).** This teaching of Christ reminds us of the power of words (James 3:1-12). Christians should be careful to speak blessings, not curses. When we are mistreated or persecuted, our perfect example is the Lord. While hanging on the cross, Jesus prayed for God to forgive those who were putting Him to death (Luke 23:34). Believers should follow their Lord's example and meet harsh treatment and persecution with prayers and blessings rather than with cursing. Stephen, like Jesus, prayed for those who tortured him for his faith. Stephen's prayer just before he died most likely was instrumental in turning *Saul*, the persecutor, into *Paul*, the apostle and missionary (Acts 7:54-60). Blessing those who hurt us is a way of returning good for evil.

- **Be happy or sad with people when they are happy or sad (Rom. 12:15; 1 Cor. 12:26).** Verse 15 teaches us to share the feelings of everyone. The Holy Spirit enables believers to have a great capacity for empathy for others. As a result, they are able to identify with others' successes, victories, and laughter, as well as with their failures, hurts, sorrows, and tears. It may be easier to mourn with those who mourn than to rejoice with those who rejoice. We may be tempted to envy the successes and victories of those who are rejoicing. Christians, however, are called upon to enter into the joy as well as the grief of others.

- **Be friendly with people in all stations of life (Rom. 12:16).** A Christlike life and an exalted opinion of one's self do not go together. The admonition here is to be willing to associate with all people, even with those who are considered by society to be lowly, without societal distinction, power, or honor. Jesus is a marvelous example: He had fellowship with public contractors for the Roman government, many of whom were dishonest tax collectors; also He associated with sinners, so that He might win them for the kingdom of God (Matt. 9:10; Mark 2:15-16). Rather than being highminded (*ta hupsela*, the "high things," Rom. 12:16), Jesus was willing to associate with humble folk. Paul urges believers to be likeminded: "Let this mind be in you which was also in Christ Jesus" (Phil. 2:5).

The Christian church is to be a place of equality, and it is no place for individuals to expect or demand superior status or privileges (James 2:1). The body of Christ is to be free of conceit. People of all ethnicities, nationalities, and backgrounds—employers and employees, people with wealth and those with financial struggles, those who have formal education and those who do not, healthy and physically strong people and those with physical challenges, those for whom life is going smoothly and those who are having problems, and those who have known Christ a long while and those who are new Christians—sit side by side in equality within the body of Christ. "God is no respecter of persons" (KJV)—"God shows no partiality" (Acts 10:34-35; cf. 2:9-11; Gal. 3:28).

- **Do everything possible to live in peace with everyone (Rom. 12:18).** Paul recognizes that it is not always possible to be at peace with everyone, even when you put forth your best effort. Observe that the apostle qualifies his injunction with "*If it is possible*, as much as depends on you, live peaceably with all men." **When individuals have character flaws, deep emotional and spiritual problems, or do outright evil, it limits the ability of Christians to remain at peace with them.** Taking a stand for what is right may bring us into conflict and disturb the peace. Again, the Lord is our example. During His time on earth, Jesus demonstrated the love and grace of God with gentleness; but when it was appropriate, He was also firm, dramatically chasing the money changers out of the Temple (John 2:13-22).

Seeking Peace When There Is Abuse in a Relationship

Much of the Bible is about relationships, not only with God but also with one another. From experience, we have learned that any human relationship can become toxic and ugly when it is used to abuse, degrade, harass, bully, or humiliate. Sadly, it is not uncommon for dedicated Christians to experience being battered or to be recipients of some other type of abuse, just like anyone else. Christians, along with their children, may suffer from abuse from another family member, acquaintance, or stranger. Being in an abusive relationship raises questions such as these: How far do I go in turning the other cheek? When do I stand up? When do I say to the abuser it is enough? No one can live under constant abuse and maintain the quality of life and spiritual, mental, and physical health that God desires for us.

All of us have the right to protect ourselves and others (see Ex. 17:8-16; Judg. 6:33-40; 1 Sam. 7:3-13). To tolerate abuse only encourages an abuser's negative behavior and does not benefit that person's spiritual health. In order for abusers to see their need for God and for help, they must be told the truth about their behavior. We are to be wise when dealing with any abuser, by seeking counsel from knowledgeable people and taking action in the safest manner for us and our family. **If we are in an abusive relationship, we are to speak the truth in love (Eph. 4:15), even if we must do so in a court of law against the abuser.**

Forgiveness is to play a role when Christians seek justice. Jesus counsels the Christian to go the second mile (Matt. 5:38-41). **While going the second mile with others does incorporate forgiveness (releasing one who has wronged us into God's hands), it does not include condoning or enduring abusive behavior.** In light of Paul's insistence on his rights as a Roman citizen, Christians may properly maintain their legal rights (Acts 16:35-39). **When an abuser seeks and receives help and there is much work on the part of everyone involved, healing and reconciliation can occur, but as Paul implies, it is impossible to live at peace with some people.**

- **Do not try to get revenge when someone mistreats you, but be kind and allow God to take care of things (Rom. 12:19).** God is ultimately in control of our lives. Romans 8:28 states it this way: "God causes all things to work together for good to those who love [Him]" (NASB). We leave the final outcomes in the hands of God and avoid acts of revenge against those who have hurt and done us wrong. The right to punish does not belong to us but to the Lord. Only God can handle vengeance. It is not revenge to report crimes and to allow courts to pronounce justice. Bitterness is the fruit of a vengeful heart. To insist on taking vengeance is to lack trust in God as Judge. Our maintaining love and self-control in hostile human relationships allows the Holy Spirit to work in the situation and in the lives of others. The Christian's duty is to counter evil with love, not to try to get even.

The Christian Life

On the basis of Proverbs 25:21-22, Paul urges Christians to be kind to their enemies. If an enemy needs food and drink, they are to give to him freely (Matt. 5:43-47). To do good to their enemy, they "will heap coals of fire on his head" (Rom. 12:20). An Egyptian ritual may help us understand the phrase *coals of fire*. In the ritual, a person carried a basin of burning coals on his head as a symbol of penitence. Paul's point seems to be that being kind to one's enemy will make him ashamed of his previous deeds and bring him to repentance. Therefore, kindness (*coals of fire*) is not a disguised punishment of an enemy, but is for his redemption. Deeds of love can turn an enemy into a friend and even bring that person to salvation.

- **Do not let evil overwhelm you, but overcome evil with good (v. 21).** Verse 21 sums up Paul's emphasis on God's impartial love in Christians' relationships with others. No doubt, the eyes of many in the city of Rome were on the church, and Paul wanted the Christians to be known for love. The same challenge faces the church today as Christians encounter nonbelievers in their neighborhoods, on their jobs, or in the marketplace. ***Agape* love demands that we love and treat everyone kindly.**

ROMANS 12:14-21

KEYWORDS

Evil (see p. 80)

Forgiveness (see p. 47)

God as Judge (see p. 86)

Humility
The essence of saving faith that excludes pride regarding one's race, religion, social status, or person. According to the teachings of Christ, a child provides the model for humility (Matt.18:1-4).

Love (*agape*) (see p. 144)

Peace (Hebrew *shalom*, Greek *eirene*) (see p. 144)

Repentance/Penitence (see p. 84)

SUMMARY

Christians are to extend love to all people. How is that to be done? Repay good for evil, share in the feelings of everyone, seek to be at peace with all, do not seek revenge, leave the righting of wrongs to God, and seek the conversion of enemies through the power of love.

There is the qualifying phrase, "if it is possible, as much as depends on you," (Rom. 12:18). Paul recognizes that we live in a hostile world. Standing for what is right will bring dissension.

LIFE APPLICATION

Good can overcome evil and hatred. Our Lord Jesus Christ taught about the power of love in the Sermon on the Mount and demonstrated it on the cross. Paul urges us to emulate our Savior. As Paul knew, there is always the temptation to judge our enemies and to retaliate against them. Christians motivated by love do not do so, but instead they bless their adversaries, seeking their well-being. If adversaries have fallen into misfortune, we are to grieve with them; or if they have good fortune, we are to rejoice with them.

Love strives to preserve harmony and build a basis for unity. There may arise disagreements because of personal preferences and prideful attitudes of superiority, but love always remains humble, desires what is best for others, and stands for what is right and good.

However, loving Christians must be realistic and recognize that under certain circumstances it may be impossible to keep the peace, especially in abusive situations. In those situations, love demands its rights for the safety and fair treatment for people who are being abused.

We are to love others as God has loved us—He cares about us even when we have rejected or opposed Him. The Bible instructs us to love all people, even our enemies. This means that we are to care about their souls and eternal well-being, even though it may be wise for us to confront them, to oppose their behavior, or to stay away from them. Endeavoring to love our enemies as God loves them may lead them to repentance.

CHRISTIANS AND CIVIL GOVERNMENT
ROMANS 13:1-7

¹ Let every soul be subject to the governing authorities. For there is no authority except from God, and the authorities that exist are appointed by God. ² Therefore whoever resists the authority resists the ordinance of God, and those who resist will bring judgment

The Christian Life

> on themselves. ³ For rulers are not a terror to good works, but to evil. Do you want to be unafraid of the authority? Do what is good, and you will have praise from the same. ⁴ For he is God's minister to you for good. But if you do evil, be afraid; for he does not bear the sword in vain; for he is God's minister, an avenger to execute wrath on him who practices evil. ⁵ Therefore you must be subject, not only because of wrath but also for conscience' sake. ⁶ For because of this you also pay taxes, for they are God's ministers attending continually to this very thing. ⁷ Render therefore to all their due: taxes to whom taxes are due, customs to whom customs, fear to whom fear, honor to whom honor.

In chapter 12, Paul has urged Christians to fulfill their duties, which have their origin in Christ. Among those duties is the use of a variety of spiritual gifts with which God has endowed them (vv. 3-8).

Moral Obligations of Christians

Following his explanation of spiritual gifts, Paul gives some moral instructions. These instructions can be divided into two groups:

- **The first group of instructions applies to Christians and their relationships with God (12:1-3) and with one another (vv. 4-13).**
- **The second group applies to Christians and their relationship with people who are outside the church (vv. 14-21; 13:1-7).**

Belonging to this second group, Romans 13:1-7 focuses on believers' obligation to the authorities in government. Note that Paul has been dealing with the ordering of relationships (government) for some time. Chapter 12 has addressed the government of the kingdom of God. Chapter 13 addresses the government of this age. **God in His sovereignty rules both His Kingdom and this world. Civil government is an aspect of the common grace of God.**

Though Christians' citizenship is in heaven and their ultimate allegiance is to God, this does not free us of our duties to the society in which we live. As citizens of heaven, we are "not [to] be conformed to this world" (12:2), and our new life in Christ makes special moral demands on us. We have responsibilities to the Present Age and to civil government. **Christians are to be "instruments of righteousness" (6:13) as long as this Present Age lasts. Our responsibilities include being good citizens out of conscientious obedience to God's will.**

Historical Context of Paul's Statements About Government

Before considering verses 1-7, a couple of observations may be helpful regarding their historical background.

1. **Paul may be defending the church against accusation that the church was advocating political revolution.** In 6 BC, Judea was declared to be a Roman province. Soon afterward arose a group of Jewish, religious militants called the Zealots, who advocated the "sole rule of God" and were known for insurrection. They were convinced that Israel should not be ruled by a king, and their aim was to destroy civil government. Not only did they oppose Roman government, but they wrecked the homes, burned crops, and assassinated the families of fellow Jews who paid taxes to Rome. The payment of taxes to Caesar was an issue for the Zealots. This Zealot sentiment against paying taxes could have been present in Rome (Simmons, 2008, 89-96). Later in AD 49, some Jews residing in Rome were involved in an uprising in the city and as a consequence, the Emperor Claudius issued a decree excluding all Jews from the city (Acts 18:1-3). The exact nature of the rioting is unknown, but it centered around a man called "Chrestus" (Christ). This probably indicates that Christianity had been introduced in Rome, and dissension had arisen about it within the Jewish community in the city (Suetonius, "Life of Claudius," 25, 4).

Though some of Paul's people felt that the governing authorities deserved respect, he knew that many shared the attitude of the Zealots toward the state, disputing the authority of Rome and holding the unyielding belief that God's children were only responsible to God. Paul was not for anarchy; and knowing that the Christians could have been seen as a threat to law and order, he encourages the Christians in Rome to support the state, insisting that there is a place for earthly authority.

2. **Nero reigned as emperor of Rome from AD 54 to 68. Because he was notorious for his cruelty, many have wondered**

why Paul considered the governing authorities to be "appointed by God" (Rom. 13:1) and urged the Christians in Rome to submit to them.

There may be several reasons why Paul encouraged the church's submission to the Roman government:

- **Since some Roman citizens may have seen the church as a movement that opposed law and order, Paul wanted the church to live in such a way that would invalidate their claims.** Many could have perceived the church as a strange Jewish sect that had little or no respect for political leaders and government. After all, the Jews had become known for insurrection.
- **Paul wrote Romans about AD 58, which fell during the period in which Nero's rule was more just and humane.** It is a well-known fact that the first five years of Nero's rule were years of good government; but as time went on, he became more despotic. In AD 64 (well after Paul wrote his letter to the Romans), there was the disastrous fire in Rome. Nero sought to blame the Christians for this disaster and had many of the Christians tortured and executed (Simmons, 2008, 234-37). Nero's persecution of the church still lay in the future when Paul wrote Romans.
- **Paul may have been urging obedience to government as a leadership structure rather than urging obedience to an individual ruler.** Paul often speaks in absolutes without mentioning exceptions to the general truth. God wills government, but this fact does not obligate us to every command of godless leaders (Acts 5:29). Scripture instructs children to obey their parents (Col. 3:20), but this instruction does not mean that a child should steal if his father tells him to do so. In human society, God has arranged for authority and government just as He has for relationships in the human family.

God, the Establisher of Authority

Because of the controversial ways Romans 13:1-7 has been used, our interpretation of this passage should be kept within the context of Paul's world. In his appeal to believers in Rome, he places their relationship to government on the highest level. Paul states that God is the source of all authority. **God himself has ordained government, and civil order exists because He wills it.** The Divine mandate to govern is founded upon affirming that which is just and rejecting that which is unjust. When a government ceases to affirm that which is good and punishes that which is evil, it has abrogated its right to govern. **The authority of political leaders has been granted to them by God, and they are to exercise their authority as *ministers* (*diakonos*, "servant"—the same word used to describe ministers of the gospel) of God (v. 4).** As long as they use their authority for the common good, they are servants of God. As they function as representatives of God, governing authorities do not punish those who do good, but only those who do evil (vv. 3-4). **Their duty is not only to restrain evil and punish evildoers but also to support the good, thereby ensuring the health of the whole society.**

Additional Reasons to Respect Government

Up to this point, Paul has urged the Christians in Rome to be subject to civil authorities because these authorities are God's servants charged with maintaining law and order. As Paul moves on in the discussion, he gives two additional reasons for the church to be respectful toward the government: "because of wrath" and "for conscience' sake" (v. 5).

- **"Because of wrath" (v. 5).** Officers of the government have the authority to reward those who do good (v. 3) and to inflict punishment (wrath) on evildoers. In their punishment of someone for evil, they act as administrators of divine justice. **Government is for the purpose of restraining evil.**
- **"For conscience' sake" (v. 5).** As citizens, Christians also are to follow governmental leadership on the basis of conscience. **Followers of Christ are not to be motivated to obey civil law only because of fear of punishment, but they are also to have internal reason for their obedience. Conscience commends obeying civil law as being a wise and prudent course of action.** In addition to receiving punishment from civil authorities, breaking moral law can

The Christian Life

result in condemnation from our own consciences. Paul does not leave the believer with fear of punishment, but elevates the Christian response to government to the level of conscience, honor, praise, and respect.

In the Roman Empire, one way that Christians had respect and support for the government was by their payment of taxes. The apostle Paul wanted the church to fulfill their social responsibilities in the context of their faith in God. He has indicated that **all of life is to be lived as an act of worship (12:1). Support of the government and the paying of taxes are ways of worshiping God in the everyday world (Käsemann, 1980, 359).** God deserves our devotion in the political sphere as well as in the church. God is everywhere—He is in public life, as well as in places of worship.

Applying Paul's Teachings About Government to Our Time

Paul's view of law and order for the Christians in Rome in AD 58 does not diminish its relevance for today. **There are some basic ways that Paul's understanding of government speaks to us.**

- **The authority of those who govern has been entrusted to them by God.** Since their authority comes to them from God, they are accountable to Him to govern wisely and benevolently.
- **Governing authorities are to be representatives of God on the earth and are to administer civil justice.** When government becomes abusive, it ceases to be an instrument of God; and its leaders are no longer functioning as servants of God. Tyrants do not have a legitimate place in government. The New Testament recognizes that with the wrong leadership the state can become apostate as well as the church. To commit apostasy, the state must fall away from the "ordinance of God" (13:2).
- **Governing authorities are not necessarily good or evil by nature, but they are to support good and restrain**

evil. Paul does not envision a perfect government or society in This Age. This Old Age with its institutions is passing away, and one day in its place will be the eternal kingdom of God.

- **Christians owe allegiance to the governing authorities, but first and foremost they are to obey God (Acts 5:29).** Christians' allegiance to the state is not absolute; they owe absolute allegiance only to their Lord. Caesar is not their Lord; Jesus Christ is their Lord (Rom. 10:9; 13:14). The Lord instructs us to "render to Caesar the things that are Caesar's, and to God the things that are God's" (Mark 12:17), reminding us that we have obligations to the Present Age, for the Coming Age has not fully come. Rendering to Caesar what belongs to him is one way of worshiping and serving God. We, as followers of Christ, are to always put God first.

ROMANS 13:1-7

KEYWORDS

Conscience (see p. 91)

Evil (see p. 80)

Ordinance of God
Something that God has put into place, such as governmental authority appointed and ordained by God. God's ordinance of government is the basis for submission to governmental authority, even for Christians, because it is an authority willed by God. Such submission expresses Christians' relation to God. Paul, in expressing the importance of respect for civil government, does not lose sight of Christian freedom in Christ (see Eph. 5:21), which may call for disobeying civil law when it violates God's law.

Servant/Minister (*leitourgos*)
Civil authorities are God's servants. Romans 13:6 refers to the collection of taxes, indicating that those who perform such services for the state are active in the service of God.

SUMMARY

God is the supreme authority, and He grants authority to civil government. The responsibility of leaders in government is to promote good and restrain evil. As leaders fulfill this responsibility, they are ministers of God.

Christians should not only be good citizens because of fear of punishment, but also out of regard and respect for God's will and a conscientious desire to be obedient to Him.

The question is whether Paul is teaching absolute obedience to all government authority. Other passages of Scripture show that God approves of Christians' disobeying the government, but only when obedience is contrary to God's will (Ex. 1:17, 21; 1 Kings 18:4-16; Dan. 3:12-18; Matt. 2:12; Acts 5:29: Heb. 11:23).

LIFE APPLICATION

The God who sent Christ into this world is the same God who gives authority to government officials in order to maintain an orderly society (family→community→state→nation→international relations). As government fulfills this purpose, it does God's will. This passage indicates that the command to "live peaceably with all men" (Rom. 12:18) includes political authorities. As well as desiring us to be faithful to Him, as part of our loving our neighbors, God wants us to be good citizens and have respect for leaders in government.

When civil leaders are in direct opposition to God, as Christians we must follow God rather than civil government. An example of an unjust government is one that rewards evildoers and punishes law-abiding citizens. Where that happens, government leaders have ceased to be ministers of God. Regarding submission to them, we are first obligated to please God and to be as good citizens as possible.

Good citizenship requires those of us who have the privilege to vote for our leaders to make an effort to become knowledgeable about civic affairs. This knowledge includes exploring candidates' leadership beliefs and practices, then prayerfully voting and maybe even working to help get someone elected. Government officials are to be God's implementers of good in the public sphere. In free societies in which we are allowed to offer input into governmental decisions, following elections, we have a responsibility to communicate our ideas for improving life in our communities, districts, states, nation, and international relations.

LOVE FULFILLS THE LAW
ROMANS 13:8-10

⁸ Owe no one anything except to love one another, for he who loves another has fulfilled the law. ⁹ For the commandments, "*You*

> shall not commit adultery," "You shall not murder," "You shall not steal," "You shall not bear false witness," "You shall not covet," and if there is any other commandment, are all summed up in this saying, namely, "You shall love your neighbor as yourself." [10] Love does no harm to a neighbor; therefore love *is* the fulfillment of the law.

Our Debt of Love

Here is another example of the Christian's obligation. **Our obligation as followers of Christ is not merely just to meet the minimal societal standard of fearing and respecting the government and paying our debt to society, but to extend ourselves even further by loving our neighbors.** So God's command to love one another is stated once again in this section of Scripture (v. 9; cf. 12:10; Lev. 19:18; Matt. 19:19; 22:31; Gal. 5:6, 13, 22). Paul has urged the Christians to pay what they owe to the civil authorities (Rom. 13:7), and now he addresses their relationship with their neighbor. **Although believers owe respect and taxes to the government, they also have a debt to love their neighbor.** Unlike legal debts, our debt of love to our neighbor can never be paid in full because of all of the love that Christ has shown and continues to show us. *Neighbor* (*heteros*) means "the other person" with whom we have a relationship, the stranger, and especially anyone in need.

The command to love our neighbor—one another—comprehends and brings to realization the entire moral code of the Bible. This command was not a new discovery for Paul; it was already written in the Old Testament (Lev. 19:18). **The way Christians fulfill the law and keep the commands to love one's neighbor is by acting with love in daily life (cf. Rom. 8:4).** Love is the complete fulfillment of what God's law demands, but love is an obligation that we will always owe, though we pay on it daily.

Commandments in the Law to Love One's Neighbor

The apostle Paul cites what is called the "second table" of the Ten Commandments, omitting the fifth commandment (honoring of parents), but implies it when he says, "if there is any other commandment" (13:9). The "first table" of the Decalogue is directed to the love of God; the "second table," to the love of neighbor, and forbids adultery, homicide, theft, lying, and coveting.

- *Adultery*—**Genuine love honors the commitment of the marital relationship.** If a person loves his neighbor, he will not violate the marriage bond. When people are unfaithful to their marriage vows, it is not due to love but to their allowing their physical passions, loneliness, or anger to control them. Love seeks to solve marital difficulties through prayer, humility, seeking wise counsel, and doing the challenging work that is necessary to change and build a healthy relationship. Love always maintains restraint and respect for the other person.
- *Homicide*—**Love does not seek to destroy and kill, but seeks to pray for and encourage others.** If a person loves his neighbor, he will not murder him. Murder may be unthinkable to us, but character assassination may not.
- *Theft*—**Love is concerned with giving and does not take what rightly belongs to others.** If a person loves his neighbor, he will not take the possessions of others.
- *Lying*—**Love does not cause harm through untruthful, careless, or vindictive words, but seeks to use words to uplift others.** If a person loves others, he will not bear false witness against them. Outright lying may be one thing, but what about the careless repeating of damaging gossip?
- *Covetousness*—**Love cleanses the heart of envy, jealousy, and the desire to have what others have.** If a person loves others, he will not covet. He will not be jealous of what others have and will not desire to possess their belongings. We may claim to be free of coveting while trying to outdo the people next door or to outshine our coworkers or our peers.

These five commandments demand that we not sin against or with others. There is no overthrowing of God's moral law—meaning that difficult circumstances do not justify our breaking God's commands to our neighbor. In addition to our willfully breaking the commandments, we may also inadvertently cause harm to our neighbor by ignoring or neglecting him or her. In either case, we are to ask God's forgiveness and to seek to reconcile with our neighbor, if possible. Only love that comes from God can empower us to keep His commandments and help us to repair damage within our relationships.

As Christians, our debt to love others never ceases, and we must continue to pay on it daily. We are to love to the limit, with the understanding that we will never be finished. Should we reach our goal in loving, we would cease loving. Never reaching the objective, however, does not cause us to fall into despair, but rather we are to live in confidence that God's love flows on and on through us to our neighbor (Schweizer, 1970, 252). **God will use the love that we express in our daily lives to accomplish His purposes.**

ROMANS 13:8-10

KEYWORDS

Covet (see p. 190)

The Law (*Torah*) (see p. 48)

Love (*agape*) (see p. 144)

Neighbor (*heteros/plesion*)
Any person—regardless of nationality, ethnicity, or religious background—with whom one has a relationship or happens to encounter.

SUMMARY

Christians are to engage in the practice of love without ceasing. Our debt of love is ongoing; it can never be fully paid.

Love fulfills the law, because it addresses the real intent behind each of God's divine commandments. Love secures proper relationships between individuals. No one acting out of love, under normal conditions, will do harm to others or will infringe on their rights.

Paul has consistently denied that the law can save a person, but he does not deny the moral law's value for guiding life.

LIFE APPLICATION

Faith works itself out through Christian love (*agape*). This love enables us to embrace all human beings, including those who are different from us. God pours out His love in our hearts through the

> Holy Spirit, and that love prompts us to pursue all that is good in life and all that is useful and helpful to others. The love of God upholds all that the Mosaic law stands for, and we are to express this love to others every day.

END-TIME URGENCY
ROMANS 13:11-14

> 📖 ¹¹ And do this, knowing the time, that now it is high time to awake out of sleep; for now our salvation is nearer than when we first believed. ¹² The night is far spent, the day is at hand. Therefore let us cast off the works of darkness, and let us put on the armor of light. ¹³ Let us walk properly, as in the day, not in revelry and drunkenness, not in lewdness and lust, not in strife and envy. ¹⁴ But put on the Lord Jesus Christ, and make no provision for the flesh, to fulfill its lusts.

Paul has presented the practical commands for living the Christian life (12:1-13). **In 13:11-14, Paul explains that the practice of these commands of God has become even more urgent because the church is living in the End Time.** Like Paul's Roman readers, those of us who are alive today live in the End Time—the period between the First and the Second Coming of Christ. The next great event in the history of salvation will be the return of Christ. We need to awaken out of spiritual sleep and be ready for Christ's Coming (v. 11). **Paul's letters abound with warnings about the nearness of Christ's return and the Final Judgment (Phil. 3:17—4:1; Col. 3:4, 6; 1 Thess. 5:1-11).** The End Time and ethics are never separated from each other in Jesus' or Paul's teachings. Paul now links the theme of *sanctification*, started in Romans 6, to the theme of *eschatology* (the study of the Last Days, the final events in history).

The modern Pentecostal Movement has shared Paul's sense of urgency—understanding that we are living in the End Time, which arrived with the First Coming of Christ, as Joel's prophecies were fulfilled on the Day of Pentecost. This arrival was then confirmed by Peter in his sermon on that day (Joel 2:28-32; Acts 2:17), and there was a call to repentance, allowing God to change people's behavior and attitude (Acts 2:38). As a result of our living during the Last Days, Pentecostals have emphasized the importance of holy living and utilizing the time remaining for the preaching of the gospel. **The urgency of the times calls for living Spirit-filled lives and using our time wisely as we wait in anticipation for our Lord to return.**

Preparation for The Coming Age

Every day that passes we are a day closer to the Coming of Christ. As Paul reminds the believers in Rome, "our salvation [glorification] is nearer than when we first believed" (13:11; cf. 8:12-36). During this End Time the future reality of salvation has become nearer. **We live in the final stage of the process of salvation. In a sense, salvation is already an accomplished fact (Eph. 2:8), but it still has a present ongoing dimension (1 Cor. 1:18). The process of salvation will not reach completion until Christ returns.** Therefore, behind the already/not yet view of salvation stands Paul's idea of the two ages—*This Age* and *the Coming Age*. Already the Coming Day of salvation has dawned, but the darkness of this world still stands opposed to it. The final day of salvation has not yet arrived, but the light of that day is already shining. **The coming of that heavenly day calls for believers to "cast off the works of darkness, and [to] put on the armor of light" (Rom. 13:12).** We as Christians are already experiencing the benefits of salvation and must stand in opposition to the evil in the world.

Cautions

Christians are to prepare for the Coming of Christ. **For those people who are not yet prepared for Christ's return, as a warning, Paul gives a list of typical sins that will interfere with their being ready (v. 13).** All of these sins were present in the Corinthian church. Paul arranges them in three pairs:

The Christian Life

- **Revelry and drunkenness.** These two vices are actions that result in people lowering themselves by disturbing the peace of others and making themselves a nuisance. Reveling and drunkenness were indecencies that nonbelievers would have condemned in Paul's day.
- **Lewdness, licentiousness, and lust.** These are actions that are a result of a person being controlled by harmful passions. People who engage in these behaviors place little value on virtue and have little or no shame about their gross immorality. They are given to excesses and generally do not care what others think about them.
- **Strife and envy.** Ungodly competition gives rise to quarreling and strife and may grow out of a refusal to take second place. Unrestrained aspirations for prestige and position can prompt a spirit that begrudges others what they have and a spirit of envy and jealousy.

Paul's final appeal is to "put on the Lord Jesus Christ, and make no provision for the flesh" (*sarx*, v. 14). In these Last Days, the suit of armor for the believer is Christ himself, which requires us to live in close personal fellowship with Him (Eph. 6:10-20). For indeed, "the night is far spent, the day is at hand" (Rom.13:12). Therefore, we are living in the End Time, and Christ may come at any time. In terms of the calendar, we do not know when, for "with the Lord one day is as a thousand years, and a thousand years as one day" (2 Peter 3:8). According to the Scriptures, we are in the Last Days—in the last chapter of salvation, but no human knows how long the chapter is. Our final salvation is closer now than in Paul's day. **Christ may come any day.**

ROMANS 13:11-14

KEYWORDS

Already/Not Yet Doctrine (see p. 47)

End Times (End Time, End of Time, Last Day, Last Days)
- **The Present Age** (the Old Age, This Age, the Current Age, this Present Evil Age, the Age of Adam)

- **The Coming Age** (the Future Age, the Age to Come, the Coming Day, the New Day, the Age of Christ. *Initiated by*: the Second Coming, Christ's Coming, the Second Advent)

These terms relate to eschatology, the *End Times*, covering a broad range of subjects such as the present and future reign of God (the two ages), the return of Christ, the rapture of the church, resurrection, the Millennium, and judgment of humankind. Terms like *Last Day* and *Last Days* are broad references to the events of the *End Times*, whereas concepts such as *Coming Day*, *New Day*, *Coming Age*, and the *Age to Come* are different ways of indicating that believers live now spiritually in the age that will be consummated when Christ returns. The *Age to Come* overlaps the *Present Age*, which is variously referred to as the *Old Age*, *This Age*, and this *Present Evil Age*. Now believers await the return of Christ to the earth "in the clouds with great power and glory" (Mark 13:26), which is often spoken of as *Second Coming* or *Christ's* Coming.

Eschatology

The study of the Last Days, the final events in history, which involve the unfolding of God's redemptive purpose in Christ

Final Judgment (see p. 84)

Flesh (see p. 58)

Jesus Christ (see p. 59)

Salvation (see p. 23)

SUMMARY

The next event in the salvation story is the return of Christ. The Roman Christians lived during the End Time, and so do we. This fact makes it urgent for us to prepare for the Second Coming of Christ by living godly lives and sharing with others the Good News of salvation.

Our final salvation draws nearer day by day. The Old Age is drawing to a close, and the Coming Age is already dawning. It is urgent that we put on the character of Christ and end the old way of life.

LIFE APPLICATION

We live in critical times. Our final salvation is still a thing of the future. It is urgent that we remain vigilant and conduct ourselves as Christians, putting off the deeds of darkness and putting on the armor of light. Our warfare is to be relentless against the enemy of our souls. At stake in this godly warfare is our eternal destiny. We know that the return of the Savior and the completion of our salvation are nearer than when we first believed. The signs of the times point to the nearness of His coming again. Our Savior desires that we live in eager expectation, being prepared to welcome Him as our Lord.

The Christian Life

PERSONAL FREEDOM AND RESPECT FOR OTHERS
ROMANS 14:1-12

> 📖 ¹ Receive one who is weak in the faith, but not to disputes over doubtful things. ² For one believes he may eat all things, but he who is weak eats only vegetables. ³ Let not him who eats despise him who does not eat, and let not him who does not eat judge him who eats; for God has received him. ⁴ Who are you to judge another's servant? To his own master he stands or falls. Indeed, he will be made to stand, for God is able to make him stand.
>
> ⁵ One person esteems one day above another; another esteems every day alike. Let each be fully convinced in his own mind. ⁶ He who observes the day, observes it to the Lord; and he who does not observe the day, to the Lord he does not observe it. He who eats, eats to the Lord, for he gives God thanks; and he who does not eat, to the Lord he does not eat, and gives God thanks. ⁷ For none of us lives to himself, and no one dies to himself. ⁸ For if we live, we live to the Lord; and if we die, we die to the Lord. Therefore, whether we live or die, we are the Lord's. ⁹ For to this end Christ died and rose and lived again, that He might be Lord of both the dead and the living. ¹⁰ But why do you judge your brother? Or why do you show contempt for your brother? For we shall all stand before the judgment seat of Christ. ¹¹ For it is written:
>
> *"As I live, says the Lord,
> Every knee shall bow to Me,
> And every tongue shall confess to God."*
>
> ¹² So then each of us shall give account of himself to God.

Following his more general exhortations in 12:1—13:14, in chapter 14, Paul addresses a specific problem among the Roman church, explaining to them the need to moderate one's own personal Christian liberty out of love and concern for others. The problem among the believers in the church in Rome was conflict over food laws and holy-day observances.

The Strong and Weak in Faith

This section in Romans begins Paul's pastoral response to the conflict over personal freedom, which involved two

contending groups of people within the church. Since Paul is so specific in his comments, someone (perhaps Phoebe) must have informed him about the friction that had developed there. **These two groups of people are often referred to as *the strong in faith* and *the weak in faith*.** The group whom Paul first addresses considered themselves to be stronger. This group insisted they were free to eat meat and to drink wine and did not think that it was necessary to observe Jewish holy days. On the other hand, those whom Paul describes as being "weak in the faith" (v. 1) insisted in the necessity of strict compliance to certain religious rules, including vegetarianism and treating certain days as being more holy than others.

The disagreement between the two groups seems to have stemmed from Gentile-Jewish differences in the church. The two groups are not addressed by name in 14:1—15:6, but in the concluding section (15:7-13), there is direct reference to both the Jewish and Gentile believers. **The Gentile believers, who did not wish to be obligated to follow Jewish laws, viewed themselves as being enlightened and, therefore, stronger. As a result, they criticized the Jewish believers, whom they thought of as being *weak*, because they practiced dietary restrictions and elevated some days above others.** No doubt, some Jews, like Paul, held beliefs that were similar to those of the Gentiles who practiced more liberty, while some Gentiles who had been attached to a synagogue before Christian conversion favored the Jewish practices. **Paul warned the two groups not to despise or to look down on each other.** The strong were not to look down on those who were weaker in faith, and the weak were not to judge those who were stronger in faith. Any contempt and negative behavior toward each other showed their own immaturity in Christ.

Respect and Unity in the Body of Christ

Morally speaking, the religious practices in question fell in the sphere of amoral practices—practices that in and of themselves are not sinful—but take on moral significance when there is conflict over the observing of them. By no means was the problem trivial. Was the observance of Jewish food laws and holy days just a matter of culture, or were these practices theologically significant and essential to faith in Christ? The conflict was not just a problem because it was a question of liberty from Jewish practices; **the disagreement struck at the heart of the church's unity. Much was at stake, including the salvation of souls.**

Paul counts himself among those who were strong in their faith. He begins his comments about the conflict by first addressing those believers who were stronger, urging them to accommodate the weaknesses of those who were "weak in faith" (14:1). *The weaker* were those whose consciences asserted that in order for them to be faithful to God, they must follow Jewish food laws and special holy days without exception. **The duty of both *the strong* and *the weak* was to stop judging one another and to mutually accept each other in the interest of love.** The reason why there is no need for judgment is because, as noted, no moral issue is at stake except for the false judgments. Criticism of one another would leave no room for mutual communication and understanding (v. 3).

Paul lays down a great principle: Neither is to judge the other. The ones who ate anything were not to criticize those who ate only vegetables. Those who ate only vegetables were to remember that God had received both groups as His servants. Who gives people the right to judge another man's servant? The master decides whether his servant keeps his position or loses it (v. 4). **The Christian, whether strong or weak, is God's servant and is not to be judged by other believers.** Only God has the right to decide when worship is acceptable, and only God can make a person's spiritual life successful (for only "God is able to make him [her] stand") (v. 4). Paul's statement implies that those who were weaker thought that the strong had fallen because they were not following the same religious rules. **God's grace is stronger than human weakness, and only God can decide whether or not His servants are being faithful.**

Our Actions as Expressions of Worship and Service

The strong and the weak were both trying to achieve the same thing in different ways; **they were both trying to be faithful in their service to the Lord.** In verse 5, Paul observes that the problem included a dispute over sacred days, including the Sabbath and other days in the Jewish religious calendar. Whatever days Christians may consider holy and whatever food they may eat, "let each be fully convinced in his own mind" that what is done is according to God's will. **Whatever is done or whatever is avoided in the Christian life is to be "to the Lord" (v. 6).** The place for resolution is the individual conscience, not on the public/corporate level. If Christians observe a day or not, they are called to do it to the pleasure of the Lord. If Christians eat meat or only vegetables, they are to do it with thanksgiving to God. Here Paul seems to place the controversy in the context of worship, elevating the infighting between the two groups of people to a higher concern, which is the worship of God. **Quality of worship can be evaluated only by God. Sincere worship is acceptable to God, regardless of mode. All of life is to be offered in worship (12:1).**

Both *strong* and *weak* Christians take spiritual risks when they condemn and judge others. This is particularly true when the acts that they are questioning are not actually sinful. **As in the case of the church in Rome, Christians may be actually criticizing acts of worship, through which fellow believers are offering themselves as living sacrifices to God.** Paul points out that while their approaches may have been different, both groups in Rome were servants of God.

Our Accountability to God

Again Paul emphasizes that the entire life of the Christian is to be devoted to the worship and service of God (14:7-8). Whether a believer lives or dies, he does it "to the Lord" (v. 8). Life and death are the extremes of human experience. Both bear witness to the sovereign rule of the Lord and to our dependence on Him. The ultimate test of being a Christian is not whether we eat meat or only vegetables, but living and dying to the Lord. Whether strong or weak, believers do not look to themselves in life or in death. They look to God and belong to Him. **All servants of God have the responsibility to determine for themselves how they will offer their lives to God in worship.**

The basic fact remains that the Lord Jesus died and arose so "that He might be Lord of both the dead and the living" (v. 9). The lordship of Christ made it senseless for believers to judge one another. Both those who are strong in their faith and those who are weak will stand before Jesus Christ as defendants (1 Cor. 3:10ff.). As defendants, neither group has the qualifications to judge the other. **No one has the right to usurp the authority of Christ in order to judge others.**

No matter what divides us on the earth, "we shall all stand before the judgment seat of Christ." Paul asks two questions: "Why do you judge your brother? Or why do you show contempt for your brother?" (Rom. 14:10). To strengthen his point about Christian compassion and unity, Paul cites Isaiah 45:23, which indicates that the final judgment is yet to come. Paul's final appeal here is for those who are strong and those who are weak to resolve their differences. They are to avoid being stumbling blocks to one another (Rom. 14:13).

Relevance for the Modern Church

Although Romans 14:1-12 is part of Paul's pastoral response to a particular problem among the believers in Rome many years ago, Paul's inspired advice is still relevant for the church and pastoral ministry today.

The issue in Rome was not a dispute about how to be saved or about fundamental Christian doctrine, but it was about how to live as a Christian. In the city of Rome, the Gentile and Jewish believers did not agree on eating meat or observing holy days. Their dispute was a threat to the unity of the church and could have become fatal to some of the believers' relationships with Christ.

Observations

Following are some observations for today's church.

1. **Controversy Over Non-Crucial Practices.** In many congregations over the years, the insistence on following certain holiness practices as the only way to live the Christian life has introduced tension and factions into the church. Many of the practices

on which people have insisted do not have the clear support of the Bible and fall in the amoral area of behavior. Since they are not commanded in Scripture, these practices are not righteous nor sinful in and of themselves, for their benefit rests on the intent and attitude of the person who practices them. **Controversy over non-crucial matters has proved to be very divisive when imposed on other believers who do not see them as being essential for living a devoted Christian life.**

2. **Freedom of Worship.** Pentecostals have been known for advocating freedom in worship, which has included outward expressions, such as the raising of hands, enthusiastic praising of God, shouting, praying in the Spirit, and sometimes being overcome by the Spirit's power, falling to the floor and resting in the Spirit. To some people, any worship service that does not conform to this style of worship is not spiritual. Out of such a conviction emerges the attitude of spiritual superiority toward those whose worship is not as outwardly dynamic and is more reserved.

No doubt, there are times in worship services when the Holy Spirit moves in extraordinary ways and gifts of the Spirit are manifested; but on other occasions of worship, the Spirit accomplishes His work through the preaching of the Word or through deep quiet times of prayer and praise with no outward demonstration of His presence. **Space needs to be given for the moving of the Spirit and for a variety of styles in worship. Worshipers need liberty to worship God in a context of order and in an atmosphere free of criticism.** Flexibility in styles of worship and allowance for spontaneity in worship will serve the unity of the church well.

3. **Inclusion of Both Mature and Less Mature Christians. Wherever Christians assemble, among them there will be the spiritually more mature (those stronger in faith) and the spiritually less mature (those weaker in faith). As a result, there will be differences in thinking and priorities, which may lead to conflict in congregations. There is plenty of room in the household of faith for both weak and strong Christians.**

All of us are on a journey of spiritual development and growth, but we are all in different places in that process. **Paul charges both**

The Christian Life

stronger and weaker Christians to show mutual tolerance and respect for each other. The weaker are not to condemn the stronger as being evildoers. Those who are strong are not to despise those who are weak as though they are ignorant. Though they do not see "eye to eye," neither has the right to judge the other (v. 4). It is all right to have our convictions, but it is our Christian duty to let other people have their convictions, too, and not impose ours on them.

ROMANS 14:1-12

KEYWORDS

Freedom in Christ (see p. 170)

Judgment by God/God's Judgment (see p. 68)

Judgment by Humans (see p. 84)

Judgment Seat of God
A raised place or stage from which God, as Judge, issues official verdicts. *Judgment seat of God* is a way of speaking of the reality of divine judgment.

Moral Practices/Amoral Practices
Moral Practices—Practices that are ethically correct according to the laws of God
Amoral Practices—Belief or behaviors that are morally neutral—not moral or immoral
The weaker in faith among the Roman Christians were committed to Old Testament food regulations and vegetarianism. These kind of beliefs and practices were morally neutral and were of minor significance. They could be observed without jeopardizing the integrity of the faith. If their observance is insisted on, amoral practices can become divisive in the church.

Strong in Faith/Weak in Faith
The phrase *weak in the faith* refers to a group of Jewish Christians in the church in Rome who were committed to observing food laws and eating only vegetables. The *strong in faith* did not observe such practices, feeling their freedom in Christ did not require them to follow such strict religious practices. The diversity of opinion and practice among the Roman Christians created tension and conflict in the church. Christians who are more mature and those who are weaker in their faith, despite their differences, are to show respect for each other and nurture unity within the body of Christ.

SUMMARY

Paul instructed the Roman Christians, who were stronger in their faith and those who were weaker in their faith, to show respect for one another. They were to avoid criticizing each other for differences in their religious practices.

Those who were considered to be weak in their faith were those who insisted on a more rule-based approach to the Christian life, with strict observance of Jewish food laws and holy days. They were looking to things of no authentic spiritual significance in an effort to secure their relationship with God. Those who were considered to be stronger placed more emphasis on freedom in Christ and did not consider strict observance of Jewish laws to be necessary in one's relationship with God.

In dealing with the dispute, Paul suggested:

- Every Christian is a servant of God; only God determines if His servants are faithful.
- Every Christian's service and worship are devoted to God.
- Every Christian must one day appear before God and give an account of himself or herself to Him.

Neither the weak nor the strong have the right or the qualifications to judge the other.

LIFE APPLICATION

The clear truths of the Scriptures must not be compromised, but there are areas that allow for flexibility and diversity. Such areas do not involve essential doctrine and moral teachings. God is merciful and gracious to allow for different convictions in doubtful and secondary matters, and He may even appreciate diverse modes of worship. Even so, despite God's acceptance, it is not uncommon for such matters to become controversial and to divide the church whenever we attempt to assign primary importance to our own personal ideas and cultural heritage. A clear sign of this problem is when the more strict Christians and the more flexible ones become critical of each other. The question is, What business do we have in judging our brothers and sisters in the Lord?

Whenever we engage in this kind of controversy, we have lost sight of a larger matter: All Christians belong to Christ and to the same family. Christ rules over all believers, both the enlightened and the unenlightened. In secondary amoral matters, not one of them is qualified to judge the other. When Christians judge one another in inconsequential issues, they are trying to do what only Christ is competent to do. Let us live at peace with one another in regard to such matters.

ACTING IN LOVE TOWARD ONE ANOTHER
ROMANS 14:13-23

> 13 Therefore let us not judge one another anymore, but rather resolve this, not to put a stumbling block or a cause to fall in our brother's way.
>
> 14 I know and am convinced by the Lord Jesus that there is nothing unclean of itself; but to him who considers anything to be unclean, to him it is unclean. 15 Yet if your brother is grieved because of your food, you are no longer walking in love. Do not destroy with your food the one for whom Christ died. 16 Therefore do not let your good be spoken of as evil; 17 for the kingdom of God is not eating and drinking, but righteousness and peace and joy in the Holy Spirit. 18 For he who serves Christ in these things is acceptable to God and approved by men.
>
> 19 Therefore let us pursue the things which make for peace and the things by which one may edify another. 20 Do not destroy the work of God for the sake of food. All things indeed are pure, but it is evil for the man who eats with offense. 21 It is good neither to eat meat nor drink wine nor do anything by which your brother stumbles or is offended or is made weak. 22 Do you have faith? Have it to yourself before God. Happy is he who does not condemn himself in what he approves. 23 But he who doubts is condemned if he eats, because he does not eat from faith; for whatever is not from faith is sin.

The Role of Love in Christian Relationships

Paul continues his discussion about handling differences in the body of Christ, emphasizing the importance of our not offending or causing a fellow Christian to stumble. His main point is that **Christian liberty must be balanced and tempered by Christian love.** *Love (agape)* **is more than affection and sympathy; it is a deep concern for the welfare of others.**

Once again, in this passage, Paul basically agrees with a group in the church that recognized that the Christian life was more about faith and less about keeping religious rules. This group, considered to be stronger in the area of faith, consisted primarily of Gentile Christians. In his comments to this stronger group, Paul is concerned about how their attitudes were affecting another group who were not as strong in their understanding of faith and freedom in Christ. This second group, consisting mostly of Jews, felt that adherence to strict dietary and holy-day laws was necessary if one was to be faithful to God.

Paul's primary interest is in preserving the unity of the Christian community and for the stronger Christians to avoid becoming a spiritual hindrance and causing the Christians who tended to be more rule-oriented in their approach to lose their faith. True love will put the interest of others above our own. Paul advises Christians, "Each of you should look not only to your own interests, but also to the interests of others" (Phil. 2:4 NIV).

Respecting Other Peoples' Decisions of Conscience

At this point, Paul's discussion focuses on the eating of meat. In verse 14 of the text, he states, "I know and am convinced by the Lord Jesus," which is a reference to the words of the historical Jesus. He is absolutely certain by the authority of Christ that there is no such thing as morally unclean food. He asserts, though, that if one is convinced that certain food is unclean, he has an obligation to follow his conscience and not eat it. The eating of meat is neither right nor wrong in itself, but it is morally wrong if it violates one's conscience or genuinely offends another. Conscience plays a critical role in the Christian life. Never does Paul advise anyone to do anything contrary to the voice of conscience. **Disregard for one's conscience can lead people to engage in actions that for them are sin, because they are violating their own sense of right and wrong.**

It is a serious matter when a strong Christian displays his freedom, causing grief to a weaker Christian. To do so shows that although the stronger Christian is considered to be enlightened, he or she is "no longer walking in love" (v. 15). The basis for Christian conduct is not knowledge but love, a theme Paul develops in 1 Corinthians. The value of each person prompts Paul to address directly those who are strong in faith: "Do not destroy with your food the one for whom Christ died" (v. 15).

To put it another way: If Christ died for your brother or sister who has religious convictions against eating certain food, why can you not give up the right to eat what you please for his or her sake? **The misuse of Christian freedom can do harm, causing a weaker believer to stumble and to turn away from Christ.**

Being Positive Representatives for Christ

Another danger of living in freedom without respect for others is that one's Christian liberty (*to agathon*, the good) might be seen as being evil (v. 16). This perception by people who are part of the body of Christ, as well as those outside the church, may cause them to doubt the truth of the gospel and Christ's ability to change lives. Inevitably, this disrespect for others would be a poor reflection of the grace of God, the source of Christian freedom. **Conflict in the church always has the potential to bring reproach from the onlooking world and to be a spiritual hindrance to others.**

The Kingdom of God and Unity in the Church

Continuing, Paul tells both Gentile and Jewish Christians that God's kingdom is not about eating and drinking, "but righteousness and peace and joy in the Holy Spirit" (v. 17). The phrase "kingdom of God" rarely appears in Paul's letters and usually speaks of those who will not inherit the kingdom of God. Verse 17 is Paul's only positive use of the phrase "kingdom of God." When Paul does use the phrase, the meaning is similar to Jesus' use of it as recorded in the Gospels. This phrase is used to indicate the presence of God's rule now, but implies that His rule will only reach complete fulfillment when Christ returns. God's rule will be fully realized in this world at the Second Advent of Christ.

Righteousness, Peace, and Joy

Paul defines *the kingdom of God* in terms of relationships in the Christian community: "righteousness and peace and joy in the Holy Spirit" (v. 17). The phrase "in the Holy Spirit" here modifies the three nouns—*righteousness*, *peace*, and *joy*—indicating the various aspects of living in the Spirit, and these three terms refer to our relationship with others.

- ***Righteousness in the Holy Spirit* refers to right relations with our fellow human beings.** In the earlier parts of Romans, the term *righteousness* refers to a right relationship with God (justification by faith). However, the focus here is not on how to get into right relationship with God, but on right living. The key to this kind of lifestyle is to allow oneself to be led by the Holy Spirit. The Spirit's guidance assures us that our conduct will be proper in relation to fellow believers and others.
- ***Peace in the Holy Spirit* is the peace we have with one another.** For the Christian, liberty does not mean freedom to do as we please, but the freedom to give up certain things that offend weaker Christians, so that peace may be maintained. For Paul, the greatest use of Christian liberty is not to use it to demand one's legitimate rights, but to give up such rights; whenever doing so will foster peace without violating God's moral laws (1 Cor. 9:1ff.). This way of living requires us to pick up our cross and deny ourselves.
- ***Joy in the Holy Spirit* is the joy we have as a result of peace with others.** Tension and conflict among believers work against joy in the community of faith, as well as against the joy of individual believers. True Christian freedom is the freedom to live a life directed by the Holy Spirit. The result is true joy.

The kingdom of God is manifested in the fellowship of believers. Serving Christ in righteousness, peace, and joy opens the door to both pleasing God and winning the respect of people (Rom. 14:18). **Therefore, Paul's admonition to the strong and to the weak is to pursue peace and mutual edification (v. 19) by being good representatives of their Lord and building up one another in the faith.** All things are clean, including food, but that does not mean that the stronger Christians should eat it. They have the right, but are not bound to it. The determining factor is whether it is good or bad for the weaker Christian. If it is bad for the weaker believer, then it is bad for the stronger one. No Christian should hesitate to abstain from meat or wine or anything that might cause someone to fall away from Christ.

Paul broadens his warnings about the danger of misusing Christian liberty, emphasizing its effect not only on the individual soul, but also "the work of God" (v. 20). **Paul's concern is not only with the spiritual welfare of the individual, but also with that of the body of Christ. Harm done to an individual also affects the community of believers as a whole (1 Cor. 12:12-27).**

Faith and Conscience in Our Decisions

Our conscience remains important whether we are strong or weak in our faith (Rom. 14:22-23). It is good that those who are stronger in the area of faith can act in faith (with a clear conscience) and enjoy their freedom in Christ. They are blessed to be able to live free of a distressed conscience and self-judgment. Stronger Christians who are more mature in their faith are able to make sound decisions that do not discredit them. In their freedom, they are also in a position to accommodate those who are weaker by not asking them to violate their consciences or by creating a stumbling block for the weak.

In addition to his advice to the more mature Christians, **Paul advises those Christians who are not as far along in their faith journey to be attentive to their conscience and not violate it.** He puts this way: "He who doubts is condemned if he eats, because he does not eat from faith; for whatsoever is not from faith is sin" (v. 23). If believers are convinced that something is wrong and do it anyway, to them it is sin. **Whatever believers may do without being fully persuaded that it is in harmony with God's will, is wrong for them.** They are sinning when they do something contrary to their convictions. Although their compliance may be out of desire to follow social convention or fear of unpopularity within the church, if their action did not come from faith, then it is wrong. Weaker Christians may be tempted to impose their convictions on those who are stronger, while those who are stronger may want to force their insight on those who are weaker. What the strong and the weak need to remember is that God has received them both as His servants, and He requires that they accept each other in spite of their differences.

Relationships in the Church Today

The apostle Paul broadens the relevance of his inspired wisdom beyond the immediate problem of eating meat and of observing holy days when he adds "[Do not] do anything by which your brother stumbles" (v. 21). The church has always had new issues that introduce tension into the body of Christ and threaten to split the church. Paul's pastoral wisdom and advice regarding matters of unity are still relevant for the church today. **God makes us responsible for one another, especially the stronger for the weaker. We are to love one another in ways that promote spiritual growth rather than hinder it. At the same time, the essential teachings of the faith must not be compromised but preserved and defended.** An urgent need for the church is to take a hard look at our differences in light of eternal truth. **When we keep our focus on what is truly important, many of our differences will diminish in significance. The church will not go wrong if we listen to Paul's pastoral wisdom and engage in generous compassion for others.**

ROMANS 14:13-23

KEYWORDS

Condemnation (see p. 155)

Evil (see p. 80)

Faith (see p. 23)

Judgment by Humans (see p. 84)

Kingdom of God
The rule and reign of God. God's kingdom is the realm in which His rule is exercised. At the present, the church realm is primarily where God reigns, but His kingdom has both a present (Luke 11:20) and a future dimension (Matt. 6:10; 25:31-46). Christ's life and death were the in-breaking of God's redemptive rule, but at the end of the Current Age we expect the culmination and victory of the divine rule. Never is the essence of God's kingdom eating and drinking, but it is the life through the presence and power of the Holy Spirit.

Love (*agape*) (see p. 144)

Peace (Hebrew *shalom*, Greek *eirene*) (see p. 144)

The Christian Life

Righteousness (see p. 48)

Unclean (see p. 80)

SUMMARY

Paul cautions that stronger Christians must be careful not to become a stumbling block or hindrance to weaker Christians. A Christian with a mature conscience knows that no food is "unclean" in itself, but it can be for those whose conscience indicates otherwise. Therefore out of respect, Christians who feel free to eat various foods or to engage in certain actions should refrain from eating foods or engaging in actions that might offend others. Their motivation is to show their love for others and their desire to avoid undermining the faith of a brother or sister for whom Christ died.

The essence of the kingdom of God is not what one eats or drinks; the kingdom of God centers on righteousness, joy, and peace in the Holy Spirit. God's reign is promoted through the wise use of Christian freedom. The strong are to rejoice in their enlightened faith, and the weak are to be careful not to violate their conscience. When individuals have convictions about certain matters and go ahead and violate their convictions, they sin—not necessarily because their action is evil in itself, but because they think that they are going against God's will for them. Their action is sin because they act out of a doubtful conscience, rather than out of their faith.

LIFE APPLICATION

God expects us to do more than tolerate unenlightened Christians. Even though we may be more mature and enlightened in our own faith, we have a responsibility to care for other people's souls and an obligation to love them. For us to avoid becoming a stumbling block to each other, we must use discretion in our use of Christian freedom. If we are not careful, what we do can entice a believer to violate his or her conscience. Such a violation of conscience would be sin because it would not come from the person's faith and convictions. Christian freedom can be used in such a way to express a callous indifference to the spiritual damage it does to others.

Still, making a major issue out of minor things can also be very perplexing and disrupt fellowship in the church. Even so, enlightened Christians are to follow the example of Christ and show interest in the welfare of fellow believers who "major in minors." For the stronger Christians to insist on their personal freedom would risk destroying harmony and the effectiveness of the church. Christ calls for us to pick up our cross and deny ourselves. At times, our personal sacrifice may be necessary, even in insignificant matters.

CHARACTERISTICS OF CHRISTIAN FELLOWSHIP
ROMANS 15:1-13

> 📖 ¹ We then who are strong ought to bear with the scruples of the weak, and not to please ourselves. ² Let each of us please his neighbor for his good, leading to edification. ³ For even Christ did not please Himself; but as it is written, *"The reproaches of those who reproached You fell on Me."* ⁴ For whatever things were written before were written for our learning, that we through the patience and comfort of the Scriptures might have hope. ⁵ Now may the God of patience and comfort grant you to be like-minded toward one another, according to Christ Jesus, ⁶ that you may with one mind and one mouth glorify the God and Father of our Lord Jesus Christ.
>
> ⁷ Therefore receive one another, just as Christ also received us, to the glory of God. ⁸ Now I say that Jesus Christ has become a servant to the circumcision for the truth of God, to confirm the promises made to the fathers, ⁹ and that the Gentiles might glorify God for His mercy, as it is written:
>
> *"For this reason I will confess to You among the Gentiles,*
> *And sing to Your name."*
>
> ¹⁰ And again he says:
> *"Rejoice, O Gentiles, with His people!"*
>
> ¹¹ And again:
> *"Praise the Lord, all you Gentiles!*
> *Laud Him, all you peoples!"*
>
> ¹² And again, Isaiah says:
> *"There shall be a root of Jesse;*
> *And He who shall rise to reign over the Gentiles,*
> *In Him the Gentiles shall hope."*
>
> ¹³ Now may the God of hope fill you with all joy and peace in believing, that you may abound in hope by the power of the Holy Spirit.

Paul continues to deal with issues that have arisen between those who were stronger in faith and those who were weaker. In particular, he speaks to the strong—those who have more experience and maturity—emphasizing their responsibility. The cardinal teaching here is that although the strong were in the right regarding their liberty in Christ, they were not free to use that Christian freedom to please themselves.

Christ, Our Model for Relationships (15:1-6)

The key to understanding Paul's viewpoint is to realize that he had real knowledge about the life of the historical Jesus. Such knowledge is evident in the first part of verse 3: "For even Christ did not please Himself." **Having agreed with the beliefs of those who experienced more freedom in Christ, Paul urges them to bear the weaknesses of the weak and give them a helping hand.** The way they are to do this is to set out to please their neighbor (*plesion*), rather than to please themselves (v. 2). This intent recalls the command of Leviticus 19:18, "You shall love your neighbor as yourself." Loving our neighbor cannot be done by ignoring our neighbor, but only by doing those things that will lead to that person's edification and spiritual growth. **The call is not for those who are stronger to tolerate doctrinal error or compromise moral standards, but to build up and strengthen the weaker in their faith.** As in Paul's day, in many churches today there are those who are not yet spiritually mature. Mature Christians have a special responsibility to them.

Christians who have gained insight and maturity are to follow Jesus Christ as their model. Christ was unselfish and did not live to please Himself. He was despised by men, suffering selflessly (Isa. 53:1ff.), and on Him fell abuse and reproaches, just as the Scriptures had predicted (Rom. 15:3). Those strong in their faith must do likewise, even if it means risking exposing themselves to insults from those who are weaker, the ones in need of their help. The point is that Christ did so much for us, and we are to be conformed to His passion and suffering. Any sacrifice Christians make is so small in comparison with the cross. **Those who are strong, by being patient with weaker Christians and enduring their misunderstandings or criticism, will please God, just as Christ pleased God, His Father.** The cross-death of our Lord teaches us to lay aside legitimate, personal rights in order to help the spiritually weak and immature. When doing so, we will not cause harm to others. The spiritually weak should not be allowed to abuse or slander people, just because those who are more mature are trying to be patient with them. **Loving those who are weaker makes it easier to help them to grow in their faith and to become mature Christians. So, Paul places relational responsibilities on both parties, the weak and the strong.**

Paul's Use of Old Testament Teachings

Once again, the apostle Paul turns to the Old Testament to support his pastoral wisdom. He reminds his readers that **what was written previously in the Scriptures was "written for our learning" (Rom. 15:4; cf. 1 Cor. 10:6-11; 2 Tim. 3:16).** This statement from the text explains why Paul has appealed to the Old Testament Scriptures throughout his letter to the Romans. The Old Testament is not out-of-date and continues to have relevance for Christians today, offering us hope and guidance. The inspired Scriptures offer encouragement and give patience to believers, encouraging them to persevere in their faith.

No doubt, the controversy in the church in Rome was perplexing, and those who considered themselves more mature in their faith were probably tempted to denounce those whom they considered to be defective in their faith. **The Old Testament Scriptures gave strength and patience to those who were stronger, enabling them to hold fast to their hope of final salvation. Believers' hope of eternal salvation is grounded in the Old Testament.** Without any doubt, the Scriptures are adequate for all of life because they focus our attention not only on how we should live but also on our destiny in Christ. As Christians study Scripture and follow the teachings of Paul, who points us to Christ, we are to take these teachings and practice and teach them to others. Our Lord Jesus Christ speaks to us through His Word. From His lips we receive instruction about how to live and about the promises of God that make sure our future hope.

Paul's Prayer for Unity

In verses 5-6, Paul prays a prayer for the Christians in Rome to be in harmony. This prayer for unity may indicate that

Paul intended for his letter to be read during a worship gathering. In the prayer, Paul asks God to enable the Roman believers to bring their differences into subjection to Jesus Christ. **The result of submissiveness to Christ is that Christians are able to speak "with one mind and one mouth" (v. 6).** Therefore, the significance of their differences are diminished and that brings harmony to their community life. They are also able to worship God and the Lord Jesus with single-minded praise. The implication is that without harmony and love, worship is unacceptable to God.

The Church, a Community of Unity

In verses 7-13, Paul sums up his previous exhortations about the Christian way of life (12:1—15:6). Again, he stresses the need for believers in Rome to accept one another "just as Christ also received us, to the glory of God" (15:7). Christ did not wait until we were perfectly good and had an adequate grasp of Christian doctrine and ethics to welcome us into God's family (4:5; 5:6-8). He received us when we were sinners. **During His time on earth, Jesus Christ always welcomed all people,** including both Jews, who were known for being very moral people, and Gentiles, people identified with idolatry and corruption— two groups of people, who had little in common except that they needed a Savior. The Savior, as Paul observes, became a servant to show God's faithfulness to His promises to "the circumcision" (the Jews), and He also made it possible for the Gentiles to share in God's saving mercy (15:8). **Christ was patient with people in their weaknesses and ministered to them.** So why shouldn't those who are stronger in faith accommodate others' religious practices, even though those practices may seem strange or unnecessary? The only hope for an answer lies with the strong, not with the weak.

Throughout Paul's discussion about the conflict over religious practices, he has used the terms *weak* and *strong* to refer to the two parties involved, but in verses 8-12, he refers simply to *Jews* and *Gentiles*, which may indicate that throughout the first century, church tensions existed between Jewish and Gentile

believers. This passage seems to return us briefly to Jewish-Gentile relations, which Paul has dealt with at length in chapters 9-11. As Paul has already made clear, **both Jews and Gentiles are to share in the blessings of God, and they will one day be united in praise to God.** Christ's saving work will enable both Jews and Gentile believers to worship and to give thanks to God for His mercy. The inclusion of the Gentiles is not something that God decided to do when He sent Christ into the world. Salvation of the Gentiles had always been God's plan and was foretold in the Old Testament (Gen. 12:3; Ps. 2:8; Isa. 42:1, 6; 66:12, 19-23). The Old Testament Scriptures that Paul selects predicted that Gentiles would one day place their hope in the Jewish Messiah, "a root of Jesse" (Rom. 15:9-12).

Paul's discussion about the responsibilities of the strong and the weak ends with a prayer for his readers (v. 13). The goal of our faith is not "eating and drinking" (14:17) and following laws perfectly, but joy and peace as we trust in Christ. **When the love of Christ is our goal, there will be an overflow of hope, which will not just result in peace and joy in our souls but also in peace and joy in our relationships with other believers. This outcome is only possible through reliance on the power of the Holy Spirit (14:17).** The mighty work of the Spirit in the hearts of believers and the manifestation of His gifts in the community of faith and in the world intensify the hope of God's people.

Observations About Unity in the Church

The apostle Paul will soon bring his letter to a close; but before we look at the closing of the letter, a few observations are in order regarding his pastoral wisdom for Christians who are stronger in faith and for those whose faith is less developed.

1. **Paul has called for harmony and unity, but not at any cost.** The focus has been on matters that are neither moral nor immoral. In speaking to the enlightened Christians, he does not ask them to achieve harmony by surrendering their basic moral convictions or by lowering doctrinal standards to the lowest common denominator. Doctrine and high morals have not been under discussion, as Paul has dealt with the conflict between those who were stronger in their faith and those who were weaker.

2. **The weaker Christians' actions were motivated by religious reasons.** For example, they abstained from alcohol (wine) not because it was harmful to their health or could cause accidents or other suffering, but because they thought it would give them a higher standing with God. Paul consistently teaches that no one can stand before God on the merits of his religious works, but only on divine grace through faith in Christ. Keeping the law in regard to abstaining from meat and wine or observing holy days will not save anyone. In short, the Christian life is not determined by law, but by the work of Christ and is lived out in the power of the Spirit.

3. **The strong have a special responsibility to weaker and more immature Christians.** It must be remembered that the weak in faith are Christians; Paul calls both the strong and weak "brethren" (1:13; 7:1, 4; 8:12, 29; 9:3; 10:1; 11:25; 12:1; 15:14, 15, 30; 16:14, 17). The weak cannot be instructed or won to a better mind-set by denying that they are Christians. Mature believers may be tempted to denounce those who are weak, considering them to be legalists without faith. Weaker Christians' standing with God (as well as stronger Christians' standing) does not depend on what anyone else may think about them. Christ has welcomed them all into the family of God. The Scriptures give us the strength and patience to bear the weaknesses of the weak. We do that because of love, and it gives those who are weak time to grow strong in their faith (Lenski, 1960, 850).

4. **It must be remembered that the weak have consciences and that their consciences, though misguided, tell them to obey certain religious rules.** If stronger believers flaunt their freedom, the weak will be hurt and there may be three possible results: First, they may be simply grieved because they feel unloved, since their convictions have been disregarded by other Christians (14:15). Second, division in the church may occur. The resulting disunity, in addition to putting individuals at risk, also has the potential to destroy "the work of God" (v. 20). Third, the most dangerous of all, criticism of those who are weaker in faith may make them do what their consciences condemn, and that is sin.

Being Christlike calls for us always to show love and respect and to seek unity in the body of Christ.

ROMANS 15:1-13

KEYWORDS

Fellowship (*koinonia*)
The deepest, highest, and broadest expression of believers' communion with Christ and one another

Gentiles (see p. 29)

Glory to God (see p. 75)

Jews/Israelites/Hebrews (see p. 29)

Strong in Faith/Weak in Faith (see p. 373)

SUMMARY

Paul appeals to the stronger Christians, the ones with more experience and insights, to be patient and support those who are weaker, rather than living selfishly to satisfy their own desires. The apostle lifts Christ up as the supreme model of one who considered others first, placing the salvation of others above His own rights.

The Old Testament foretold that Christ would live unselfishly and would endure great suffering for the benefit of others. Besides providing prophetic affirmation of who Christ is, the Old Testament also provided instruction and encouragement for followers of Christ. Paul's reference to the Old Testament clearly implies that the words God inspired to be written down, in addition to being for the people living at that time, were meant to speak across the centuries in order to fulfill God's purposes. The Old Testament offers Christians instruction and hope, showing us how God intends for us to live.

Again Paul appeals to Christ as our example and urges the strong and the weak to receive one another just as Christ had received them, welcoming both Jews and Gentiles. Jesus demonstrated God's faithfulness to His promises to the Jews, and through Him God's mercy was also extended to the Gentiles. The Old Testament plainly predicted salvation of the Gentiles. God intends for the church to be inclusive, welcoming people from all walks of life who believe in Christ into the body of Christ, the church.

LIFE APPLICATION

Paul has identified with the enlightened Christians ("the strong"). Christ was a marvelous example for them to follow in the use of Christian freedom. Christ did not live to please Himself. God has

The Christian Life

> called us to do likewise. This may require us to put up with the weaknesses and criticisms of unenlightened believers.
>
> It is through the inspired witness of the Scriptures that we learn about patience and receive comfort in order to bear the burdens of others. Indeed we find encouragement and strength in God's Word through its promises and its record of spiritual struggles of God's people. The way Christ accepted us when we were sinners is our model. His actions of grace obligate us to welcome others who confess Christ as Savior, but who may have different opinions regarding minor issues. There is room in the household of faith for both the enlightened and the unenlightened. If we are honest with ourselves, each of us will find that in some areas of our lives we are more mature and enlightened, and in others we are weaker and need to grow spiritually. We are all in need of each other's patience and encouraging support.
>
> The members of God's family will have different convictions regarding secondary matters, but their life together can preserve harmony in relationships, even though they may differ in their opinions.

REFLECTION—PART SIX
Romans 12:1—15:13

1. In what ways does Romans 12:1-2 warn Christians against reverting to pre-conversion patterns of behavior?

2. How should we understand the church as the body of Christ in terms of its unity and diversity and gifts of the Spirit?

3. What do you understand by "you will heap coals of fire on his head" (Rom. 12:20; Prov. 25:21-22)?

4. State your understanding of Paul's idea of living peaceably with all people as far as possible (Rom. 12:18).

5. What questions have been raised in your mind as you have studied what Paul says about the obligation of Christians to their government?

6. Could information about the Zealots and Nero help us in reconstructing the background of Romans 13:1-7? Explain.

7. How does love fulfill the law? What did Jesus teach about the relationship between love and the law?

8. What is one way that you have received selfless love from another person, which has fulfilled the intent of the law?

9. List and discuss at least two ways Christians can prepare for the return of Christ.

10. What is your understanding of *the weak* and *the strong* in the church in Rome?

11. How are those Christians who are stronger in faith and those who are weaker in faith to treat each other?

12. Are there areas of your Christian life in which you consider yourself stronger in faith, and areas in which you consider yourself weaker? How have these affected your relationships with other Christians?

13. What is your interpretation of the statement, "Whatever is not from faith is sin" (14:23)?

14. What is Paul's view of the Old Testament's offering instruction and encouragement to Christians? What value do you think Old Testament teachings have for us today?

Prayer

God our Father, we cry out for a mighty demonstration of Christian living among Your people.
May we be a people:
who honor You as God,
who know that You are sovereign,
whose hearts are filled with Your love,
who are empowered by the Holy Spirit,
who are wise and mature in Your ways,
who have love, respect, and compassion for one another,
who strive for unity in the church, and
who are holy in living and serving. Amen.

PART SEVEN—Romans 15—16:27

Closing of Paul's Letter

- **Paul's Travel Plans**
  Romans 15:14-33
- **Commendation of Phoebe**
  Romans 16:1-2
- **Personal Greetings**
  Romans 16:3-16
- **Final Caution**
  Romans 16:17-20
- **Greetings From Paul's Fellow Workers**
  Romans 16:21-24
- **Closing Words of Praise**
  Romans 16:25-27

As Paul closes his letter to the church in Rome, he offers some final personal remarks. Planning to travel to Rome soon, Paul wishes to prepare the Christians there for his visit. Paul started his letter with some personal remarks about himself and his ministry (1:1-7). He now returns to personal matters. He explains a reason for his letter, discusses his travel plans, commends Phoebe, greets various friends, gives a final caution, and closes with words of praise and blessing.

PAUL'S TRAVEL PLANS
ROMANS 15:14-33

Paul opened his letter to the Romans with information about his travel plans (1:8-15), and as the letter is coming to a close, he gives the church more details about those plans. Paul's plans for the future have figured prominently in his letter because they were related to his purpose for writing to the Roman Christians. **From the beginning of the letter, the apostle declared his intention to preach the gospel in Rome (v. 15) and his hope of seeing fruit produced among the people of Rome**

like he had seen among other Gentiles (v. 13). In his closing remarks, Paul expresses his confidence that his coming to them will be in the fullness of Christ's blessings, so his closing echoes his opening.

PAUL'S MISSION
ROMANS 15:14-24

> 14 Now I myself am confident concerning you, my brethren, that you also are full of goodness, filled with all knowledge, able also to admonish one another. 15 Nevertheless, brethren, I have written more boldly to you on some points, as reminding you, because of the grace given to me by God, 16 that I might be a minister of Jesus Christ to the Gentiles, ministering the gospel of God, that the offering of the Gentiles might be acceptable, sanctified by the Holy Spirit. 17 Therefore I have reason to glory in Christ Jesus in the things which pertain to God. 18 For I will not dare to speak of any of those things which Christ has not accomplished through me, in word and deed, to make the Gentiles obedient— 19 in mighty signs and wonders, by the power of the Spirit of God, so that from Jerusalem and round about to Illyricum I have fully preached the gospel of Christ. 20 And so I have made it my aim to preach the gospel, not where Christ was named, lest I should build on another man's foundation, 21 but as it is written:
>
> > "To whom He was not announced, they shall see;
> > And those who have not heard shall understand."
>
> 22 For this reason I also have been much hindered from coming to you. 23 But now no longer having a place in these parts, and having a great desire these many years to come to you, 24 whenever I journey to Spain, I shall come to you. For I hope to see you on my journey, and to be helped on my way there by you, if first I may enjoy your company for a while.

At the beginning of this letter, Paul commended the Roman church for its reputation of faith throughout the world (1:8). Again he pays tribute to the church for being "full of goodness, filled with all knowledge, able also to admonish one another" (15:14). **Paul was confident that the Roman Christians were kind and conciliatory and had sufficient knowledge of Christ's teaching** to proceed with the Christian life. Even so, he wrote boldly to them about some points of doctrine.

Paul's Christ-Centered and Spirit-Empowered Ministry to the Gentiles

Paul had expressed his interest in them, explaining that God had appointed him to minister to the Gentiles and that it was God's grace that conferred on him the authority to write to them (v. 15; cf. 1:5; 12:3; Gal. 1:15-16). Drawing from the Jewish sacrificial system, **Paul described himself as a *minister* (*leitourgos*), which indicates that he functioned as a priest. He did priestly work under Christ through his preaching of the gospel and in preparing the Gentiles (*ta ethne*, the nations) to be an offering "acceptable, sanctified by the Holy Spirit" (Rom. 15:16).** By Paul's leading them to faith in Jesus Christ, the Gentile believers were Paul's priestly offering to God.

The apostle Paul could have rightly spoken about his own accomplishments in ministry among the Gentiles, but he did not do so since his desire was to point only to what Christ had accomplished through him (vv. 17-18). **Paul's ministry was Christ-centered, and the nature of his ministry was that of leading Gentiles to obey God (cf. 1:5).** In Paul's ministry, Christ worked through him by the Holy Spirit.

Paul summarizes his ministry by saying that Christ accomplished His work through him "in word and deed" (15:18). **It was through the preaching of the gospel and miraculous deeds that Paul carried out his ministry. His preaching was regularly accompanied by mighty signs and wonders performed by the power of the Holy Spirit.** These miracles functioned as signs which pointed to the truth of the gospel and strengthened the faith of those who witnessed them. As wonders, they amazed people and made them aware that God was present and was at work (Acts 4:30; 5:12; 14:3; 2 Cor. 12:12; Heb. 2:4).

The Spirit provided the power for Paul's entire ministry, including not only power for miracles but also power for his preaching of the gospel. No wonder Paul wrote earlier that the gospel is the power of God (Rom. 1:16). Paul fulfilled his mandate to preach the gospel to the Gentiles from Jerusalem to Illyricum (a Roman province north of Macedonia, including most of the Balkan area of what is now Albania and formerly Yugoslavia—see map: Appendix A on page 424). We have no record of Paul's ministry in Illyricum in the biblical account. He may have gone there during his time in Corinth (Acts 18:1-17) or during the missionary journey mentioned in 20:1ff.

Paul's Cross-Cultural Ministry—an Example for Today

The cross-cultural ministry of the apostle Paul, characterized by the Spirit-anointed preaching of the gospel and miraculous demonstrations of the Spirit's power in the marketplace, is much needed in evangelism today. A return to such a ministry can have, as in Paul's day, a tremendous impact on our pluralistic world. **Through the Holy Spirit's power, Christians can live and tell about the love of Christ in such a manner that people from other religions come to understand the grace, forgiveness, and hope that are available to them through Christ.**

Paul's Missionary Strategy

Paul's missionary strategy was to go to urban centers and preach the gospel. Then from those centers, his converts would tell others about their experience with Christ throughout the surrounding areas (cf. 1 Thess. 1:8-10). Such a strategy resulted in the gospel being planted throughout the eastern half of the Roman Empire—Palestine, Cyprus, Asia Minor, and Greece. **In his many travels, Paul determined not to preach the gospel where churches already existed. Paul deliberately avoided building on the work of others (Rom. 15:20), since his specific aim was to break new ground and plant churches where the gospel had not been preached. His missionary strategy fulfilled the prophecy of Isaiah 52:15: "To whom He was not announced, they shall see; and those who have not heard shall understand" (Rom. 15:21).**

The Roman Church as a Mission Base

Paul's laboring in areas where people had not heard about Jesus Christ explains why he had not already paid Rome a visit.

But his decision also indicates that he did not try to exert authority in churches which had been founded by others. He was not planning to go to Rome to interfere with matters of the church. The church was mature enough to deal with their day-to-day functions and issues, and they did not need him or any other apostle to do so. Paul, therefore, made it clear that **his plan was to come to Rome on his way to an area where no one had preached about Jesus Christ, and that he anticipated just a short stay in Rome.** He expected that Rome could serve as a new base for missionary endeavors in the West, like Antioch had done in the East.

The apostle Paul felt that his ministry in the East had come to its end. **He wanted the Roman church to become a new base of support for his Spanish mission and expressed his desire for their assistance.** The word translated "to be helped" (*propemphthenai*, v. 24) was a technical word used for supporting Christian missionaries. **Paul expected that in addition to prayer and goodwill, the church in Rome would provide practical assistance, including money, recruitment of believers willing to go with him, and help with his travel plans to a region with which he was unfamiliar.** The reason why Paul chose Spain is not stated, but it was a strategic location from which he could evangelize. No visit of Paul's to that country is recorded in the New Testament. First Clement 5:7[1] reports that he reached Spain, but many scholars doubt that the journey to Spain ever took place. The information we have falls short of clear proof that Paul actually preached in Spain. It is possible that Paul went there after his release from his first imprisonment in Rome (Acts 28:30-31). If he did, he arrived in that country only after a long delay. Upon reaching Jerusalem, Paul was arrested and spent the next four years in confinement in Caesarea and Rome.

---

[1] *1 Clement* is a letter written by Clement of Rome in AD 96 to foster peace in the church of Corinth.

> **ROMANS 15:14-24**
>
> **KEYWORDS**
>
> **Evangelism**
> Derived from the noun *euanggelion* (gospel) and the verb *euaggelizomai* (to proclaim good news), this term means to share and spread throughout the world the Good News about Jesus Christ and eternal life, inviting all people to a relationship with Christ and salvation (Acts 1:8). Jesus commissioned the church to bring light to a spiritually dark world (Matt. 5:14-16) and to make disciples (28:18-20).
>
> **Gentiles** (see p. 29)
>
> **Gospel** (see p. 23)
>
> **Grace (*charis*)** (see p. 23)
>
> **Holy Spirit/The Spirit** (see p. 25)
>
> **Jesus Christ** (see p. 59)
>
> **Obedience to the Gospel/Obedience of Faith** (see p. 185)
>
> **Sanctification** (see p. 171)
>
> **SUMMARY & LIFE APPLICATION**
> See ROMANS 15:25-33 on pages 399-401.

THE COLLECTION OF FUNDS FOR THOSE IN NEED
ROMANS 15:25-33

> 25 But now I am going to Jerusalem to minister to the saints. 26 For it pleased those from Macedonia and Achaia to make a certain contribution for the poor among the saints who are in Jerusalem. 27 It pleased them indeed, and they are their debtors. For if the Gentiles have been partakers of their spiritual things, their duty is also to minister to them in material things. 28 Therefore, when I have performed this and have sealed to them this fruit, I shall go by way of you to Spain. 29 But I know that when I come to you, I shall come in the fullness of the blessing of the gospel of Christ.

> ³⁰ Now I beg you, brethren, through the Lord Jesus Christ, and through the love of the Spirit, that you strive together with me in prayers to God for me, ³¹ that I may be delivered from those in Judea who do not believe, and that my service for Jerusalem may be acceptable to the saints, ³² that I may come to you with joy by the will of God, and may be refreshed together with you. ³³ Now the God of peace be with you all. Amen.

Paul had a pressing duty to perform before going to Rome. His immediate task was to deliver money (known today as "the Pauline Collection"), given by Gentile churches for the Christians in Jerusalem who were in need (1 Cor. 16:1-4; 2 Cor. 8—9). Paul had been involved in this project for several years. Fourteen years after his conversion, he had visited Jerusalem. On that occasion he made an agreement with the apostles that required him to "remember the poor," which he was eager to do (Gal. 2:1-10). There were a number of factors that may have contributed to the Jerusalem Christians' economic need, including the devastation of a famine (Acts 11:27-30), the hosting of visitors to the city for the celebration of annual Jewish feasts, the Sadducees' control of the Temple, and lack of employment.

Giving as a Service of Love That Fosters Unity and Fellowship

The raising of money from the Gentile churches had been a long-standing obligation of Paul's. The offering was not only a practical act of Christian love that provided relief for the poor; it also had great theological significance, since it was a means of fostering unity and fellowship between the Jewish church in Jerusalem and the Gentile churches. The funds came from churches that were predominantly Gentile. Most of the money had been given by churches in the Roman provinces of Macedonia and Achaia, located in such cities as Philippi, Thessalonica, and Corinth. The delivering of this offering to Jerusalem occurred during the climax of Paul's ministry in the East, indeed an appropriate act before setting out for a new field of ministry.

The financial gift to the church in Jerusalem was an act motivated by divine grace (2 Cor. 8—9) and was a means of

giving recognition to the spiritual debt that the Gentile believers owed to the Jews (Rom. 15:27).** The Gentile believers enjoyed the spiritual blessings of the Jewish people. After all, it was Jewish people, such as Paul, who had brought the Good News about Christ to them. **Paul reminded the Gentile believers, "You do not support the root [Israel], but the root supports you" (11:18).** Moreover, once Paul had delivered the financial gift to Jerusalem, he would have fulfilled the promise he made to the apostles to help the poor (2 Cor. 8:1—9:15; Gal. 2:9-10). Then he would be free to go on his way to Spain.

Paul's Request for Prayer

In visiting Rome, Paul was confident that his visit would have Christ's fullest blessing (Rom. 15:29), but he also recognized the perils of returning to Jerusalem. Very concerned, he wanted the earnest prayers of the Roman believers while he was in Jerusalem. He had a premonition of encountering trouble in this center of the Jewish world. **His prayer request related to two matters (v. 31).**

- **First, Paul needed protection from unbelievers.** As modern readers, we know that Paul's fears were well-founded. When he arrived in the Holy City, the Christians welcomed him, though cautiously. But some unbelieving Jews mobbed him, accused him of desecrating the Temple, and almost put him to death before they had him put in prison (Acts 21:17-36).
- **Second, Paul wanted prayer that the offering would "be acceptable to the saints [Christians]" (Rom. 15:31).** The apostle had deep-seated concerns that the Jewish believers might not accept the funds from the Gentile churches. The Gentiles had contributed with gladness, without any sense of compulsion (vv. 26-27), but the Jewish believers who still held some of their earlier beliefs could have possibly seen the offering as a bribe. There was the possibility that they may have thought that by accepting the money, they would be obligated to allow Paul to preach a law-free gospel, or they could have seen the gift as being "unclean" since the money came from Gentiles. Paul hoped that the

offering would be received in a positive manner. Acts 24:17 suggests that the offering was received in Jerusalem.

Paul's Troubles as Inspiration for Others' Preaching

To Paul's delight when he arrived in Rome, his imprisonment had inspired others to preach the gospel. He found that some preached the gospel out of pure motives, whereas others did so out of selfish motives (Phil. 1:12-18). They preached as rivals to Paul in order to gain converts for themselves, assuming that they could add to Paul's afflictions in prison. But Paul wrote from the house where he was held as a prisoner (Acts 28:16, 23), "Whether in pretence or in truth, Christ is preached; and in this I rejoice, yes, and will rejoice" (Phil. 1:18). **The apostle Paul lived by the words of Romans 8:28—"all things work together for good."**

Paul's Prayer for Peace

Verses 32 and 33 bring chapter 15 to an end. When dangers in Jerusalem were behind him, the apostle Paul expected to come to the Roman Christians with a relieved heart in the will of God. He expected that they would enjoy a mutual refreshing. **Paul prayed for God's blessings of peace on the Roman believers, hoping that a renewed peace among the body of Christ would be the outcome of his visit to Jerusalem.**

ROMANS 15:25-33
KEYWORDS
Gentiles (see p. 29)
Gospel (see p. 23)
Holy Spirit/The Spirit (see p. 25)
Jesus Christ (see p. 59)
Saints (*hagioi*) (see p. 59)
SUMMARY
Paul knew of the good qualities of the Roman Christians. He had written to them in the manner that he had because of his calling as

an apostle to the Gentiles. Speaking about the divine character of his special mission, he observed that Christ had accomplished His work in the East through preaching of the Good News and through mighty works.

The apostle had plans for journeys to Rome and Spain, but first he was setting out for Jerusalem to deliver the funds from the Gentile churches to poor Christians in the Holy City. He requested that the Roman Christians pray that he would be delivered from danger during his return to Jerusalem. Once he fulfilled his mission to Jerusalem, he intended to go to Spain by the way of Rome.

LIFE APPLICATION

Kindness to One Another. Christian courtesy has a vital place in the Christian life. Convinced of that, Paul commends the Christians in Rome for their spirituality, noting that they were full of kindness, as well as doctrinal and ethical wisdom. Having confidence in the Roman Christians opened the door for Paul to instruct and advise them in the faith, and to address a dispute that had risen between those who were stronger in the faith and those who were weak. Just as Paul boldly addressed the dispute among the Roman Christians, ministers of the gospel today have a solemn responsibility to speak candidly about faith issues. The authority for our boldness is the grace that has been given to us by God.

In our efforts to engage in responsible ministry to others, we are to be caring and grateful. We are to view those to whom we minister as sacred trusts and then to lead them to God for His love and eternal life. No matter where life has taken them or what they have done, we can bring all people to God as offerings acceptable to Him, because God loves them and His Holy Spirit consecrates them (v. 16). For successes in ministry, we need to give thanks to God and celebrate, praise, and give glory to Christ, not to ourselves.

Spirit-Empowered Ministry. Self-confidence comes from knowing that our ministry is Spirit-empowered and is carried out through the help of divine grace. We are instruments in the salvation of people, but the Holy Spirit is the One who enlightens them, bringing them to the conviction of their sin and to conversion. Success in evangelism is the fruit of preaching and teaching the gospel, which is confirmed by signs and wonders wrought by the Holy Spirit. Our challenge is like that of Paul—to spread the gospel far and wide—so God can use us to help bring as many to Christ as possible.

Our evangelistic efforts need not be confined to the church. We should share God's love and the Good News about Christ in our daily lives—in our homes and neighborhoods, and in the marketplace. Evangelism is simply living out the love of Christ moment to moment and telling others our personal story about how Jesus Christ has changed and helped us.

Giving to Those in Need. Christians not only have a responsibility to share the gospel with others, but also to share their material things with those in need. Paul described the financial gift that he planned to take to the needy Christians in Jerusalem as a "contribution," which is the translation of the significant word *koinonia*, meaning "sharing." Paul's sharing of finances with the Jewish Christians of Jerusalem was a completely voluntary act, but it did honor a responsibility that Gentile Christians have to express gratitude to those from whom they have received spiritual benefits. Of course, our obligation reaches beyond those who have blessed us with the gospel. The sharing of our material things with the poor is a tangible expression of Christ's and the church's love and care for them, and helps them to understand and receive the blessings of forgiveness, joy, and eternal life that Christ has for them.

Supporting Missions. We, as individuals and church congregations, have an obligation to support evangelists and missionaries with our prayers, finances, and other practical assistance. Paul wanted to inspire the Roman Christians' vision for supporting his missionary efforts. It is easy for churches to settle into a state of self-satisfaction and lethargy. The gospel in its love and concern for others requires that those of us who have experienced the blessings of Christ do what is necessary to spread the Good News about Christ and His blessings to those who have not yet heard or understood.

COMMENDATION OF PHOEBE
ROMANS 16:1-2

¹ I commend to you Phoebe our sister, who is a servant of the church in Cenchrea, ² that you may receive her in the Lord in a manner worthy of the saints, and assist her in whatever business she has need of you; for indeed she has been a helper of many and of myself also.

Near the end of his letter, Paul communicates some important personal messages. In Paul's day, travel was common, and so he had acquaintances and friends in the church in Rome. **Among Paul's acquaintances were a number of women who were respected coworkers and to whom Paul gave honorable mention along with his male coworkers. Women, such as Chloe (1 Cor. 1:11)**

and Lydia (Acts 16:11-15), had an important place in the early church, and Paul valued their ministry. In bringing his letter to a close, Paul's first item of business was to introduce one of these women, Phoebe, to the Roman Christians.

Phoebe's Ministry in the Church

Paul identifies Phoebe as being a deacon (diakonos) of the church in Cenchrea (a port town located six and a half miles to the east of Corinth; see the map Appendix D on page 427). In his reference to Phoebe's role, he uses the masculine form of *deacon*, not the feminine, making it less likely that there was a separate order of "deaconesses" in the church. In Paul's letters, *diakonos* is often used in a general sense as "one who serves." Scholars debate whether Phoebe served as a deacon, holding a church office (Phil. 1:1; 1 Tim. 3:8, 12). The word *diakonos* does not give us a clue what her precise responsibilities had been in the church in Cenchrea. Paul's statement is more helpful: "She has been a helper of many and of myself also" (Rom. 16:2). The word rendered "helper" (*prostatis*) literally means "one who stands before," suggesting that she had served as a leader of the church in Cenchrea (perhaps a house church). **It is evident from his statement in verses 1 and 2 that Paul considered Phoebe to be an important person in the Cenchrean church, as well as in his own ministry, as she ministered to the sick, widows, orphans, and Christians arriving and departing from Cenchrea.**

We know that Phoebe was a minister of the church in Cenchrea, but the precise nature of her ministry is hard to determine since during Paul's time there were few rigid lines drawn between the roles of men and women in the church. (Today we tend to distinguish too much between the work that men and women do in the church, and such distinctions can be a real hindrance to accomplishing the Lord's work.) **As many other Christian women and men of her day, Phoebe simply did the ministry to which God had called her. Paul's description of Phoebe underscores his view of ministry—that every believer is brought into the service of the Lord.** "Insofar as Phoebe has a permanent and recognized ministry as is emphasized by the [present] participle [ousan] and the place name [Cenchrea], one may see an early stage of what later became an ecclesiastical office"

(Käsemann, 1990, 411). **It is very possible that the office of deaconess was emerging within the church.**

Paul's Request

The apostle Paul urges the Roman Christians to welcome Phoebe as a minister of the church in Cenchrea. She was setting out on a long trip from Cenchrea to Rome. When she arrived, she would be in a strange and distant place. He wanted the Christians there to receive her, offering her lodging and whatever help she needed. He knew how other Christians traveling to Rome had been welcomed, and so he desired her to be received in the same manner and to be granted every spiritual privilege. After all, this woman had rendered distinguished service to the church. **The introduction that Paul gave Phoebe was consistent with her devotion, character, and service. It is commonly assumed that Phoebe carried this letter to Rome.** There is no conclusive proof that she did. If she did, it only added weight to Paul's commendation.

ROMANS 16:1-2

KEYWORDS

Deacon/Deaconess (*diakonos*)
Both terms have to do with personal service, involving the care of orphans and widows, and deeds of charity. In the New Testament, *deacon* was an office in the church (1 Tim. 3:8-13), and the mention of Phoebe in Romans 16:1 as a *deacon* may imply that deaconess was beginning to emerge as an office in the church.

Helper (*prostatis*)
A person who has the gifted ministry of helping others. Such a person is the source of assistance that benefits believers in terms of fellowship, finances, and hospitality.

Saints (*hagioi*) (see p. 59)

Servant/Minister (*diakonos*) (see p. 358)

SUMMARY

Phoebe was a leading Christian woman who had rendered outstanding service in the church in Cenchrea. Paul held her in highest esteem and strongly encouraged the Roman Christians to receive her as a genuine servant of the Lord and to help her, probably with financial assistance and hospitality.

LIFE APPLICATION

What a high compliment Paul pays to Phoebe, identifying her as his sister in the Lord, as a deacon, and one to receive treatment "worthy of the saints" (v. 2). Also, what a privilege this woman had, for most likely she was the bearer of Paul's message to the Romans.

As believers in Christ, we have the same privilege open to each of us. We have the blessed opportunity of sharing with others the gospel that Paul so eloquently explains in Romans. There is no task—no mission—which is as supremely important. Nothing but the gospel of Jesus Christ has the power to save us.

PERSONAL GREETINGS
ROMANS 16:3-16

3 Greet Priscilla and Aquila, my fellow workers in Christ Jesus, 4 who risked their own necks for my life, to whom not only I give thanks, but also all the churches of the Gentiles. 5 Likewise greet the church that is in their house.

Greet my beloved Epaenetus, who is the firstfruits of Achaia to Christ. 6 Greet Mary, who labored much for us. 7 Greet Andronicus and Junia, my countrymen and my fellow prisoners, who are of note among the apostles, who also were in Christ before me.

8 Greet Amplias, my beloved in the Lord. 9 Greet Urbanus, our fellow worker in Christ, and Stachys, my beloved. 10 Greet Apelles, approved in Christ. Greet those who are of the household of Aristobulus. 11 Greet Herodion, my countryman. Greet those who are of the household of Narcissus who are in the Lord.

12 Greet Tryphena and Tryphosa, who have labored in the Lord. Greet the beloved Persis, who labored much in the Lord. 13 Greet Rufus, chosen in the Lord, and his mother and mine. 14 Greet Asyncritus, Phlegon, Hermas, Patrobas, Hermes, and the brethren who are with them. 15 Greet Philologus and Julia, Nereus and his sister, and Olympas, and all the saints who are with them. 16 Greet one another with a holy kiss. The churches of Christ greet you.

In this last chapter of Romans, Paul sends greetings to twenty-five people by name and greetings to two families. As we have read and studied Romans, we may have asked ourselves to what kind of people did Paul write this letter. Here Paul gives us a brief sketch of several of them. The fact that Paul directly greets several people shows that he valued individuals. We are thankful for what he tells us about them, but how we wish he had told us more. No doubt, each one of them was an important, honorable Christian. His brief descriptions are worthy of careful study.

Paul's Greetings
Priscilla and Aquila—A Jewish Missionary Couple

The first two persons who are named, Priscilla ("diminutive," Prisca) and her husband, Aquila, were former residents of Rome. In AD 49 the emperor Claudius had "commanded all the Jews to depart from Rome" (Acts 18:2). Among the Jews who fled the city were Priscilla and Aquila. They later met Paul in Corinth after they fled Rome, but we do not know if they were Christians before becoming his friends. From Corinth, they went with Paul to Ephesus, where both of them remained behind when Paul took a ship for Caesarea (Acts 18:18-19).

Both Priscilla and Aquila had worked closely with Paul. This Jewish Christian couple was among the leading missionaries. On one occasion, the couple had even risked their lives (Rom. 16:4). The Bible gives us no details about that event. We could assume that it took place either in Corinth (Acts 18:1-10) or in Ephesus (1 Cor. 15:32).

Paul places Priscilla and Aquila first in his list and heaps upon them extraordinary praise. When mentioning this couple in Romans 16:3, he lists Priscilla's name before her husband's— a practice uncommon in the first century. Priscilla was apparently very gifted and, of the two, was more involved in ministry, serving as an important leader in the church. Priscilla's name also stands first in one of the three places in Acts where both of them are mentioned (18:18).

Wherever Priscilla and Aquila lived, they must have had a church in their home. In Paul's letter to the Corinthians, he had sent greetings from the church in Asia to the church that met in the home of Aquila and Priscilla (1 Cor. 16:19), and also in Romans he indicates that the couple held a church in their home

(16:5). There may have been in actuality many house churches in the great city of Rome. **Today, like in Priscilla's and Aquila's day, small-group meetings and hospitality expressed in the home can be ways of sharing the Good News of Christ and expressing Christ's love to others.**

Epaenetus—The First Gentile Convert

Next, Paul mentions the Gentile Christian, Epaenetus, who is called "the firstfruits" (first convert) of the entire Roman province of Achaia (v. 5). What a great thing! Just think about it: the first convert in a large part of Asia Minor and in a huge population—the first to stand and declare; "Jesus is Lord."

Mary—A Devoted Worker

Also, there is Mary who is described as having *labored* (*kopiao*) near the point of exhaustion in doing Christian work such as preaching, caring for the needy, and encouraging fellow believers (v. 6). We would like to know more about these people, but they were like many who do work for the Lord, serving in humility without fellow Christians fully realizing all that they do for the body of Christ. Much valuable Christian service goes unrecorded, but God blesses it and knows and appreciates all our efforts.

Andronicus and Junia—Fellow Jewish Christians

Paul refers to Andronicus and Junia as "countrymen" ("kinsmen," KJV; "relatives," NIV), meaning that they were fellow Jewish Christians (v. 7). They were already followers of Christ before Paul became a believer. Besides being Christians for many years, they had also suffered imprisonment with Paul. None of the details of their imprisonment with Paul are provided, but it is not hard to fit their imprisonment into the list of Paul's sufferings in 2 Corinthians 11:23ff. Of special interest is Paul's reference to them as ones "who are of note [*episemoi*, prominent] among the apostles" (Rom. 16:7). Scholars have debated whether the name "Junia" is masculine or feminine. Until modern times it was assumed to be a female name. Furthermore, there is no evidence for the male form *Junia*. Along with Andronicus, she was prominent among the apostles. (The term *apostle* was a common designation for the Twelve and Paul, but it was not used exclusively to refer to them. The term was also used to describe those who had distinguished themselves in the ministry.) **Andronicus and Junia had left their marks as missionaries by founding and building up churches.** They were outstanding workers for the Lord.

Rufus—A Devoted Christian; and Rufus' Mother—A Woman Beloved by Paul

Among some of the others who were greeted is Rufus, whom Paul described as an outstanding Christian. Paul also greets Rufus' mother, whom he considered to be his mother, as well (v. 13). **This woman had befriended the apostle Paul and had treated him as her own son.** This fact is touching. Paul is grateful for her thoughtfulness and kindness; he expresses his appreciation publicly.

House Churches

Paul's greetings to households and the people "with them" reveal that there were a number of house churches in Rome. The existence of house churches is suggested by "the household of Aristobulus" (v. 10), "the household of Narcissus" (v. 11), and "all the saints who are with them" (v. 15). The apostle would not have known all the names of individual Christians within the church in Rome. It is possible that Aristobulus and Narcissus each was a leader of a house church and were possibly converts of Paul's, who had previously moved to the capital.

Diversity Within the Roman Church

It is important that both Jewish and Gentile names appear in the list and that many of the names mentioned were common among the lower classes of Roman society. The diversity within the church might be one of the reasons why details about individuals were given in Romans 9—11. **The descriptions of individuals clearly indicate that the Roman church was a diverse group of people from different religious and socioeconomic backgrounds, just as the church is today.** Each of these people apparently had found their place in Christ.

Especially noteworthy is the important role women had in the church. Paul mentions twice as many men as women, but he commends twice as many women as he does men. This fact should answer the charge that Paul was ill-disposed toward women and is a clear testament to their prominence in the early church.

Valuing Individuals in the Body of Christ

The apostle Paul encourages the Roman believers to "greet one another with a holy kiss" (16:16). In the ancient world this practice expressed affection and greetings. The "holy kiss" was also a greeting used among early Christians, just like it was in the broader culture (1 Cor. 16:20; 2 Cor. 13:12). **It was Paul's way of encouraging genuine friendship among believers.**

In his greetings to individuals and families, Paul has shown the value of every person in the church and kingdom of God. A great deal of effort by scholars has gone into trying to link names with the same names elsewhere in Paul's letters and in Acts. Aside from Timothy, a well-known companion of Paul (Acts 16:1-3), and Priscilla and Aquila (Acts 18:1-3; 1 Cor. 16:19), their efforts have been fruitless. At that time all the names were quite common, but each of them was special and important to God and to the body of Christ, no matter their social class or occupation or how obscure they may have been.

Paul knew a number of people in Rome and had a warm appreciation for them and his coworkers. Since he had preached the gospel for about twenty-five years, it is not surprising that he knew as many as he did in Rome. Some to whom he sent greetings, Paul may have known only by the virtue of their reputation.

ROMANS 16:3-16

KEYWORDS

Apostle (*apostole*) (see p. 29)

Church (*ekklesia*) (see p. 17)

Labor (verb, *kopiao*)
A verb that Paul used to indicate diligent service by missionaries or local church leaders

Closing of Paul's Letter

SUMMARY

We must not underestimate the amount of travel in Paul's day. Perhaps many of the people to whom Paul sends greetings had met him on his missionary journeys, and some had been members of Pauline churches before they relocated to Rome. It seems Paul was greeting several of his personal contacts in Rome in order to renew his ties with them. Looking at the people to whom he sends greetings reminds us of the diversity of people Paul touched with the gospel. In almost every case, he adds a word of warm affection and commendation. His greetings show how much he valued individuals.

LIFE APPLICATION

Do we wish that more was known about the Christians to whom Paul sent greetings? Many of their names do not appear in any other place in the historical records, but the mention of them in Romans has immortalized them in history. **The appearance of individuals' names in the final chapter of Paul's great letter to the Roman Christians reminds us of two things:**

1. **What really matters is the inclusion of our names in God's Book of Life.** In the world and even in the church, we may be unknown. No matter how obscure we may be, we are precious in the sight of the Lord. We observe that a number of those whom Paul greeted are described as "beloved." Nothing is said about their accomplishments, talents, or abilities, but each one of them was a recipient of God's love, as is each one of us.

2. **It is important to have friends in the church, as Paul did.** The gathering of the church provides us with the opportunity to have fellowship with dear brothers and sisters in Christ. Christian friends have a way of sticking as close or perhaps closer than a brother or sister.

FINAL CAUTION
ROMANS 16:17-20

[17] Now I urge you, brethren, note those who cause divisions and offenses, contrary to the doctrine which you learned, and avoid them. [18] For those who are such do not serve our Lord Jesus Christ, but their own belly, and by smooth words and flattering speech deceive the hearts of the simple. [19] For your obedience has become known to all. Therefore I am glad on your behalf; but I want you to be wise in what is good, and simple concerning evil. [20] And the God of peace will crush Satan under your feet shortly.

The grace of our Lord Jesus Christ be with you. Amen.

False Teachers

Paul breaks off his greetings rather abruptly to offer some final counsel to the church in Rome. Perhaps before Paul closed the letter, he received some new information about the Roman church; this prompted him to give a strong warning about troublemakers who were trying to intrude into the church. We are not told whether the troublemakers were Christians or unbelievers. **Paul wants the Christians to be alert because some divisive people and false teachers in the Christian church were advocating doctrine contrary to what the Roman believers had learned.** The troublemakers had deserted sound Christian doctrine. Paul chooses not to counsel the church to confront and correct such people, but to avoid them (v. 17). They are not servants of Christ, but servants of "their own belly" (v. 18), literally "their own appetites" (NIV). These phrases could indicate that these people were merely greedy and self-indulgent; but when we compare these phrases with the phrases that Paul used in Philippians 3:17-19, **we can conclude that the people to whom Paul is referring may have seen Christianity in terms of material things, power, or prestige, rather than in light of the cross. If so, they were enemies of the cross and advocated what is known today as the "prosperity gospel."**

The weapons that the false teachers used were "smooth words and flattering speech [to] deceive the hearts of the simple [*hoi akakoi*, the innocent, unsuspecting]" (v. 18). **When they spoke, they employed words that were gentle and engaging, but were untrue so as to deceive innocent people.** These false teachers were at the door of the church knocking on it, but the Roman believers were to have no dealings with them. These believers in the Roman church had a good record of obedience to sound Christian doctrine (cf. 1:8), and Paul warns them to be careful not to spoil their good reputation (16:19).

Discernment Among the Faithful
Paul's Advice

The apostle Paul was delighted that the Roman believers were faithful, and he rejoiced as a proud parent would over the success of a child. **Paul advised that for the church's continued success,** they would need to be wise and to discern between what was good and what was contaminated by evil (v. 19). The Roman church, while taking the necessary precautions of removing themselves from those who were deceptive but still continuing to pray for their souls, could rest in God's promise that one day the Evil One would have no more power (v. 20). They would soon see how God would destroy Satan, and they would share in God's victory by setting their feet on this archenemy and trampling on him (cf. Gen. 3:15). **Ultimately and finally, this victory will come to pass when Christ returns.** Then God will bring the defeat of Satan and will truly bring peace. Paul adds a blessing: "The grace of our Lord Jesus Christ be with you all."

Discernment in the Church Today

Paul's warning alerted the Romans Christians to the danger of false doctrine and false teachers, and his warning is also important for us today. The Christian faith is based on revealed truths recorded in the Bible and handed down through the centuries. **In every generation there is the danger that the gospel will be compromised and abandoned for a message that is not the gospel of the cross. Such a message may be packaged for us in religious and culturally appealing language and may promote religiosity, but be devoid of the full truth of the gospel, which is preserved for us in the Scriptures. Christians need to examine religious trends, new revelations, and new doctrines in light of the Word of God.**

ROMANS 16:17-20

KEYWORDS

Discernment—Judgment of Spiritual Matters
To distinguish or discern (John 7:24). Jesus' use of the term, as recorded in the Gospel of John, indicates that we are responsible for evaluating or discerning certain matters in life.

Doctrine (see p. 25)

Evil (see p. 80)

Obedience to the Gospel/Obedience of Faith (see p. 185)

Peace (Hebrew *shalom*, Greek *eirene*) (see p. 144)

Prosperity Gospel

An unbiblical emphasis on material prosperity. As a result, pressure is on believers to demonstrate their faith by owning or displaying their culture's material symbols of success—such as owning a fine car, living in an extravagant home, wearing elegant clothes, or taking exotic vacations. How can one reconcile this type of lifestyle with the simple life of our Lord (Matt. 8:20)? For a biblical perspective on the prosperity gospel, 3 John 2 is used as the basic text: "Beloved [Gaius], I pray that you may prosper in all things and be in health, just as your soul prospers." The definition of *prosperity* within the kingdom of God is the growth and the fullness of the fruit of the Spirit within our souls. To extend this prayer for Gaius' prosperity to refer to the financial and material prosperity for all believers is foreign to the meaning of this text. The argument that God wills that all Christians be wealthy is a gross misinterpretation of Scripture. God desires for us an abundance of eternal spiritual riches, such as love, joy, and peace.

Satan/Devil

The chief antagonist of God and humankind

SUMMARY

The apostle Paul alerted the Roman Christians to the danger of those who cause divisions by teaching doctrines contrary to the faith. He instructed them to turn away from such people who were out for personal gain and were trying to deceive innocent and trusting believers. Paul warned that false teachers often are attractive in speech, but they are motivated by selfish desires. Looking forward to the ultimate defeat of Satan, Paul offered his readers a final word of encouragement.

LIFE APPLICATION

Satan is a troublemaker. Working through false teachers and heretics, Satan's purpose is to create dissension in the church and to trip up Christians in their faith and practice.

From time to time, people who are driven by impure motives may slip into a congregation and begin to sow their ungodly doctrines and practices. Through their smooth talk and flattery they deceive innocent souls. The proper response is to keep away from them. They serve their own carnal nature and are dishonest and selfish people.

Such people are not servants of Christ. Their purpose is not to please Him, even though they claim to come in His name and may appeal to the Bible for their doctrines. Their targets are usually Bible-believing churches and unsuspecting believers. A safeguard

> against their deception and enticements is to be well-grounded in the Scriptures and Christian doctrine.
>
> With God's guidance and assistance of the leadership of the congregation, troublemakers must be removed from its midst, if they will not correct their ways. Sound doctrine and practical godliness are vital to the well-being of the church.

GREETINGS FROM PAUL'S FELLOW WORKERS
ROMANS 16:21-24

> 📖 ²¹ Timothy, my fellow worker, and Lucius, Jason, and Sosipater, my countrymen, greet you.
>
> ²² I, Tertius, who wrote this epistle, greet you in the Lord.
>
> ²³ Gaius, my host and the host of the whole church, greets you. Erastus, the treasurer of the city, greets you, and Quartus, a brother.
> ²⁴ The grace of our Lord Jesus Christ be with you all. Amen.

Of people mentioned at the end of Paul's letter to the Romans are some of Paul's associates who also send greetings to the Roman Christians. **The apostle made it a practice to pass along greetings from his coworkers at the end of his letters.** Sometimes he identified the individuals as a group: "the saints" (2 Cor. 13:13; Phil. 4:22), "the brethren" (1 Cor. 16:20; Phil. 4:21), or "all who are with me" (Titus 3:15). **In his closing, here as at other times, Paul mentions individual believers (Col. 4:10-14; 2 Tim. 4:21; Philem. 23-24).**

Timothy—Paul's Fellow Worker

Standing at the head of this list of greetings is Timothy, who is identified as Paul's fellow worker. Timothy had been a great helper in Paul's ministry in Macedonia and Achaia (Acts 17—18) and was particularly helpful in dealing with the opposition in Corinth (1 Cor. 4:17; 16:10-11). Indeed, Timothy was a beloved colleague in the ministry and a constant companion of Paul.

Lucius, Jason, and Sosipater—Travel Companions

The next three—Lucius, Jason, and Sosipater—may have accompanied Paul in carrying the collection to Jerusalem. As he has already identified three others (Rom. 16:7, 11), he refers to these three as his "kinsmen" (v. 21 KJV)—probably not blood relatives, but Jewish Christians.

Tertius—Paul's Scribe

The man who wrote down Romans as Paul dictated it was Tertius, about whom little is known. He seems to have been a Christian, and he took the liberty to include his own greeting in the letter that he was transcribing. It was a common practice for Paul to use a Christian scribe, and at the end of his letters Paul would also add his own personal touch (1 Cor. 16:21; Gal. 6:11; 2 Thess. 3:17; Philem. 19).

Gaius—A Hospitable Christian; Erastus—A Municipal Treasurer; and Quartus—A Brother

Others who sent their greetings were Gaius, Erastus, and Quartus.

- *Gaius* **was known for his hospitality.** He had opened his home to many traveling Christians, including Paul, providing them accommodations.
- *Erastus* **is identified as a city treasurer (*oikonomos*, from which we get the word *economist*).** He probably was a Roman patron who helped support others financially. It is clear that this man had some kind of financial position in the city of Corinth. It evidently was a distinguished post, and he apparently had some contacts in Rome.
- *Quartus* **is the last person to send greetings to the Christians in Rome. All that we know about him is that he was a "brother."** The *New King James Version* translates *ho adelphos* as "a brother," but the Greek literally means "the brother," perhaps meaning that he was a believer in Christ. Exactly why Quartus is described in this way, when all the others who sent greetings were Christians as well, is unknown. Perhaps the others were known by some Christian names in Roman, but Quartus was not.

Paul's personal greetings and the greetings from some of his coworkers expressed their gratitude to the Roman Christians and remind us that the outcome of Christian community—fellowship, unity, gifts of the Spirit—is service to the Lord. Community among believers transcends racial, social, economic, and educational differences. Our cooperation with one another and work for the Lord are accomplished in community. **The particular ministry we do, while it may feel solitary, is actually a combined outcome (the result) of all the people who have contributed to our lives. We stand on the shoulders of others, and therefore our roots in serving the Lord are planted in the soil of community. Indeed, community is the soil for an effective ministry and for a fruitful and Spirit-filled church.**

ROMANS 16:21-24

KEYWORDS

Church (*ekklesia*) (see p. 17)

Epistle
A letter written from one person to another person or group for a definite purpose in order to meet definite needs

Fellowship (*koinonia*) (see p. 388)

Patron, Roman
The Roman social structure in which a wealthy or influential person helped an institutional cause or individual. A master in ancient times could free slaves and retain social rights over them, an arrangement that benefited them both.

SUMMARY

Those who were with Paul at the time of his completion of his letter to the Romans send their greetings to the Roman believers. We note that among those who sent greetings was Timothy, the most well-known and beloved colleague of Paul.

LIFE APPLICATION

Paul's fellow workers join in sending greetings to the believers in Rome. Deep bonds of fellowship often exist among those who are in Christian ministry. The confession of Jesus Christ as Savior and

> the joys and burdens of the work of the Lord are held in common by all of us. Holding the same basic convictions and mutually sharing in the work of the gospel cement bonds of fellowship. We are to cherish this kind of fellowship, not only those of us who are colleagues in full-time ministry, but all of God's people. Local congregations have much in common for building deep relationships.

CLOSING WORDS OF PRAISE
ROMANS 16:25-27

> 📖 ²⁵ Now to Him who is able to establish you according to my gospel and the preaching of Jesus Christ, according to the revelation of the mystery kept secret since the world began ²⁶ but now made manifest, and by the prophetic Scriptures made known to all nations, according to the commandment of the everlasting God, for obedience to the faith— ²⁷ to God, alone wise, be glory through Jesus Christ forever. Amen.

Words of praise bring this letter to a close. Verses 25-27 form a single sentence, and the themes of this doxology recall the opening of Romans (1:1-7); so the whole epistle is wrapped in praise.

Themes in Paul's Doxology
Many of the themes of Paul's letter reappear in this ascription of praise.
- **The gospel had been entrusted to Paul (v. 25; 1:1).** Paul describes the gospel as "my gospel" (2:16; 16:25)—not to claim that the gospel was his own personal possession, but that it was a true expression of the gospel. The preaching of the true gospel gave Paul his authority.
- **Although Paul describes the gospel as a "mystery," he indicates that this mystery has already been revealed to believers as being God's plan to bring salvation to all nations (v. 25; 11:25).**
- **The gospel had been promised by God through the Old Testament prophets (16:26; 1:2).**

- **Now the promised Good News of salvation is no longer hidden away (16:26).** The gospel has become clear through the life, death, and resurrection of Jesus Christ and the preaching about the Good News of grace and eternal life.
- **The gospel has been extended to all people—both Jews and Gentiles (v. 26).** Therefore, it is God's will that this gospel go to all nations and everyone who is obedient to it will be saved (1:16-17).
- **The intent of the gospel is to bring everyone into faithful obedience to God (16:26; 1:5).** Through the gospel, God granted salvation to the Roman Christians and strengthened their faith in the face of the false teachers, just as He does for us today.

Words of Praise to God
Paul's Praise

At this point, Paul comes to the main purpose of his doxology—praise to God, who in His great wisdom gave the world the plan of salvation. To the only wise God "be glory through Jesus Christ forever. Amen" (16:27).

Our Praise to God and Our Application of the Book of Romans

We, too, can praise and worship God by allowing this magnificent letter to inspire us to grow in our relationship with Christ and to move forward in our Christian life . . .

- accepting God's love and forgiveness through Jesus Christ
- being grateful to God
- serving Him through the power of the Holy Spirit
- growing in our relationship with Him and becoming more like Him
- sharing the Good News and love of Christ with others
- promoting unity in the body of Christ
- treating all people with dignity and compassion.

Let us join the church of Rome in saying, "To God, alone wise, be glory through Jesus Christ forever. Amen."

ROMANS 16:25-27

KEYWORDS

Doxology
A hymn or words that express praise to God

Glory to God (see p. 75)

God/Godhead (see p. 58)

Gospel (see p. 23)

Jesus Christ (see p. 59)

Obedience to the Gospel/Obedience of Faith (see p. 185)

Preach (see p. 294)

SUMMARY

Being all-wise and powerful, God has a marvelous plan of salvation, and He has made it known through Jesus Christ. Paul invited the Christians of Rome to praise God for His great wisdom and His saving work in Christ, for God was the source of their strength and the only One who was able to establish them and make them firm so that they would not fall.

The gospel that Paul and other apostles preached was from and about Jesus Christ—it was the *Good News*. This gospel was a mystery for many ages, but now it has been disclosed and made known to all the nations of the earth. However, God's plan of salvation in Christ was not a new innovation during New Testament times, for it was in accord with the ancient predictions in the Old Testament.

The purpose for Paul's (and our) preaching the gospel is not merely to inform others so they can accept the message intellectually, but to inspire them to seek God and to respond to the Holy Spirit's voice with obedience. Responding in obedience of faith to the Spirit's call will lead others to receive God's forgiveness and healing through Christ, resulting in a changed life devoted to doing His will. Because of His grace and mercy toward all of us, God is due praise both now and forever.

LIFE APPLICATION

We owe praise to God for His great plan of salvation. God is the only One who has the power to establish us in the truth of the gospel and is the source of all our strength and constancy in believing the gospel. The gospel that we have believed is the same gospel that Jesus and Paul proclaimed.

> The gospel is the Good News to those who believe because it has effectively become the power of God to lead us to salvation (Rom. 1:16). As an instrument of the Holy Spirit the gospel is grace, forgiveness, and eternal life. It is not the message of self-appointed teachers who bring their own traditions and opinions. On the contrary, the true gospel is a fulfillment of the Old Testament and the proclamation that we are saved only through faith in Jesus Christ, followed by a life of obedience and discipleship.
>
> This magnificent gift of salvation has been made possible for us by the only wise and everlasting God through His Son, our sin-bearer. May we all praise the one and only true God.

REFLECTION—PART SEVEN
Romans 15:14—16:27

1. How does Paul characterize his ministry among the Gentiles in the eastern part of the Roman Empire?

2. What were Paul's plans for ministry once he left Corinth on his way to Jerusalem?

3. Why do you think Paul did not work where others had preached the gospel and had already established churches?

4. Explain the ways Paul wanted the church in Rome to support his mission to Spain.

5. What is your understanding of the Pauline Collection and its importance to the church in Paul's day?

6. Why did Paul request the Roman Christians to pray earnestly for him while he was in Jerusalem?

7. Paul identified Phoebe as a "deacon." How should we understand her function in the church in Cenchrea? Did she hold a church office?

8. How was it possible for Paul to know as many people as he did since he had never visited Rome?

9. In light of the biblical account in Acts and Romans, discuss the ministry of Priscilla and Aquila and their association with Paul.

10. Do you feel that Paul was convinced that the gospel about which the Roman Christians had learned was completely sufficient? Explain your answer.

11. In light of your study of Romans, how would you describe the Good News about Christ and eternal life (the gospel) to someone who is not yet a follower of Jesus Christ?

13. What impact has Paul's letter to the Romans had on you?

Prayer

Holy God, loving Father, we bow in Your presence with our hearts filled with thanksgiving for the written Word of God.

We thank You for the eternal living Word, Your Son . . .
- *through whom Your plan of salvation is fulfilled and made known*
- *to whom we may look in faith and be justified as Paul teaches us in Romans.*

Help us to understand the inspired wisdom recorded in Romans . . .
- *to apply it in our lives*
- *to be moved to a new spiritual awakening*
- *to experience a deep hunger for a fresh outpouring of the Holy Spirit.*

Father, Son, and Holy Spirit, You have done great things in the lives of Your people throughout all the world. Today, Triune God, may we receive You in our lives and, through Your guidance and power, become instruments of Your love and mercy in the world. Amen.

Supplemental Resources

APPENDIX A

The Apostle Paul, Author of Romans	
Name	Jewish Hebrew name at birth—Saul
	Roman Latin name—Paul
	Referred to by the Christian church as "the apostle Paul" or "Saint Paul"
Birth	Born around AD 3, during the reign of Caesar Augustus
	Citizenship—Rome (only official citizenship)
	Place—Tarsus, a Greek city in Cilicia, Asia Minor
Death	Died around AD 67, martyred in Rome toward the end of the reign of Nero
Family	Born to Jewish family, rich in religious traditions and heritage
	Father was a Pharisaic Jew with Roman citizenship
	Member of the tribe of Benjamin
Marital status	Unknown
Education, Profession	Studied Hebrew Scriptures and traditions
	Language—Hebrew and Greek
	Trade—tentmaker
Religion	Before conversion to Christianity: • Pharisaic Jew, devout in keeping the Jewish law • Enthusiastic about protecting the integrity of the Jewish faith • Persecutor of followers of Christ After conversion to Christianity: • Devout follower of Christ • Enthusiastic about preaching and teaching about the good news of forgiveness and eternal life available through faith in Christ • Martyred for his faith

APPENDIX B

Paul's Missionary Work and His Letters

The apostle Paul's three missionary journeys covered about ten years, with his ministry occurring mainly in provinces in the Roman Empire: Galatia, Macedonia, Achaia, and Asia, with concentration on key cities. His strategy was to first preach the gospel in synagogues in the cities, establishing a pattern for his missionary work.

AD 33	Paul's conversion to Christ (Acts 9:1-17)
around AD 44	Early Ministry: Damascus (Acts 9:20-22)
	Returned to Tarsus, the city of his birth, and remained about ten years—known as the *Silent Period* (Acts 9:29-30)
	Barnabas brought Paul to Antioch in Syria.
AD 47-49	First Missionary Journey
	Influx of Gentiles into the church
	Wrote Galatians before Jerusalem Council; place uncertain
AD 49	Jerusalem Council
AD 49-52	Second Missionary Journey
AD 51 or 52	Wrote 1 and 2 Thessalonians from Corinth
AD 53-58	Third Missionary Journey
AD 56	Wrote 1 Corinthians from Ephesus

Appendices

6 months later	Wrote 2 Corinthians from Macedonia
AD 58	Wrote Romans from Corinth
AD 61-63	First Roman Imprisonment
	In prison
AD 64	Wrote 1 Timothy, probably from Macedonia
Soon after	Probably wrote Titus (place uncertain)
AD 67	Second Roman Imprisonment
	Wrote 2 Timothy, his last spiritual testament
	Executed in Rome

The Greatest Letter Ever Written

APPENDIX C

Paul's First Missionary Journey

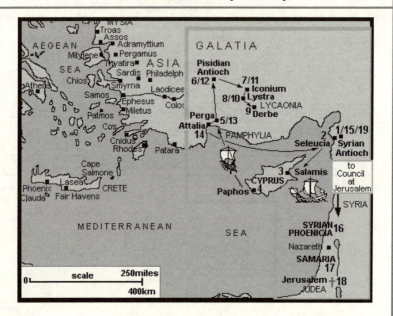

Around AD 47, Paul and Barnabas were sent by the church of Antioch in Syria on their First Missionary Journey to the cities of Pisidian Antioch, Iconium, Lystra, and Derbe, where they helped to found churches. These cities were located in the south of the Roman province of Galatia.

APPENDIX D

Paul's Second Missionary Journey

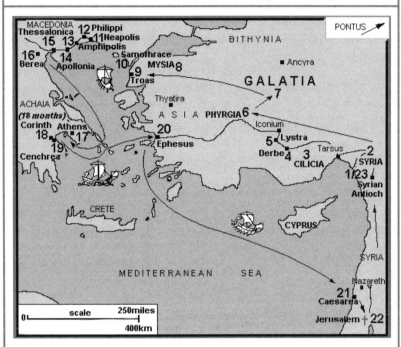

In AD 49 or 50, back in Antioch in Syria, Paul and Barnabas had a disagreement, and the two parted ways. Paul set out on his Second Missionary Journey, during which he crossed into Europe, and founded churches in Philippi, Thessalonica, and Corinth. In Athens, he had only limited success. Only a few of the Athenians received the gospel.

APPENDIX E

Paul's Third Missionary Journey

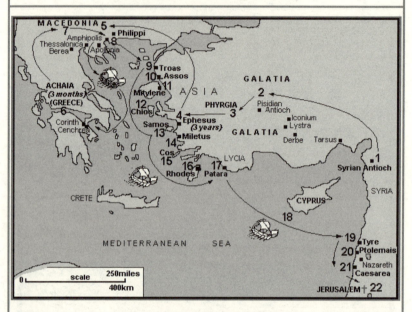

In AD 53 or 54, Paul revisited Jerusalem and returned to Antioch. Then he set out on his Third Missionary Journey, during which he spent three years in Ephesus. The Book of Acts does not mention any churches established during this journey. In AD 58, Paul revisited Greece and spent three months in Corinth, at which time he wrote his letter to the Roman church.

Completing the third journey, Paul returned to Jerusalem with money he had collected for the poor. Roman soldiers rescued him from almost being lynched in the Temple. He was tried before the Sanhedrin (Acts 22), and due to a plot against him, he was sent to Caesarea, where he remained in prison for two years. In AD 60, he appealed his case to Caesar and was sent to Rome. In Rome, he spent two years in custody. He then was probably released and later imprisoned again and executed.

APPENDIX F

Justification	Sanctification
Accepting Christ	Walking with Christ and becoming more like Him
A result of faith	A result of faith and daily nurture of our faith relationship with God
Right relationship with God	Fruit of our right relationship with God—right living for God
Being declared "righteous" by God and given a holy spiritual designation—the result is *positional sanctification*.	Maturing in holy living—honoring our status of *positional sanctification* by living a life that is focused on God, expressing the fruit of the Spirit (*practical sanctification*)
Being adopted into God's family	Fulfilling the responsibilities of being a member of God's family
Submitting to the initial call of the Holy Spirit	Submitting to the initial call and ongoing guidance of the Holy Spirit
Spiritual initiation	Spiritual designation and spiritual maturation
Our initial repentance and God's forgiveness for our shortcomings and sins	Our daily repentance and God's ongoing forgiveness for our shortcomings and sins
Freedom from sin	Daily empowerment by the Holy Spirit to resist temptation and sin
Freedom from death	Freedom to live a whole, full life of purpose for Christ that will never end
Assurance of an eternal life of glory and joy with Christ	Learning to live in the glorious, joyous life with Christ that has been promised to us

APPENDIX G

Practices That Nurture Our Faith and Holy Living

"Draw near to God and He will draw near to you" (James 4:8).

Romans 2:10; 6:4, 11, 13, 19; 7:4; 8:14; 12:1-2;
Luke 10:27; 14:27-30; John 15:5; 1 Corinthians 9:24-26;
2 Corinthians 9:8; Galatians 5:16-17, 22-23; Colossians 3:1-4;
1 Timothy 4:7-8; 2 Timothy 1:7

Time With God in Solitude

Matthew 14:23; Mark 1:35; 6:31, 46; Luke 4:42; 5:16; 6:12;
Isaiah 30:15; Psalm 46:10

Bible Reading and Study regular reading and thoughtful examination and consideration of God's written message to us	Romans 12:2; John 8:31-32; 2 Timothy 2:15; 3:16-17; Hebrews 4:12; 5:12-14; Deuteronomy 30:14; Psalm 119:103-105
Meditation on God and Scripture focusing our minds on who God is and His teachings	Romans 8:5-6; Luke 24:8; Philippians 4:8; Joshua 1:8; Psalm 1:2; 19:14; 63:6; 77:12; 104:34; 119:97, 111; 130:6
Prayer conversing with God, including both talking and listening to Him	Romans 8:26-27; Matthew 7:7; 6:9-13; Acts 1:14; Ephesians 6:18; 1 Thessalonians 5:17; 1 Peter 4:7; Psalm 69:13
Confession and Repentance to God asking God to forgive us for our wrongdoings and allowing Him to change us	Romans 6; 10:9; 12:1-2; Matthew 9:12; Luke 15:7, 10; Acts 2:38; 3:19; 1 John 1:9; 2:1-2; Psalm 32:5; 51:1-2, 10; Proverbs 28:13
Silence and Listening to God removing ourselves from busyness and noise in order to be attentive to God and to receive His love, teaching, and guidance	Mark 1:35; 2 Thessalonians 3:5; 1 Kings 19:11-13; Psalm 46:10; 62:1, 5; 130:5-6; Lamentations 3:25-28

Simplicity and Humility responsible and unpretentious living that expresses undivided devotion to Jesus Christ	**SIMPLICITY:** Romans 12:2; Matthew 5:37; 6:33 (vv.19-34); 18:2-3; 19:21; Luke 3:11; 12:15; 2 Corinthians 1:12; 11:3; Philippians 4:11-13; Colossians 3:1-3; 1 Thessalonians 2:3-7; 1 Timothy 6:6-10; Hebrews 12:1; James 4:8; Psalm 62:10; 116:6; Proverbs 11:28 **HUMILITY:** Romans 10:12-13; 12:3, 16; 14:1-4; Matthew 6:1-6; 18:4; Ephesians 2:8-10; James 4:6; Proverbs 16:19; Micah 6:8
Fasting refraining from food or drink, as an act of self-denial that helps us to be open to God and to focus on spiritual matters	Matthew 4:1-2; 6:16-18; 9:14-15; 17:19-21; Luke 2:36-37; 5:35; Acts 10:30-31; 13:3; 14:22-23; Nehemiah 1:4; Esther 4:16; Isaiah 58:3-10
Rest pausing from work to focus on God, to enjoy His blessings, and to be refreshed	Matthew 11:29-30; Mark 6:30-32; Hebrews 4:9-10; Genesis 2:1-3; Exodus 16:23-30; 20:8-11; Leviticus 25:2-5; Psalm 23

Time With God in Community
Luke 24:13-15; John 17:23; Galatians 6:2, 10; Ephesians 5:2, 19; Colossians 2:2; 3:16; 1 John 1:3, 7; Psalm 55:14

Worship engaging in honor, praise, and devotion to God	Romans 12:1-8; Matthew 4:10; John 4:23-24; Acts 13:14-15; 1 Corinthians 14:12, 23, 26; Colossians 3:16; Hebrews 10:25; 13:15; Revelation 19:10; Psalm 5:7; 86:9; 95:6
Celebration of God's Goodness rejoicing in God's blessings and observing special days and seasons to honor God	**REJOICING:** Romans 5:2-3; 8:15-17, 38-39; 8:28; 12:12; 15:13; 1 Corinthians 5:8; Philippians 4:4 (vv. 4-13); 2 Samuel 6:14; Psalm 5:11; 16:7, 9, 11; 28:7; 47:1; 98; 100; 107:8-9; 118:24; 122:1; 126:2; 139:14; 145:7 **SPECIAL CELEBRATIONS:** Romans 14:5-7; Luke 14:12-14; 15:23-32; Exodus 5:1; 12:14; Leviticus 23; Esther 9:22

Holy Communion observing together the Lord's Supper, celebrating God's provision for our salvation through the sacrificial death of Jesus Christ	Matthew 26:26-28; Mark 14:22-24; Luke 22:19-20; Acts 2:46-47; 1 Corinthians 10:16-17; 11:24-26
Stewardship and Giving wise use and management of the resources with which God has blessed us; includes use of funds, goods, and time in service to God—compassionately caring for other people and God's world	**Management of Resources (Including Finances):** Romans 13:6-9; Matthew 6:19-21; 25:14-30; Mark 12:41-44; 1 Timothy 6:17-19; Leviticus 27:30; Deuteronomy 8:17-18; Proverbs 3:9 **Use of Resources to Care for People:** Romans 12:10-13; 13:9; 15:25-27; Matthew 5:7; Acts 6:1-3; 2 Corinthians 8—9; James 1:27; Deuteronomy 14:28-29; Proverbs 22:9; Malachi 3:5 **Care for God's Creation:** Romans 8:19-22; Acts 17:24; Genesis 1:29, 31; 2:15; Numbers 35:33-34; Psalm 24:1
Service actions and work that benefit others and the world God created	Romans 12:4-8, 11; Matthew 20:26-28; 22:37-39; 25:44-46; Mark 9:35; 10:42-45; Luke 10:25-37; John 12:26; 13:12-16; 1 Corinthians 12:1-26; Galatians 6:2; Ephesians 2:10; 4:11-13; 6:6-7; 1 Peter 4:10; Exodus 36; 1 Samuel 12:24
Witnessing/Testifying telling others about Christ and His work in our lives through our words and actions	Romans 1:9, 16-17; 15:19; Matthew 5:13-16; Mark 16:15; Acts 1:8; 20:20-21; Proverbs 11:30
Discipling/Mentoring instructing, encouraging, and walking with another in the spiritual journey of growing in faith in Christ	Romans 1:11-13; Matthew 28:19; John 14:26; 15:15; Acts 9:27; Colossians 3:16; 2 Thessalonians 2:15; 1 Timothy 1:18; 2 Timothy 2:2; Titus 2:3-5; Psalm 71:18; 145:4; Proverbs 22:6; 27:17; Isaiah 50:4

Repentance and Restitution to Others, and Accepting Forgiveness From Others apologizing, engaging in healing actions, and graciously accepting others' kindness in response to the wrongs or hurts we have committed against them	Romans 12:18; Matthew 5:23-25; James 5:16; Numbers 5:7
Forgiving Others being merciful, releasing others from obligation for wrongs or hurts that they have committed against us, while continuing to stand for what is true, honorable and good	Romans 12:14; 14:19; Matthew 5:43-44; 6:12; 18:21-23; Mark 11:25; Ephesians 4:32
Fellowship friendship and unity with other followers of Christ	Romans 12:10; 14:1-13, 19; Acts 2:42, 46; 20:7; Philippians 4:14-20; Hebrews 10:24-25; 1 John 1:7
Hospitality being welcoming and creating an atmosphere in which friends or strangers can come and experience the love of Christ through relationship	Romans 12:13; 15:7; Matthew 25:34-40; Mark 12:30-31; Hebrews 13:1-2; 1 Timothy 3:1-2; 1 Peter 4:9

GLOSSARY

Using This Glossary
This glossary contains both short definitions and longer explanations for terms selected from the Book of Romans (NKJV) and from the author's comments in this book, *The Greatest Letter Ever Written*. At the end of each definition are listed the main parts of this book where this term appears, as well as related glossary terms.

Additional Resources
For more explanation of terms, additional terms, or for locating particular passages or keywords in the Bible, the following on-line resources are recommended:

Dictionary
Baker's Evangelical Dictionary of Biblical Theology www.biblestudytools.com/dictionaries

Bible Search
BibleGateway.com www.biblegateway.com
BibleStudyTools.com www.biblestudytools.com/search
Interlinear Bible (English/Hebrew/Greek) www.biblestudytools.com/interlinear-bible

ABBREVIATIONS

AD   Latin: ***Anno Domini*** **(in the year of our Lord).** Designating the years after Christ's birth. Example: *AD 49 during the reign of Claudius.*

BC   ***Before Christ.*** Designating the years before Christ's birth. Example: *68 BC*

cf.   ***Confer.*** Compare, consult, see also. Example: (*Rom. 15:4; cf. 1 Cor. 10:6-11*).

ff.   ***Folios, following.*** When read aloud: "and following," used to indicate biblical passages following the one cited. Example: (*Isa. 53:1ff.*).

LXX   **The Greek translation of the Hebrew Old Testament.** This version known as the Septuagint (LXX), the Greek word for *seventy*, was made during the second and third centuries BC.

ACCOUNT/IMPUTE (*verb logizomai*)—Greek bookkeeping term—translated "account," "reckon," "impute" or "credit." This term basically means "to set down to one's account," that is, God credits

to the account of the believer the righteousness of Christ. This is a gift of righteousness apart from human virtue, merit, or works. God declares that the believer is righteous in His sight because of the believer's faith in Christ. At the heart of justification by faith stands *logizomai*, the doctrine of *imputation*. PART 3. (See also IMPUTATION OF RIGHTEOUSNESS; IMPUTATION OF SIN)

ADOPTION—Literally means "placed as a son or daughter." Adoption is an act of grace by God, which bestows on believers the status and blessings of membership in His family. This gracious blessing of adoption is received by all who trust in Jesus as their Savior and prepares them to live a new life in the family of God. PARTS 1, 4- 5. (See also CHILDREN OF GOD/SONS OF GOD; CHOSEN BY GOD)

ALREADY/NOT YET DOCTRINE—Through the First Coming of Christ and His ministry on earth, the beginning of the Future Age has moved into the Present Age. Until Christ returns, the Future Age penetrates the Present Age and the two ages overlap. From the perspective of the New Testament, Christ's life, death, and resurrection were the turning point in all human history. Since that time, believers *already* enjoy many blessings of salvation, but *not yet* have they received these blessings in their fullness and will not until Christ's Second Coming. OVERVIEW; PARTS 4, 6. (See also THIS AGE/THE COMING AGE; END TIMES)

AMORAL PRACTICES (See MORAL PRACTICES/AMORAL PRACTICES)

ANTINOMIAN PERVERSION—A system of thought that erroneously teaches that Christians are entirely free of moral law as a rule for life, due to the fact that they are justified by faith alone. Antinomianism literally means being opposed to God's law, and it maintains that justified believers have no obligation to keep the Ten Commandments. PART 2. (See also LAW, the Torah)

APOSTLE (*apostolos*)—A person whom a sender dispatches with authority to fulfill a mission. An apostle is sent with a definite responsibility to act in behalf of the sender with full authority to carry out a mission. Paul received a direct appointment by Christ to preach the gospel to the Gentile world (Gal. 1:1, 16; 2:8). *The Twelve* were most often called *disciples*, but they were also called *apostles*, because Jesus gave to them the authority to preach the gospel, heal the sick, and cast out demons. OVERVIEW; PARTS 1, 7. (See also DISCIPLE)

ATTRIBUTES OF GOD (See DIVINE ATTRIBUTES)

BAPTISM IN THE SPIRIT—The powerful Pentecostal anointing by the Spirit that one may experience subsequent (after) conversion. To be Spirit-anointed is to be endowed with power for witnessing and evangelizing (Luke 4:18; Acts 1:8). PART 3. (See also HOLY SPIRIT/THE SPIRIT; GIFT OF THE SPIRIT; PENTECOST/DAY OF PENTECOST; SPEAKING IN TONGUES)

BAPTISM INTO CHRIST JESUS—A phrase that refers to inward spiritual conversion. Water baptism, a symbol of *baptism in Christ Jesus*, has

Glossary

no power to save, but it pictures what happens at the time Christ is received in faith. PART 4. See also (SALVATION; GIFT OF THE SPIRIT; WATER BAPTISM)

BELIEVE—An attitude of the heart to accept something as being true and to rely on particular persons or things. In the New Testament, *to believe* is to have an active, personal trust in Jesus Christ and to depend on Him for salvation (Rom. 4:5; 10:10). PARTS 1- 5. (See also FAITH)

BELIEVER (See CHRISTIAN/BELIEVER)

BIBLE—The collection of holy writings (Scriptures) that Christians use as their guide for life, which consists of sixty-six books (thirty-nine in the Old Testament and twenty-seven in the New Testament). The word *Bible* is derived from the Greek *biblion* ("roll" or "book"). Today this word refers to the Bible, which is recognized as the inspired record of divine revelation. God's revelation is a combination of what He has said and done. His words and actions are woven together in the Bible, neither being complete without the other. The revealed message of God was recorded in the Bible by people inspired by the Holy Spirit (2 Tim. 3:16). *Revelation* makes truth known, whereas the word *inspiration* means "God-breathed" or "inspired of God," guaranteeing and preserving truth.

The Bible was written over 1,500 years. Already by the time of Jesus, the Jews had accepted the Old Testament (also referred to today as the *Hebrew Bible*) as a set of holy, authoritative Scriptures. The Christian church, following the example of Jesus and His disciples, also accepted the authority of the Old Testament. The early church added a second part, the New Testament, the inspired record of God's revelation in the teaching and ministry of Jesus and in the life and ministry of the church. This process did not take place at once, but over a period of time. By the end of the second century, the task was mainly completed, but an authoritative list of the twenty-seven books in the New Testament did not appear until AD 367.

Though written over a long period of time and by many authors inspired by the Holy Spirit, the Bible reveals a marvelous unity in thought. The value of the Bible rests in the fact that it is the Word of God, recording God's mighty acts in the history of Israel and in the life and ministry of both Jesus and the early church. A superb example of this unity in the Bible is Paul's letter to the Roman Christians. INTRODUCTION. (See also LAW, the Torah; GOSPEL; EPISTLE; ROMANS)

BODY OF CHRIST (See CHURCH)

BODY OF SIN/BODY OF DEATH—The human body (the whole personality) ruled by the power of sin. This expression refers to slavery to sin. The new life in Christ delivers the believer from the dominion of sin and from the bondage of following the dictates of any will but the will of Christ. PART 4. (See also SIN; UNGODLINESS; DEATH; FLESH; OLD MAN; SINNER; UNDER SIN; FREEDOM FROM SIN; FREEDOM IN CHRIST)

BONDSERVANT/SLAVE (*doulos*)—A person who renders service freely or because of obligation. In the New Testament, the emphasis is on obedience to Christ. Paul uses the term *bondservant* or *slave* to describe his total dedication to Christ. Such dedication is called for in Romans 12:1 as our "reasonable service." PARTS 1, 4

BOOK OF ROMANS (See *ROMANS*)

BRETHREN—A term used to refer to members of the same family (Mark 1:16), a race (Rom. 9:3), or a neighbor (Matt. 7:3), but the distinctive use in the New Testament is to express a spiritual relationship. All members of the Christian community are brothers (sisters). This relationship is not merely figurative, but is based on spiritual birth (2 Peter 1:4). PARTS 1, 4, 5, 7. (See also *ISRAEL; JEWS/ISRAELITES/HEBREWS; CHILDREN OF GOD/SONS OF GOD; ADOPTION*)

CALLED BY GOD
1. **Called to Salvation (*kaleo*)—God's invitation to participate in the blessings of salvation.** This invitation comes through the preaching of the gospel (2 Thess. 2:14); it is God's invitation to accept His grace, forgiveness, and gift of eternal life through Jesus Christ, and to then live a holy life that is sanctified by the Lord. The person who refuses the call rejects not man, but the Holy Spirit (1 Thess. 4:7-8). PARTS 4-6. (See also *CHOSEN BY GOD; ELECT OF GOD; PREDESTINATION; GIFT OF THE SPIRIT*)
2. **Called/Sent to Service (*apostolosin*)—God's invitation to engage in particular service.** In addition to being called to participate in the blessings of salvation, individuals are given one or more spiritual gifts. God may call them to use those gifts in particular functions and ministries (Acts 13:2; 16:10; Rom. 1:1; Heb. 5:4). Such a call may involve full-time service. PARTS 5-7. (See also *GIFT OF THE SPIRIT*)
3. **Called/Sent to Preach (*apostolosin*)—God's invitation and authorization to preach the gospel.** The preacher's mission is not from those to whom he or she delivers the gospel, but from a higher authority—God himself (Rom. 1:1). Though divine sending or authorizing legitimizes the proclamation of the gospel, being called by God does not make anyone infallible. Those who preach the gospel may err in what they say. This possibility of human error is why it is always important for us to compare human teachings to God's teachings recorded in the Bible. PARTS 5, 7. (See also *PREACH*)

CARNAL (*sarkinos*, unspiritual)—A worldly orientation which manifests itself in opposition to God. PART 4. (See also *FLESH; SIN*)

CHILDREN OF GOD/SONS OF GOD—The status and resulting privileges of sons and daughters received by people who have been adopted into the family of God. This is made possible for all people through faith in Christ (Gal. 3:26) and is attested by the Holy Spirit (Rom. 8:14, 16). Children of God are born again by the Spirit (John 3:3-7) and have the privileges of being members of God's family. On the earth, believers' status as God's children remains incomplete until resurrection at the return of Christ (Rom. 8:21, 23, 29; 1 John 3:2). PARTS 1, 2, 4. (See also *ADOPTION; BRETHREN; CHURCH*)

CHOSEN BY GOD
1. **Chosen (People of Israel)—The nation whom God chose to be His light to all nations, and through whom He sent His Son, the Messiah Jesus Christ, into the world to offer grace, healing, and salvation to all people.** As God's chosen, Israel received all the blessings and privileges of being His people (Deut. 4:37; 7:6-7;

1 Kings 3:8). Being chosen is a corporate idea and requires the human cooperation of personal faith. *PARTS 2, 5.* (See also *ELECT OF GOD; ISRAEL; COVENANT*)

2. **Chosen (Christians)—People who are trusting in Christ and are obedient to Him.** God has chosen to save the body of Christ (the church) through His Son Jesus Christ. Membership in the body of Christ is determined by personal repentance and faith in Christ (2 Cor. 7:10). (See also *ELECT OF GOD; ADOPTION; PREDESTINATION; COVENANT*)

CHRISTIAN/BELIEVER—A follower of Jesus Christ and His teachings, one who is personally devoted to Him and has the features of His character. In the true sense, a true Christian has a genuine saving faith in Christ. *INTRODUCTION; OVERVIEW; PARTS 1-7.* (See also *DISCIPLE; SAINTS*)

CHRISTIAN SERVICE (See *SERVICE*)

CHURCH (*ekklesia*)—The family of God, created by the Holy Spirit. The Christian church stands in unity with the people of God in the Old Testament (Matt. 8:11; Rom. 11:16-28). **In the New Testament, *ekklesia* is mainly used in two ways:**

1. **The Body of Christ/One Body in Christ—The whole redeemed fellowship in heaven and earth (Matt. 16:18; Eph. 1:22).** This theological term pictures the church as a fellowship similar to the human body. The members of the church are members of one another (Rom. 12:5). As believers, they have all been joined to the church by the Holy Spirit at the time of their conversion and have mutual fellowship and unity (1 Cor. 12:13). Each believer has been given a spiritual gift(s) with which to minister in the body (vv. 5, 7, 11). For unity to exist within the body of Christ (the Christian church) respect must be given to differences among individuals, including those differences of opinion that might occur among more mature and less mature believers (Rom. 14:1ff.; 1 Cor. 3:1ff.). Under Christ's leadership and the power of the Holy Spirit, Christ is manifested in the world through the lives and service of God's people. *INTRODUCTION; PART 6.* (See also *CHILDREN OF GOD/SONS OF GOD; GIFT OF THE SPIRIT*)

2. **A Gathering of Worshipers—An assembly, a gathering of people who meet to worship the Lord (Acts 19:32, 39, 41).** Examples of such gatherings were the church in Jerusalem (8:1, 3) the churches in Syria and Cilicia (15:41), and churches who met in homes in Rome and Ephesus (Rom. 16:5; 1 Cor. 16:19). *INTRODUCTION; PARTS 6-7.* (See also *WORSHIP*)

CHURCH IN ROME (See *ROMANS*)

CIRCUMCISION—The removal of the foreskin on the male organ. For the Jewish people, this holy ritual had the distinct meaning of being the sign of the covenant that God made with Abraham. Circumcision was a confirming seal/sign of the salvation Abraham received by faith (Gen. 17:11). In Romans 3:30, Paul refers to "the circumcised by [*ek*, out of] faith and the uncircumcised through [*dia*, through] faith." These are two ways of expressing the same truth—that *true circumcision* is primarily a condition of the heart that is the result of faith in the one *true* God. Circumcised (Jews) and uncircumcised (Gentiles) both stand in a right relationship with God on the basis of faith. The entire human family's access to righteousness is through Christ. *PARTS 2-3.* (See also *SEAL/SIGN*)

COMING AGE, THE (See *THIS AGE/THE COMING AGE*)

COMMANDMENT, THE (See *LAW, the Torah*)

COMMUNION—A common sharing or participation in something.
1. **Communion with God/Communion of the Saints**—In the present life, communion finds its highest realization in the fellowship of believers with the triune God (1 Cor. 1:9; 2 Cor. 13:14; 1 John 1:3). This blessed communion with God and with one another will reach its fulfillment through eternal fellowship in unity together with the triune God (Matt. 8:11; Heb. 12:22-24). *PARTS 4, 7.* (See also *FELLOWSHIP*)
2. **Holy Communion/The Lord's Supper**—Believers have a fellowship with God and one another that is visibly portrayed in Holy Communion, the Lord's Supper. When Jesus gave the bread and wine to His disciples, He was inviting them to share in the blessings of the new covenant and to have fellowship with Him, a foretaste of full salvation in heaven (Matt. 26:26-29; 1 Cor. 11:23-26). *APPENDIX (G)*

CONDEMNATION—An unfavorable decision or sentence by a human or divine agent. People who love darkness rather than light come under God's holy displeasure or judgment. For those who are in Christ, there remains no holy displeasure or divine judgment. For them Christ has borne God's holy displeasure toward their sins. *PARTS 2-4, 6.* (See also *JUDGMENT BY GOD/GOD'S JUDGMENT; WRATH OF GOD; GRACE; FORGIVENESS*)

CONFESS—Meaning "to testify, acknowledge, declare." In certain contexts this term may mean "to admit," such as the confessing of sin and asking God to forgive us of wrongdoing and to change us. *PART 5; APPENDIX (G).* (See also *REPENTANCE/PENITENCE; FORGIVENESS*)

CONSCIENCE—Moral awareness, the faculty in humans that makes them aware of right and wrong and is a dimension of the image of God in humankind. It urges people to do what they recognize as being morally right and restrains them from doing what they recognize as being morally evil. The conscience can be influenced by environment, training, and education. *PARTS 2, 6*

CORPORATE SOLIDARITY—The principle of the human race being in unity with Adam in his sin (Rom. 5:12-21; 1 Cor. 15:22, 45). Being united with Adam in his disobedience to God, the entire race suffered the dire consequences of Adam's sin. What Adam did was more than an act of an individual; it was a corporate act of the human race. *PART 3.* (See also *SIN*)

COVENANT (*diatheke*)—A compact or agreement between two parties that is mutually binding on each other. In the biblical covenant (*diatheke*), God took the initiative and established the terms of the relationship with His chosen people, the nation of Israel. God also put in place the new covenant through His Son, Jesus Christ, and the blessings

Glossary

of that covenant are through faith in Christ's saving death. OVERVIEW; PARTS 2, 5. (See also PROMISE; CHOSEN BY GOD; ISRAEL)

COVET—Excessive desire for something that rightfully belongs to another person. Such desire often lies in the realm of money, position, power, or honor. Since the intensity of desire and worship are closely related, *covetousness* is labeled "idolatry" (Col. 3:5). PARTS 4, 6

CREATION—The world and everything in it, which God made by command, without using any previously existing material that He did not create. God created the heavens and the earth and all living things and beings, including humans. The entire universe is the direct result of the creative power of God (Gen. 1:1—2:25). PARTS 2, 4. (See also GOD, THE FATHER/THE CREATOR; SOVEREIGNTY OF GOD)

CREATOR, THE (See GOD, THE FATHER/THE CREATOR)

CROSS, THE—The Roman Empire's instrument for the most cruel and shameful punishment, and the climax to Christ's suffering for the salvation of humankind. Through His death on the cross, Christ bore the consequences of our sins (2 Cor. 5:21) and made peace between God and us (Col. 1:20). Christ calls on all believers to take up their cross by being ready to deny themselves of self-interest and to serve God daily (Mark 8:34-38). PARTS 2-7 (see footnote) (See also RESURRECTION; SALVATION; JESUS CHRIST)

CRUCIFIXION (See CROSS, THE)

DAY OF PENTECOST (See PENTECOST/DAY OF PENTECOST)

DEACON/DEACONESS—Both terms have to do with personal service, involving the care of orphans and widows and deeds of charity. In the New Testament, *deacon* was an office in the church (1 Tim. 3:8-13), and the mention of Phoebe in Romans 16:1 as a *deacon* ("servant") may imply that *deaconess* was beginning to emerge as an office in the church. PART 7. (See also SERVANT/MINISTER; SERVICE)

DEATH—Disunion of soul and body, or a state of separation from God. Adam's transgression of God's will brought death as a penalty. Since sin is universal, the presence of death is a necessary consequence (Rom. 5:12-14). PARTS 1-6. (See also SIN; BODY OF SIN/BODY OF DEATH; LIFE)

DISCERNMENT (See JUDGMENT)

DISCIPLE—Any person who follows Jesus Christ and His teachings and endeavors to continue to learn more about His ways and to grow in their relationship with Him. The term *disciples* also refers to *the twelve* followers of Jesus, who traveled and worked with Him during His life on earth. OVERVIEW; PART 4. (See also CHRISTIAN/BELIEVER; APOSTLE)

DIVINE ATTRIBUTES—The perfections or characteristics of God. From the Bible we learn what the living God is like. There is no attempt in the Bible to give a complete list of divine attributes. Biblical scholars have classified them under two major headings: (1) *attributes reflected* *in humankind* (knowledge, wisdom, goodness, love, grace, mercy, faithfulness, holiness, justice, will, power) and (2) *attributes not reflected in humankind* (self-existence, eternity, omnipresence, immutability). Each attribute describes God in His total being. PART 2. (See also GOD/GODHEAD; HOLY; LOVE (agape); RIGHTEOUSNESS)

DOCETISM—Teaching that denied that Christ had a physical body and erroneously proposed that Christ was sinful. PART 4. (See also INCARNATION)

DOCTRINE—A body or system of beliefs and teachings; also refers to the central theological themes of Scripture, particularly including the teachings given by Jesus and the apostles. "Sound doctrine" is vital to the Christian life (1 Tim. 1:10; Titus 2:1). The early Christians devoted themselves to "the apostles' doctrine" (Acts 2:42). INTRODUCTION; PARTS 4, 7.

DOXOLOGY—A hymn or words that express praise to God. PART 7. (See also WORSHIP)

ELECT OF GOD—The term elect of God refers to believers in Christ and the chosen nation of Israel. The biblical term *elect* (*election*) is a corporate category, and does not indicate the selection of specific individuals for salvation. In the Old Testament, God chose the nation of Israel as *one* people to be His servant in a special way. Likewise in the New Testament, not arbitrarily excluding anyone, *the elect* are the people who belong to *one* body (the church) by faith in Christ (Eph. 1:3-14). PARTS 4-5. (See also CHOSEN BY GOD; CALLED BY GOD; PREDESTINATION)

END TIMES
- **End Times (End Time, End of Time, Last Day, Last Days)**
- **The Present Age (the Old Age, This Age, the Current Age, this Present Evil Age, the Age of Adam)**
- **The Coming Age (the Future Age, the Age to Come, the Coming Day, the New Day, the Age of Christ)** *Initiated by*: **the Second Coming (Christ's Coming, the Second Advent)**

These terms relate to eschatology—the *End Times*—covering a broad range of subjects such as the present and future reign of God (the two ages), the return of Christ, the rapture of the church, resurrection, the Millennium, and judgment of humankind. Terms like *Last Day* and *Last Days* are broad references to the events of the *End Times*, whereas concepts such as *Coming Day*, *New Day*, *Coming Age*, and the *Age to Come* are different ways of indicating that believers live now spiritually in the age that will be consummated when Christ returns. The *Age to Come* overlaps the *Present Age*, which is variously referred to as the *Old Age*, *This Age*, and this *Present Evil Age*. Now believers await the return of Christ to the earth "in the clouds with great power and glory" (Mark 13:26) which is often spoken of as the *Second Coming* or *Christ's Coming*. PART 6. (See also THIS AGE/THE COMING AGE; ALREADY/NOT YET DOCTRINE; ESCHATOLOGY)

Glossary

EPISTLE—**A letter written from one person to another person or group for a definite purpose in order to meet definite needs.** *PART 7*

ESCHATOLOGY—**The study of the Last Days, the final events in history, which involve the unfolding of God's redemptive purpose in Christ.** *PART 6.* (See also *END TIMES; THIS AGE/THE COMING AGE*)

ETERNAL LIFE (See *LIFE/ETERNAL LIFE*)

EVANGELISM (*evanggelismos*)—**Derived from the noun *euanggelion (gospel), and the verb euaggelizomai*–(to proclaim good news), this term means to share and spread throughout the world the good news about Jesus Christ and eternal life, inviting all people to a relationship with Christ and salvation (Acts 1:8).** Jesus commissioned the church to bring light to a spiritually dark world (Matt. 5:14-16) and to make disciples (28:18-20). *PART 7.* (See also *GOSPEL*)

EVIL—**The opposite of good and is the cause of loss and suffering. Several kinds of evil can be identified:**
1. **Religious evil**—the evil that corrupts religion, motivating religious expression to become sin through legalism and oppression, the opposite of righteousness and love
2. **Moral evil**—motivator of actions that are contrary to what is right and good
3. **Social evil**—the root of societal problems, such as drug addiction, cheating in business, corrupt politics, and poverty
4. **Natural evil**—the force behind loss and suffering caused by natural events, such as earthquakes, fire, floods, and disease

PARTS 2-7. (See also *SIN; PRINCIPALITIES AND POWERS; SATAN/DEVIL*)

EXHORTATION, GIFT OF (*paraklesis*)—**A particular ministry of pastors and others to comfort, strengthen, and encourage fellow believers.** It is one of the gifts of the Spirit (Rom. 12:8), and a message given through prophecy may offer comfort and exhortation (1 Cor. 14:3). *PART 6*

EXPIATION (See *PROPITIATION*)

FAITH—**A response of a person to God, in which there is a trusted reliance on Him and faithfulness in life to Him.** In the New Testament, *faith in God* is defined as "faith in Christ." Paul shows that faith in Christ is the only way to have a right relationship with God. Using Abraham as his model for salvation, Paul speaks of "righteousness of faith" (Rom. 4:11). This phrase means that neither circumcision nor good works saved the patriarch Abraham. Nothing but faith secured for him a righteous standing before God. From start to finish, salvation is a matter of faith (1:17). Faith is the means by which a person receives Jesus Christ as his/her personal Savior. Assent to the truth of the gospel is necessary, and, therefore, saving faith involves active, personal trust and the commitment of oneself totally to the Savior. While the apostle Paul denies that good works will save a person, he teaches that faith animates both love and good works. *INTRODUCTION; PARTS 1-7; APPENDIX (G).* (See also *OBEDIENCE TO THE GOSPEL/OBEDIENCE OF FAITH; JUSTIFIED BY FAITH; BELIEVE; RIGHTEOUSNESS; MEASURE OF FAITH*)

FATHERS (See *PATRIARCH/FATHER*)

FELLOWSHIP (*koinonia*)—The deepest, highest, and broadest expression of believers' communion with Christ and one another. Such relationships emerge out of the new life in Christ (John 3:1-12) and occur only among those who are "in Christ" (2 Cor. 5:17). This blessed fellowship binds us to Jesus Christ and to one another, and will reach its perfection in our eternal fellowship with the triune God (Rev. 5:9-14; 7:9-17). PARTS 6-7. (See also *COMMUNION; LOVE (philadelphia); RECONCILIATION*)

FINAL DAY (See *FINAL JUDGMENT*)

FINAL JUDGMENT—The occasion when God will reward the righteous and condemn the ungodly. The Final Judgment is universal and includes the living and the resurrected dead. While Paul sees the Final Judgment as in the future, he understands that it has already begun—the *already/not yet* biblical structure. God, through Christ, will be the Judge of all humankind. God has ordained Christ to be the judge of the living and the dead (Acts 10:42; 17:31; 2 Tim. 4:1). The Final Judgment will determine the Christian's reward but not his or her salvation. Christians will not be judged before the Great White Throne of God with the unsaved because their names are written in the Book of Life (Rev. 20:11-15). For the unsaved, judgment will be based entirely on works. PARTS 1-6. (See also *GOD AS JUDGE; JUDGMENT BY GOD/GOD'S JUDGMENT; JUDGMENT SEAT OF GOD*)

FIRSTFRUIT—A term that describes the products of human labor, especially those that come from the soil at the beginning of the harvest, such as grain, flour, and fruit. The term is used figuratively in the New Testament. The first converts to Christ were described as *firstfruits* (Rom. 16:5; 1 Cor. 16:15), and the works of the Spirit are also described as *firstfruits* (Rom. 8:23). PARTS 4-5, 7. (See also *OLIVE TREE, THE*)

FLESH
1. **Sinful living**—Life "in the flesh" implies sinful living, the results of relying on human strength (flesh), which is weak, rather than relying on God. Paul discusses this kind of lifestyle in contrast to life in the Spirit and describes it as walking "according to the flesh" (Rom. 8:4-11). Existence in the flesh is not the same as having a physical body. Flesh is a power that gives rise to sinful passions, ungodly desires for honor, and excessive zeal for keeping the law and forcing others to observe it. A highly religious person may be motivated by the flesh (Gal. 1:13-14). (See also *CARNAL; SIN; UNGODLINESS; BODY OF SIN/BODY OF DEATH; OLD MAN; UNDER SIN; FREEDOM FROM SIN; HOLY LIVING*)
2. **Physical body or lineage**—In some passages, *flesh* may refer to the physical body (Rom. 2:28) or to lineage (1:3; 4:1).
3. **Natural human limitations**—Humans with the weaknesses of their mortal bodies cannot inherit the kingdom of God through their own efforts (1 Cor. 15:50). They must rely on God. PARTS 1-6

FOREKNOWLEDGE—The foresight of an all-knowing God. Scripture presents God as knowing all things past, present, and future. It also describes humans as having freedom and moral responsibility. No attempt is made in the Bible to explain this mystery. PARTS 4-5. (See also *PREDESTINATION*)

Glossary

FORGIVENESS
1. **Forgiveness by God—God's act of pardon or remission of sin.** Divine forgiveness is accomplished by faith and repentance as part of God's program of salvation and results in the restoration of fellowship with God. The ground for the forgiveness of sin is the death of Christ. *INTRODUCTION; OVERVIEW; PARTS 1-7.* (See also *CONFESS; REPENTANCE/PENITENCE; FREEDOM IN CHRIST; FREEDOM FROM SIN; JUSTIFICATION; RECONCILIATION*)
2. **Forgiveness of Humans for Each Other—Our response to God's forgiveness of our own sins by our becoming loving and forgiving toward others.** To forgive is to be merciful, releasing others to God and from obligation to us for the wrongs that they have committed against us. It is, however, a mistake to think that *forgiveness* requires us to allow any kind of wrongdoing to go unchallenged and uncorrected, such as the abuse of women and children. *PART 6; APPENDIX (G).* (See also *RECONCILIATION*)

FREEDOM FROM SIN—Putting out of operation the dominion of sin in the life of the believer. It is liberation from the human plight of servitude to sin. The Holy Spirit is the power behind making *freedom from sin* a reality. *PART 4.* (See also *SIN; FREEDOM IN CHRIST; FORGIVENESS; HOLY; HOLY LIVING*)

FREEDOM IN CHRIST—A supernatural blessing which delivers believers from destructive influence, such as sin, Satan, power of darkness, and condemnation by the law. This freedom is the grace that Christ preached (Luke 4:16ff.) and offered. *PARTS 4, 6.* (See also *FREEDOM FROM SIN; FORGIVENESS; JESUS CHRIST*)

FRUIT OF THE SPIRIT—A cluster of gracious virtues produced by the Holy Spirit in the life of the Christian (Gal. 5:22-23; Eph. 5:9). The result is a Christlike life evident in one's words and deeds, including one's loving treatment of others. *PART 6.* (See also *LOVE (agape); HOLY LIVING; GIFT OF THE SPIRIT*)

GENTILES—A biblical term used to describe people who were not Jews. Paul at times in his letter to the Romans, rather than referring to Jews and Gentiles, refers to Jews and Greeks (Rom. 1:14, 16; 2:9-10; 3:9; 10:12). In his day, the term *Gentiles* was considered to be a more disparaging term among general society. Most likely, in order to avoid the negative connotation at points in his correspondence, Paul chose the designation *Greeks* instead. Today the use of the term *Gentiles* is simply used to designate people who are not born into the Jewish heritage or who have not converted to the religion of Judaism. *OVERVIEW; PARTS 1-7.* (See also *JEWS/ISRAELITES/HEBREWS*)

GIFT—The basic meaning is gratuity, a free gift. In the New Testament, the term *gift* signifies God's supreme gift of His Son to humankind (John 3:16; 2 Cor. 9:15). Furthermore, the Holy Spirit is the promised gift of the Father, sent by His Son to believers (Acts 2:33, 38). *PARTS 3-6.* (See also *GIFT OF THE SPIRIT*)

GIFT OF THE SPIRIT
1. **The Spirit in Salvation—The reception and work of the Spirit in salvation,** which includes *calling* (Rom. 8:30; 1 Cor. 1:9), *new birth/*

regeneration, John 3:2ff.; 4:14; 7:37-39), *adoption* (Rom. 8:15-16; Gal. 4:5), *sanctification* (Rom. 8:3-4; 15:16), and *resurrection* (8:11). (See also *HOLY SPIRIT/THE SPIRIT; BAPTISM INTO JESUS CHRIST; CALLED BY GOD; SALVATION*)
   2. **Baptism (Immersion) in the Spirit—An additional blessing received subsequent to one's salvation**—referred to as "baptism" or "immersion" in the Spirit (Acts 2:38; 10:45; 19:1-7). *PART 3.* (See also *HOLY SPIRIT/THE SPIRIT; BAPTISM IN THE SPIRIT; SPEAKING IN TONGUES*)
   3. **Spiritual Gift for Christian Service (*Charisma*, plural *Charismata*)**—A special gift given to individuals to empower them to do Christian service in the body of Christ and world (Rom. 1:11; 12:6; 1 Cor. 12:4, 9, 28, 30-31; 1 Tim. 4:14; 2 Tim. 1:6; 1 Peter 4:10). *PARTS 1, 6.* (See also *HOLY SPIRIT/THE SPIRIT; CALLED BY GOD; FRUIT OF THE SPIRIT*)

GIVING, GIFT OF—A gift of the Spirit that enables a believer to share his or her resources for the benefit of others, whether food, clothing, money, or possessions. *PART 6*

GLORIFICATION OF HUMANS (See *GLORY—GLORIFICATION OF HUMANS*)

GLORIFY (See *GLORY—GLORY TO GOD*)

GLORY
   1. **Glory of God**
      - **The sum total of God's perfections (attributes).** The term refers to God's splendor, brilliance, awesomeness, and majesty. It represents a manifestation of God's presence. Christ in the believer is the hope of glory (Col. 1:27), and in heaven the believer will be more conformed to the glorified Savior. (See also *DIVINE ATTRIBUTES*)
      - **A special manifestation of God.** It is not limited to some outward sign, but expresses God's inherent majesty such as Isaiah's vision in which the prophet perceived the holiness of God (6:1-3).
   2. **Glory to God—An act of praise and worship by human beings for God.** To give glory to God (glorify God) is to take delight in His majesty, power, and presence. (See also *WORSHIP*)
   3. **Glorification of Humans—The resurrection state of the believer.** To some extent, the believer shares now in glory (2 Cor. 3:18; 4:6). In the future state, the believer will have a new body on the order of Christ's glorified body (Phil. 3:21). *PARTS 2-7*

GOD/GODHEAD—**The spiritual entity and social being comprised of three persons: Father, Son, and Holy Spirit, who is all-powerful, all-knowing, infinite, eternal, and unchangeable in being, wisdom, and glory.** The Bible stresses God has revealed Himself in His creation, human conscience, and historical events. The divine disclosure reached its climax in Jesus Christ. The decisive source of the knowledge of God is the prophetic-apostolic witness of the Bible. The Old Testament hints at the one God existing in three persons; but in the New Testament, that teaching becomes clear. The word *Godhead* refers to the sum-total of the divine attributes (characteristics) common to all three divine persons (Father, Son, and Holy Spirit). Many of God's attributes can be seen in the world around us (Ps. 19:1-3; Rom. 1:19-20). *INTRODUCTION; OVERVIEW; PARTS 1-7.* (See also *GOD, THE FATHER; GOD, THE SON; JESUS CHRIST; HOLY SPIRIT/THE SPIRIT; DIVINE ATTRIBUTES; HOLY*)

Glossary

GOD, THE FATHER / THE CREATOR—God is Father and the Creator (originator and maker) of all things in the universe. God is Father to humankind by creation (Acts 17:28-29), Father of Israel (Isa. 63:16) because He created the nation, Father of Christ in a special sense because His Son is a revelation of the Father (Matt. 11:27; John 14:6-7), and Father of believers because they are children of God (Rom. 8:15). The term *Father* indicates a relationship. PARTS 1-7. (See also GOD/GODHEAD; LORD OF SABAOTH; GOD, THE SON)

GOD, THE HOLY SPIRIT (See HOLY SPIRIT/THE SPIRIT)

GOD, THE SON—A title indicating that Jesus shares the nature of God, united in being with the Father. The Son and the Father are one (John 5:19, 30) in will (4:34; 6:38), in activity (14:10), and in giving eternal life (10:28-30). The church knew Jesus as the *Son of God* (Acts 9:20; Rom. 1:3-6; Gal. 2:20), worshiped Him as *Lord* (Acts 2:36; Rom. 10:9-13), and applied to Him the title *Lord* (*Jehovah*) used for God in the Old Testament (Phil. 2:10-11; cf. Rom. 14:10-12 and Isa. 45:23; 1 Peter 2:3; cf. Ps. 34:8). Jesus shared the nature of God. He claimed to come from God and spoke of God in a unique personal sense as His *Father* (Matt. 11:25-27). PARTS 1-7. (See also GOD/GODHEAD; JESUS CHRIST; MESSIAH; INCARNATION; GOD, THE FATHER)

GOD AS JUDGE—God is the absolute judge of all the earth (Gen. 18:25; Rom. 3:6). His decisions are without prejudice or partiality. God always judges according to truth (Rom. 2:2) and "will render to each one according to his deeds" (v. 6). His perfect will is the standard of His judgments. OVERVIEW; PARTS 1-6. (See also FINAL JUDGMENT; JUDGMENT BY GOD/GOD'S JUDGMENT; JUSTIFICATION)

GOD'S WRATH (See WRATH OF GOD)

GODLY/UNGODLY—*Godly* people have great respect for God and for sacred things, but the *ungodly* is Paul's picture of all who are without Christ. They are too weak to live a disciplined, godly life and persist in rebellion against God, showing no real respect for Him. PARTS 2-6. (See also HOLY LIVING; UNGODLINESS)

GOOD NEWS (See GOSPEL)

GOSPEL—Good News about Christ and eternal life. The word *gospel* is a noun that comes from the Greek verb *euaggelizo*, which means "to bring good news, to announce glad tidings." **In the Old Testament**, *euaggelizo* was used for any kind of good news about God's kindness—sin in particular, about the blessings and deliverance that the Messiah would bring upon His arrival. **In the New Testament**, *euaggelizo* is used especially of the joyous proclamation of God's redemptive activity in Jesus Christ on behalf of humans enslaved in sin. *Gospel* is also used to refer to the books of the Bible, written by Matthew, Mark, Luke, and John, which contain the story of Jesus Christ and His Good News. INTRODUCTION; OVERVIEW; PARTS 1-7. (See also EVANGELISM; JESUS CHRIST; BIBLE)

GRACE (*charis*)—Unearned favor and blessings from God. Grace (*charis*) emanates from God. Paul uses this term fourteen times in

Romans to characterize what God has done in Christ to save humankind. It is God's grace in Christ that calls us to salvation and sustains us as we live the Christian life by the help of the Holy Spirit and finally will bring us to heaven. *OVERVIEW; PARTS 1-7.* (See also *MERCY OF GOD*)

GREEKS (See *GENTILES*)

GROAN—There are several uses of the word groan in the Bible:
1. **Oppression**—In the Old Testament, *groaning* is a sign of oppression and bondage and of the hope of deliverance (Ex. 2:23f.; 6:5; Ps. 6:6).
2. **Holy Spirit**—The Spirit *groans* on our behalf, clearly indicating the Spirit's prayerful intercession on behalf of believers. Believers do not pray alone, for the Spirit comes alongside and helps them (Rom. 8:26-27). *PART 4.* (See also *INTERCESSION*)
3. **God's Creation**—Creation now utters concerted *groans* because it is under the burden of the consequences of man's sin and is waiting with eager longing for deliverance from that burden (Rom. 8:19-22). *PART 4*

HEBREW BIBLE (See *BIBLE*)

HELPER (*prostatis*)—A person who has the gifted ministry of helping others. Such a person is the source of assistance that benefits believers in terms of fellowship, finances, and hospitality. *PART 7.* (See also *SERVICE*)

HELPS, GIFT OF (See *SERVICE*)

HOLY
1. **Applied to God—God's separation from sin in any form or degree.** To refer to "the Almighty God as *holy*" speaks of His supremacy, majesty, and awesome glory, as well as His perfection and spotlessness in ethical character (Lev. 11:44; 1 Peter 1:16). *PARTS 1-7.* (See also *DIVINE ATTRIBUTES; RIGHTEOUSNESS*)
2. **Applied to the Law and God's Word—The sacred nature of God's law and word.** As the primary author of the Scriptures, God's recorded word has a divine quality of its own. Holy people were moved by the Holy Spirit of God (2 Peter 1:21), and as they spoke or wrote, they gave forth heavenly instructions and truth. *PARTS 1, 4-5.* (See also *BIBLE; LAW, the Torah*)
3. **Applied to humans—God sets individuals or groups apart to serve Him, and as a result they have a holy standing.** At a deeper level, these people, through God's help and their obedience, become *holy in character*. In the New Testament, God gives a *holy standing* to those people who are joined to Christ by faith, and they are to endeavor through the help of the Holy Spirit to be Christlike in character and actions. *PARTS 1, 4-7.* (See also *SAINTS; HOLY LIVING; SANCTIFICATION; FREEDOM FROM SIN*)

HOLY LIVING—Living according to the teachings and example of Jesus Christ. Through the guidance of the Holy Spirit and the striving for moral excellence, Christians attain to the ideal—holy living (practical sanctification). *PARTS 4, 6; APPENDIX (G).* (See also *HOLY; SANCTIFICATION; FREEDOM FROM SIN; GODLY/UNGODLY; LIVING SACRIFICE; FRUIT OF THE SPIRIT*)

Glossary

HOLY SPIRIT/THE SPIRIT—The third person of the Godhead. The Spirit is equal to and works with the Father and the Son, calling people to Christ and His saving grace, bestowing spiritual gifts, and giving guidance, power, and peace for the Christian life. The New Testament writers describe that there are many works of the Spirit and indicate that the Spirit comes to us with unique and extraordinary power. The Spirit was a powerful presence in the ministry of Jesus and of the early Christians. He gives believers a new form of life (Gal. 5:22-23) and bestows on them special and diverse gifts for service and ministry (Rom. 12:6-8; 1 Cor. 12:7-11, 28-31; 2 Cor. 13:14; 1 Peter 1:2). *INTRODUCTION; OVERVIEW; PARTS 1-7.* (See also *GOD/GODHEAD; BAPTISM IN THE SPIRIT; GIFT OF THE SPIRIT; PENTECOST/DAY OF PENTECOST*)

HOLY TRINITY (See *GOD/GODHEAD*)

HOPE—Confidence that God will do what He has promised. The focus of hope is on the future. God has given His people hope through the gospel (Col. 1:23); and by Christ indwelling them through the Holy Spirit, they have "hope of glory" (v. 27). Hope is oriented toward the future, but is not merely human expectation for better days. Biblical hope anticipates the consummation of salvation in the resurrection and the second coming of Jesus. This hope is variously described as "laid up for you in heaven" (v. 5), "hope of eternal life" (Titus 1:2), and "living hope" (1 Peter 1:3). It is also associated with patience and adversities. *PARTS 3-4, 6.* (See also *PROMISE; PERSEVERANCE*)

HOSPITALITY (*philoxenia*)—Compassion and generosity expressed toward others. In the biblical world, hospitality was focused primarily toward aliens, travelers, strangers, and those in need. A few examples: in the Old Testament—Abraham and Lot (Gen. 18:2-8; 19:1-8); in the New Testament—Jesus' parable of the good Samaritan (Luke 10:25-37). Hospitality ("the love of strangers") is treated as a Christian virtue (Rom. 12:13) and is a Christian duty (1 Peter 4:9). *PART 6*

HUMILITY—The essence of saving faith that excludes pride regarding one's race, religion, social status, or person. According to the teachings of Christ, a child provides the model for humility (Matt. 18:1-4). *PART 6.* (See also *MEASURE OF FAITH; STRONG IN FAITH/WEAK IN FAITH; SELF-RIGHTEOUSNESS*)

IMPUTATION OF RIGHTEOUSNESS—An act of God by which the believer is declared righteous before the holy God. It is a divine reckoning and forgiveness of sin. Believers are declared justified by faith. Abraham and David are examples in the Old Testament. *PART 3.* (See also *ACCOUNT/IMPUTE; JUSTIFICATION; FORGIVENESS; RIGHTEOUSNESS*)

IMPUTATION OF SIN—God's holding humans accountable for their sins. It is the opposite of being declared righteous and forgiven of sin. God holds humans responsible for doing wrong. *PART 3.* (See also *ACCOUNT/IMPUTE; CONDEMNATION*)

IMPUTE (See *ACCOUNT/IMPUTE*)

INCARNATION—The once-and-for-all action by which the eternal Son of God (second person of the Godhead) became a man (John 1:14).

Being born as a man, He was fully God and fully man. That is, He thought, willed, and acted as God, and He thought, willed, and acted as man. In His earthy life He had all the divine attributes and was completely identified with humankind except He was free of sin. (See also GOD, THE SON; JESUS CHRIST)

INTERCESSION
1. **Intercession by the Holy Spirit—The Spirit lends assistance for believers in their weakness in prayer (Rom. 8:26-27).** Believers are capable of praying, but may not know how to pray for exact needs. Vital is the Spirit's prayerful intercession for them. PART 4. (See also GROAN)
2. **Intercession by Jesus Christ—At the right hand of God, the risen Christ intercedes on behalf of believers (Heb. 7:25).** Christ and the Holy Spirit, as well as believers, are in the position to converse with the heavenly Father, who hears and is attentive to them and the needs they express. We need Christ's intercession because His prayers assure us that He is not in heaven to condemn us, but to help us. PART 4. (See also JESUS CHRIST)

INVISIBLE ATTRIBUTES (See DIVINE ATTRIBUTES)

ISRAEL
1. **Personal Name for Jacob—A personal name divinely bestowed on the biblical patriarch Jacob and is interpreted as meaning one who "struggled with God" (Gen. 32:28).**
2. **Chosen People—*Israel* became the covenant name for the descendants of Jacob, whom God chose to be His people.** The name was applied collectively and nationally to the twelve tribes, identifying them as either the *children* or *sons* of Israel.
3. **Nation of Israel—*Israel* is also a modern designation for a republic founded in 1948 in Palestine, on the eastern seaboard of the Mediterranean Sea.** PARTS 1-7. (See also JEWS/ISRAELITES/HEBREWS; CHOSEN BY GOD; COVENANT)

JESUS CHRIST—The Son of God who suffered and died for the sins of humankind (Mark 1:1; 15:33-39). The double name "Jesus Christ" implies the life story of Jesus of Nazareth. Without ceasing to be what He had been eternally, Jesus came into this world as a human being. He submitted Himself to be born as a baby with all the limitations and sufferings of this life on earth, so that He could demonstrate His love for us. The name given to God's Son before His birth was *Jesus*, meaning "the Lord is salvation." After His resurrection, it became a common practice to link His human name *Jesus* with the titles *Christ* and *Lord*. The word *Christ* is the equivalent of the Hebrew word *Messiah*, meaning "the Anointed One." The early Christians did not hesitate to acknowledge Jesus as the *Christ*. Peter's sermon on the Day of Pentecost affirmed Jesus as "both Lord and Christ," thereby identifying Him as deity (Acts 2:36). The resurrection of Jesus declared Him to be the Son of God, the Christ of God (Rom. 1:4; Phil. 2:9-11). INTRODUCTION; OVERVIEW; PARTS 1-7. (See also MESSIAH; GOD, THE SON; LORD; GOD/GODHEAD; INCARNATION; CROSS, THE; GOSPEL)

**JEWS/ISRAELITES/HEBREWS—The *Jews* were Abraham's descendants, who were also called *Hebrews* or *Israelites*. The term *Jews*

Glossary

refers to national origin, while the term *Israelites* indicates membership in the covenant community based on God's promises to Jacob. In Scripture, Abraham is the first person spoken of as a **Hebrew** (Gen. 14:13), apparently because his ancestor was *Eber* (11:16-26). The term must have a covenantal meaning since Moses spoke of God as "the God of the Hebrews" (Ex. 5:3; 7:16; 9:1). Early on, the term *Jews* referred to the descendants of Judah, but over time came to be applied to all *Israelites*. Paul properly called himself a Jew. God chose the nation of *Israel* to be a kingdom of priests and to teach other nations about Himself. All other nations in the Bible are referred to as *Gentiles*. INTRODUCTION; OVERVIEW; PARTS 1-7. (See also ISRAEL; GENTILES)

JUDGMENT BY GOD/GOD'S JUDGMENT—Being held accountable by God for one's wrongdoings (sins). For those who reject Christ's love and salvation, divine judgment will hold them accountable for their sins. Whatever good they have done will not be sufficient for their salvation. For followers of Christ, their sins were judged at the cross, and there remains only the evaluation of their works and their rewards for faithfulness, since Christ suffered and died in their place. OVERVIEW, PARTS 1-6. (See also GOD AS JUDGE; WRATH OF GOD; CONDEMNATION; FINAL JUDGMENT; JUDGMENT SEAT OF GOD; JUSTIFICATION)

JUDGMENT BY HUMANS—In the New Testament, the verb *judge* has two meanings:
1. **One Person's Judgment of Another—To condemn or harshly criticize.** Scripture forbids us from taking a self-righteous spiritual attitude toward others, hypocritically judging or harshly criticizing them (Matt. 7:1; Rom. 2:1). Some in the Roman church were judging the Gentiles' spiritual condition by setting themselves up as God (a type of idolatry) and assuming that they had the right to determine the destiny of the Gentiles. PARTS 2, 6. (See also SELF-RIGHTEOUSNESS; HUMILITY; STRONG IN FAITH/WEAK IN FAITH)
2. **Judgment of Spiritual Matters—To distinguish or discern (John 7:24).** Jesus' use of the term, as recorded in the Gospel of John, indicates that we are responsible for evaluating or discerning certain matters in life. PARTS 2, 7

JUDGMENT DAY (See *FINAL JUDGMENT*)

JUDGMENT SEAT OF GOD—A raised place or stage from which God, as Judge, issues official verdicts. "Judgment seat of God" is a way of speaking of the reality of divine judgment. The word *seat* (*bema*) is used in Romans 14:10 "of God" (NASB) and in 2 Corinthians 5:10 "of Christ." PART 6. (See also JUDGMENT BY GOD/GOD'S JUDGMENT; FINAL JUDGMENT)

JUSTIFICATION (*dikaiosune*)—God's act of declaring a person to be righteous. The word *justification* is a noun that comes from the Greek verb *dikaioo*. *Justification* is the act through which God pronounces one righteous. Through the grace and forgiveness of Christ, God puts a person in right standing with Himself. This right relationship and standing is the condition that God desires for all people whom He has created. The process of justification includes God's forgiving sin by declaring or pronouncing a person to be just and righteous in His sight on the condition of faith in Christ.

The two terms *righteousness* and *justification* both can be a translation of the same Greek word (*dikaiosune*). Justification is God's gracious action of accepting individuals as *righteous* as a result of their faith in His saving work in Christ. At the heart of *justification* is the idea that God treats sinners as though they are not sinners. INTRODUCTION; OVERVIEW; PARTS 1-6; APPENDIX (F). (See also RIGHTEOUSNESS; PROPITIATION; JUSTIFIED BY FAITH; FORGIVENESS; IMPUTATION OF RIGHTEOUSNESS; SALVATION)

JUSTIFIED BY FAITH (*dikaioo*)—The condition of having been forgiven and pardoned by God due to one's trusting in Christ for salvation. INTRODUCTION; OVERVIEW; PARTS 1-6. (See also JUSTIFICATION; FAITH)

JUSTIFY GOD—Declaring God to be right. To justify God is to acknowledge that He is just and His ways are right. PART 2

KINGDOM OF GOD—The rule and reign of God. God's kingdom is the realm in which His rule is exercised. At the present, the church realm is primarily where God reigns, but the Kingdom has both a present (Luke 11:20) and a future dimension (Matt. 6:10; 25:31-46). Christ's life and death were the in-breaking of God's redemptive rule, but at the end of the Current Age we expect the culmination and victory of the divine rule. Never is the essence of God's kingdom eating and drinking, but it is the life through the presence and power of the Holy Spirit. PART 6

LAST DAY (See END TIMES)

LAW, THE (*Torah*)—Sacred Scriptures recorded in the Hebrew Bible (Old Testament) that give Jewish religious rules for living and authoritative regulations, specifying the relationship between God and His people. The Law (*Torah*) was delivered by an authorized spokesman, such as Moses, a prophet, or priest. The moral law, essentially summarized in the Ten Commandments, had a prominent place in biblical revelation. OVERVIEW; PARTS 2- 6. (See also ORACLES OF GOD; BIBLE)

LEADERSHIP, GIFT OF (verb–"lead," *proistemi*)—A gift of the Holy Spirit, giving one the authority to lead and to provide guidance in the church (Rom. 12:8). The Bible is clear that in addition to following leaders, people need to depend on the Lord for guidance (Ps. 24:4-5, 9). The Holy Spirit guides God's people directly (John 16:13-15; Rom. 8:14, and also uses individuals to lead His people (Ex. 6:13; 1 Chron. 11:1-3; Acts 26:16-18; Eph. 4:11-15). PART 6. (See also SERVICE)

LEGALISM—Having hope for salvation based on human effort, rather than relying on God's grace. The term *legalism* is not found in either the Old or New Testaments, but the concept of persons trying to earn salvation through excessive devotion to the law appears throughout the Bible. Thinking that salvation can be earned by strict adherence to a moral code, the legalist tries to win God's favor and get to heaven by doing good works. OVERVIEW; PART 4. (See also LAW, The Torah; FAITH)

LIFE/ETERNAL LIFE—A quality of being and living which is derived from God and is eternal. Such life is imparted to those who follow

Glossary

Christ in faith (Rom. 6:4; 1 John 5:12) and extends into eternity beyond physical death. The word *life* may refer to physical life (Acts 17:25; 1 Cor. 15:19) or to God's life (Rom. 5:10: Eph. 4:18). As a quality from God, it is the life of Christ in the believer (2 Cor. 4:10-11) and is received through faith (John 3:16). This life is a present possession (5:24) and is eternal (6:51). *PARTS 1-7.* (See also *SALVATION; DEATH*)

LIVING SACRIFICE—The placing of one's life on God's altar in daily life; that is, living one's whole life for God. The word *living* implies a bloodless sacrifice and emphasizes daily submission to the lordship of God. Christians do not offer animal sacrifices to God but, rather, offer themselves and their conduct to Him. *PART 6.* (See also *HOLY LIVING*)

LORD—A term that expresses the nature of deity as the Sovereign of heaven and earth. The New Testament writers apply *Lord* to Jesus as a divine title, which identifies Him as God and as having divine authority and glory. His divine nature and authority call for us to worship Him and to render obedient service to Him. *PARTS 1-7.* (See also *JESUS CHRIST; GOD/GODHEAD*)

LORD OF SABAOTH, THE—Lord of Hosts; God of all beings and forces, which He created and maintains. *PART 5.* (See also *GOD, THE FATHER*)

LOVE (*agape*)—The expression of God's good will and mercy for everyone, initiated and lived by deliberate choice, rather than by mere emotions or affection. God is the source of *agape love*, and without Him, this Christian love is impossible. *Agape love* "is the bond of perfection," binding all things together in perfect unity (Col. 3:14), and in itself is the fulfillment of the law (Rom. 13:10). The word *agape* describes a new attitude, a new quality of life that is only made possible through fellowship with God. *Love* is a fruit of the Spirit (Gal. 5:22-23) and is manifested among devoted Christians. Rather than an emotion or feeling, Christian love, being patterned after God's love, has the ability to love the unlovely and unlovable and even our enemies. *Agape love* involves a double relationship and a double commitment—relationship with Christ and a relationship with humankind; a commitment to Christ and a commitment to humankind. Love is not passive; it calls for intention and action. Paul told the Christians at Colosse to "put on love" (Col. 3:14). We speak of a person putting on a garment, but the Christian is to be clothed in the beauty of sincere good will toward all people. *PARTS 3, 6.* (See also *FRUIT OF THE SPIRIT; DIVINE ATTRIBUTES*)

LOVE (*philadelphia*)—Love of believers for one another. Initially, *philadelphia* referred to familial love; but in the New Testament, it extends beyond the family to include fellow believers (1 Thess. 4:9-10). This affectionate reality is to stand in opposition to cliques among members of a Christian congregation. *PART 6.* (See also *FELLOWSHIP; CHURCH*)

MEASURE OF FAITH—A standard by which a Christian is to estimate himself/herself. A realistic appraisal of ourselves prevents us from thinking too highly or lowly of ourselves. The reference is not to miracle-working faith of 1 Corinthians 13:2 since Paul's exhortation is to all the Roman Christians. The gift of miracle-working faith is only given to some (1 Cor. 12:7-10). Every Christian has a charismatic gift (vv. 7, 11).

Paul was aware of the dangers of pride in regards to one's gifts, so he warns against conceit and condescension (Rom. 12:3ff.). *PART 6*. (See also *HUMILITY; FAITH*)

MERCY, GIFT OF—**A Spirit-given capacity to express empathy in concrete ways to those who are in need, such as caring for the sick, providing for the poor, and tending to the elderly and those with disabilities.** *PART 6*

MERCY OF GOD—**A characteristic or attribute of God that expresses God's love and compassion to those who are in trouble and victims of sin.** The supreme expression of God's mercy was God's provision of salvation at Calvary. *PARTS 2-3, 5-6*. (See also *GRACE*)

MESSIAH—**The Anointed One.** In its early usage, *messiah* often referred to a high priest as God's anointed (Lev. 4:3, 5, 16) or to a king as the Lord's anointed (1 Sam. 26:11; Ps. 89:20). The Old Testament prophets spoke about a specially anointed One who was to come from the throne of David and who would have an eternal government in an unlimited rule (Isa. 9:2-7; Mic. 5:2). The New Testament writers later declared that such prophecies were fulfilled in the first coming of Jesus, the Messiah. *PART 5*. (See also *JESUS CHRIST; GOD, THE SON*)

MINISTRY, GIFT OF (See *SERVICE*)

MISSIONARY—**A person who is especially sent by God to preach the gospel and to do the work of the church.** Such ministry springs from love and obedience to Jesus Christ. The greatest of the early missionaries was Paul, the apostle to the Gentile world. He traveled over land and sea preaching the gospel. His three missionary journeys recorded in Acts are models of missionary work. *OVERVIEW; APPENDICES (B, C, D, E)*. (See also *EVANGELIZE; GOSPEL*)

MORAL PRACTICES/AMORAL PRACTICES
- *Moral Practices*—**practices that are ethically correct according to the laws of God**
- *Amoral Practices*—**belief or behaviors that are morally neutral; not moral or immoral** The weaker in faith among the Roman Christians were committed to Old Testament food regulations and vegetarianism. These kind of beliefs and practices were morally neutral and were of minor significance. They could be observed without jeopardizing the integrity of the faith. If their observance is insisted on, amoral practices can become divisive in the church. *PART 6*. (See also *STRONG IN FAITH/WEAK IN FAITH*)

NEIGHBOR (*heteros/plesion*)—**Any person, regardless of nationality, ethnicity, or religious background, with whom one has a relationship or happens to encounter.** In the Old Testament, a *neighbor* (*plesion*) was a fellow Israelite (Prov. 27:10; Jer. 31:34; Hab. 2:15), but Jesus broadened the word *plesion* to mean anyone in need (Luke 10:25-37). Paul refers to the person who is being loved as "another" (*heteros*): "He who loves another has fulfilled the law" (Rom. 13:8). In verses 8-10, *neighbor* and *another* are used interchangeably and refer to the love of believers beyond one's small circle, opening the door to the discussion of the strong and the weak in 14:1—16:23. *PART 6*

Glossary

NEW TESTAMENT (See *BIBLE*)

OBEDIENCE TO THE GOSPEL/OBEDIENCE OF FAITH—A positive response and true respect for God's redemptive activity in Christ on behalf of humankind. The gospel is glad news which tells about Christ and His saving work. When it is obeyed (believed), the gospel becomes the power of God for salvation (Rom. 1:16). *PARTS 4-5, 7.* (See also *BELIEVE; FAITH*)

OLD AGE, THE (See *THIS AGE/THE COMING AGE; THE TWO AGES*)

OLD MAN—The sinful self. It is the self that is dominated by sin and is crucified at the moment of conversion. *Old man* refers to the part of ourselves that is dominated by sin and then dies at the moment of conversion. At that point, the tyranny and domination of sin is broken within those who believe in Christ. Dying and rising with Christ is the end of dominion of sin and is the foundation of the new life in Christ. Believers are no longer enslaved to sin and death. The phrase *old man* is closely related to "the body of sin," which indicates being under the rule of sin. *PART 4.* (See also *SIN; SINNER; UNDER SIN; UNGODLINESS; BODY OF SIN/BODY OF DEATH; FLESH; FREEDOM FROM SIN; FREEDOM IN CHRIST*)

OLD TESTAMENT (See *BIBLE*)

OLIVE TREE, THE—A metaphor for Israel. This tree, including root and branches, represents Israel. Israel's existence provided the vehicle by which the Christian church came into existence. In the olive-tree metaphor, some of the natural branches of the garden olive became broken off (those Jewish people who did not accept Jesus as their Messiah), and wild branches (Gentiles who followed Christ) were miraculously grafted in. Extraordinary benefits have come to the Christian church because of its connection to and participation with Israel. God's ultimate plan is to one day reunite all of His people who believe (both Jews and Gentiles). The Jews will be restored alongside Gentile believers to the holy olive tree. Through His power, God is able to transform both Jews and Gentiles by the miracle of grace. *PART 5.* (See also *FIRSTFRUIT*)

ORACLES OF GOD—Hebrew Scriptures. In Jewish writings, refers to the Old Testament. *PART 2.* (See also *LAW, The Torah; BIBLE*)

ORDINANCE OF GOD—Something that God has put into place, such as governmental authority appointed and ordained by God. God's ordinance of government is the basis for submission to governmental authority, even for Christians, because it is an authority willed by God. Such submission expresses Christians' relation to God. Paul, in expressing the importance of respect for civil government, does not lose sight of Christian freedom in Christ (Eph. 5:21), which may call for disobeying civil law when it violates God's law. *PART 6*

PATRIARCH/FATHER—Head or founder of a family or tribe. The term is used to describe Jewish ancestors prior to the time of Moses. The New Testament identifies Abraham, the twelve sons of Jacob, and David as patriarchs. *PART 5*

PATRON, ROMAN—**The Roman social structure in which a wealthy or influential person helped an institutional cause or individual.** A master in ancient times could free slaves and retain social rights over them, an arrangement that benefited them both. PART 7

PEACE (Hebrew, *shalom*; Greek, *eirene*)—**A condition of being whole or of being complete and sound.** The Greek verb *to be at peace* (*eireneuo*) can be static, meaning "to be complete"; or it can be dynamic, meaning "to live well," or to reconcile those who are quarreling. The Greek noun *peace* (*eirene*) refers to a right relationship or harmony between two groups or people, often established by a covenant. The Hebrew word for *peace (shalom)*, which is quite broad in usage, has greatly influenced the Greek word for *peace* (*eirene*) in the New Testament. PARTS 3, 6-7. (See also RECONCILIATION)

PENITENCE (See REPENTANCE/PENITENCE)

PENTECOST/DAY OF PENTECOST—**One of the three major feasts in early Israel. It was also known as the Feast of Harvest, the Feast of Weeks, and the Feast of Pentecost.** This feast was celebrated in early summer, fifty days or seven weeks after the first day of unleavened bread. On the first Pentecost after the resurrection of Jesus, the Holy Spirit was poured out on the church. This event was the beginning of the fulfillment of Joel's prophecy (Joel 2:28-29). PART 3. (See also HOLY SPIRIT/THE SPIRIT; BAPTISM IN THE SPIRIT)

PERSEVERANCE—**The supreme value of fortitude and endurance despite the disadvantages caused by circumstances.** A person who perseveres does so through the grace of God, receiving courage to continue in affliction and suffering. PART 3. (See also HOPE)

POSITIONAL SANCTIFICATION (See SANCTIFICATION)

POWER (*dunamis*)—**The ability to perform.** In the New Testament, God manifested His power in Christ. Paul recognized the preaching of the cross as the power of God (1 Cor. 1:23-24) and that God's power succeeds in saving humans who have faith in Christ. The gospel as God's power is capable of achieving its purpose, the salvation of souls (v. 18). PART 1

POWERS AND PRINCIPALITIES (See PRINCIPALITIES AND POWERS)

PRACTICAL SANCTIFICATION (See SANCTIFICATION)

PRAY/PRAYER—**An element of worship, and the communication between God and His people.** True prayer is spiritual, emphasizing the inwardness of communion with the heavenly Father. Jesus directs believers to pray with perseverance and in faith (Mark 11:20-24; Luke 18:1-8). PARTS 1, 4, 6-7; APPENDIX (G). (See also WORSHIP)

PREACH—**To proclaim God's Word.** True preaching is done by a person who has received his or her assignment and message from God. In the New Testament, the primary message is the historical fact of Christ's life, death, resurrection, ascension, and return to earth, linked with the call to repentance and faith. OVERVIEW; PARTS 5-7. (See also CALLED BY GOD)

Glossary

PREDESTINATION—Divine foreordination of the future. Scripture leaves this doctrine undeveloped and does not teach that God determines the actions of an individual in advance. Both *foreknowledge* and *predestination* refer to the fact that God has an eternal plan which He has carried out by making provision for the salvation of all who receive Christ. *PART 4.* (See also *FOREKNOWLEDGE; CALLED BY GOD; ELECT OF GOD; CHOSEN BY GOD*)

PRINCIPALITIES AND POWERS—Demonic forces and agencies. The overthrow of these opposing powers reached its climax at the cross (Col. 2:15). Though defeated, Paul describes the present struggle of Christians against these demonic powers (Eph. 6:12). *PART 4.* (See also *EVIL*)

PROMISE—In Scripture, that which God declares that He will bring to pass. There is a wide range of divine promises, beginning with Genesis 3:15 and including: God's covenant with Israel, especially with Abraham, remedying the distance that had occurred between God and His people (Jer. 31:31-34); the outpouring of the Holy Spirit (Joel 2:28-32); and ultimately, new heavens and earth (Isa. 65:17; 66:22). God fulfills His promises through Christ: "For no matter how many promises God has made, they are 'Yes' in Christ. And so through him the 'Amen' is spoken by us to the glory of God" (2 Cor. 1:20 NIV). *PARTS 3, 5.* (See also *COVENANT; HOPE*)

PROPHECY—A message from the Holy Spirit given directly to a prophet. The message may be a prediction of the future, or it may have to do with present issues and local matters. The gift of prophecy is a gift of the Spirit, which gives edification, exhortation, and comfort (1 Cor. 14:1, 3). The word prophet was used to describe God's messengers prior to Jesus Christ's birth, as well as to describe people in the early church through today who have been prompted by the Holy Spirit to communicate a message from God. Such a message always agrees with God's written word recorded in the Bible. *PARTS 5-6.* (See also *REVEALED*)

PROPHECY, GIFT OF—A spiritual gift that enables a believer to speak words inspired by the Holy Spirit. A prophetic message may be predictive, referring to future events, or it may speak to a need or situation in the church at the time. *PART 6*

PROPITIATION—The act of atoning or of satisfying the wrath of God against sin. The need for propitiation arose because the sin of humankind offended the holiness of God. In the New Testament, the cross is the place of propitiation, since there the death of Christ fully satisfied the holy demands of God. In the Old Testament, the place of propitiation is the mercy seat where high priests sprinkled blood in atoning for the peoples' sins. *PART 3.* (See also *REDEMPTION; JUSTIFICATION; CROSS, THE*)

PROSPERITY GOSPEL—An unbiblical emphasis on material prosperity. As a result, pressure is on believers to demonstrate their faith by owning or displaying their culture's material symbols of success—such as owning a fine car, living in an extravagant home, wearing elegant clothes, or taking exotic vacations. How can one reconcile this type of lifestyle with the simple life of our Lord (Matt. 8:20)? For a biblical perspective on the prosperity gospel, 3 John 2 is used as the basic text: "Beloved [Gaius], I pray that you may prosper in all things and be in health, just as your soul prospers." The definition of *prosperity* within the kingdom of God is the growth and the fullness of the fruit of the Spirit within our souls. To extend this prayer for Gaius' prosperity to refer to the financial and material prosperity for all believers is foreign to the meaning of this text. The argument that God wills that all Christians be wealthy is a gross misinterpretation of Scripture. God desires for us an abundance of eternal spiritual riches, such as love, joy, and peace. *PART 7*

PROTESTANT REFORMATION—A Christian religious movement in the sixteenth century under the leadership of Martin Luther's teaching, which resulted in the reconstruction of Western Christianity according to the norms of Scripture and the separation of Protestant churches from the Roman Catholic Church. Opposition from the Roman Catholic leadership led Luther to emphasize the sole authority of the Scriptures and Paul's doctrine of justification through faith. *INTRODUCTION*

PUNISHMENT (See *CONDEMNATION*)

RECONCILIATION (*katallage*)—A restoration of personal relationship between God and human beings (Rom. 5:1-11; 2 Cor. 5:18-21) or between human beings. Through rebellion against God, humankind has forfeited relationship with God; but through Christ, God restores the relationship between Himself and rebellious humans. God initiates the whole reconciling process and it reaches even to His enemies. Humans may now be reconciled to God through faith in Christ. As reconciliation is realized, it also restores peace and fellowship among humankind. *PARTS 3, 5.* (See also *FORGIVENESS; PEACE; FELLOWSHIP*)

REDEMPTION—Deliverance from some form of bondage secured by the payment of a ransom. Throughout the New Testament, redemption is a divine activity; its primary spiritual significance lies in the price that God paid to deliver humankind from the death that sin brings—through the death of His Son Jesus Christ on the cross. *PARTS 3-4.* (See also *PROPITIATION; CROSS, THE*)

REMNANT, THE—*In the Old Testament*, the portion of the Jewish community who truly believed in God and were faithful. *In the New Testament*, in the first century, a minority of Christian believers among the Jewish people. While many Jews continued to rely on keeping the law rather than relying on faith and the grace of Jesus Christ, there was a small number who understood Jesus' message of forgiveness and accepted in faith His free gift of eternal life. The *theology* (*doctrine*) *of the remnant* teaches that there have always been some true believers throughout human history. *PART 5.* (See also *TRUE ISRAEL*)

REPENTANCE/PENITENCE
The two words are closely related in meaning, being used as almost synonyms:
- **Repentance—turning from sin and self-centeredness to God, asking for His forgiveness.**
- *Penitence*—**a deep remorse and contrition for misdeeds or sins and a humbling of oneself, begging for pardon.** *PARTS 2, 6.* (See also *CONFESS; FORGIVENESS*)

Glossary

RESURRECTION—The coming forth from the dead in a resurrected body. The literal resurrection of Christ and the spiritual resurrection of believers have already occurred and should continue to occur as believers live the Christian life, but the literal resurrection of believers will not occur until the return of Christ. PART 4. (See also CROSS, THE)

REVEALED
1. **Revealed/Revelation (verb–*apokaluptetai*)—This verb implies God's divine action to make effective salvation.** God revealed His salvation plan in a historical manner through Christ and the preaching of the gospel. This revealed plan takes effect through the conversion of believers. PARTS 1, 3, 5. (See also GOSPEL)
2. **Revealed/Revelation (verb–*pephanerotai*)—Similar to revealed (*apokaluptetai*), this term emphasizes God's making His truths visible.** God manifested His salvation plan in a public manner through Christ's life and ministry. What was invisible became visible. God's provision of salvation was not done in secret; it was done in a public event—the cross. PART 3. (See also PROPHECY)

RIGHTEOUSNESS (*dikaiosune*)
1. **Righteousness of God/God's Righteousness (God's Nature)—God's good, perfect, and holy nature.** The phrase "that He might be just" (*dikaios*, righteous) (Rom. 3:26) affirms God as being righteous. Paul teaches that God always acts according to His nature, even in providing salvation through the cross. In 14:17, *righteousness* describes the kingdom of God and is a synonym for *holiness*, describing the new life of believers. PARTS 1-3. (See also HOLY; DIVINE ATTRIBUTES)
2. **Righteousness of God/Righteousness of Faith (for Believers)—The state of being in right relationship and standing with God, which is a gift from God to all believers.** God gives to the believer a spiritual and moral quality of life that extends beyond physical death into eternity (2 Cor. 5:4; 2 Tim. 1:10). God's verdict of righteousness declares the ungodly as just or righteous in His sight because of their faith in Christ. The word *righteousness* is a noun that comes from the Greek noun *dikaiosune*. This term refers to God's intention for the state of how a person ought to be, that is, being in true relationship and right standing with God (Rom. 1:17; 3:24; 2 Cor. 5:21; Phil. 3:9). OVERVIEW; PARTS 1- 5. (See also JUSTIFICATION; FAITH; IMPUTATION OF RIGHTEOUSNESS)
3. **Human Righteousness—Humans' personal striving to live according to the law of God.** Righteousness may be thought of in an ethical sense, that is, as derived from keeping law (Phil. 3:9). Paul described it as his own righteousness and as insufficient for salvation. PARTS 1, 4-5. (See also SELF-RIGHTEOUSNESS)
4. **Righteousness in the Holy Spirit—Right living, holy living (Rom. 14:17).** PART 6. (See also HOLY LIVING; SANCTIFICATION)

ROMAN CHURCH (See ROMANS)

ROMANS
Rome—The capital of the Roman Empire, which dominated Europe and the Mediterranean world from 44 BC to AD 1453, commanding

respect of millions of people. Early in the second century, the city of Rome had reached a population of about 1.5 million people. By AD 58, the time period in which Paul wrote his letter to the church in Rome, the people of the Empire had lived under a number of emperors: Augustus (27 BC–AD 14), Tiberius (AD 14-37), Gaius ("Caligula") (AD 37-41), Claudius (AD 41-54), and Nero (AD 54-68). As the Empire grew, commerce flourished as roads were built and travel increased. Most people living in Rome participated in pagan religions, serving the Roman gods, familiar to us today through accounts from Roman mythological literature. There was also a minority of Jews and Christians in the city of Rome and throughout the Empire. Although from time to time there was political unrest among the Romans, generally peace prevailed, which allowed for the preaching of the gospel. OVERVIEW

Roman Church/Christian Church in Rome—The church to whom Paul writes the Book of Romans. The beginning of the church remains unknown. Paul speaks of having long desired to visit the church (Rom. 15:23) and that its faith was well known. Probably the church was established by Jewish missionaries who went to Rome after being converted on the Day of Pentecost (Acts 2:10). The majority of the Roman Christians were Gentiles, many of whom were from the lower strata of society. At the time that Paul wrote to the church, there were also some Jewish Christians among the church members. Paul had a number of friends and acquaintances in the church, although most of the believers in Rome had never met Paul. OVERVIEW; PART 1. (See also CHURCH)

Book of Romans/Letter to the Romans/Epistle to the Romans— Paul's pastoral letter to the Christian church in Rome around AD 58. It is generally agreed that Romans is the most important letter that Paul wrote from a theological point of view. Written from Corinth during Paul's third missionary journey, his explanation of salvation is profound, and he applies the truths of God's grace and salvation broadly. There is no dispute among biblical scholars that the letter's claim of Paul being its author is true. Similarities between Galatians and Romans help to establish Romans as coming from Paul's pen. INTRODUCTION. (See also BIBLE)

SACRIFICIAL LIVING (See LIVING SACRIFICE)

SAINTS (*hagioi*)—The people of God, holy or dedicated ones. Paul uses the term *saints* to refer to the nation of Israel and to Christians as being God's people. The term implies God's choice and His favor, as well as conformity to God's will and character (Eph. 5:3). God is holy, and His people are to be holy and faithful to Him. PARTS 1, 4, 6-7. (See also HOLY; ISRAEL; CHRISTIAN/BELIEVER)

SALVATION—God's work in bringing people to eternal life. *Salvation* is the total work of God to bring humankind from a state of sin to a state of eternal life through Jesus Christ. People are saved when they believe in Christ. From that time, their salvation progresses; and finally in the future when Christ returns, the fullness of their salvation is realized. INTRODUCTION; OVERVIEW; PARTS 1-7. (See also BAPTISM INTO JESUS CHRIST; JUSTIFICATION; CROSS, THE; LIFE/ETERNAL LIFE)

Glossary

SANCTIFICATION—The process of being made holy. Sanctification arises from a direct relationship with God, and its fruits are ethical and personal purity. In light of Scripture, in a positional sense, sanctification is complete; but in practice, it is still ongoing and a goal that can only be reached by the guidance of the Holy Spirit.
- **Positional Sanctification**—The status of anyone who, by faith, has been joined to Christ, breaking the dominion of sin.
- **Practical Sanctification**—Result of a believer's being joined to Christ and striving, through the help of the Holy Spirit, for moral excellence in character and actions, following the teachings and example of Jesus Christ. *PARTS 4, 6-7; APPENDICES (F), (G).* (See also *HOLY; HOLY LIVING*)

SATAN/DEVIL—The chief antagonist of God and humankind. In Scripture, Satan has a close connection to the government of the evil world system (Dan. 10:13; Eph. 6:12). Satan has a past career as "Lucifer" (Isa. 14:12-15; Ezek. 28:12-15) and caused the fall of the human race (Gen. 3). His emissaries (demons) are so numerous that Satan is practically everywhere. Though Satan was judged through Jesus Christ's death on the cross (Col. 2:15) and eventually will be cast into the lake of fire (Rev. 20:10), he continues to attempt to take over Christ's realm, tempting and accusing people, and spreading massive destruction (2 Cor. 4:4; Rev. 12:10). *PART 7.* (See also *EVIL*)

SCRIPTURES (See *BIBLE*)

SEAL/SIGN—In the ancient world, a seal or stamp served to give authenticity or authority to letters, documents, or commands. At times, the imprints of seals were placed on merchandise or other items as proof of ownership. **Circumcision** was a confirming seal/sign of the salvation Abraham received by faith. The visible sign or mark of circumcision was given to Abraham as a seal/proof of his right relationship with God. Likewise, *water baptism* serves as a seal/sign of believers' right standing with God through faith in Christ. *PART 3.* (See also *CIRCUMCISION; WATER BAPTISM*)

SELF-RIGHTEOUSNESS—A critical and *holier-than-thou* attitude of being morally better than others. The self-righteous are sanctimoniously sure of their own righteousness. *PART 2.* (See also *HUMILITY; JUDGMENT BY HUMANS*)

SENT/CALLED BY GOD (*apostolosin*) (See *CALLED BY GOD*)

SEPARATED—A term often used to make a distinction between God's people and those who are not. Sin disrupted fellowship between God and humankind. In restoring fellowship, God sets apart for holy living those who come to faith in Christ. In the case of Paul, he was separated not only to holy living but also to a special ministry as an apostle. *PART 1*

SERVANT/MINISTER
1. **Servant/Minister (*diakonos*)—A person who serves God in a particular capacity. There were two orders of ministers in local churches in the first century: *elders* and *deacons*.** The origin of the order of deacons probably reaches back to Acts 6, though that is never said in the New Testament. The qualifications of a deacon are given in 1 Timothy 3:8-13, and their function had to do with the

service of love, such as caring for the needy and other practical duties. PART 7. (See also DEACON/DEACONESS; SERVICE)
2. **Servant/Minister (*leitourgos*)—Civil authorities are God's servants.** Romans 13:6 refers to the collection of taxes, indicating those who perform such services for the state are active in the service of God. PART 6. (See also ORDINANCE)

SERVICE
1. **Christian Service (by all believers) (*diakonia*)—Actions and work through which followers of Christ express God's love, peace, and joy, benefiting others and the world God created.** The idea is that of ministry, rather than servitude (i.e., bondage or slavery). In response to God's great love, Christians are prompted to serve God and their fellow humans. Such service requires believers to devote themselves to God daily, submitting their talents, spiritual gifts, and lives to Him, then using their gifts to help others. INTRODUCTION; PART 6; APPENDIX (G)
2. **Service/Ministry, Gift of (*diakonia*)—A spiritual gift that enables one to do deeds of service (Rom. 12:7).** This gift includes various kinds of spiritual service, such as ministry to the poor, preparing meals, assisting the disabled, and providing other practical services as opportunities present themselves. PART 6. (See also DEACON/DEACONESS; SERVANT/MINISTER; HELPER)
3. **Service/Ministry in Leadership, Gift of (*diakonia*)—A spiritual gift that enables one to give leadership in the church (Rom. 12:8).** Paul speaks of "those who . . . are over you in the Lord" (1 Thess. 5:12). In Romans 12:8, the word translated **"he who leads" (*proistemi*)** may also suggest the idea of "to care for" or "to give aid." Often, giving care or assistance is involved in leadership in the church. The ministry of the seven deacons in Acts 6:1-7 involved the leadership of caring for the needs of widows. Indeed, these seven Spirit-filled men were servant leaders. PART 6. (See also LEADERSHIP; WORK; DEACON/DEACONESS; SERVANT/MINISTER)
4. **Service/Helps, Gift of (*antilepseis*)—A Spirit-given capacity to be helpers (1 Cor. 12:28).** The precise ministry of those who have this gift is not indicated in the New Testament. The gift of helps overlaps in its function with the gift of service, and is a special spiritual endowment of individuals as servants and helpers of those in need. PARTS 6-7. (See also HELPER)

SIGN/SEAL (See SEAL/SIGN)

SIN—Anything contrary to the will and character of God. A variety of terms are used in the New Testament for *sin*. In light of the terms, the essential nature of sin is rebellion against God and a transgression of His standards. OVERVIEW; PARTS 1-6. (See also TRANSGRESSION; UNGODLINESS; UNRIGHTEOUSNESS; BODY OF SIN/BODY OF DEATH; FLESH; OLD MAN; SINNER; UNDER SIN; DEATH; EVIL; FORGIVENESS; FREEDOM FROM SIN)

SINNER—A person who has violated God's will (God's law). This person is usually thought of as being devoted to sinning (wrongdoing). Apart from Christ, all people are *sinners* (fall short of keeping all of God's law) and are in need of forgiveness and salvation. PARTS 1-6. (See also SIN; UNDER SIN; BODY OF SIN/BODY OF DEATH; OLD MAN; FORGIVENESS)

Glossary

SLAVE (See *BONDSERVANT/SLAVE*)

SOLIDARITY (See *CORPORATE SOLIDARITY*)

SON OF GOD (See *GOD, THE SON*)

SONS OF GOD (See *CHILDREN OF GOD/SONS OF GOD*)

SOVEREIGN WILL OF GOD (See *WILL OF GOD*)

SOVEREIGNTY OF GOD—God's control of every area of His creation. Being the Most High God, God the Creator is "the blessed and only Potentate, the King of kings and Lord of lords" (1 Tim. 6:15). Nothing lies outside of the realm of His rule. Humans can make choices because God wills that they be free to do so. God's sovereignty always operates in accordance with His divine wisdom and mercy. *PART 5.* (See also *WILL OF GOD*)

SPEAKING IN TONGUES—Speaking in a language unknown by the speaker. In the Book of Acts, this manifestation is prompted by the Holy Spirit when a believer is filled with or baptized in the Spirit (2:4; 10:44-46; 19:1-7). In 1 Corinthians 12—14, speaking in tongues is one of the gifts of the Spirit. When this gift operates in worship, interpretation should follow so that the church will understand what the Spirit says and be blessed. *PART 4.* (See also *BAPTISM IN THE SPIRIT; GIFT OF THE SPIRIT; PENTECOST/DAY OF PENTECOST*)

SPIRIT, THE (See *HOLY SPIRIT/THE SPIRIT*)

SPIRITUAL
1. **Spiritual realm—This realm has two dimensions:**
   - **God and His realm,** which is governed by the Holy Spirit and Christian spirituality and are characterized by the conditions of heaven and eternity. (See also *KINGDOM OF HEAVEN*)
   - **Satan and his realm,** which is governed by demons (Eph. 6:10-20), and also characterized by idolatry, immorality, and human wickedness (1 Cor. 10:20; Rev. 9:20-21). (See also *POWERS AND PRINCIPALITIES*)
2. **Spiritual growth—The growth of Christians to maturity resulting from an ongoing deepening of relationship with God.** Such growth is brought about through daily spiritual practices that nurture God's grace, love, peace, and joy in our lives and create a desire for a fuller knowledge of Him. New believers are to endeavor to grow to maturity (1 Peter 2:2). Being rooted in Christ, they are to grow in grace, becoming more like Him as they mature. As they do so, they become more stabilized in the Christian life and their behavior, though they are to never think of themselves as having arrived to a place of total maturity (Phil. 3:12-15). A *spiritual person* is the Christian who has come to maturity (1 Cor. 2:15; 3:1; Gal. 6:1). The characteristics of being truly spiritual are walking in the Spirit, being filled with the Spirit, bearing the fruit of the Spirit, and using the spiritual gifts one has been given. *PART 4; APPENDIX (G).* (See also *SANCTIFICATION; HOLY LIVING*)

SPIRITUAL GIFT (See *GIFT OF THE SPIRIT*)

STRONG IN FAITH/WEAK IN FAITH—The phrase "weak in the faith" refers to a group of Jewish Christians in the church in Rome who

were committed to observing food laws and eating only vegetables. The "strong in faith" did not observe such practices, feeling their freedom in Christ did not require them to follow such strict religious practices. The diversity of opinion and practice among the Roman Christians created tension and conflict in the church. Christians who are more mature and those who are weaker in their faith, despite their differences, are to show respect for each other and nurture unity within the body of Christ. PART 6. (See also *HUMILITY; MORAL/AMORAL PRACTICES*)

TEACHING, GIFT OF—**The Spirit-given ability to instruct others in the Christian faith.** PART 6. (See also *DOCTRINE*)

TEMPTATION—**The enticement to sin, that is to do what is contrary to the perfect will of God.** External circumstances are subjective conditions that may incite a person to sin. Enticement to sin and rebellion is the work of Satan (1 Peter 5:8-9; Rev. 2:9) and is contrary to God. The Bible is full of warnings to be watchful because there is always a danger of falling into temptation. Just because someone is being tempted does not mean that person is guilty of sinning at that moment, or that he or she is not in relationship with God. Even Jesus was tempted (Matt. 4:1-11; Mark 1:12-13; Luke 4:1-13). To be able to stand firm during times of temptation, Christians are to nurture in an ongoing manner their relationship with God and with other believers, and are to rely on God's Spirit for guidance for healing, maturity, and strength. PART 4; APPENDIX (G)

THIS AGE/THE COMING AGE (THE TWO AGES)—**The biblical view of history in which there are two orders of existence: this age of sin and death and the coming age of grace and life.** *This Age*, also referred to as *the Age of Adam*, is dominated by sin, evil, and demonic powers and is doomed to pass away. *The Coming Age* (*the Future Age*), which was initiated into *This Age* during Christ's first coming, will be fully realized when Christ returns in glory. Now the two ages overlap, and there is an already/not yet distinction. This overlap will continue until Christ returns in power and glory. At that time, *This Age* of sin and death will be destroyed (1 Cor. 2:6-9), *the Coming Age* will be fully realized, and those who believe in Christ will share in the full benefits of salvation. *OVERVIEW; PARTS 3, 6.* (See also *ALREADY/NOT YET DOCTRINE; END TIMES*)

TONGUES (See *SPEAKING IN TONGUES*)

TORAH (See *LAW, the Torah*)

TRANSFORMATION—**The process of God's changing and renewing a believer's mind, enabling that person to live a holy life, dedicated to God.** *PARTS 4, 6; APPENDIX (G). (See also SANCTIFICATION; HOLY LIVING)*

TRANSGRESSION—**A deliberate violation of a revealed command.** PARTS 2-3. (See also *SIN*)

TRESPASSES (See *SIN*)

TRIBULATION
   1. **Life's Trials and Tribulation**—**Trouble and suffering in this life.** Some troubles are part of life: pain, weariness, health problems, economic

Glossary

distress, natural disasters, and death. Other troubles may be in part or in full the result of choices, such as these: moral failures that lead to personal stress or relationship problems; various behaviors that lead to addiction; or the breaking of civil laws, which then leads to imprisonment. God's grace and hope, expressed directly or through His people, can help us through all of life's tribulations. *PARTS 2-3, 6.* (See also *HOPE; PERSEVERANCE*)

2. **The Period of Tribulation—A period of time during the End Times thought to last for seven years, between the Rapture of the church and the return of Christ to the earth.** During the Tribulation, God will pour out His judgment without measure (Rev. 6—11). The Tribulation will end with the Second Advent (Coming) of Christ. (See also *END TIMES*)

TRINITY, THE (See *GOD/GODHEAD*)

TRUE ISRAEL—Those people who were descendants of Abraham, with whom God made a special covenant, promising that He would bless them and bring the Messiah to the earth through them. Those Israelites who continued to be faithful and true to God and put their hope in the promises He made to them are often referred to by scholars as "true Israel." *PART 5.* (See also *REMNANT, THE; FAITH*)

TWELVE, THE (See *DISCIPLE*)

UNCLEAN—Contamination by physical, ritual, or moral impurity; the opposite of purity and sanctity in relation to God and His will. In Jewish tradition, the term *unclean* referred to certain foods that were not to be eaten, such as animals that did not have their blood drained, for blood was only to be used to make atonement for sin (Lev. 17:10-14). Other animals and foods were also specified as being unclean (ch. 11). The term *unclean* was also used to describe items or people not properly ritually purified for worship. In Jesus' teaching and in apostolic practice, these distinctions were set aside (Matt. 15:10-20; Acts 11:1-12; Titus 1:15). In the church in Rome, the strong and weak Christians were adversaries in regard to what was clean and unclean. Paul wanted both to be sober-minded and to stop judging one another. In the New Testament, uncleanness is understood in terms of internal spirituality and is opposed to goodness, justice, and uprightness. *PARTS 2, 6*

UNDER SIN—To be in a Christless condition, controlled and dominated by the oppressive power of evil. *PARTS 2, 4.* (See also *SIN; SINNER; BODY OF SIN/BODY OF DEATH; FLESH; OLD MAN; GODLY/UNGODLY*)

UNGODLINESS—A lack of reverence for God. Such a lifestyle shows disrespect for God and sacred things and manifests itself in a wide range of evil works. Ungodliness is at the root of many sins and manifests itself in behavior and attitudes that are contrary to God's character, which is holy, pure, and upright. Such a lifestyle pays no attention to God and shows a lack of reverence for God and sacred things (Rom. 1:24-32; 2 Peter 2:1-6). *PARTS 2-5.* (See also *SIN; BODY OF SIN; FLESH; OLD MAN; GODLY/UNGODLY; UNRIGHTEOUSNESS*)

UNITY IN THE BODY (See *CHURCH*)

**UNRIGHTEOUSNESS—An indication that one is not in right relationship with God due to one's wickedness and unbelief, including a lack of both a right attitude and right conduct. The range of the works of unrighteousness is broad and comprehensive. Romans 1:24-32 explains the kind of sins that are involved in both ungodliness and unrighteousness, emphasizing thoroughgoing evil and wrongdoing. Both *ungodliness* and *unrighteousness* separate from God and attract divine punishment and wrath. PART 2. (See also SIN; UNGODLINESS; RIGHTEOUSNESS)

VESSELS OF WRATH/VESSELS OF MERCY—Analogy that distinguishes between those who embrace a real relationship with God (true Israel), as demonstrated through Jesus Christ's gift of grace and forgiveness (the gospel), and those who do not desire a relationship with God. God's desire is to change the "vessels of wrath" into "vessels of mercy" through the power of the gospel. Paul's explanation indicates the predominance of divine mercy over divine wrath (Rom. 9:22-23; cf. 11:26-32) and reconciles the roles of human responsibility and God's sovereign power in salvation. PART 5. (See also WRATH OF GOD)

WATER BAPTISM—An ordinance of the church, which is a sign of death to the old life and resurrection to a new life with Christ (Rom. 6:1-6). Water baptism also serves as a seal/sign of believers' right standing with God through faith in Christ. As it is known by us, baptism began with John the Baptist. Jesus himself, by example (Matt. 3:13) and precept (28:19), gave authority for its observance, which is commonly administered in the name of the Trinity. The term *baptism* means "to dip" or "immerse." Baptism bears witness to Christ's atoning death and to His bodily resurrection. PARTS 2-4. (See also SEAL/SIGN; BAPTISM INTO JESUS CHRIST)

WEAK IN FAITH (See STRONG IN FAITH/WEAK IN FAITH)

WILL OF GOD—God's eternal plan and sovereign purpose. God's will is absolute and unchangeable and completely in harmony with His character. The divine will for a person is always in agreement with what is revealed in the Bible. In determining God's will, the believer is wise to depend on the leading of the Holy Spirit, the clear teaching of Scripture, and the wisdom of mature Christians. PARTS 5-6. (See also SOVEREIGNTY OF GOD)

WITNESSING (See EVANGELISM)

WORK (verb, *kopiao*)—A verb that Paul used to indicate diligent service by missionaries or local church leaders. PART 7. (See also SERVICE)

WORKS (See RIGHTEOUSNESS—HUMAN RIGHTEOUSNESS)

WORSHIP—The act of giving honor and deference to someone or something. Worship is due the true and living God who has revealed Himself in Christ (Matt. 4:9-10). Christian worship is, therefore, the pure praise and adoration of God as we contemplate His holy character and serve Him. PART 5; APPENDIX (G). (See also GLORY TO GOD; PRAY/PRAYER)

WRATH OF GOD—God's displeasure with rejection of Him; God's opposition to sin, the results of which are correction and punishment, from which God in His grace forgives and releases anyone who repents. God's reaction to sin and His judgment of it are unlike human

Glossary

anger, which is spasmodic and unpredictable. God's wrath is constant and unchanging against evil and wickedness and remains against those who refuse to accept His love and forgiveness, expressed through the death and resurrection of Jesus Christ. All who believe in Christ are delivered from divine wrath (Rom. 5:9). *PARTS 2-6.* (See also *CONDEMNATION; JUDGMENT BY GOD/GOD'S JUDGMENT; SIN; VESSELS OF WRATH/VESSELS OF MERCY; FORGIVENESS*)

Bibliography

Arrington, French L. *Christian Doctrine: A Pentecostal Perspective.* 3 vols. Cleveland, Tenn.: Pathway, 1992-94.

_____. *Encountering the Holy Spirit: Paths of Christian Growth and Service.* Cleveland, Tenn.: Pathway, 2003.

_____. *Unconditional Eternal Security: Myth or Truth?* Cleveland, Tenn.: Pathway, 2005.

Barclay, William. *The Letter to the Romans.* Philadelphia: Westminster, 1957.

Barrett, C. K. *A Commentary on the Epistle to the Romans.* New York: Harper & Row, 1957.

_____. *From First Adam to Last.* New York: Charles Scribner's Sons, 1962.

Barth, Karl. *A Shorter Commentary on Romans.* Richmond, Va.: John Knox, 1959.

Beker, J. Christiaan. *Paul the Apostle: The Triumph of God in Life and Thought.* Philadelphia: Fortress, 1980.

Bloesch, Donald G. *The Crisis of Piety.* Grand Rapids: Eerdmans, 1968.

Bruce, F. F. *The Epistle to the Romans.* Grand Rapids: Eerdmans, 1963.

Cranfield, C. E. B. *Romans: A Shorter Commentary.* Grand Rapids: Eerdmans, 1985.

Deissmann, Adolf. *Paul: A Study in Social and Religious History.* New York: Harper & Row, 1957.

Dodd, C. H. *The Meaning of Paul for Today.* New York: World Publishing, 1970.

Earle, Ralph. *Word Meanings in the New Testament.* Vol. 3. Grand Rapids: Baker, 1974.

Furnish, Victor Paul. *Theology and Ethics of Paul.* Nashville: Abingdon, 1968.

Gause, R. H. *The Preaching of Paul: A Study of Romans*. Cleveland, Tenn.: Church of God, General Department of Education, 1986.

Goold, G. P., ed. *Augustine Confessions* (Loeb Classical Library, vols. I-VIII). Cambridge: Harvard University, 1999.

Hallett, Judith P. "Roman Attitudes Toward Sex," in *Civilization of the Ancient Mediterranean: Greece and Rome*. Vol. 2. New York: Charles Scribner's, 1988.

Henderson, Jeffery. "Greek Attitudes Toward Sex," in *Civilization of the Ancient Mediterranean: Greece and Rome*. Vol. 2., New York: Charles Scribner's, 1988.

Johns, Cheryl Bridges. *Pentecostal Formation: A Pedagogy Among the Oppressed*. Sheffield, England: Sheffield, 1993.

Johnson, Van. "Romans," in *Full Life Bible Commentary to the New Testament*. Ed. French L. Arrington and Roger Stronstad. Grand Rapids: Zondervan, 1999.

Käsemann, Ernest. *Commentary on Romans*. Grand Rapids: Eerdmans, 1980.

Krenkel, Werner A. "Prostitution," in *Civilization of the Ancient Mediterranean: Greece and Rome*. Vol. 2. New York: Charles Scribner's, 1988.

Lenski, R. C. H. *The Interpretation of St. Paul's Epistle to the Romans*. Minneapolis: Wartburg, 1946.

Luther, Martin. *Commentary on the Epistle to the Romans*. Grand Rapids: Zondervan, 1954.

Moo, Douglas. *The Epistle to the Romans: The New International Commentary*. Grand Rapids: Eerdmans, 1996.

Morris, Leon. *The Epistle to the Romans*. Grand Rapids: Eerdmans, 1988.

Nygren, Anders. *Commentary on Romans*. Philadelphia: Muhlenberg, 1949.

Rienecker, Fritz. *A Linguistic Key to the Greek New Testament*. Vol. 2. Grand Rapids: Zondervan, 1980.

Schweizer, Eduard. *The Good News According to Mark.* Richmond, Va.: John Knox, 1970.

Scroggs, Robin. *Paul for a New Day.* Philadelphia: Fortress, 1977.

Simmons, William A. *People of the New Testament World.* Peabody, Mass.: Hendrickson, 2008.

Smart, James D. *Doorway to the New Age: A Study of Paul's Letter to the Romans.* Philadelphia: Westminster, 1972.

Stifler, James M. *The Epistle to the Romans.* Chicago: Moody, 1960.

Thielicke, Helmut. *The Evangelical Faith.* Grand Rapids: Eerdmans, 1982.

Whiteley, D. E. H. *The Theology of Paul.* Philadelphia: Fortress, 1972.